The Decision-Making Process of Investor-State Arbitration Tribunals

International Arbitration Law Library

VOLUME 46

Editors

Professor Julian D.M. Lew QC has been involved with international arbitration for more than forty years as counsel, as arbitrator and as an academic. He is the founder and has been the Head of the School of International Arbitration, Centre for Commercial Law Studies, Queen Mary University of London since its creation in 1985. He is now an independent international arbitrator at 20 Essex Street, London.

Stavros Brekoulakis is Professor at Queen Mary University of London and an associate member of 3 Verulam Buildings (Gray's Inn). He is a leading academic in international arbitration and has led, or been involved in, several projects with ICCA, ICC Commission and ILA. He also acts as an independent arbitrator and has been appointed as chairman, sole arbitrator, co-arbitrator and emergency arbitrator under the rules of all the major arbitration rules.

Introduction

Since its first volume published in 1993, this authoritative practitioner-oriented series has published in-depth and analytical works on niche aspects of international arbitration, authored by specialists in the field.

Objective

This authoritative and established series covering in-depth analyses of niche areas appeals to both practitioners and academics. The series includes specific monographs and PhD dissertations of high quality, which are practical and cover issues not fully explored in general texts.

Frequency

A volume is published whenever an interesting topic presents itself.

The titles published in this series are listed at the end of this volume.

The Decision-Making Process of Investor-State Arbitration Tribunals

Mary Mitsi

Wolters Kluwer

Published by:
Kluwer Law International B.V.
PO Box 316
2400 AH Alphen aan den Rijn
The Netherlands
E-mail: international-sales@wolterskluwer.com
Website: lrus.wolterskluwer.com

Sold and distributed in North, Central and South America by:
Wolters Kluwer Legal & Regulatory U.S.
7201 McKinney Circle
Frederick, MD 21704
United States of America
Email: customer.service@wolterskluwer.com

Sold and distributed in all other countries by:
Air Business Subscriptions
Rockwood House
Haywards Heath
West Sussex
RH16 3DH
United Kingdom
Email: international-customerservice@wolterskluwer.com

Printed on acid-free paper.

ISBN 978-90-411-9600-2

e-Book: ISBN 978-90-411-9657-6
web-PDF: ISBN 978-90-411-9671-2

Printed in the United Kingdom.

To my parents. To my father, Andreas – a constant source of inspiration –, and to my mother, Magda – an endless source of support. With love and gratitude

Table of Contents

Foreword			xiii
Preface			xv
List of Abbreviations			xvii
Introduction			1
I	Connecting Practice and Theory		1
II	The Importance of the Arbitral Decision-Making Process		3
III	Argumentation and Decision-Making		6
	[A]	Origins of Argumentation Theories	6
	[B]	Legal Argumentation	9
	[C]	Legal Argumentation in Judicial Decision-Making: Logic–Rhetoric–Dialectic	10
	[D]	Legal Argumentation in Arbitral Decision-Making: Language–Rhetoric–Dialogue	12
IV	Structure of the Book		16
Part I Arbitral Decision-Making			19
Introduction to Part I			21
Chapter 1 Decision-Making and Legal Argumentation			23
§1.01	Dispute Resolution Function: A Transnational Perspective		23
§1.02	Genres of Arbitral Decision-Making		28
	[A]	Attitudinal/Behavioural Genre	29
	[B]	Economic Genre	31
	[C]	Strategic/Institutional Genre	32

[D] Legal Genre 34
[1] Legal Decision-Making: Interpretation and Application of the Law 34
[2] The Science and Art of Legal Interpretation 36
[3] Legal Interpretation and Arbitral Discretion 37
[4] Legal Interpretation and Argumentation 40

Conclusion to Part I 43

PART II
Language 45

Introduction to Part II 47

CHAPTER 2
Arbitral Legal Language 49
§2.01 Normative Functions of Legal Language 49
§2.02 Arbitral Vocabulary: Standards of Conduct–Principles–Rights 52
[A] Standards 53
[1] Sketching Their Legal Content 53
[2] Between Standards and Principles 55
[B] Principles 60
[1] Sketching Their Legal Content 60
[2] General Principles of Law and Principles of International Law 62
[3] Interchangeability: Principles as Sources of Law and as Interpretive Arguments 63
[4] Transnational Law Method for Identifying General Principles of Law as a Source of Law 65
[5] General Principles of Investment Law and Arbitration 68
[C] Rights 72
[1] Sketching Their Legal Content 73
[2] Substantive Rights and Standards 77
[3] Substantive Rights as a Source of Substantive Law 80

Conclusion to Part II 83

PART III
Rhetoric 85

Introduction to Part III 87

Chapter 3
The Dynamics of Reasoning 89
§3.01 The Amorphous Reasoning Requirement for Investment-Arbitration Awards 89
§3.02 Dynamics of Reasons in the Investment-Arbitration Framework 92
[A] Acceptability 92
[B] Internal Audience 95
[C] External Audience 97
[D] Legitimacy 99

Chapter 4
The Functions of Reasoning 103
§4.01 Persuasion-Oriented Function: Reasoning as a Rhetorical Technique 103
[A] High Rhetoric Standards 104
[B] Low Rhetoric Standards 106
§4.02 Development-Oriented Function: Reasoning as a Means for Normative Development 110
[A] Errors of Law 112

Conclusion to Part III 117

Part IV
Dialogue 119

Introduction to Part IV 121

Chapter 5
Dialogical Network: Theory 123
§5.01 Dialogical Networks 123
[A] Dialogue 124
[B] Networks 125
§5.02 Assessing Legal Arguments 128
§5.03 From Legal Transplants to Legal Dialogues 133
§5.04 Legal Pluralism and Adaptation 135

Chapter 6
Dialogical Network: Practice 141
§6.01 Narrative Arguments 141
[A] Dialogue Between the Parties 142
[B] Dialogue Between the Parties and the Tribunal 146
[C] Dialogue Between the Arbitrators of the Tribunal 149
[D] Expanding the Dialogue Through Third Parties 152
§6.02 Convention Arguments 155
[A] The Use of the VCLT by Investment-Arbitration Tribunals 156

[B] Effectiveness of the VCLT in the Investor-State Arbitration Disputes 161
§6.03 Precedent Arguments 164
[A] A Doctrine of Precedent? 165
[B] Precedential Value of Investment Arbitration Awards 167
[C] The Need to Interpret Precedents 169
[D] Dialogue with International Legal Orders 172
[1] Specialised International Legal Orders 172
[2] The Role of 'Systemic Integration' in Investment Arbitration 175
[3] Dialogue with International Judges 177
[4] Reciprocal Communication 183
[E] Dialogue with National Legal Orders 184
[1] Dialogue with National Law 185
[2] Dialogue with National Judges 186
[3] Reciprocal Communication 193
§6.04 Customary Law Arguments 196
[A] Interpreting Investment Protection Guarantees: A Cyclical Relationship 197
[B] Towards the Emergence of Customary International Investment Law 199
[1] State Practice and *Opinio Juris* Revisited 200
[2] Evolutionary Interpretation of Customary International Law 204
[C] Reciprocal Communication 211
§6.05 Policy Arguments 214
[A] Policies Expressed in Investment Treaties 215
[1] Political Policies 215
[2] Economic Policies 217
[3] Evaluating the Effectiveness of Treaty Policies 222
[B] Policies Revealed by Tribunals in Practice 227
[1] Legal Policy Concerns 227
[a] Consistency, Predictability, Legal Stability 228
[b] Legal Policies and the Rule of Law 232
[c] Systemic Integrity 235
[2] Emerging Social Policy Concerns 238
[a] Sustainable Development-Environmental Rights 241
Conclusion to Part IV 245

Conclusions 249

Annex Interview Questions 259

Bibliography 261

Table of Cases 287

Table of Legislation 297

Index 299

Foreword

Investment arbitration has developed exponentially over the past forty years. At the early stages of investment arbitration, which did not see many disputes, the arbitrators derived their authority from contractual arbitration clauses and the arbitral process was not fundamentally different from the resolution of disputes arising out of commercial contracts. The steady increase in States' unilateral offers to arbitrate enshrined in international treaties, such as Bilateral Investment Treaties (BITs), changed this situation. The arbitration community was slow to adapt to this change, and there were increasing pressures from States, Non-Governmental Organisations (NGOs), media and other representatives of public interests. The changes triggered by the growth and increasing complexity of investment arbitration disputes led to controversies about the legitimacy of arbitration as a method to resolve disputes where there is arguably some inequality between the parties (investment arbitration is but one example, and similar controversies have erupted in sports-disputes, labour-disputes, consumer-disputes, etc.). 'Justice behind Closed Doors' drew harsh criticism and, at least in part, it was a lack of understanding of how the arbitral process functions that caused these controversies: novelties may cause concern, and the very success of arbitration may have led stakeholders, especially States to question whether investment arbitration presents the appropriate avenue for deciding matters of public interest.

Analysing the arbitral process and shedding light on its features may alleviate some harsh and unjustified criticisms. Is an arbitrator different from other dispute-adjudicators, especially judges? Will it fail to consider interests that a judge would? Is it less sensitive to public interest and more inclined to favour the private party in dispute? Will it reason in manners that would be abhorrent to a judge? Will it use different methods, and if so, what methods? Most of these concerns would appear unjustified given that judges and most arbitrators share similar educational backgrounds, and that some arbitrators are in fact judges or retired judges. All 'adjudicators' have to endeavour to render their decisions in a way that will make it possible for the parties to accept or at least understand: usually, the arbitrator will provide reasons for the award and hope that the addressees will read it, understand it and ideally accept it. In 'arbitration without privity', the difficulty increases given that the 'addressees' will include others than the parties, like other States, investors and, often, other circles, thus making the task of drafting the arbitral award even more arduous.

These questions attracted little attention until investment arbitration reached its adulthood and a few awards drew widespread public consideration in view of the increasing amounts of damages awarded against some States.

The initial research in the field analysed how tribunals applied investment laws, whether treaties, national laws or even case law, after some precursors referred to the steady emergence of arbitral jurisprudence. More recently, some authors have turned their attention to the sociology of arbitration, others focused on the philosophical aspects, still others on the psychology ('cognitive biases', reasons for an arbitrator's reasoning, role of legal standards, concepts, use of characterisation or redundancy of such use, etc.).

The question of how the arbitrator grapples with the applicable norms has not attracted much attention until recently. The focus of existent studies is mostly connected to issues of treaty interpretation as well as to the comparative interpretation in contractual and investment disputes. However, there remained a need for a systematic analysis of the various interpretation challenges that may arise in the decision-making process of investment treaty tribunals. Dr Mitsi's book successfully closes this gap by explaining how arbitrators adjust to the new issues that this kind of disputes generate. An example: How are arbitral awards reasoned? On what basis would the Vienna Convention on the Law of Treaties (VCLT) apply? Should it apply and in which manner? What is the role of general principles of law, precedent, customary law and policies in the decision-making process? How do the narrative techniques of the parties shape the interpretation process? Do social actors influence the legitimacy of the investment arbitration framework? The book is a substantial addition to the international arbitration scholarship introducing a thorough overview of the theory and practice of international investment arbitration. For any practitioner and academic interested in these issues, Dr Mitsi's opus will provide valuable insights into the arbitrator's decision-making process.

Laurent Lévy

Preface

The book explores the ways in which arbitral tribunals interpret the law in investor-state disputes and the emergence of a specialised way of decision-making adapted to the characteristics and needs of investment arbitration. In the course of a single investor-state dispute, an arbitrator may make numerous decisions, from interpreting the treaty or national laws to taking into account precedents, customs and policies.

The understanding of how tribunals deal with these interpretational issues is important not only because tribunals address questions of public interest but also due to considerable legitimacy criticisms regarding how awards are rendered and reasoned. Consequently, unveiling the legal decision-making process is critical for the well-being of the whole dispute resolution procedure as an effective and acceptable process.

Nonetheless, such an understanding requires taking into account the transnational characteristics of the investment-arbitration framework within which decision-making takes place. Investment arbitration encompasses both private and public interests and lies at the intersection of the national and international legal cosmos. Structurally it is positioned at the crossroads of national and international, and private and public law. The emergence of private authority with cross-border aspects and the challenges arising from the questioning of the legitimacy and transparency of investor-state arbitration, question the use of traditional interpretive methodologies such as the Vienna Conventions on the Law of Treaties. In this case, theory should keep up with practice as a means for enhancing the legal theory of international arbitration.

Given such specificities, the book examines the legal decision-making process analysing the legal arguments tribunals use when interpreting the law. Legal argumentation theories and specifically the triptych of language–rhetoric–dialogue constitute the theoretical framework for such an analysis. The language aspect will show that arbitrators have developed a specialised language when interpreting the law, while the rhetoric aspect discusses the distinctive functions of an award's reasoning. Lastly, the dialogue aspect will reveal the idiosyncratic interactions of legal orders, judges and arbitrators in decision-making. It is therefore asserted that arbitral tribunals have gradually developed a distinctive way of decision-making which is connected to the interpretive needs that arise in the decision-making process and the transnational elements of investment arbitration. This is a book about the theory of practice.

List of Abbreviations

AG	Attorney General
AI&L	Artificial Intelligence and Law
AJ	Arbitration Journal
AJIL	American Journal of International Law
AJLP	Australian Journal of Legal Philosophy
All ER Rep	All England Reports Reprint
AmEconRev	American Economic Review
AmJCompL	American Journal of Comparative Law
AmPolSciRev	American Political Science Review
AmUIntlLRev	American University International Law Review
AnnuarioDirComp	Annuario Di Diritto Comparato E Di Studi Legislativi
ArbIntl	Arbitration International
ASIL PROC.	American Society of International Law Proceedings
AUP	Amsterdam University Press
BCSC	British Columbia Supreme Court
BerkeleyJIntlL	Berkeley Journal of International Law
BIICL	British Institute of International and Comparative Law
BIT	Bilateral Investment Treaty
BrJPoliticalSci	British Journal of Political Science
BULRev	Boston University Law Review
BYIL	British Yearbook of International Law
BYULRev	Brigham Young University Law Review

CCJ	Caribbean Court of Justice
CETA	Comprehensive Economic and Trade Agreement
ChiJIntlL	Chicago Journal of International Law
CIL	Customary International Law
CLPE	Comparative Research in Law and Political Economy
CMLRev	Common Market Law Review
CMP	Conference of the Kyoto Protocol State Parties
ColumJTransnatlL	Columbia Journal of Transnational Law
ColumLRev	Columbia Law Review
CornellLRev	Cornell Law Review
CUP	Cambridge University Press
CYArb	Czech (& Central European) Yearbook of Arbitration
DispResolJ	Dispute Resolution Journal
DJILP	Denver Journal of International Law and Policy
DR-CAFTA	Dominican Republic–Central America–United States Free Trade Agreement
DukeLJ	Duke Law Journal
ECJ	European Court of Justice
Ecology LQ	Ecology Law Quarterly
ECT	Energy Charter Treaty
ECtHR	European Court of Human Rights
EFILA	European Federation for Investment Law and Arbitration
EJIL	European Journal of International Law
ERRJ	Employee Responsibilities and Rights Journal
EU	European Union
EUP	Edinburg University Press
EurEconRev	European Economic Review
FET	Fair and Equitable Treatment
FinnishYBIL	Finnish Yearbook of International Law
FlaStULRev	Florida State University Law Review
FordhamIntlLJ	Fordham International Law Journal
FordhamLRev	Fordham Law Review

FPS	Full Protection and Security
FTA	Free Trade Agreement
FTC	Free Trade Commission
GAR	Global Arbitration Review
GLJ	German Law Journal
GPL	General Principles of Law
GWashIntlLRev	George Washington International Law Review
HagueRec	Hague Recueil
HarvIntlLJ	Harvard International Law Journal
HarvIntlLJ Online	Harvard International Law Journal Online
HarvLRev	Harvard Law Review
HKUP	Hong Kong University Press
HLJ	Hastings Law Journal
HUP	Harvard University Press
IACtHR	Inter-American Court of Human Rights
IBA	International Bar Association
ICC	International Chamber of Commerce
ICCA	International Council for Commercial Arbitration
ICCt	International Criminal Court
ICJ	International Court of Justice
ICJ Reports	International Court of Justice Reports
ICLQ	International and Comparative Law Quarterly
ICSID	International Centre for Settlement of Investment Disputes
ICSID Rev	International Centre for Settlement of Investment Disputes Review
ICTR	International Criminal Tribunal for Rwanda
ICTY	International Criminal Tribunal for the former Yugoslavia
IIA	International Investment Agreements
IILJ	Institute for International Law and Justice
IISD	International Institute for Sustainable Development

ILC	International Law Commission
ILC YB	International Law Commission Yearbook
IntlConstrLRev	International Construction Law Review
IntlJConstL	International Journal of Constitutional Law
IO	International Organization
ISDS	Investor-to-State Dispute Settlement
JACM	Journal of the Association for Computing Machinery
JC	Journal of Computers
JIDS	Journal of International Dispute Settlement
JIEL	Journal of International Economic Law
JIntlArb	Journal of International Arbitration
JL&Soc'y	Journal of Law and Society
JLB	Journal of Law & Business
JLS	Journal of Legal Studies
JPragmat	Journal of Pragmatics
JWTL	Journal of World Trade Law
LCIA	London Court of International Arbitration
LegalStudF	Legal Studies Forum
LGDJ	Librairie Générale de Droit et de Jurisprudence
LIEI	Legal Issues of Economic Integration
LSE	London School of Economics
MaxPlanckUNYB	Max Planck Yearbook of United Nations Law
MFN	Most Favoured Nation Treatment
MichJIntlL	Michigan Journal of International Law
MinnLRev	Minnesota Law Review
ModLRev	Modern Law Review
NAFTA	North American Free Trade Agreement
NBER	National Bureau of Economic Research
NCLRev	North Carolina Law Review
NebLRev	Nebraska Law Review
NGOs	Non-Governmental Organisations

NJILB	Northwestern Journal of International Law and Business
NSAIL	Non-State Actors and International Law
NT	National Treatment
NUP	Northwestern University Press
NYIL	Netherlands Yearbook of International Law
NYU School, PubLaw&LT	New York University School, Public Law & Legal Theory
NYUJIntlL&P	New York University Journal of International Law and Politics
NYUL&Econ	New York University Law and Economics
NYULRev	New York University Law Review
OECD	Organisation for Economic Co-operation and Development
OJLS	Oxford Journal of Legal Studies
OSCA	Organization of Supreme Courts of the Americas
OsgoodeHallLJ	Osgoode Hall Law Journal
OSSA	Ontario Society for the study of Argumentation
OUP	Oxford University Press
PCIJ	Permanent Court of International Justice
PCIJ Rep series	Permanent Court of International Justice Report Series
Ph&Rh	Philosophy and Rhetoric
PUF	Pressses Universitaires de France
QB	Queen's Bench, commercial court
RecDesCours	Recueil Des Cours
RECIEL	Review of European Community and International Environmental Law
RESLA	Revista Española de Lingüística Aplicada
Rev Litig	Review of Litigation
RevArb	Revue de l'arbitrage
RevEcon&Stat	Review of Economics and Statistics
S	Syllogism
SantaClaraIntlLRev	Santa Clara International Law Review
SantaClaraLRev	Santa Clara Law Review

SCalLRev	Southern California Law Review
SCC	Stockholm Chamber of Commerce
SIEL	Society of International Economic Law
SSRN	Social Science Research Network
StatuteLRev	Statute Law Review
SuffolkTransnatlLJ	Suffolk Transnational Law Journal
TDM	Transnational Dispute Manager
TexIntlLJ	Texas International Law Journal
TLR	Texas Law Review
TTIP	Transatlantic Trade and Investment Partnership Agreement
UCDJInternl'L&P	University of California Davis Journal of International Law and Policy
UCLA L Rev	University of California, Los Angeles Law Review
UCP	University of Chicago Press
UMiamiLRev	University of Miami Law Review
UN	United Nations
UNCITRAL	United Nations Commission of International Trade Law
UNCTAD	United Nations Conference on Trade and Development
UPa J Int'lL	University of Pennsylvania Journal of International Law
UPaLRev	University of Pennsylvania Law Review
US	United States
US Reports	United States Reports
USGL&Econ	University of Saint Gallen Law and Economics
Utrecht L Rev	Utrecht Law Review
VaLRev	Virginia Law Review
VandJTransnatL	Vanderbilt Journal Transnational Law
VCLT	Vienna Convention on the Law of Treaties
WAMR	World Arbitration Mediation Review
WashUJL&P	Washington University Journal of Law and Policy
Wm&MaryLRev	William and Mary Law Review
WTO	World Trade Organization

YaleJIntlL	Yale Journal of International Law
YaleLJ	Yale Law Journal
ZaöRV	Zeitschrift für ausländisches öffentliches Recht und Völkerrecht
Zbornik Radova	Zbornik Radova Ekonomskog Fakulteta u Rijeci

Introduction

I CONNECTING PRACTICE AND THEORY

There exists a double aspect of things: for at times the one rises alone from the many, yet at others, the many are born of one.[1]

Empedocles

Empedocles' fundamental thesis about the cyclic relation of elements and forces could have very well been written to describe the polymorphous decision-making process of investment-arbitration tribunals. Investment arbitration is one of the many dispute resolution bodies that operate in an international framework. However, are there any specific characteristics and policies that make arbitration differentiate or in other words, rise from the many?

This book examines the legal decision-making process of investor-state arbitration tribunals. It particularly analyses the ways in which tribunals interpret the law in the context of a specific dispute. The analysis draws upon the theories of legal argumentation, specifically, upon the triptych of 'logic, 'rhetoric' and 'dialogue'.

Arbitral decision-making is an important and topical issue as various economic, political and legal interests depend on the arbitral award. However, due to the case-specific approach governing the investor-state arbitration framework, arbitrators resolve each dispute on an ad hoc basis, with the Vienna Convention on the Law of Treaties as the only guidance on the methodology of interpreting the law. This ad hoc mandate, coupled with the generality characterising the investment-treaty terms, accounts for the wide discretion of arbitrators when deciding on a specific dispute. In addition, given the fact that there is no formal doctrine of precedent governing the arbitration framework, any convergence of the arbitral decision-making patterns would, at first sight, seem a goal not easy to attain. In this context, the process

1. Empedocles, cited in Mireille Delmas-Marty, *Ordering Pluralism* (Hart 2009) 2.

arbitrators follow to render an award raises important issues regarding the consistency of decisions, as well as the predictability and legitimacy of the decision-making process in general.

This book purports to critically analyse these issues connected to the methodology arbitrators use to interpret the law, from a transnational perspective.[2] The investment-arbitration framework within which decision-making takes place presents certain transnational characteristics that should be taken into account when theorising over the legal decision-making process of investment tribunals. Picturing investment arbitration as solely a party-centred dispute resolution process makes it hard to describe properly its place in the international and domestic scene. Investment arbitration can be understood as 'part of a transnational system of justice', which cannot be positioned entirely either in the sphere of national, international or in the field of private or public law.[3] The investment-arbitration framework has idiosyncratic characteristics and needs since it is comprised of interactions between public and private actors coming from various legal and political systems. Additionally, it operates in a multilayered legal framework of different sets of laws including public international law, administrative decisions and host State regulations.

All these transnational elements question the use of traditional interpretive methodologies such as the VCLT. The codified customary international law canons of interpretation contained in the VCLT constitute a starting point guiding the way arbitral tribunals interpret the law in investment-arbitration disputes. However, arbitral case law is not always consistent with the public international law interpretive methodology pronounced in the VCLT.[4] The complex interpretive issues that may arise in investment-arbitration disputes call for a specialised methodology of interpretation developed in practice by arbitral tribunals. The diversification of the interpretive methodology is consistent with the idea that interpretation methods may change depending on the specialised nature of each international treaty.[5] Going a step further, the need to interpret not only treaties but also precedents, policies, general principles and customary international law, constitutes a further basis for approaching the legal interpretation process from a specialised lens.

Within this background, what becomes important is the need to reveal the gap between the obvious target of dispute resolution and what exists in symbiosis with it. As an example, symbiotic issues that may arise are the way national and international legal orders interact in the context of interpretation and the role of policy and third parties therein. For this reason, and in an attempt to offer a broader insight on how decision-making in investment arbitration takes place, this book approaches the legal decision-making process of arbitral tribunals through the wider perspective of transnational dispute resolution. This approach will place arbitral decision-making at the

---

2. *See* §1.01 'Dispute Resolution Function: A Transnational Perspective'.
3. David Caron and others, *Practising Virtue: Inside International Arbitration* (OUP 2015) 2.
4. *See* §6.02 'Convention Syllogism'.
5. Jan Klabbers, 'Virtuous Interpretation', in Malgosia Fitzmaurice, Olufemi Elias and Panos Merkouris (eds) *Treaty Interpretation and the Vienna Convention on the Law of Treaties: 30 Years on* (Brill/Nijhoff 2010) 17–37.

crossroad of international and national legal orders and the intersection of private and public interests.

In this context, the main questions the book addresses are: How do investment-arbitration tribunals interpret the law from a transnational perspective? How is the interaction between the various actors and legal orders pictured in the legal decision-making process? The hypothesis of the book is that investment-arbitration tribunals have developed a specialised process of legal decision-making adapted to the interpretational needs that arise in the context of an investor-state dispute, and to the transnational characteristics of the investment-arbitration framework.

II THE IMPORTANCE OF THE ARBITRAL DECISION-MAKING PROCESS

The reasons underlying the choice of focusing on the decision-making of investment-arbitration tribunals can be summarised in three main points: the popularity of investment arbitration for the resolution of investor-state disputes which has led to the emergence of a large body of case law; the idiosyncratic characteristics of this framework and the public policy issues entailed which expand the interest in the arbitral award to a broader audience; and last but not least, the legitimacy and consistency concerns connected to the decision-making process of arbitrators which may threaten the attractiveness of the dispute resolution process.[6]

Foreign direct investments constitute source of a State's economic development. They are linked to the development of public and private services such as telecommunication, water, gas and electricity supply, contributing not only capital but also technology and know-how. The creation of an investment-friendly climate, essential to attract foreign investors, depends on the State's economic, political and legal environment.[7] From an economic perspective, what is important is economic stability, market access, taxation and the existence of infrastructure.[8] From a political perspective, essential elements are stability, transparency and an effectively operating public administration.[9]

The legal environment also plays a crucial role in the investor's decision to invest in a foreign country. The dispute resolution mechanisms offered to an investor in the

6. The decision of the Court of Justice of the European Union in the *Achmea* case pictures clearly these concerns. The Court held that the arbitration clause contained into the Netherlands-Slovakia BIT has 'an adverse effect on the autonomy of EU law, and is therefore incompatible with EU law'. The Court was concerned with the issue of how the EU Law is interpreted by arbitral tribunals and whether the founding principles of the EU Law would be respected. It concluded that arbitration tribunals are not courts of Member States and as such have no power to request a preliminary ruling to the CJEU (Article 267 TFEU). The latter is the mechanism for ensuring the consistency and autonomy of EU Law. Case C-284/16, *Slovakia Republic v. Achmea B.V.*, (6 Mar. 2018) paras 31 et seq.
7. Christoph Schreuer, 'The Future of Investment Arbitration' in Mahnoush Arsanjani and others (eds) *Looking to the Future: Essays on International Law in Honor of W. Michael Reisman* (Nijhoff 2011) 1.
8. *See* §6.05[A][2] 'Economic Policies'.
9. *See* §6.05[A][1] 'Political Policies'.

case a State will not respect its obligations is a decisive factor.[10] Local courts and the road of diplomatic protection may be considered ineffective ways of resolving investor-state disputes due to the perceived 'cultural' bias of domestic courts and the indirect nature of protection offered through diplomatic protection.[11] Investment arbitration, on the other hand, constitutes a more suitable and effective framework for the resolution of investor-state disputes. The parties have the opportunity to select experienced arbitrators who will decide the dispute and profit from a strong enforcement regime for arbitral awards.

However, the popularity of investment arbitration[12] has been challenged. Important criticisms regarding the functioning of the investor-state arbitration dispute resolution framework are brought to the surface not only by the legal society but also by the civil and political circles. Such issues include the questioning of the legitimacy of the investment-arbitration framework in general and of the decision-making process in particular. The concept of individuals acting as judges in million dollar disputes which concern issues of public interest is neither an easy one to conceive nor to accept.[13] The issues of how arbitrators interpret and apply the law, whether an award should contain adequate reasons, and the case-specific or systemic approach to arbitral decision-making have revealed concerns of the precariousness of the investment-arbitration framework.

All these criticisms are closely connected to the interpretation process of arbitrators. Investor-state arbitration is requested to give answers to complex issues linked to the public interest of a State and its economic development. The outcome of an arbitral

10. David Gaukrodger and Kathryn Gordon, 'Investor-State Dispute Settlement: A Scoping Paper for the Investment Policy Community' (2012) OECD Working Papers on International Investment, 2012/03, OECD Publishing <http://dx.doi.org/10.1787/5k46b1r85j6f-en> (accessed 28 Jun. 2018) (stating that: 'an investor who is trying to resolve a dispute with a host government will keep in mind the prospects offered by international arbitration when determining strategy and tactics in other dispute settlement procedures. This underscores the importance of appropriate design for ISDS, since it is likely to influence all other dispute resolution processes'); For the debate on whether the incorporation of arbitration clauses in investment treaties is linked to the promotion of inbound investment, *see*: Lauge N Skovgaard Poulsen, *Bounded Rationality and Economic Diplomacy: The Politics of Investment Treaties in Developing Countries* (CUP 2015); Luke Nottage, *International Investment Treaties and Arbitration Across Asia* (Brill 2017); Thomas Schultz and Cedric Dupont, 'Investment Arbitration: Promoting the Rule of Law or over-Empowering Investors? A Quantitative Empirical Study' (2014) 25 EJIL 1147.
11. There is the concern that domestic courts may not be impartial when dealing with disputes between the State and a foreign investor. They are also considered to lack important expertise and experience for the resolution of investment disputes. On the other hand, diplomatic protection is left at the discretion of the investor's home State. For the evaluation of investment arbitration as an alternative to domestic courts, *see* Tom Ginsburg, 'International Substitutes for Domestic Institutions: Bilateral Investment Treaties and Governance' (2006) University Illinois Law & Economics Research Paper No. LE06-027, 28.
12. According to the ICSID Caseload Statistics, as of 31 Dec. 2017, ICSID had registered 650 cases under the ICSID Convention and Additional Facility Rules, 'The ICSID Caseload Statistics' (Issue 2018-1) Table 1 <https://icsid.worldbank.org/en/Documents/resources/ICSID%20Web%20Stats%2020181(English).pdf> (accessed 30 Jun. 2018).
13. For example, Pia Eberhardt and Cecilia Olivet, 'Profiting from Injustice: How Law Firms, Arbitrators and Financiers Are Fuelling an Investment Arbitration Boom' (2012) Corporate Europe Observatory and the Transnational Institute <https://www.tni.org/en/briefing/profiting-injustice> (accessed 10 Jun. 2018).

award may also affect the public works and the everyday life of the State's citizens. From a legal point of view, the legitimacy critique generally focuses on the inconsistent interpretations by arbitral tribunals,[14] the lack of an appeal mechanism supervising the interpretation of the law and the lack of predictability in arbitral decision-making.[15]

This book purports to shed light and critically analyse these issues connected to the legal decision-making process of arbitrators. It aims at untangling the process of interpretation of the law by the arbitrator revealing the methodology arbitrators use in order to complete this process.

The motivation for this research is derived from the need to reconcile the obvious gap between the outward show and the actual activity. As such, the fact that there is no formal doctrine of precedent in arbitration does not mean that arbitrators do not refer to case law in their reasoning.[16] Likewise, the existence of the VCLT as an authoritative text for the interpretation of treaties does not automatically lead to the conclusion that the Convention is the only effective interpretation tool that arbitrators use.

It is hoped that this book will contribute in reconciling conventional wisdom on interpretation and the reality of investment arbitration. Clarifying what arbitrators actually do in practice and how they interpret the law becomes a matter of knowledge; knowledge of how private judges decide important disputes and ultimately knowledge of how the entire investment-arbitration framework operates. Decodifying the methodology arbitrators use to interpret the law is important for comprehending how the investment-arbitration framework develops and what kind of relationships – if any – it has formed with national and international legal orders. It will also constitute an indicator of the level of systemic coherence of investment arbitration. From a practitioner's perspective, the challenges that an arbitrator may confront during the interpretation process may also be confronted by counsel when drafting the parties' submissions. Being aware of how arbitrators interpret the law will constitute a road map for the counsel's arguments and approaches when dealing with cross-border

14. As an example, *see Lauder v. Czech Republic* and *CME v. Czech Republic* decisions. The Tribunals in these two parallel arbitration cases concerning an investment in a Czech television broadcaster dealt with the same dispute arising out of a contract termination but reached differing decisions. *Lauder v. Czech Republic*, UNCITRAL, Final Award (3 Sep. 2002), *CME Czech Republic B.V. v. Czech Republic*, UNCITRAL, Partial Award (13 Sep. 2001); In the Symposium co-organised by ICSID, OECD and UNCTAD it was mentioned that: 'While there is no guarantee that the inconsistencies would have been avoided if these awards had been submitted subsequently to an appeal, the chances for consistency would be reinforced by the existence of a common appeals body which would handle not only ICSID awards, but also UNCITRAL awards and awards rendered by ICC, SCC and other ad hoc arbitral tribunals', Symposium co-organised by ICSID, OECD and UNCTAD: 'Improving The System of Investor-State Dispute Settlement: An Overview' (12 Dec. 2005) para. 38, <https://www.oecd.org/investment/internationalinvestmentagreements/35808448.pdf> (accessed 28 May 2018); *See also* discussion in §402[A]'Errors of Law'.
15. UNCTAD Report, 'Reform of Investor State Dispute Settlement: In search of a roadmap' (2013) IIA Issues Note No. 2.
16. Perelman defines legal reasoning as 'judicial reasoning as disclosed in a judgment or order which justifies a decision'. Chaim Perelman, *Droit, morale et philosophie* (2nd edn, LGDJ/Pichon et Durand-Auzias 1976) 93.

disputes. A methodology for decision-making seen from a transnational perspective links arbitration and decision-making with the globalised legal environment it operates in.

On a further note, analysing the legal decision-making process may facilitate those affected by the arbitral decision to understand how complex political issues such as the exercise of State powers and administrative decisions comprising economic and legislative policies, are approached. In addition, the acceptance of the award by the wider audience which constantly assesses and criticises the consistency and predictability of arbitral decisions may also be facilitated. Such an audience includes potential users of arbitration, international organisations and domestic actors, NGOs and think tanks.

Although investment arbitration's history is very recent with the largest bulk of case law being produced throughout the last twenty years, its rapid expansion raises issues of internal cohesiveness and external effectiveness which can be addressed mainly through the analysis of the legal decision-making process. Addressing these issues is significant for the long-term viability of the whole dispute resolution process. An effective dispute resolution process requires a transparent and reliable decision-making process that will be solidified as an alternative to court proceedings. The topic of this book is relevant for both academics and practitioners, and its significance is only growing with the use of investor-state arbitration.

III ARGUMENTATION AND DECISION-MAKING

The theoretical framework of the book is inspired from legal argumentation theories. The analysis of arbitral decision-making is effectuated through the analysis of the arbitrators' legal arguments as pictured in the arbitral decision.

Argumentation can be generally defined as 'a verbal, social and rational activity aimed at convincing a reasonable critic of the acceptability of a standpoint by advancing a constellation of propositions justifying or refuting the proposition expressed in the standpoint'.[17] The Argumentation theory is interested in the various aspects of argumentation including the structure of argumentation, the consequences of advancing specific arguments as well as the analysis and assessment of argumentative discourse.[18] The main argumentation types are three: 'logic', 'rhetoric' and 'dialectic'.

[A] Origins of Argumentation Theories

Argumentation techniques and the specific role 'logic', 'rhetoric' and 'dialectic' plays in the argumentation process was first identified by ancient Greek philosophers. The

17. Frans van Eemeren (ed.), *Crucial Concepts in Argumentation Theory* (AUP 2001) 11; Frans van Eemeren and others, *Fundamentals of Argumentation Theory: A Hand-Book of Historical Backgrounds and Contemporary Developments* (Lawrence Erlbaum 1996) 3.
18. Frans Van Eemeren and Rob Grootendorst, *A Systematic Theory of Argumentation: The Pragma-Dialectical Approach* (CUP 2004) 2.

political success in the Athenian participatory democracy largely depended on persuasion and argumentation skills. The Sophists were the teachers of argumentation techniques preparing young promising students for public speaking and engagement. Argumentation techniques were initially studied as a particular epistemic field with theoretical interest by the Greek philosopher Aristotle of Stagira, Macedonia.[19] Starting from a separate approach to these concepts, the logical reasoning focused on revealing the truth, the dialectical reasoning emphasised on the debating of personal opinions, and the rhetorical reasoning was linked to the persuasive power of communicating personal beliefs. Eventually the functions of these three concepts were presented in an interconnected way revealing the strong links formed amongst them.

Aristotle depicted logic through an analytical process of reasoning that would help identify what can be called 'true' or 'false' as well as what is the connection between an argument and its conclusion. The first type of logical reasoning he identified is called 'deduction' (συλλογισμός). 'Deduction' is a speech (λόγος) in which specific things have been supposed and a specific conclusion is derived from these premises as a necessity, or in other words as a logical consequence.[20] The second type of logical reasoning is called induction (επαγωγή) and describes the reasoning process which starts from the particular and ends to the general.[21]

Aristotle's approach to logic and reasoning is particular as it considers these issues in a dialectical context, a form of question-answer dialogue much alike the Socratic method of questioning.[22] The dialectic method of Socrates, called 'maieutic', constitutes a means of contesting the interlocutor's arguments. Specific questions are posed to the interlocutor in order to reveal the inconsistencies of his arguments and eventually lead him to adopt the opposing view.[23]

For Aristotle, however, dialectic is not only concerned with practical conflicts in which only personal opinions are accepted or rejected and not real knowledge.[24] He distinguishes three functions of dialectic: 'mental training', 'conversation' and the 'philosophical sciences'.[25] 'Mental training' is connected to the methodology of arguing whereas 'conversation' is useful 'when we shall want to persuade them to give up assertions which will seem to us openly unacceptable'.[26] The function of 'philosophical sciences' connects the art of dialectic with the acquisition of knowledge or as called at that time, science.[27] In this context, 'dialectic' includes 'the process of examining, probing and reorganising forms so as to reach the right definitions and whatever else

19. *See* Jaakko Hintikka, *Analyses of Aristotle* (Kluwer Academic Publishers 2004).
20. Aristotle, 'Prior Analytics' ch.I.2, 24B18-20 <http://classics.mit.edu/Aristotle/prior.1.i.html> (accessed 3 Jan. 2018).
21. Aristotle, 'Posterior Analytics' ch.1.1, 71a6 <http://classics.mit.edu/Aristotle/posterior.html> (accessed 4 Jan. 2018).
22. Hintikka, *Analyses of Aristotle* (n 19) 1.
23. James Zappen, *The Rebirth of Dialogue: Bakhtin, Socrates, and the Rhetorical Tradition* (State University of New York Press 2004).
24. Marta Spranzi, *The Art of Dialectic between Dialogue and Rhetoric: The Aristotelian Tradition* (John Benjamins Publishing Company 2011) 19.
25. *Ibid.* citing Aristotle, *Topics* Ch. I.2, 101a25–101b4.
26. *Ibid.* Ch. I.2, 101a33–34.
27. 'Science', the Greek word 'episteme', is defined by Aristotle as acquaintance of knowledge: 'We think we know (epistasthai) a thing simpliciter [...] whenever we think that we know

may be needed as first premises of a science'.[28] As a result, dialectic constitutes, *inter alia*, a means, a methodology of defining principles which constitute the starting points of sciences.[29] As the great saga states:

> Again, [dialectic is useful] with regard to the starting points of each science; for it is impossible to say anything about them from the principles special to the science proposed since the starting points are the principles of everything, and it is necessary to discuss them through the endoxa pertaining to each. This is unique, or most proper, to dialectic, for being able to inquire in relation to the starting points of all studies, it has a way to proceed.[30]

Aristotle's logic and dialectic are enhanced by the third element of the legal argumentation triptych: 'Rhetoric'. The philosopher defined rhetoric as the 'ability [of a person, group, society, or culture] in each [particular] case to see [perceive] the available means of persuasion'.[31] The persuasive power of the speaker depends on the use of either 'extrinsic' or 'intrinsic' methods.[32] The former draw on existing sources such as laws or documents. The use of 'intrinsic' means of persuasion, which depend on the speaker's skills, includes 'logos' (logical reasoning), 'ethos' (the virtue of the speaker) and 'pathos' (emotion).[33] Argumentation theories mostly concentrate on the concept of 'logos'.

'Rhetoric', which is mostly audience-oriented, is presented as having a very close connection to 'Dialectic', in the sense of them constituting two 'coordinate opposites'.[34] 'Rhetoric' and 'Dialectic' are both described as methods of proof, however employing different instruments of proof: the former 'draw[s] its inferences by the abbreviated, imperfect, conversational enthymeme, never complete in form, and by the single example in the place of the general induction' whereas the latter 'conclude[s] by the formal syllogism, and by the regular induction, assumed complete'.[35] Drawing on this way of thinking, in 'Dialectic', the individuals advance claims seeking to point out the logic behind them and also respond to the questions of their counterparties. On this basis, while 'Dialectic' proceeds by question and answer, 'Rhetoric' proceeds by continuous exposition – a relatively uninterrupted discourse – aiming at persuading the audience rather than the counterparty.[36]

(ginôskein) that the cause, due to which the thing is, is its cause, and that it is not possible for this to be otherwise'. Aristotle, 'Posterior Analytics' (n 21) I.2 (71b9-2).

28. Hintikka, *Analyses of Aristotle* (n 19) 68.
29. Orna Harari, *Knowledge and Demonstration: Aristotle's Posterior Analytics* (Springer 2004) 117–118.
30. 'Endoxa' has the meaning of 'what is acceptable'; Julie Ward, *Aristotle on Homonymy: Dialectic and Science* (CUP 2008) 50, 51 citing Aristotle, *Topics* Alpha 2 (101a36–b4).
31. Richard Rieke, Malcolm Sillars, and Tarla Peterson (eds) *Argumentation and Critical Decision Making* (6th ed., Peachpit Press 2013) 20 citing Aristotle, *On Rhetoric*.
32. Van Eemeren and Grootendorst, *A Systematic Theory of Argumentation* (n 18) 43.
33. John Dryzek, 'Rhetoric in Democracy: A Systemic Appreciation' (2010) 38(3) Political Theory 319, 320.
34. Edward Meredith Cope and John Sandys (eds), *Aristotle: Rhetoric*, vol. 1 (CUP 2009) 2.
35. *Ibid.*
36. *Aristotle: On Rhetoric* (George Kennedy tr, 2nd ed., OUP 2007) 28; George A Kennedy, *Aristotle. On Rhetoric* (2nd ed., OUP 2007) 28; Rieke, Sillars, and Peterson (eds) *Argumentation and Critical Decision Making* (n 31) 19.

For Aristotle, the arts of 'Logic', 'Rhetoric' and 'Dialectic' have different functions and are achieved through different means. Aristotle connected logic with 'reasoning related to truth', dialectical reasoning with opinions and beliefs, and the so-called *topoi* with 'the ways in which these beliefs are conveyed and shared (that is to say, rhetoric)'.[37] However, they are also presented as interrelated processes. The following quote from Aristotle's 'Posterior Analysis' illustrates the way he analyses deductive and inductive logical reasoning in connection to dialectical and rhetorical reasoning:

> All instruction given or received by way of argument proceeds from pre-existent knowledge. This becomes evident upon a survey of all the species of such instruction. The mathematical sciences and all other speculative disciplines are acquired in this way, and so are the two forms of dialectical reasoning, syllogistic and inductive; for each of these latter make use of old knowledge to impart new, the syllogism assuming an audience that accepts its premises, induction exhibiting the universal as implicit in the clearly known particular. Again, the persuasion exerted by rhetorical arguments is in principle the same, since they use either example, a kind of induction, or enthymeme, a form of syllogism.[38]

The functions of 'Logic', 'Dialectic' and 'Rhetoric' as well as the relationship between them becomes more complex especially when this triptych is transferred into the legal context.

[B] Legal Argumentation

Argumentation plays an important role in the legal world. Legislators, judges and lawyers advance legal statements to propose a legislative act, to render a decision or to support the case of their client. These legal statements require reasoning that, in its turn, plays a major role for their acceptability.

The interest in legal argumentation as a field of research studied in its own right developed in the 1970s. The evolving legal argumentation studies mainly focused on the criteria for the rational justification of legal judgments. Research in the field has produced a rich selection of themes, methodologies and approaches.[39] Kalinowski (1972) proposed a classification of the types of legal reasoning, Alexy (1989) developed a legal argumentation theory based on analytic moral philosophy and Rieke (1982) surveyed the use of legal arguments in the context of communication functions.[40]

---

37. Pompeu Casanovas, 'Legal Electronic Institutions and ONTOMEDIA: Dialogue, Inventio, and Relational Justice Scenarios' in Pompeu Casanovas and others, *AI Approaches to the Complexity of Legal Systems Complex Systems, the SemanticWeb, Ontologies, Argumentation and Dialogue* (Springer 2010) 192.
38. Richard Orsinger, *The Role of Reasoning and Persuasion in Legal Argumentation* (2013) 9 <http://www.orsinger.com/PDFFiles/constructing-a-persuasive-argument-version-three.pdf> (accessed 2 Oct. 2018) citing Aristotle, *Posterior Analytics* 1.1. Aristotle's writings on Logic are found in six different books: Categories, On Interpretation, Prior Analytics, Posterior Analytics, Topics, and On Sophistical Refutations, Collectively Called the Organon.
39. Eveline Feteris, 'A Survey of 25 Years of Research on Legal Argumentation' (1997) 11 Argumentation 356.
40. Georges Kalinowski, *La Logique des norms* (Pressses Universitaires de France 1972); Robert Alexy, *A Theory of Legal Argumentation. The Theory of Rational Discourse as Theory of Legal*

Chaïm Pelerman, one of the most well-known legal argumentation theorists, strongly connects the practice of legal argumentation with the process of legal reasoning and the art of rhetoric:

> Argumentation is the technique that we use in controversy when we are concerned with criticizing and justifying, objecting and refuting, of asking and giving reasons. It is to argumentation that we have recourse when we discuss and deliberate, when we try to convince or persuade, when we give reasons for or against, when we justify our choices and decisions.[41]

In legal theory, legal argumentation theories have been described as arising as 'an echo of the argumentative turn in philosophy of language and as a middle way between the idea of a mechanistic judge and an arbitrary judge with absolute discretion'.[42] They focus on suggesting criteria for the reasonableness and rationality of judicial decisions and for facilitating the public scrutiny of the adjudication process.[43]

[C] Legal Argumentation in Judicial Decision-Making: Logic–Rhetoric–Dialectic

Legal argumentation can be studied in various contexts varying from the legislative process to the process of legal decision-making.[44] In this setting, judicial deliberation, court-room negotiations and treatment of legal questions in a legislative context can all be the object of legal argumentation studies.[45] What becomes important in such studies is the theoretical approach of the study as well as the methodology employed to conduct the research.

Aristotle's approach to 'Logic', 'Rhetoric' and 'Dialectic' has influenced the development of epistemology in contemporary argumentation theories. These classic antiquity concepts are transferred into the legal context constituting the theoretical framework usually employed in argumentation studies. Embarking from this way of thinking, argumentation theorists distinguish three main approaches to legal argumentation in the decision-making of judges: the logical approach, the rhetorical approach and the dialectical approach.

Justification (Clarendon Press 1989); Richard Rieke 'Argumentation in the Legal Process' in Robert Cox and Charles Arthur Willard (eds) *Advances in Argumentation Theory and Research* (Southern Illinois University Press 1982).

41. Chaim Perelman, *Justice, Law and Argument* (Reidel 1980) 108; For the construction of the structure of an international legal argument *see* Martti Koskenniemi, *From Apology to Utopia. The Structure of International Legal Argument* (Reissue with a New Epilogue) (CUP 2006) 503 et seq.
42. Christian Dahlman and Eveline Feteris (eds), *Legal Argumentation Theory: Cross-Disciplinary Perspectives* (Springer Science + Business Media Dordrecht 2013) 1 citing Flavia Carbonell, 'Reasoning by Consequences: Applying Different Argumentation Structures to the Analysis of Consequentialist Reasoning in Judicial Decisions'.
43. *Ibid.* 1.
44. *See* Part Introduction section III[A] 'Origins of Argumentation Theories'.
45. Dieter Flader, 'Aspects of Legal Argumentation' (2007) 4(1) TDM 1; *See also* Stephen Toulmin, *The Uses of Argument* (CUP 1958) (referring to argument phases and which features of arguments are field-invariant or field-dependent).

The concept of 'Logic' covers the intellectual analysis of the way people communicate between them, putting emphasis on the process of reasoning rather than the content of the communication.[46] The logical approach emphasises on the criteria for a logically valid argument. Formal validity interpreted in the terms of a logically valid argument constitutes a decisive criterion for the rationality of legal argumentation. In this context, the acceptability of a legal justification requires that the arguments underlying the justification could be reconstructed in a rational way and are acceptable according to specific legal standards.[47] The conclusion of a decision follows from the legal rules and the facts (premises) only when an argument is logically valid.[48]

The rhetorical approach connects the acceptability of legal arguments with their effectiveness to persuade a specific audience. The argumentative techniques used by judges in order to convince the audience for the acceptability of the legal decisions may vary from the use of certain legal principles such as good faith, fairness, equity and freedom, to the use of argumentation schemes such as analogy and *a contrario*.[49] Inspired from Aristotle's Topics, the German legal argumentation theorist, Viehweg, argues that justifications which are based on general viewpoints (topoi) such as general principles have the power to convince a legal audience.[50] The rhetorical approach is seen by various authors as an alternative to the formal validity of the logical approach.

While rhetoric echoes speeches in judicial frameworks, dialectic reflects 'legal dialogical controversies'.[51] The dialectical approach considers legal argumentation from the perspective of a discussion procedure aiming at defending a certain legal position. Based on this approach, the acceptability of a legal argument is assessed in the context of a dialogue.[52] The dialectical approach could also be seen as an answer to logical systems which mainly reconstruct monologues.

However, in certain studies, the elements of logic and rationality remain present as a means to emphasise on the rationality of the communication. Prakken, for example, developed a logical system within which it is possible to proceed to a dialectical analysis of legal arguments comparing the arguments for and against conflicting conclusions.[53]

46. Orsinger, *The Role of Reasoning and Persuasion in Legal Argumentation* (n 38) 9.
47. Eveline Feteris, *Fundamentals of Legal Argumentation: A Survey on Theories of the Justification of Judicial Decisions* (Springer-Science + Business media B.V. 1999) 15.
48. Feteris, 'A Survey of 25 Years of Research on Legal Argumentation' (n 39) 355, 358.
49. *Ibid.* 359.
50. Feteris, *Fundamentals of Legal Argumentation* (n 47) 18; *See also* Ivor A Richards, *The Philosophy of Rhetoric* (OUP 1936) describing rhetoric as the study of misunderstandings and its remedies); Chaim Perelman, *The New Rhetoric and the Humanities: Essays on Rhetoric and Its Applications* (Reidel 1979).
51. Casanovas, 'Legal Electronic Institutions and ONTOMEDIA' (n 37) 192.
52. Robert Alexy, *A Theory of Legal Argumentation. The Theory of Rational Discourse as Theory of Legal Justification* (Ruth Adler and Neil MacCormick tr, Clarendon Press 2009). A similar approach is the pragma-dialectics encompassing a consensus oriented analysis of reasoning and argument. The process of legal argumentation is considered as a contribution to a rational discussion.
53. Henry Prakken, *Logical Tools for Modelling Legal Argument: A Study of Defeasible Reasoning in Law* (Springer 1997).

In this dialectical setting, legal argumentation theorists depend the acceptability of the arguments of a legal decision on whether they meet certain formal, material and procedural criteria of rational justification.[54] The formal criterion requires that the argument is reconstructed as a logically valid argument which consists of the premises (facts and law) and the decision as a conclusion. The material aspect deals with the question of whether the rules and facts used in the premises can be considered acceptable. According to the procedural criterion, the acceptability of a legal decision requires the observation of rules such as consistency, efficiency, coherence and generalisability.

The three theoretical approaches of legal argumentation theories have inspired the theoretical framework of this book albeit used in the present context with alterations and adaptations as revealed in the next section.

[D] Legal Argumentation in Arbitral Decision-Making: Language–Rhetoric–Dialogue

Drawing on the concepts developed in legal argumentation studies, this book examines the legal arguments of investment-arbitration tribunals. Legal argumentation is studied in the context of the legal interpretation by arbitrators. Consequently, legal arguments are viewed as a means to effectuate and justify a legal interpretation in the context of a specific dispute.

The scope and purpose of the book, however, differs from the focus of legal augmentation theories as presented above.[55] The latter constitute a source of inspiration for the book; specifically the triptych of 'Logic', 'Rhetoric' and 'Dialectic', as well as the analytical methodology employed in such theoretical argumentation studies.[56] Nonetheless, the objective of the research is to reveal the process of interpretation

54. Feteris, 'A Survey of 25 Years of Research on Legal Argumentation' (n 39) 362–363.
55. *See* Part Introduction section III[C] 'Legal Argumentation in Judicial Decision-Making: Logic-Rhetoric–Dialectic'.
56. From a methodological perspective, legal argumentation theories follow various approaches. These methodologies, that can also be used in a combined way, are divided into six approaches: the philosophical, the theoretical, the practical, the empirical, the normative, and the analytical. The analytical methodology can be parallelised with an uncultivated piece of land. The situations that may arise in practice may not always be clear and ready to use. For this reason, a helping hand is required in order to prepare the land for cultivation. The required work may either be simple or more complicated depending on the theoretical plan and its purpose. In general, the analytical reconstruction may include different forms of 'transformational operations' such as 'selecting, supplementing, and rearranging to reformulating relevant elements of the original discourse'. The reason that this method is selected over the others lies in the fact that it is the most suitable for analysing the legal arguments contained in arbitral decisions. These arguments do not regularly follow a clear-cut subsumption of the facts to the law, resulting into blurring the methodology of legal decision-making. The chosen methodology is a process of selecting and rearranging – rather than transforming – the interpretive arguments in a way that permits the understanding of the process of interpretation and application of the law by the arbitrators. *See* Van Eemeren and Grootendorst, *A Systematic Theory of Argumentation* (n 18) 12; Feteris, 'A Survey of 25 Years of Research on Legal Argumentation' (n 39) 367; Ingo Venzke, *How Interpretation Makes International Law: On Semantic Change and Normative Twists* (OUP 2012) 198.

followed by arbitrators through the analysis of the legal argumentation process without getting into the discussion of whether the argumentation methods followed are rationally justified or not.

In this context, the book does not aim to investigate the criteria under which the interpretation of a legal rule can be rationally justified. In addition, the study will not get into the discussion of the types of reasoning – deductive reasoning, inductive reasoning, and reasoning by analogy – neither will it be concerned with the correctness of the arbitrators' normative statements.

The objective of the book is to explain the process arbitrators use in order to interpret the law. Legal argumentation in the arbitration context is treated mostly as a methodology of legal decision-making, rather than a pure theory of rational legal arguments.

In tune with the above and for the purpose of the book, the first perspective through which the interpretation of the law is examined is that of 'Language' rather than 'Logic'. Instead of focusing on the logical validity of the arguments, the emphasis is put on the language that arbitrators use when interpreting the law. What is examined is the legal vocabulary arbitrators use and the meaning they give to legal concepts such as 'rights', 'principles' and 'standards'.

The analysis of arbitral decision-making based on the rhetorical approach will focus on the function of the legal reasoning as a means to persuade a specific audience. The analysis of interpretation methods from this perspective is mostly connected to the externalisation of the interpretation process or in other words to the reasoning of arbitral awards. This part will examine the quality of the reasoning of arbitral awards, the communicative functions of reasoning and its importance for the legitimacy of the investment-arbitration framework.

Approaching the interpretation process from a dialogical perspective, the book develops a 'dialogical network' approach. The term 'Dialogical' is preferred over the term 'Dialectical' as having a wider content. The dialectic process is mostly connected to the aim of exposing the other speaker's weakness of arguments in order to persuade for the validity of one's own arguments. On the contrary, the dialogical approach provides an analysis of legal decision-making translating the interpretation process arbitrators use into the various dialogues formed in the decision-making process. This approach reveals the relations and dialogues formed between legal rules, principles, case law, customary international law and narrative techniques in the context of legal interpretation and justification.

Studies following a multidisciplinary approach combining legal argumentation theories and international arbitration are mostly limited to commercial arbitration.[57]

57. Degano studied the functional variety of linguistics as indicators of argumentation in arbitral awards, Chiara Degano, 'Indicators of Argumentation in Arbitration Awards: A Diachronic Perspective' in Vijay Bhatia, Christopher Candlin and Maurizio Gotti (eds), *The Discourses of Dispute Resolution* (Peter Lang 2010) 193; Degano also co-edited the volume *Arbitration Awards: Generic Features and Textual Realisations* which analyses the contextual and discourse data of arbitral awards in order to examine the extent to which arbitration practices are influenced by litigation procedures, Vijay Bhatia, Giuliana Garzone and Chiara Degano (eds), *Arbitration Awards: Generic Features and Textual Realisations* (Cambridge Scholars Publishing

This field of study is rather new since the majority of the literature made its appearance within the last seven years with the majority of the authors having a linguistic rather than a legal background. The focus is restricted to the linguistic and rhetorical analysis of awards and arbitration laws.[58]

In the field of investment-arbitration studies using legal argumentation theories mainly focus on the types of reasoning of arbitral judgments.[59] This book is distinguished from and complements the existing literature in various ways. First, it uses legal argumentation theories as the main theoretical framework in order to explore decision-making in investment arbitration. The existing studies are valuable contributions to the literature in this field but they do not focus on providing a systematic account of the interpretation process in investment arbitration from the perspective of language, rhetoric and dialogue.[60] Second, the interpretation process is strongly connected to the transnational characteristics of the arbitration framework within which decision-making takes place.[61]

Third, this book also differs in its methods. It does not only draw on international law and legal theory literature but also on case law and empirical data. The case law covers the publically available awards and decisions of investment-arbitration tribunals dealing with either procedural or substantive issues, both ad hoc and institutional

2012); The editors of the volume *Discourse and Practice in International Commercial Arbitration* seek to identify whether litigation affects the aspects of arbitration that are considered vital for its integrity as an institution and its independence as a professional practice, Vijay Bhatia, Christopher Candlin and Maurizio Gotti (eds) *Discourse and Practice in International Commercial Arbitration* (Ashgate 2012).

58. Vázquez-Orta compares the pattern of judicial and arbitral reasoning as pictured in judgments and awards, Ignacio Vázquez-Orta, 'Authoritative Intervention in Legal Discourse: A Genre-Based Study of Judgments and Arbitration Awards' (2013) RESLA 91; The same linguistic and rhetoric approach was followed by Han Zhengruia and Li Xiaoyu. The two linguistic theorists examine Chinese arbitration discourse through the analysis of arbitration awards, arbitration rules and laws, and lawyers' accounts, Han Zhengruia, and Li Xiaoyu, 'Discourse of International Commercial Arbitration: The Case of Mainland China' (2011) 43 JPragmat 1380; The editors of the volume *Legal Discourse Across Cultures and Systems* direct the attention to the 'linguistic and discoursal properties of legal documents used in international commercial arbitration', Vijay Bhatia, Christopher Candlin and Jan Engberg (eds) *Legal Discourse Across Cultures and Systems* (HKUP 2008); Walker and Daniels compare the role of argument in three alternative dispute resolution systems: arbitration, mediation, and multiparty facilitation, Gregg Walker and Steven Daniels, *Argument and Alternative Dispute Resolution Systems* (1995) 9 Argumentation 693.
59. Gilles Sourgens, in his book *A Nascent Common Law,* makes reference to Aristotle's *Rhetoric* in order to describe the inductive and synthetic nature of the reasoning of arbitral judgments and concludes that investment arbitration functions like a common law, Frédéric Sourgens, *A Nascent Common Law* (Brill/Nijhoff 2015) 29, 133–134; In a similar vein, the book *Practicing Virtue* looks at both commercial and investment arbitration from the 'inside', with an emphasis on its transnational character. Legal argumentation is limited to the issue of party submissions and its role is assessed within the context of written submissions and oral hearings, Caron and others, *Practising Virtue* (n 3); Scobbie assesses the use of rhetoric in interpretation as a method for achieving the objectives of the interpreter, Iain Scobbie, 'Rhetoric, Persuasion, and Interpretation in International Law' in Andrea Bianchi, Daniel Peat, and Matthew Windsor (eds) *Interpretation in International Law* (OUP 2015).
60. *See* Part Introduction section III[D] 'Legal Argumentation in Arbitral Decision-Making: Language–Rhetoric–Dialogue'.
61. *See* §1.01 'Dispute Resolution Function: A Transnational Perspective'.

as well as arbitrations under BITs and multilateral treaties (NAFTA, ECT). It also covers decisions of national, international and regional courts and tribunals in order to demonstrate the interaction of investment arbitration with these legal orders. This research does not purport to offer an exhaustive résumé of all the awards available but rather it aims to select and analyse the most important awards in terms of doctrinal development connected to the research questions of each chapter.

Going a step further, the book also draws on empirical research, in particular, on open-ended, semi-structured interviews.[62] It is a confirmatory study which aims at confirming or rejecting views about the legal decision-making process. The total number of arbitrators interviewed is ten including two women and eight men.[63] The interview subjects were selected by a 'purposive' or 'judgmental' sampling keeping in mind that the arbitrators are best fit to answer questions about arbitral decision-making. As Berg points out: 'When developing a purposive sample, researchers use their special knowledge or expertise about some group to select subjects who represent this population.'[64]

The research paradigm is interpretive in the sense that it focuses on subjective interpretations with no universal conclusions. It is an interpretive paradigm because the understanding of the issues involved in the decision-making of investment-arbitration tribunals emerges from the analysis of the individual responses and allows 'the subjective world of human experience' to arise.[65] This paradigm is characterised by 'a concern for the individual' and his interpretations of the world.[66] This is the case due to the subjective nature of the data gathered, as they are perceived views coming from the individuals immediately involved on the topic examined. Since a small

62. The interview design is detailed in Annex 'Interview Questions'. The interview included seven open-ended questions. This semi-structured interview style gives the freedom to the interviewees to develop any point that they feel is relevant to the questions. The arbitrators had the chance to expand on their answer and develop any information they considered appropriate. For purposes of structure and continuity, all the interviewees were asked the same questions. However, during the interview some sub-questions where posed drawing directly on the specific answers of each interviewee. The data derived from the interviews is qualitative. *See* Bruce Berg, *Qualitative Research Methods for the Social Sciences* (Pearson 2007) 44; Jaber Gubrium and James Holstein (eds) *Handbook of Interview Research* (Sage 2002) 37.
63. Regarding the use of the interview data, full anonymity is retained and the arbitrators are referred to using letters: Arbitrator A, Arbitrator B, Arbitrator C, Arbitrator D, Arbitrator E, Arbitrator F, Arbitrator G, Arbitrator H, Arbitrator I, Arbitrator J. For this reason, the full interview transcripts are not included. The disproportionate analogy of men and women interviewed is a factor that can easily be understood if someone takes into account that the appointments of female arbitrators are fewer than those of male arbitrators. A study of 254 concluded ICSID cases, from 1972 to 2012 revealed that from 746 arbitrators that were appointed, 42 (5.63%) of those appointments were of female arbitrators. *See* Lucy Greenwood and Mark Baker, *Getting a Better Balance on International Arbitration Tribunal* (2012) 28(4) ArbIntl 653, 654; Gus Van Harten, 'The (Lack of) Women Arbitrators in Investment Treaty Arbitration' (2012) Columbia FDI Perspectives No. 59 <http://ccsi.columbia.edu/files/2014/01/FDI_59.pdf> (accessed 6 Feb. 2018).
64. Berg, *Qualitative Research Methods for the Social Sciences* (n 62) 92–95.
65. Louis Cohen, Lawrence Manion, and Keith Morrison, *Research Methods in Education* (6th ed., Routledge, 2007) 21; Dawn Watkins and Mandy Burton, *Research Methods in Law* (Routledge 2013).
66. Louis Cohen and others, *Research Methods in Education* (n 65) 21.

population of arbitrators is tested, the data coming from the interviews are 'non-parametric', as they do not assume knowledge about the general population's tendency.[67]

Therefore, the book takes a novel approach. On the one hand, it uses an interdisciplinary analysis combining the core epistemology of legal argumentation theories and legal interpretation in international law and investment arbitration. On the other hand, it attempts to identify the personal views of investment arbitrators on the way they interpret the law. Finally, the book proposes a new methodological approach to interpretation which is the analysis of interpretation methods through a dialogical network.

IV STRUCTURE OF THE BOOK

The book is divided into four parts. Part I is comprised of Chapter 1 and describes the dispute resolution function of investor-state arbitration tribunals from a transnational perspective. In particular, it examines the transnational characteristics of the investment-arbitration framework and how these may influence arbitral decision-making. After placing investment arbitration in this transnational setting, it analyses the various decision-making types of arbitral tribunals such as the attitudinal, economic, strategic and legal decision-making genres. Going a step further, it delimits the scope of this book to legal decision-making which focuses on the process of legal interpretation.

Part II of the book analyses the legal decision-making process of arbitrators from the first legal argumentation perspective, that of 'Language'. What is examined here is the arbitral language, meaning the legal vocabulary arbitrators use in the interpretation process. The use of language, the interpretation of terms and the arguments used to assert the meaning of words are all interconnected processes. This part is comprised of Chapter 2.

Chapter 2 initially analyses the general normative functions of legal language, in particular of 'rules', 'standards', 'principles' and 'rights'. As a next step, the chapter examines arbitral case law in order to identify what meaning arbitrators give to the above-mentioned legal terms. The objective of the part's analysis is to reveal whether arbitrators have developed a specialised interpretation language adapted to the interpretation needs that arise in the context of a specific dispute and the characteristics of investment arbitration.

The way arbitrators use legal terms when interpreting the law may also be linked to the aim of persuading a specific audience, which is exactly the aim of rhetoric. As such, Part III of the book examines how arbitral tribunals externalise their legal decision-making process through the reasoning of their awards from a rhetorical perspective. 'Rhetoric' appears to be strongly linked to an audience-oriented legal argumentation scheme. The legal arguments of arbitral awards will be analysed so as

67. *Ibid.* 503; *See also* Anthony Bradney, 'The Place of Empirical Research in the Law School Curriculum' in Peter Crane and Herbert Kritzer (eds), *The Oxford Handbook of Empirical Legal Research* (OUP 2010).

to reveal the functions of the reasoning process for specific audiences and for the investment-arbitration framework in general. This part is divided into Chapter 3 and Chapter 4. Chapter 3 particularly examines the reasoning requirement as provided for in the investment treaties as well as the dynamics of reasoning based on the characteristics of the investment-arbitration framework. These dynamics touch upon the concepts of 'acceptability', 'audience' and 'legitimacy'. Chapter 4 aims at elucidating the functions of reasons in arbitral practice. These are divided into a persuasion-oriented function and a development-oriented function. What is purported is to reveal whether arbitrators approach the issue of reasoning in an idiosyncratic way based on the specific needs and characteristics of investment arbitration.

Part IV of the book approaches the legal decision-making process from a dialogical perspective. It is comprised of Chapters 5 and 6. Chapter 5 develops a novel 'dialogical network' approach to interpretation introducing the interaction of legal arguments as an interpretation method. It identifies five types of legal arguments which play their own role in the decision-making process: Narrative, Convention, Precedent, Custom, and Policy. While Chapter 5 introduces a theoretical perspective of the 'dialogical network' approach, Chapter 6 demonstrates how each one of the five syllogisms appears in arbitral practice. The Narrative arguments examine the role of the dialogues formed between the legal arguments of the parties and the tribunal. The Convention-based arguments focus on the effectiveness of the VCLT in the investment-arbitration legal decision-making process. The Precedent arguments explore the dialogues formed between arbitrators and domestic and international legal orders. The Customary law based arguments analyse the interaction of arbitrators with customary international law. Last but not least, the Policy arguments examine the role of policy in interpretation and the dialogues formed between the decision-makers and the policies of the investment-arbitration framework.

At this point a note about style is necessary since Part IV is the largest part of the book and this may create the image of an uneven analysis. The reason this part is so large is because it develops a novel framework for the analysis of legal decision-making through the perspective of 'Dialogue'. As such, it was necessary to present both the theoretical underpinnings of such an analysis as well as its application in practice. In this sense, it was important to describe and delimit the 'Dialogue' function and conceptually separate it from similar terms. Last but not least, the 'dialogical network' methodology was crafted in detail since it was formed with the intention to be useful for future studies on the legal decision-making of international courts and tribunals and the relationships formed between international and domestic legal orders.

PART I Arbitral Decision-Making

[k]nowledge of the law consists in large part of an understanding of prevailing interpretive practices within the legal community. [68]

68. Cass Sunstein, *Legal Reasoning and Political Conflict* (OUP 1998) 33.

Introduction to Part I

The decision-making process signifies the specific process in which arbitrators engage in order to resolve a specific dispute. In international investment law there is no central authority empowered with a dispute resolution function. Dispute resolution is decentralised and spread throughout the investment framework by the provisions of individual treaties.[69] The investment treaties mainly provide for four forms of dispute resolution including: (a) consultation between the State parties to a treaty; (b) state-to-state arbitration; (c) consultation and negotiation between the foreign investor and the host State; and (d) arbitration between a private investor and a State.[70] This book focuses on the last type of dispute resolution analysing decision-making in investor-state arbitration disputes.

Part I sets the conceptual framework of the book thus delimiting its scope. It is comprised of Chapter 1. The first section of the chapter analyses the decision-making function of arbitral tribunals from a transnational perspective. It describes the transnational characteristics of a dispute resolution process and the interactions taking place therewith. It also examines the types of decision-making through a genre approach dividing arbitral decision-making into four genres: legal, attitudinal, strategic and economic. The genre approach constitutes the basis for narrowing down the scope of the research in order to place the focus on the legal genre of arbitral decision-making. The latter comprises both the processes of interpreting and applying the law. Even though the present study recognises that the separation of these two processes is not always an easy task, the book focuses on the interpretation process.[71]

69. Jeswald Salacuse, *The Law of Investment Treaties* (OUP 2010) 10.
70. *Ibid.*
71. For the purposes of this research, the concepts 'interpretation process' and 'methodology of interpretation' are used interchangeably. They both signify the broader hermeneutic process used to derive the meaning of legal rules. This process may include multiple interpretation methods/canons such as contextual, historical, teleological or systematic interpretation. *See also* the analysis on the concept of 'interpretation' below in §1.02[D][1] 'Legal Decision-Making: Interpretation and Application of the Law'.

CHAPTER 1
Decision-Making and Legal Argumentation

§1.01 DISPUTE RESOLUTION FUNCTION: A TRANSNATIONAL PERSPECTIVE

The direct function of international courts and tribunals, including investment-arbitration tribunals, is the resolution of a particular dispute.[72] Sir Hersch Lauterpacht connects this particular dispute resolution function with the fundamental role of international courts in rendering international law an effective and complete law through filling gaps and concretising obligations.[73] Such a function is further linked to 'the individualised and isolated maximization of the parties' satisfaction'.[74]

The process of decision-making is effectuated with connection to the ad hoc dispute settlement function of arbitral tribunals. What is important, however, is to identify and address the issues that are intertwined with this function. Such issues are for example the ways national and international legal orders interact in the context of interpretation or the role of policy, custom and third parties therein. In a broad sense, international courts and tribunals are better viewed as 'instruments of the parties in a state-centred world order, as organs of a value-based international community, and as institutions of specific legal regimes'.[75]

72. David Caron, 'International Courts and Tribunals: Their Roles Amidst a World of Courts' (2011) 26(1) ICSID Foreign Investment Law Journal 3.
73. Hersch Lauterpacht, 'The Function of Law in the International Community' in Caron, 'International Courts and Tribunals' (n 72) 2.
74. Thomas Schultz, 'The Three Pursuits of Dispute Settlement' (2010) 1 CYArb 227, 227; But *see* Caron stating that the traditional approach of viewing arbitrators as the agents of the parties has been described as taking us back to 'the days of the Mosaic law, and to a systematically individualistic conception of law, which is almost the exact contrary of international solidarity', Caron, 'International Courts and Tribunals' (n 72) fn 7.
75. Armin Von Bogdandy and Ingo Venzke, 'On the Functions of International Courts: An Appraisal in Light of the Burgeoning Public Authority' (2012) Amsterdam Law School Legal Studies Research Paper No 2012-69, 1.

The investment-arbitration framework 'exists at the intersection of multiple fields'.[76] It encompasses the interaction of divergent actors and laws. It is comprised of public and private actors coming from various legal and political systems and of different sets of laws including public international law, administrative decisions and host State regulations.[77] In this context, private investors, public States, decision-makers, NGOs, think tanks, national and international legal systems and customs all interact possessing their own role in the investment-arbitration framework.

From a functional perspective, investment arbitration is considered to have developed into a dynamic dispute resolution process with its own procedures which largely operate independently from national and international law.[78] Structurally it is difficult to position it entirely in the sphere of national, international or in the field of private or public law.[79]

This book examines the decision-making process of investor-state arbitration tribunals from a transnational perspective. The meaning of the term 'transnational' is 'cross-border' or in other words, something that extends beyond the boundaries of a

76. Anthea Roberts, 'Clash of Paradigms: Actors and Analogies Shaping the Investment Treaty System' (2013) 107 AJIL 45, 49; Schill states that 'international arbitration functions as a system of transnational governance that has an impact on society at large and that has to conform to generally accepted standards for governance, such as democracy, the rule of law, and human rights'. Stephan Schill, 'Developing a Framework for the Legitimacy of International Arbitration', Amsterdam Law School Legal Studies Research Paper No. 2017-23, 5; Similarly, Schultz notes: 'These last decades have been marked by a radical increase in the number of dispute resolution mechanisms in the international arena and by a general liberalization of national arbitration laws, leading to a decreasing control of national courts and national laws over arbitral procedures and awards, in what William Park views as a paradigm shift to "laissez-faire judicial review". These movements were accompanied by a creeping expansion of private justice systems into new territories, such as foreign investment, sports, competition matters, Internet-related disputes and, to some extent, consumer disputes. Private justice mechanisms, and in particular arbitral systems, which this article focuses on, have become numerous and more autonomous, and have extended their realm. They have acquired a growing normative power, furthering the development of their own spheres of normativity, which in certain cases may be referred to as transnational arbitral regimes.' Thomas Schultz, 'The Concept of Law in Transnational Arbitral Legal Orders and Some of Its Consequences', 2(1) JIDS (2011) 59–60; Brekoulakis also argues that: 'From this procedural standpoint, clear norms regulating the conduct of arbitration have emerged through constant arbitration practices, and with the simultaneous contribution of a variety of national and transnational sources. These sources include arbitration institutions, associations and counsel, of arbitration specialized departments of law firms, commercial organizations and chambers.' Stavros Brekoulakis, 'International Arbitration Scholarship and the Concept of Arbitration Law', 36(4) FordhamIntlLJ (2013) 778.
77. Pieter Bekker, 'Recalibrating the Investment Treaty Arbitration System Through Non-Compartmentalized Legal Thinking' (2013) 55 HarvIntlLJ Online 1, 12; *See also*: Emmanuel Gaillard, 'The Sociology of International Arbitration' (2015) 31(1) ArbIntl 3 et seq. (speaking about the emergence of specialised actors in addition to the parties and their arbitrators, who are the essential and traditional arbitration actors); Won L Kidane, *The Culture of International Arbitration* (OUP 2017) (analysing the existing theories on international arbitration from a cultural perspective); Joshua Carton, *The Culture of International Arbitration* (OUP 2013) (identifying the legal and social norms governing an emerging culture of international arbitration, and their implications for the interpretation of contract law).
78. Caron and others, *Practising Virtue* (n 3) 2.
79. *Ibid.*

single country.[80] However, it should be noted that the term 'transnational' is not a term of the art. It has been used by different authors in different senses and contexts. In the legal field, the term 'transnational' has been used in order to express the emergence of new legal relations, legal doctrines and regimes that are not fully grasped by national or international law.[81] As such, it has stimulated thorough scholarly discourse as its meaning defers based on the specific lens through which it can be viewed and analysed. Going through the doctrinal analysis of transnational law, this research identifies three such lenses.

Through the first lens, the term 'transnational law' is used to add a new source of law to the traditional national and international sources of law. It describes the emergence of a uniform law – whether hard law or soft law – as the legal regime for international commercial transactions.[82] Transnational law was initially connected to the regulation of global commercial transactions through the emergence of *lex mercatoria*. Sir Roy Goode described the different usages of the term 'transnational law'. He particularly made reference to the emergence of international uniform sources of commercial law, and to the factual similarity in contractual patterns and contract laws applicable to international commercial transactions.[83]

The second lens describes the way transnational law emerges through the interaction of various private and public actors. Philip Jessup produced a succinct definition of the term in pursuit of a response to the interaction of rules and actors regulating issues that arise in a global context. He defined it to include both private and public international law as well as other rules which do not wholly fit into these categories.[84] Similarly, for Cotterrell, transnational law goes beyond the role of the States as traditional lawmakers. Cross-border interactions are not solely regulated by States but by different networks created in the context of corporations and civil society groups which fill in the gaps and interact in the formulation of a transnational legal framework.[85]

Transnational law under these two lenses is seen as a first step towards a global governance; a global law that will grow mainly from the social peripheries rather than from State authorities and international institutions.[86] Unlike the traditional dichotomies of law, transnational law covers a wide range of emerging governance communities which exist and function beyond the jurisdiction of a single nation State. Such

80. Roy Goode, Herbert Kronke and Ewan Mckendrick (eds), *Transnational Commercial Law: Texts, Cases and Materials* (2nd ed., OUP 2015) 4.
81. Roger Cotterrell, 'What Is Transnational Law?' (2012) 37(2) Journal of the American Bar Foundation Issue 500, 501.
82. Goode, Kronke and Mckendrick (eds), *Transnational Commercial Law: Texts, Cases and Materials* (n 80) 4.
83. *Ibid.*
84. Philip Jessup, *Transnational Law* (Yale University Press 1956) 2; *See also* Peer Zumbansen, 'Defining the Space of Transnational Law: Legal Theory, Global Governance & Legal Pluralism' (2011) Osgoode CLPE Research Paper No. 21/2011 1.
85. Cotterrell, 'What Is Transnational Law?' (n 81), 500, 514; *See also* Gralf-Peter Calliess and Peer Zumbansen, *Rough Consensus and Running Code: A Theory of Transnational Private Law* (Hart 2010).
86. Andreas Fischer-Lescano and Gunther Teubner, 'Regime-Collisions: the Vain Search for Legal Unity in the Fragmentation of Global Law' (2004) 25 MichJIntlL 999; *See also* Gunther Teubner,

governance communities are not structured around an organised government system delegated with power in the same way States are. Rather, they may be local, regional or international in nature organised for mutual benefit or for specific objectives, such as the EU and the WTO.[87]

The term 'transnational' in the legal field may also have a third meaning indicating a broader transnational process which goes beyond lawmaking and actor interaction but focuses on a methodological dimension. It describes a transnational methodology of decision-making as a means to interpret and apply the law in the context of a specific dispute. Transnational decision-making can be understood as a specialised methodology of decision-making characterised by interactions and communication networks.[88] Such an approach to decision-making also acknowledges the existence of various interpretive and epistemic communities influencing the way investment law is interpreted.[89]

A transnational perspective provokes the revision of ideas and methods of international law to keep up with the continuous development of a field of law that does not focus on traditional regulatory powers but deals with regulating transnational relations between individuals, corporations and public actors.[90] The emergence of specialised legal decision-making methodologies has gained momentum. The ICJ pictures the emergence of specialised approaches in the international decision-making scene stating that the treaties of international organisations: 'can raise specific problems of interpretation owing, *inter alia*, to their character which is conventional and at the same time institutional; the very nature of the organization created, the objectives which have been assigned to it by its founders, the imperatives associated with the effective performance of its functions, as well as its own practice, are all elements which may deserve special attention when the time comes to interpret these constituent treaties'.[91]

As eloquently put by Paulsson: 'Whatever the reason for the expansion of arbitral and other non-state methods of resolving disputes, it seems futile to resist their claims

'Global Bukowina': Legal Pluralism in the World Society, in Gunther Teubner (ed,) *Global Law Without a State* (Dartmouth Publishing 1997) 5 ('the new living law of the world is nourished not from stores of tradition but from the ongoing self-reproduction of highly technical, highly specialized, often formally organized and rather narrowly defined, global networks of an economic, cultural, academic or technological nature').

87. Larry Catá Backer, 'The Emerging Normative Structures of Transnational Law: Non-State Enterprises in Polycentric Asymmetric Global Orders' (2016) 31 BYU Journal Public International Law 1, 38.
88. Backer refers to the concept of transnational law focusing on methodology. The author describes it as focusing on 'methodology and interconnectivity, on networks and intermeshing of systems in constant communication'. Larry Catá Backer, 'The Emerging Normative Structures of Transnational Law: Non-State Enterprises in Polycentric Asymmetric Global Orders' (n 87), 1, 3.
89. Michael Waibel, 'Interpretive Communities in International Law' in Andrea Bianchi, Daniel Peat, and Matthew Windsor (eds) *Interpretation in International Law* (n 59) 149; *See* below §6.05[B][2] 'Emerging Social Policy Concerns'.
90. Roger Cotterrell, 'What is Transnational Law?' (n 81), 500, 505.
91. ICJ, Legality of the Use of Force By a State of Nuclear Weapons in Armed Conflict, Advisory Opinion (8 Jul. 1996) ICJ Reports 1996, 66–85, para. 19; Maximilian Clasmeier, *Arbitral Awards as Investments: Treaty Interpretation and the Dynamics of International Investment Law* (Kluwer 2016) 149.

to belong to the genus of legal processes.'[92] Within this background, a transnational dispute resolution process can find its theoretical basis in what Koh describes as a 'transnational legal process': 'a process whereby public and private actors, including nation-states, corporations, international organizations, non-governmental organizations, and individuals, interact in a variety of fora to interpret, enforce, and ultimately internalize, rules of international law'.[93]

As such, it calls for the evaluation of four components characterising a transnational legal process: it is non-traditional, non-statist, dynamic, and normative.[94] 'Non-traditional' refers to a process that transcends the traditional dichotomies of private-public and national-international. A 'non-statist' process indicates the existence of not only State actors but non-State actors as well. The transnational legal process is 'dynamic' transforming, mutating and percolating 'up and down, from the public to the private, from the domestic to the international level and back down again'.[95] Finally, it is a 'normative process' signifying the emergence of new rules of law through such interactions. These new rules of law are interpreted, internalised and enforced, thus activating the process from the beginning.[96]

In this setting, a transnational approach is not restricted to the type of law regulating transnational relationships. For the purposes of this study, the concept 'transnational' is connected to a decision-making process as part of a broader transnational dispute resolution process.[97] This perspective is used in order to identify the transnational elements of arbitral decision-making, the interpretive needs of the disputes and the specialised characteristics of investment arbitration.

---

92. Jan Paulsson, 'Arbitration in Three Dimensions' (2011) 60(2) ICLQ 291, 317.
93. Harold Koh, 'Jefferson Memorial Lecture – Transnational Legal Process after September 11th' (2004) 22(3) BerkeleyJIntlL 337, 339; Brekoulakis states: 'international arbitration is a community that has the capacity to engender non-state rules which the members of this community accept as normative'. Stavros Brekoulakis, 'International Arbitration Scholarship and the Concept of Arbitration Law' (n 76), 748.
94. Harold Koh, 'Transnational Legal Process' (1996) 75 NebLRev 181, 183.
95. *Ibid.* 184.
96. *Ibid.*
97. In the context of *lex mercatoria*, Gaillard approached transnational law as a method of decision-making, rather than as a list of general principles of law. Emmanuel Gaillard, 'Transnational Law: A Legal System or a Method of Decision-Making?' 17(1) ArbIntl 59, 62; Schultz refers to the 'transnationalisation' of the applicable law in the sense that it is interpreted in a different manner than it would be by a national court. The arbitration community members share a social convention – the removal of the dispute from possibly inadequate national legal orders – according to which it is desirable to interpret them differently. Thomas Schultz, *Transnational Legality: Stateless Law and International Arbitration* (OUP 2014) 125; Sourgens forms an analogy between the transnational dispute resolution process and common law. Sourgens, *A Nascent Common Law* (n 59) 91; Similarly, Dezalay and Garth, focusing on commercial arbitration and the theory of social fields, speak about the construction of a transnational legal order by arbitrators largely independent from the domestic legal orders. The interactions of various 'social players' in the development, application and interpretation of *lex mercatoria* has led to the construction of a so-called 'transnational system of private justice'. Such law that developed along the resolution of cross-border business disputes gained a type of transnational authority even in countries with weak legal traditions, Yves Dezalay and Bryant Garth, *Dealing in Virtue: International Commercial Arbitration and the Construction of a Transnational Legal Order* (UCP 1996) 31, 64.

§1.02 GENRES OF ARBITRAL DECISION-MAKING

The dispute resolution function of arbitrators is effectuated through a specific decision-making process which, for the purpose of this book, reflects a binding determination between possible outcomes through the process of interpreting and applying the law.[98]

Human behaviour could be explained through many prisms that focus on various criteria. This section identifies these criteria in the decision-making context and specifies the genres under which they fall. The genre approach has a double function: it recognises the complexity of the arbitrator's decision-making task which can be examined based on various criteria, and it helps to narrow down the scope of the research moving the focus to specific decision-making elements.

In the judicial context, the genres of decision-making range between legal formalism, that views the judge as mechanically deducing the law from abstract rules and applying them to the facts, and legal realism, that identifies the influence of extra-legal factors of social, political and economic character in the decision-making process.[99] The scholarship on decision-making in the arbitral setting largely borrows from the studies on the decision-making of judges and jurists.[100] The present study identifies five decision-making genres: the legal genre, the attitudinal/behavioural genre, the economic genre and the strategic/institutional genre.[101]

It is important to note that the genres of decision-making presented below are not disconnected from one another. The process of deciding on a particular case may, at the same time, be analysed based on the sources of legal authority referred to by the decision-maker, on policy and economic concerns, or on the personal experience of the decision-maker.

The studies that have been conducted in order to demonstrate how arbitrators decide are mostly empirical studies that focus on whether the decision-making is

---

98. As such, the concept of 'dispute resolution' is broader than the concept of 'decision-making'.
99. Ronald Cass, 'Judging: Norms and Incentives of Retrospective Decision-Making' (1995) 75 BULRev 941, 942 (analysing the systemic envisioning of a legal system running 'according to script regardless of the players. The straw man of this account is legal formalism'. On the other hand, 'the individual oriented description of judicial decision-making' relegates to legal realism); Theories on adjudication require a careful and rigorous analysis. Only indicative recent studies are referred to here; *See also* Richard A Posner, *How Judges Think* (HUP 2008) 371 (stating that 'legalism fails at a deeper level to refute the hypothesis that personal and political leanings influence judicial decisions'. However, he opposes legalism, as he calls the formalist theory, to pragmatism.); *See also* Ronald Dworkin, *Taking Rights Seriously* (reprint, A & C Black, 2013) 456 (arguing that albeit the existence of judicial discretion when deciding on a case, judges are rightly understood as searching for an internally coherent meaning of law. He formulates an adjudication theory recognising a single right answer to complex legal questions).
100. For example, Philipp Peters, 'Chapter II: The Arbitrator and the Arbitration Procedure – Presiding Arbitrator, Deciding Arbitrator: Decision-Making in Arbitral Tribunals' in Christian Klausseger and others (eds), Austrian Yearbook on International Arbitration 2011 (Manz'sche Verlags- Universitätsbuchhandlung 2011) 129–160.
101. Daphna Kapeliuk, 'Repeat Appointment Factor: Exploring Decision Patterns of Elite Investment Arbitrators' (2010–2011) 96 CornellLRev 47, 58; Richard Posner analyses 9 theories of judicial behaviour: attitudinal, strategic, sociological, psychological, economic, organisational, pragmatic, phenomenological, legalist. Posner, *How Judges Think* (n 99) 19.

affected by individual preferences.[102] Influenced by the scholarship on the US national judges,[103] the studies on arbitral decision-making focus on the extra-legal factors influencing the decision-making, namely personal policy preferences and financial incentives of the arbitrators.[104]

[A] Attitudinal/Behavioural Genre

The attitudinal or behavioural model postulates that judges decide not only in light of the facts of the case but also based on ideological preferences. This model is an amalgamation of concepts from legal realism and political and social sciences.[105] It focuses on how the personal characteristics of the decision-maker can influence the decision-making process.[106] These personal attributes may include elements such as gender, race, education, religion, previous judicial experience, political ideologies, appointment of the decision-maker by the party and presidential role of the judge.

In the arbitration scene, studies on the decision-making of arbitrators cover a wide range of matters from the way the background of the arbitrators influence their decisions to the issues of bias and the assessment of the arbitrator's ethical behaviour. From an ideological and political point of view, this genre describes the way the personal background and the individual preferences of the arbitrators affect the decision-making process.[107]

---

102. Susan Franck, 'Empirically Evaluating Claims About Investment Treaty Arbitration' (2007) 86(1) NCLRev; Susan D Franck, 'Development and Outcomes of Investment Treaty Arbitration' (2009) 50(2) HarvIntlLJ; Washington & Lee Legal Studies Paper No. 2009-04; Cf Gus Van Harten, 'Fairness and Independence in Investment Arbitration: A Critique of Susan Franck's "Development and Outcomes of Investment Treaty Arbitration"' (2011) <http://ssrn.com/abstract=1740031> (accessed 10 Jun. 2018).
103. Judge Posner notes that judges' personal characteristics such as race, sex, personality traits, professional and life experiences contribute to the development of a judge's ideology and 'thus of the political inclinations that affect judicial decisions'. Posner, *How Judges Think* (n 99) 370; C Herman Pritchett, 'Divisions of Opinion among Justices of the U.S. Supreme Court, 1939–1941' (1941) 35 AmPolSciRev, 890–98 (studying how private attitudes of the US Supreme judges become public law); Sheldon Goldman, 'Voting Behavior on the United States Courts of Appeals, 1961–1964' (1966) AmPolSciRev 60, 374 83 (researching the judicial behaviour of the appeal court judges based on attitudinal and background characteristics).
104. Stavros Brekoulakis, 'Systemic Bias and the Institution of International Arbitration: A New Approach to Arbitral Decision-Making' (2013) 4(3) JIDS 553, 571.
105. For example, Harold Spaeth, 'The Attitudinal Model' in Lee Epstein (eds) *Contemplating Courts* (CQ Press 1995) 296–315; Charles M Cameron and Lewis A Kornhauser, 'Rational Choice Attitudinalism? A Review of Epstein, Landes and Posner's The Behavior of Federal Judges: A Theoretical and Empirical Study of Rational Choice' (2015). NYU Law and Economics Research Paper No. 15-15. <http://ssrn.com/abstract=2640600> (accessed 10 Jun. 2018).
106. In his empirical analysis of the U.S. Supreme Court justices' votes, Schubert aimed at answering the following question: 'To what extent are their public acts influenced by their personal beliefs?'. Glendon Schubert, *The Judicial Mind: The Attitudes and Ideologies of Supreme Court Justices 1946–1963* (NUP 1965) 15; *See also* Harry T Edwards, 'Public Misperceptions Concerning the "Politics" of Judging: Dispelling Some Myths About the D.C. Circuit' (1985) 56 University of Colorado Law Review 619.
107. *See* David Schneiderman, 'Judicial Politics and International Investment Arbitration: Seeking an Explanation for Conflicting Outcomes' (2010) NJILB 30 383; Catherine A Rogers, 'The Politics of International Investment Arbitrators' (2013) Penn State Law Research Paper No.

It has been suggested that the arbitrator's decision-making history (award orientation) has a consistent impact on arbitral outcomes.[108] In addition, there has been a growth in empirical studies exploring the voting patterns of sole arbitrators.[109] Specific characteristics of party-appointed arbitrators have also been studied in order to demonstrate whether these have an influence on the dynamics of the panel and consequently on the final award.[110] Other factors that may influence the reappointment of arbitrators include the pre-existing relationship between the arbitrator and the appointing party, the arbitrator's reputation and the economic reward.[111] Quantitative research has also been effectuated regarding the connection between the developmental background of presiding arbitrators and control over the arbitration process.[112]

The way the above-mentioned personal preferences and values of the individual arbitrator influence the decision-making process may lead to issues of perception of bias and the rendering of compromised awards. It has been argued that, since private judges mostly depend on their appointment, they tend to 'split the baby' rendering an award that would keep both parties happy, thus augmenting their chances of being reappointed in future cases.[113] The issue of bias is also connected to the effects of

---

52-2013 (exploring how the social background, attitudinal behaviour and institutional concerns affect the decision-making of arbitrators); Catherine A Rogers, 'The Politics of International Investment Arbitrators' (2013) 12 SantaClaraIntlLRev, 2013 Penn State Law Research Paper No. 52-2013, (evaluating hypotheses about the influence of extra-legal factors, such as ideology, common law or civil law background, nature of litigants, policy reaction to other institutions, on arbitral decision-making); Michael Waibel, 'Empirical Research on International Arbitrators: Benefits and Challenges' in Stavros Brekoulakis, Julian Lew and Loukas Mistelis (eds), *The Evolution of International Arbitration* (Kluwer 2016), (studying the nationalities of ICSID Arbitrators).

108. Stephen Crow and James Logan, 'Arbitrators' Characteristics and Decision-Making Records, Gender of Arbitrators and Grievants, and the Presence of Legal Counsel as Predictors of Arbitral Outcomes' (1994) 7(2) ERRJ 169; Nels E Nelson and Sung Min Kim provide a structural model of arbitral decision-making concluding that arbitrators' biographical characteristics have a limited impact in determining the arbitral decision, Nels E Nelson and Sung Min Kim, 'A Model of Arbitral Decision Making: Facts, Weights, and Decision Elements' (2008) 47 Industrial Relations: A Journal of Economy and Society 2, 266–283.; *See also* Nels E, Nelson and Earl M, Curry, J, 'Arbitrator Characteristics and Arbitral Decisions' (1981) 20 Industrial Relations: A Journal of Economy and Society 3.
109. For example, Orley Ashenfelter and David Bloom, 'Models of Arbitrator Behavior: Theory and Evidence' (1984) 74 AmEconRev 111.
110. Daphna Kapeliuk, 'Collegial Games: Analyzing the Effect of Panel Composition on Outcome in Investment Arbitration' (2012) 31 Rev Litig 267.
111. Natalia Giraldo-Carrillo, 'The "Repeat Arbitrators" Issue: A Subjective Concept' (2011) 19 Revista Colombiana de Derecho Internacional 75.
112. Susan Franck, 'Development and Outcomes of Investment Treaty Arbitration' (2009) 50 HarvIntlLJ 2 435.
113. David Bloom, 'Empirical Models of Arbitrator Behaviour under Conventional Arbitration' (1986) 68 RevEcon&Stat 578, 578; *See also* Henry S Farber & Max H Bazerman, 'The General Basis of Arbitrator Behavior: An Empirical Analysis of Conventional and Final-Offer Arbitration' (1986) 54 Econometrica 819, 822, 842 (maintaining that arbitrators tend to avoid rendering awards that would not be acceptable to either party). But *see* Stephanie E Keer and Richard W Naimark, 'Arbitrators Do Not "Split the Baby": Empirical Evidence from International Business Arbitrations' (2001) 18 JIntlArb 573 (arguing that arbitrators do not engage in the practice of 'splitting the baby'). In the field on investment arbitration, Kapeliuk concludes that repeatedly appointed arbitrators display no biases and no tendencies to 'split the difference', Daphna Kapeliuk, 'Repeat Appointment Factor' (n 101) 47, 47.

cognitive misconceptions and heuristics in arbitral decision-making. In the first case, cognitive biases constitute psychological biases that can lead the decision-maker to inaccurate perceptions of facts.[114] Heuristics, which are not considered bias but they can lead to it, are 'mental shortcuts' that the human brain subconsciously uses in order to make complicated and difficult decisions.[115]

In arbitration practice, the issue of bias in arbitral decision-making is also associated with the ethics of the individuals acting as arbitrators.[116] Standards and rules defining the obligations of arbitrators such as impartiality and disclosure, as well as guidelines on conflict of interest have proliferated rapidly.[117] Such ethical considerations mainly derive from the need for ensuring the legitimacy and integrity of the private dispute resolution process.

[B] Economic Genre

The economic model views judges as maximising a utility function supporting the operation of successful social and economic systems.[118] This genre describes an arbitral decision-making process connected to utilitarian concerns such as money income, power, prestige, reputation, leisure and the stimulation and challenge of the work.[119]

One of the central institutional differences between public and private judges is the existence of 'competition between arbitrators and between arbitral fora'.[120] The selection of private judges by the parties may lead to view arbitrators as service

114. Christopher Drahozal, 'A Behavioral Analysis of Private Judging' (Paper prepared for a symposium on 'The Coming Crisis in Mandatory Arbitration: New Perspectives and Possibilities' Duke University School of Law, 2002) <http://papers.ssrn.com/sol3/papers.cfm?abstract_id = 380021> (accessed 11 May 2018).
115. Robert Coulson, 'The Decision-Making Process in Arbitration' (1990) 45(3) AJ 37, 37; Jan Paulsson, 'Metaphors, Maxims, and Other Mischief. The Freshfields Arbitration Lecture' (2014) 30(4) ArbIntl 615; Chris Guthrieetal, 'Inside the Judicial Mind' (2001) 86 CornellLRev 777, 780; Lucy Reed, 'The 2013 Hong Kong International Arbitration Centre Kaplan Lecture – Arbitral Decision-Making: Art, Science or Sport?' (2013) 30 JIntlArb 2 85, 86; Paulsson, Metaphors, 'Maxims, and Other Mischief – the Freshfields Arbitration Lecture' (n 115) 615.
116. For example, Catherine A Rogers, 'The Ethics of International Arbitrators' (2008) Bocconi Legal Studies Research Paper No. 08/01 <http://ssrn.com/abstract = 10O81436> (accessed 20 Jun. 2018); Carrie Menkel-Meadow, 'Ethics Issues in Arbitration and Related Dispute Resolution Processes: What's Happening and What's Not' (2001–2002) 56 UMiamiLRev 949; David A Dilts and Stanley W Elsea 'What Do Arbitrators Do: Empirical Results and Ethical Considerations in Interest Arbitration' (1992) 27(3) Indian Journal of Industrial Relations 279.
117. For example, IBA guidelines on conflict of interest in International Arbitration (2014) <http://www.ibanet.org/Publications/publications_IBA_guides_and_free_materials.aspx> (accessed 19 Jun. 2018).
118. John Drobak and Douglass North, 'Understanding Judicial Decision-Making: The Importance of Constraints on Non-Rational Deliberations' (2008) 26 WashUJL&P 131, 146.
119. For example, Richard Posner, 'Judicial Behavior and Performance an Economic Approach' (2005) 32 FlaStULRev 1259.
120. Joshua Carton, 'International Arbitration Culture and Global Governance' in Walter Mattli and Thomas Dietz (eds) *International Arbitration and Global Governance: Contending Theories and Evidence* (OUP 2014) 86.

providers competing in the arbitration business market.[121] In this context, market forces may lead arbitrators to render awards that will increase the satisfaction of the parties.[122] This in its turn will attract business, having effect on the arbitrators' market value and income.[123]

It is also suggested that the arbitral decision-making process is influenced by the aim of maximising personal financial and social interests through the establishment of a firm reputation in the field.[124] The number of arbitral appointments, the minimum number of challenges of both the awards and of the appointment, the frequent appearances in conferences and other arbitration-related ceremonials are all factors that enhance the arbitrator's positive reputation and establishment in the arbitration cosmos.

From a sociological perspective, economic forces as well as business practices are even considered capable of influencing the development of specific legal cultures.[125] Arbitration has developed certain networks of various actors including arbitrators and arbitral institutions as service providers, and international organisations and academic institutions as value providers which all may influence the decision-making process.[126] The service providers are seen as 'distribut[ing] legitimacy within the field of international arbitration; and the value providers [...] provide guidance as to the way international arbitration should develop and how arbitral social actors should behave'.[127] The economic value of such arbitral social networks may further constitute an important factor for the evaluation of a developing arbitral 'legal culture'.[128]

[C] Strategic/Institutional Genre

The strategic/institutional approach suggests that judges are influenced by the choices of other actors, mainly political, and by institutional settings.[129] The discussions behind the systemic constraints in the decision-making process are closely connected

121. Robert Cooter, 'The Objectives of Private and Public Judges' 41 Public Choice 107, 108 (The author argues that since private judges aim at income-maximising, they have to attract business and are subject to market pressure as any other service provider).
122. Kapeliuk, 'Repeat Appointment Factor' (n 101) 61.
123. Thomas Schultz, 'Arbitral Decision-Making: Legal Realism and Law & Economics' (2015) King's College London Dickson Poon School of Law Legal Studies Research Paper Series: Paper No. 2015-28, 13.
124. For example, Thomas Schultz and Robert Kovacs, 'The Law Is What the Arbitrator Had for Breakfast: How Income, Reputation, Justice, and Reprimand Act as Determinants of Arbitrator Behaviour' (2014) King's College London Dickson Poon School of Law Legal Studies Research Paper Series: Paper No. 2014-36.
125. *See* Erhard Blankenburg, 'Patterns of Legal Culture: The Netherlands Compared to Neighboring Germany' (1998) 46 AmJCompL 1–41.
126. For a description of arbitral networks *see* Emmanuel Gaillard 'Sociology of International Arbitration' (n 77) 1.
127. *Ibid.*
128. Carton, 'International Arbitration Culture and Global Governance' (n 120) 87; Anthony Ogus, 'The Economic Basis of Legal Culture: Networks and Monopolization' (2002) 22(3) OJLS 419.
129. For systemic and individual accounts in judicial decision-making *see* Pablo Spiller and Rafael Gely, 'Strategic Judicial Decision Making' (2007) NBER Working Paper No. 13321.

to the issues of systemic rather than personal bias as pictured in the behavioural/attitudinal genre of decision-making.

This decision-making genre, deals with the question of whether the arbitrator, could be influenced by various interests. These could be economic interests as described in the economic genre of arbitral decision-making. They can also be systemic interests of the broader institutional design of international arbitration. Within this genre, it is examined whether the current ecosystem of international arbitration constrains in some way the arbitral decision-making process. Structural features of arbitration such as the appointment of the arbitrators by the parties involved and the lack of tenured arbitrators may be seen as fostering collective biases.[130] Based on this way of thinking, an adjudication system promoting collective biases is likely to produce decisions that favour a particular outcome.[131]

Institutional design is a rather explicit source of interests that may affect the decision-making process. Other important sources are the 'implicit or informal institutional structures' such as 'certain legal values and ideological assumptions that conserve the status quo of international arbitration'.[132] The question here is whether the international arbitration framework has introduced mechanisms that implicitly and informally shape legal concepts, theory and practice of arbitration.[133] Under this scenario, the decision-maker or anyone wishing to enter the cosmos of arbitration may need to embrace and conserve the values of the private dispute resolution framework.

Apart from the promotion of collective interests connected to explicit and implicit features of international arbitration in general, there is also a concern that arbitral institutions in particular promote specific interests that may affect the arbitral decision-making process. The proliferation of arbitration forums has been exponential. The direct involvement of arbitral institutions in the procedure of arbitration constitutes a sort of 'legitimate power source' for the regulation of the arbitrator's conduct by these institutions. Rogers reflecting on this institutional competence of arbitral institutions eloquently marks that 'they are poised to become to international arbitrators what bar associations are to lawyers'.[134]

The issue that surfaces here is whether the institutional competences of arbitral institutions are reserved for procedural issues or if they also influence the actual decision-making process. The diverse reality of institutional arbitration makes it difficult to provide one single answer to this question. While in some cases, the measures are purely administrative and do not participate in the 'adjudication' of the dispute, certain decisions of the institutions have the ability of being outcome

---

130. Stavros Brekoulakis, 'Collective Biases and International Arbitral Tribunals' (2013) Queen Mary School of Law Legal Studies Research Paper No. 131/2013, 5 (The author studies the collective biases among arbitrators as opposed to how individual arbitrators can be biased. In his article, Brekoulakis concluded that 'the paradigm of arbitration exhibits unique forum design features that eschew collective biases and meet fundamental standards of procedural fairness').
131. *Ibid.* 8.
132. Brekoulakis, 'Systemic Bias and the Institution of International Arbitration' (n 104) 558.
133. *Ibid.* 584.
134. Catherine A Rogers, 'The Vocation of the International Arbitrator' (2005) 20(5) AmUIntlLRev 957, 1011.

determinative.[135] In the last instance, for example, the institution may provide rules for the legal framework applicable to the arbitration of small claims or expedited rules, or the application of rules of international law when the parties do not otherwise agree.[136]

[D] Legal Genre

The legal genre focuses on the fact that the judge decides based on a reasoned analysis of the law. The decision-making process is shaped by traditional principles of constitutional and statutory interpretation rather than by the personal politics of the individual. The variants of a legal decision-making process include the facts of the case in light of the interpreted rules, the intent of the framers and precedent.[137]

In a broad context, the legal genre of arbitral decision-making reflects the methodology arbitrators use to interpret and apply the law. As will be mainly demonstrated in Part IV, support for the legal model, or rather the choice to study the legal model, does not automatically lead to the exclusion of other factors influencing the legal decision-making process such as policy concerns. The discretion of arbitrators when it comes to the decision-making process as well as the specific framework in which they operate leaves the door open for embracing a legal decision-making approach that does not only adhere to facts, law and precedents.[138]

For the purposes of this research, the analysis on arbitral decision-making will focus on the legal genre of decision-making and in particular on the interpretation of legal sources. Although it may be neglected in certain cases, the distinction between the interpretation and application of the law is a central matter when examining the decision-making process since it stirs the analysis to specific directions. As a preliminary step, the next section purports to clarify the conceptual differences between the process of interpreting and applying the law.

[1] Legal Decision-Making: Interpretation and Application of the Law

When analysing the process of legal decision-making what should first come to mind is the dichotomy between interpretation and application of the law. The terms, in some circumstances, may be employed interchangeably due to the strong link that exists between them. The jurisdictional clauses in the investment treaties refer cumulatively to 'disputes over the interpretation or application of the present treaty' giving the impression of creating a 'portmanteau category' [139] that may not require the competent tribunal to distinguish the one from the other. However, this distinction is important as it creates two linked but functionally separate spheres.

135. *See* Rémy Gerbay, *The Functions of Arbitral Institutions* (Kluwer 2016).
136. *Ibid.* 210; *See* example: ICSID rules, Article 42(1).
137. Jeffrey Segal and Harold Spaeth (eds), *The Supreme Court and the Attitudinal Model Revisited* (CUP 2002) 48.
138. *See* Part IV 'Dialogue'.
139. Franklin Berman, 'International Treaties and British Statutes' (2005) 26 StatuteLRev 1, 10.

Interpretation of legal norms is a hermeneutic process through which the meaning of a norm is determined. The concept of 'application' can itself be divided into two categories: *stricto sensu* application (application in its narrow context) and *lato sensu* application (application in a broader context which contains both the process of interpretation and the process of application *stricto sensu*). As put by judge Ehrilich, interpretation is the course of 'determining the meaning of a rule' whereas application *stricto sensu* is the method of 'determining the consequences which the rule attaches to the occurrence of a given fact'.[140]

A legal decision 'is said to follow from the application of the law to the circumstances of the case'.[141] In this sense, the application of the facts and the specification of a norm, when 'vested' in a mandatory form in a judicial proceeding is called a judgment.[142] In the investment-arbitration scene, Sir Franklin Berman, in his dissenting opinion in the *Lucchetti* annulment phase, makes reference to the Tribunal's twofold task:

> [...] interpreting the BIT and then applying it; [...] whereas treaty interpretation can often be a detached exercise, it is virtually inevitable that treaty application will entail to some extent an assessment of the facts of the particular case and their correlation with the legal rights and obligations in play.[143]

However, this traditional distinction between the interpretation and application of the law is not always a straightforward task in practice. In some circumstances, the interpretation may be formed based on how this interpretation will apply to the facts.[144] In other clear-cut cases, the treaty provisions are applied to the facts directly without the need for the determination of the meaning of the provision.[145]

Nevertheless, leaving aside the practical difficulties, the dyadic approach to legal decision-making, which marks the separation between the process of interpreting and applying the law, can become crucial. As an example, the quality of reasoning may vary based on whether the arbitrators make reference only to the process of applying the law to the facts or whether there is also description of the legal interpretation process.[146] Furthermore, the fragmentation of international legal orders on the one hand but also their interconnection on the other hand, has triggered the need for

140. Anastasios Gourgourinis, 'The Distinction Between Interpretation and Application of Norms in International Adjudication' (2011) 2(1) JIDS 31, 43 citing the *Case concerning the Factory at Chorzow*, PCIJ, Claim for indemnity-Jurisdiction, (Dissenting opinion of judge Ehrilich) 39; *See* Chang-fa Lo, 'Difference and Relations Between Interpretation and Application of Treaties and the Possible Codification' in Chang-fa Lo (ed.) *Treaty Interpretation under the Vienna Convention on the Law of Treaties a New Round of Codification* (Springer 2017) 81.
141. Arthur Glass, 'Interpretation/Application/Decision-Making' (2005) 25 AJLP 97, 97.
142. Michael Reisman, *The Quest for World Order and Human Dignity in the Twenty-first Century: Constitutive Process and Individual Commitment* (Brill 2012) 177.
143. *Empresas Lucchetti, S.A. and Lucchetti Peru, S.A. v. The Republic of Peru*, ICSID Case No. ARB/03/4, Decision on Annulment, Dissenting opinion Sir Franklin Berman (5 Sep. 2007) para. 15.
144. Romesh Weeramantry, *Treaty Interpretation in Investment Arbitration* (OUP 2012) 30; Gleider Hérnandez, 'Interpretative Authority and International Judiciary' in Andrea Bianchi, Daniel Peat, and Matthew Windsor (eds) *Interpretation in International Law* (n 59) 176.
145. *Ibid.*
146. *See* Part II 'Language'.

communication between them. At the level of legal interpretation the communication is effectuated mostly through the dialogue between the judges which does not necessarily lead to the application of the interlocutor-framework to the investment dispute. For instance, investment-arbitration tribunals turn to the jurisprudence of the ECtHR for guidance on how to interpret the principle of proportionality.[147] In this context, proportionality constitutes 'a method of legal interpretation and decision-making in situations of collisions or conflicts of different principles and legitimate public objectives'.[148] As such, the analysis of legal interpretation requires a rather different approach than the analysis of law application.

[2] The Science and Art of Legal Interpretation

The process arbitrators follow to interpret the law becomes an issue of legal knowledge. Understanding the interpretation practices within a specific legal community is a first step towards knowledge of the law.[149] The concept of knowledge leads to connotations of a scientific rather than an artistic nature of interpretation.

However, the ILC Report mentions that 'the interpretation of documents is to some extent, an art not an exact science'.[150] The focus on the artistic characteristics implies that the interpretation process cannot be explained in a rational way based on strict step-by-step interpretation acts.[151] Interpretation as an art consists of 'unquantifiable elements' that do not permit the prediction of the outcome with certainty.[152] This is contrasted to science '[...] where a set of rules will predetermine the exact outcome in any given scenario [...]'.[153]

---

147. In the *Técnicas Medioambientales Tecmed SA* case, the tribunal relied on the ECtHR jurisprudence regarding Art 1 of Protocol 1 in order to draw guidance for the use of the proportionality analysis in determining whether a legitimate regulation turned in fact into indirect expropriation. *Técnicas Medioambientales Tecmed, S.A. v. The United Mexican States*, ICSID Case No. ARB(AF)/00/2, Award (29 May 2003) para. 122 (citations omitted); *See also* Tarcisio Gazzini, *Interpretation of International Investment Treaties* (Bloomsbury 2016) Ch. 10.
148. Benedict Kingsbury and Stephan Schill, 'Investor-State Arbitration as Governance: Fair and Equitable Treatment, Proportionality and the Emerging Global Administrative Law' (2009) Public Law & Legal Theory Research Paper Series Working Paper No. 09-46, 21 <http://ssrn.com/abstract=1466980> (accessed 4 Jul. 2018); Prabhash Ranjan, 'Using the Public Law Concept of Proportionality to Balance Investment Protection and Regulation in International Investment Law: A Critical Appraisal', 3(3) CJICL (2014) 853, 854.
149. Sunstein, *Legal Reasoning and Political Conflict* (n 68) 33.
150. 'Draft Articles on the Law of Treaties with commentaries' as part of the 'Report of the International Law Commission on the work of its eighteenth session' (4 May–19 Jul. 1966) ILC Draft Articles, Doc A/6309/Rev.1 (1966) ILC YB II, 218, para. 4.
151. Ulf Linderfalk, 'Is Treaty Interpretation an Art or a Science? International Law and Rational Decision Making' (2015) 26(1) EJIL 169, 169 (Linderfalk argues that the characterisation of the interpretation process as art or science is a question of fact which is tied to the approach taken by law-applying bodies in particular cases).
152. Panos Merkouris, 'Interpretation is a Science, is an Art, is a Science', in Panos Merkouris, Malgosia Fitzmaurice, and Olufemi Elias (eds), *Treaty Interpretation and the Vienna Convention on the Law of Treaties – 30 Years On* (Nijhoff 2010) 10.
153. *Ibid.* 10; *See also* Lucy Reed, 'The 2013 Hong Kong International Arbitration Centre Kaplan Lecture – Arbitral Decision-Making: Art, Science or Sport?' (n 115), 85.

Nonetheless, embarking from this way of thinking does not lead to the conclusion that the scientific nature of interpretation runs afoul of the artistic elements of the process. Interpretation has been described as being: 'dynamic and creative and transformative, not merely mechanical, and not merely an incidental or ancillary aspect of the real-world effect of a text. Interpretation is a permanent life-changing force acting on the text, constantly modifying its effect throughout its life-history'.[154]

What will gradually transpire in the book is the consideration of the interpretation process as:

> [...] one integrated operation which uses several tools simultaneously to shed light from different angles on the interpreted text; these tools should not be seen as watertight compartments or as a series of separate sub-operations but, rather, as connected (even overlapping) and mutually reinforcing parts of a whole, of a continuum or a continuous and multifaceted process that cannot be reduced to a mechanical operation and which partakes as much of art (the art of judgment) as of science (the science of law).[155]

As such, interpretation can be seen both as an artistic endeavour enhanced by the discretion of the decision-maker when deciding the dispute as well as a scientific endeavour predicated upon the use of certain interpretation principles set by the VCLT. While the public international law interpretive principles of the VCLT guide arbitral tribunals, they do not address all the interpretive needs that may arise in the interpretation practice.[156] Methodological differentiations in the interpretation process of arbitral tribunals is a question of hermeneutics 'not only in the sense of articulating different rules and different methods which will make outcomes more "appropriate" and more predictable, but also in helping to cast the very role of interpretation differently'.[157] Such a specialised interpretation process can only be conceived when recognising the artistic nature of interpretation.

[3] Legal Interpretation and Arbitral Discretion

[I]t is not a precise science law, and therefore you always exercise judgment when you take a critical view of something.[158]

154. Philip Allott, 'Interpretation – An Exact Art' in Andrea Bianchi, Daniel Peat, and Matthew Windsor (eds) *Interpretation in International Law* (n 59) 392.
155. Georges Abi-Saab, 'The Appellate Body and Treaty Interpretation' in Giorgio Sacerdoti, Alan Yanovich and Jan Bohanes (eds), *The WTO at Ten – The Contribution of the Dispute Settlement System* (CUP 2006) 453, 459.
156. *See* §6.02 'Convention Syllogism'.
157. Clasmeier, *Arbitral Awards as Investments* (n 91) 173 citing Joseph H H Weiler, 'Prolegomena to a Meso-theory of Treaty Interpretation at the Turn of the Century', IILJ International Legal Theory Colloquium, Interpretation and Judgment in International Law, 14; *See also* Catherine Brölmann, 'Specialized Rules of Treaty Interpretation: International Organizations' in Duncan B Hollis (ed.), *The Oxford Guide to Treaties* (OUP 2012) 509 arguing that specialised regimes supplement and adapt the VCLT interpretation principles to their 'special' characteristics.
158. Arbitrator B. *See* Annex 'Interview Questions' for the interview design.

It is mostly the space between the text and its interpretation that enhances the artistic elements of the process. Judicial discretionary power is described as a normative concept reflecting a state of affairs in which a judge must choose from a number of options none of which is determined to be the right one by the legal system.[159] In the case where a judge is faced with 'the penumbra of general legal terms a judge has no option but to help fix the meaning through the exercise of a discretionary authority'.[160]

The indeterminacy – whether of a high or low degree – characterising any set of rules confers a certain degree of discretion to the arbitrator when interpreting and applying the law.[161] In the investment-arbitration context, the legal terms used in the investment treaties and institutional rules are characterised by a certain degree of vagueness and generality. The reasons for this are mainly the lack of consensus on a definition by the States, the reference to standards of conduct over clear rules, the fact that a concept may not be adequately developed in general and, last but not least, the intentional generality of a term in order to leave place for its future development.[162]

On this basis, arbitrators have the discretion to apply the vague investment protection guarantees contained in the investment treaties. The ad hoc nature of arbitral tribunals and the absence of a formal doctrine of precedent are additional factors that enhance the arbitrator's interpretative discretion.[163] As such, the general investment protection guarantees contained in the investment treaties acquire a concretise meaning only through the process of interpretation.[164]

It has been argued that 'modern international arbitration requires the objective application of rules to facts and the exercise of bounded discretion to ensure that the final outcome is warranted by the applicable rules; that is, to ensure that the final outcome is justified'.[165] In this context, checks and balances are put in place to assure the integrity of the decision-making process. As far as objectivity is concerned, for example, while the parties actively participate in the selection of the arbitrators, the integrity of the decision-making process is enhanced by the duty of the arbitrator to be impartial and independent.[166] However, things are more complicated when it comes to

---

159. Aharon Barak, *Purposive Interpretation in Law* (Sari Bashi tr, Princeton University Press 2005) 208.
160. Herbert Hart, 'Positivism and the Separation of Law and Morals' (1958) 71 HarvLRev 593, 607–615.
161. *See generally* Roberto M Unger, *Knowledge and Politics* (Free Press 1975) (maintaining that the law is characterised by a large degree of indeterminacy); *See also* Berger stating: 'It would be deceptive to expect that the application of the law is a process in which the norm is applied to the facts as a mere measure stick. [...] This would pre-suppose first that the norm to be applied is definite from the outset so that its contents are beyond doubt. If this would be so, there would be no need for construction.' Klaus Peter Berger, 'The International Arbitrator's Application of Precedents' (1992) 9(4) JIntlArb, 12 citing Karl Larenz, *Methodenlehre der Rechtswissenschaft*, 6th edition, 1991; Cf Ronald Dworkin, 'Hard Cases' (1976) 88 HarvLRev 1057 (arguing that there is no indeterminacy in law since there is a right answer to all legal questions in dispute).
162. Andrés Rigo Sureda, *Investment Treaty Arbitration Judging under Uncertainty* (CUP 2012) 9.
163. For the issue of Precedent *see* §6.03 'Precedent Syllogism'.
164. Stephan Schill, 'System Building in Investment Treaty Arbitration and Lawmaking', (2011) 12 German Law Journal 1083, 1092.
165. Rogers, 'The Vocation of the International Arbitrator' (n 134) 989.
166. For these duties in the ICSID framework *see* Peter Horn, 'A Matter of Appearances: Arbitrator Independence and Impartiality in ICSID Arbitration' (2014) 11(2) JLB 249.

the actual process of interpreting and applying the law. Institutional rules and investment treaties under which arbitrators exercise their discretion make limited reference to the legal decision-making process.

From an institutional perspective, a prime example is the ICSID framework which sets out general guidelines regarding the arbitral decision-making process. Article 42(1) ICSID Convention provides that the arbitrators will decide the dispute 'in accordance with such rules of law as may be agreed by the parties'. In the absence of any such agreement, 'the Tribunal shall apply the law of the Contracting state-party to the dispute (including its rules on the conflict of laws) and such rules of international law as may be applicable'. In addition, Article 48 (3) of the Convention provides that 'the award shall deal with every question submitted to the Tribunal, and shall state the reasons upon which it is based'.[167] While the determinations of the applicable law and the requirement to provide reasons are referred to in the Convention, since they constitute essential elements of the decision-making process, there is no reference to the interpretation process, an equally important denominator. Of course such a gap is justified by the administrative and not decision-making functions of arbitral institutions.

From an investment-treaty perspective, an example is the NAFTA. In this context, there are specific mechanisms set in place to provide some guidance as to legal interpretation. Article 102 requires that the parties 'interpret and apply the provisions of this Agreement in the light of its objectives set out in paragraph 1 and in accordance with applicable rules of international law'.[168] Furthermore, Article 1131, titled 'governing law', provides that the tribunals shall decide a dispute in accordance with the rules of the NAFTA agreement and applicable rules of international law.[169] Reference to decision-making mainly turns around the concept of 'governing law'. As far as the interpretation is concerned, there are no guidelines addressed to the arbitrators. Nonetheless, the agreement gives the power to the NAFTA Free Trade Commission, comprising cabinet level representatives of the parties, to interpret provisions of the Agreement.[170] Such an interpretation is binding for the Chapter 11 Tribunals. The three States have jointly issued a note of interpretation in 2001 addressing mostly issues of procedural transparency. There was also reference to the interpretation of the minimum standard of treatment of Article 1105 NAFTA.[171]

The issue that arises here is that references to the applicable law or even the scarce issuance of interpretive notes do not directly guide or even more illuminate the

167. Article 42 ICSID Convention.
168. Article 102(2) Ch. 1 NAFTA.
169. Article 1131(2) Ch. 11 NAFTA; DR-CAFTA in a similar provision refers to the power of the Commission to interpret a provision of the Agreement in a binding manner: 'A decision of the Commission declaring its interpretation of a provision of this Agreement under Article 19.1.3(c) (The Free Trade Commission) shall be binding on a tribunal established under this Section, and any decision or award issued by the tribunal must be consistent with that decision'. Article 10.22 (3) DR-CAFTA.
170. Article 1131 (2), Ch. 11 NAFTA; DR-CAFTA in a similar provision refers to the power of the Commission to interpret a provision of the Agreement in a binding manner in Article 10.22 (3) DR-CAFTA.
171. Article 1105 (1), (2) Ch. 11 NAFTA.

process of legal interpretation in the decision-making of arbitration tribunals. Arbitrators have the mandate and discretion to decide a specific dispute through the interpretation and application of the law. The question that still remains is how arbitrators interpret the law in the context of a specific dispute. In this context, what is the importance of legal argumentation in revealing how tribunals interpret the law?

[4] Legal Interpretation and Argumentation

'Law is an argumentative discipline.'[172] The decision-maker, whether judge or arbitrator, is expected to render a decision supported with arguments. The way a legal rule is interpreted and eventually applied is determined using specific legal arguments. In certain cases, the application of the law to the facts is not a complicated process provided that the meaning of the legal rule as well as its applicability to the specific case are clear. However, in more complex situations, the application of the legal rule in the specific context may not be straightforward, requiring further interpretation. In these cases, the decision-maker should justify the specific interpretation chosen.[173]

Leaving aside the discussion regarding the blurred distinction between clear and hard cases,[174] what becomes important is focusing on the fact that legal rules do not fully determine the process of legal decision-making. Maintaining that the application of the law involves 'no more than a logical subsumption under abstractly formulated major premises' can no longer be the answer to questions concerning the methodology of the interpretation and application of the law.[175] The reasons for this are mainly the vagueness of legal language, the possibility of conflict between norms, the absence of an existing valid norm to cover certain situations and the possibility of deciding in a way that is contrary to the strict letter of the law.[176]

In practice, the legal arguments employed in order to justify a specific interpretation of a legal rule are connected to the various canons of interpretation.[177] The most common canons of interpretation are the grammatical/semantic, historical, teleological/objective and systematic methods. However, the number of canons and their rank order still remains in dispute.[178] Analysing the canons for the interpretation of statutes of various legal systems, MacCormick and Summers developed an order of

172. Neil MacCormick, *Rhetoric and the Rule of Law: A Theory of Legal Reasoning* (OUP 2005) 14.
173. Feteris, *Fundamentals of Legal Argumentation* (n 47) 7; *See also* Luiz Silveira, 'Discovery and Justification of Judicial Decisions: Towards More Precise Distinctions in Legal Decision-Making', (2014) Law and Method (discussing the distinction between discovery – how a judge actually reaches a decision – and justification – how a judge publicly justifies a decision –).
174. *See* H L A Hart, *The Concept of Law* (OUP 1961); Ronald Dworkin, *Taking Rights Seriously* (HUP 1978) (who first introduced these concepts).
175. Alexy, *A Theory of Legal Argumentation* (n 40) 1 citing Karl Larenz, *Methodenlehre der Rechtswissenschaft* (3rd ed., Springer 1991) 154.
176. *Ibid.* 1.
177. The terms 'methods of interpretation', 'canons of interpretation' and 'techniques of interpretation' are used interchangeably.
178. Alexy, *A Theory of Legal Argumentation* (n 40) 1.

the most preferred methods of interpretation which are the linguistic arguments, the systemic arguments and the teleological/evaluative arguments.[179]

When it comes to decision-making in the international arena, the authoritative text which codifies the methods of treaty interpretation is the VCLT. Articles 31 to 33 VCLT reflect the basic principles of interpretation that have been agreed on during the time of the negotiation of the Treaty. The ILC, however, emphasised the fact that the codification of the canons of interpretation was not a synonym for restricting the discretion of the decision-makers to interpret the language of a treaty taking into account a range of considerations.[180]

As will be further analysed in Part IV, the interpretation principles of the VCLT constitute a source of reference for investment arbitrators.[181] However, these principles need to be further evaluated, interpreted and applied in the context of the specific dispute. In addition, investor-state arbitration tribunals are not only confronted with the task to interpret treaties, but also customary international law which may not be codified in treaties as well as case law.

Concluding that arbitral tribunals interpret the law, drawing legal arguments solely from the VCLT would ignore the range of the arbitrators' interpretive task and the need to further determine the meaning and content of the VCLT interpretation principles. It would also ignore the fact that the VCLT does not provide an exhaustive list of interpretation principles but only the principles that were agreed upon when the treaty was drafted. In this context it is important to reveal the legal arguments arbitrators use in order to interpret the law and eventually justify the judgments they render.

179. Neil D MacCormick and Robert S Summers (eds), *Interpreting Statutes: A Comparative Study* (Dartmouth 1991) 311–358.
180. Isabelle Van Damme, *Treaty Interpretation by the WTO Appellate Body* (OUP 2009) 381.
181. *See* §6.02 'Convention Arguments'.

Conclusion to Part I

Part I of the book sketched the conceptual framework of the analysis of arbitral decision-making. At first, the dispute resolution function of arbitral tribunals was set in a transnational environment. Investment-treaty arbitration is comprised of various public and private parties and of different sets of laws including public international law, administrative decisions and host State regulations. Apart from the parties and their arbitrators, who are the essential and traditional arbitration actors, specialised actors have also made their appearance.[182] Aim of the latter is to influence in their own way the development of the arbitration framework based on their policy oriented goals. As an example, arbitral institutions develop their own procedural and administrative arbitration strategies through their arbitration rules. This way, they compete with other arbitration institutions in order to gain an important place in the arbitration market. Similarly, third-party funders, international organisations and NGOs are specialised actors that not only shape the way arbitration is conducted but also indicate how arbitration should be conducted. Issues such as the protection of the environment, the promotion of sustainable development as well as the need for greater transparency, are present in the amicus curiae submissions and the works of international organisations.[183]

With this background in mind, the ad hoc and case-specific dispute resolution process may be the obvious target of decision-making but a comprehensive analysis of the legal decision-making process cannot ignore further issues that may arise such as the consistency and predictability of the decision-making process.

As a second step, the concept of decision-making in investment arbitration was narrowed down to the genre of legal decision-making and in particular to the process

182. *See* Emmanuel Gaillard, 'The Sociology of International Arbitration' (n 77) 3 et seq.; *See also* Kidane, *The Culture of International Arbitration* (n 77) (analysing the existing theories on international arbitration from a cultural perspective).
183. *See* §6.01[D] 'Expanding the Dialogue Through Third Parties' and §6.05[B][2] 'Emerging Social Policy Concerns'.

of legal interpretation. Arbitrators have wide discretion when deciding a dispute and the process they use to interpret the law is not easy to identify. The aim of the book therefore is to analyse how arbitrators interpret the law in the context of investor-state disputes in order to reveal whether they have developed a specialised decision-making process.

PART II Language

[L]anguage varies as its function varies; it differs in different situations.[184]

184. Michael Halliday, Angus McIntosh, and Peter Strevens, *The Linguistic Sciences and Language Teaching* (Longmans 1964) 87.

Introduction to Part II

This part analyses the legal decision-making process of arbitrators through the first legal argumentation perspective, that of 'Language'. Inspiration for this part's analysis constitutes the logical approach which is one of the three approaches to legal argumentation in the decision-making of judges.[185] The logical approach emphasises on the criteria for a logically valid argument. Formal validity interpreted in the terms of a logically valid argument constitutes a decisive criterion for the rationality of legal argumentation. In this context, the conclusion of a decision follows from the legal rules and the facts (premises) only when an argument is logically valid.[186]

However, for the purpose of the book, the first perspective through which the interpretation of the law is examined is that of 'Language' rather than logic.[187] Instead of focusing on the logical validity of the arguments, the emphasis is put on the language of the arbitrators. What is examined here is the legal vocabulary that arbitrators use when interpreting the law and the meaning they give to legal concepts such as 'rights', 'principles' and 'standards'. As suggested in this part, the understanding of the distinction between 'rights', 'standards' and 'principles', and their methodologically based interpretative treatment is extremely important because the normative terminology serves specific functions in every legal framework. The overall objective is to analyse the legal terminology tribunals use in order to determine whether they have developed a specialised legal decision-making process adapted to the interpretive needs that arise in the context of the dispute and to the characteristics of investment arbitration.

This part consists of Chapter 2 which initially describes the normative functions of legal language, in particular of 'rules', 'standards', 'principles', and 'rights'. As a next step, it analyses arbitral case law to reveal what content the decision-makers give to the above-mentioned normative arrangements and how they interpret them in the context of a specific dispute.

---

185. The other two being the rhetorical and dialectical approach. *See* Part Introduction III[C] 'Legal Argumentation in Judicial Decision-Making: Logic–Rhetoric–Dialectic'.
186. Feteris, 'A Survey of 25 Years of Research on Legal Argumentation' (n 39) 358.
187. *See* III [D] 'Legal Argumentation in Arbitral Decision-Making: Language–Rhetoric–Dialogue'.

CHAPTER 2
Arbitral Legal Language

§2.01 NORMATIVE FUNCTIONS OF LEGAL LANGUAGE

Language is a tool for thinking and telling. Its two main functions are representation and processing of information about the environment, and information transferal between user's (communication).[188]

- Lauri Carlson

Legal language plays an essential role in 'the construction, interpretation, negotiation and implementation of legal justice'.[189] The use of specific legal language genres has been described as an attempt to construct a 'model world of rights and obligations, permissions and prohibitions'.[190] In investment arbitration the main models of normative arrangements contained in set rules or customary international law are primarily externalised as 'principles', 'standards' and 'rights'.[191]

The understanding of the distinction between the normative arrangements and their methodologically based interpretative treatment is essential since the normative terminology is connected to specific functions in a legal system.[192] In the private law sector, for example,[193] the 'rules' versus 'standards' dichotomy is important in

188. Lauri Carlson, *Dialogue Games: An Approach to Discourse Analysis* (Reidel Publishing Company 1983) 27 citing Wolfgang Dressler (ed.) *Current Trends in Text Linguistics* (Walter de Gruyter 1978).
189. Bhatia and others (eds) *Legal Discourse Across Cultures and Systems* (n 58) 9; *See also* Stéphane Beaulac, *The Power of Language in the Making of International Law* (Nijhoff 2004) (examining the role of language as an organic instrument of social power).
190. Bhatia and others (eds) *Legal Discourse Across Cultures and Systems* (n 58) 9.
191. Oscar Schachter, *International Law in Theory and Practice* (Nijhoff 1991) 20.
192. *See* Duncan Kennedy, 'Form and Substance in Private Law Adjudication' (1976) 89 HarvLRev 1689–1690; The concepts 'interpretive' and 'interpretative' are used as synonyms.
193. Pierre Schlag, 'Rules and Standards' (1985) 33 UCLA L Rev 379, 2.

shaping contract law norms[194] or in altering the inelastic, rule-like personal property security law into a standard-like code.[195] The use of norms over 'standards' is also considered to restrain arbitrariness and offer certainty.[196]

The issue of legal language or legal qualification remains important even if someone supposes that the legal decision-making process could be simply described as animating the following form of normative arrangement: if OF then NC (where OF are the operative facts and NC the normative consequences).[197] However, the normative consequences attached by a legal rule to specific facts require instantiation in the cadre of a specific dispute.[198] Outlining the links formed between 'if' and 'then' is not a straightforward process but requires refining the components that constitute the logical foundation of the legal decision-making process.

In this context, defining these concepts is not an easy task. In the literature, the terms are not always used distinctively.[199] However, the vocabulary employed by the decision-maker is very important as it is connected to specific interpretational consequences. All types of legal norms when materialised, mandate a certain normative conclusion and are based on fundamental values that are either external or internal to each normative arrangement.[200] As a result, the process of interpreting a rule-based legal directive is different from the way 'standards' or 'principles' should be interpreted. In this context, the fundamental values on which a rule is based are external to the rule whereas the values shaping 'principles' or 'standards' are inherent to these normative arrangements.[201] In other words, rules have external to the text values whereas 'principles' and 'standards' have an internal value.

As far as the rule is concerned, the legislator is the one that has assessed the value behind the rule, the rule's reason for existence, the policy it represents and its connection to the characteristics of the legal system within which it will perform. The legislator, being the author of the text, develops a normative conclusion from the fundamental value and confers to it the independent normative status of a rule.[202] In this case, the interpreter is not called to assess the external value of the rule as this was the task of the legislator but is called to give greater weight to the evaluation process followed by the latter. As such, rules provide decision-makers with less discretion than

194. Douglas Baird and Robert Weisberg, 'Rules, Standards, and the Battle of the Forms: A Reassessment of § 2-207' (1982) 68 VaLRev 1217, 1223–1231.
195. Grant Gilmore, 'Security Law, Formalism and Article 9' (1968) 47 NebLRev 659.
196. Kennedy, 'Form and Substance in Private Law Adjudication' (n 192) 1685, 1688; *See* §2.02[A] 'Standards'.
197. This depiction is known, as the 'hypothetical syllogism' of traditional logicians. MacCormick, *Rhetoric and the Rule of Law: A Theory of Legal Reasoning* (n 172) 24, 32.
198. *Ibid.* 37.
199. Ronald Dworkin refers to rules as 'rules' and to standards as 'principles'. Dworkin, *Taking Rights Seriously* (n 174) 22–28, 72–80; Cf the view that the distinction between rules and standards may deceptively appear to be a dichotomy as the two terms are theoretical endpoints on a continuum of greater or lesser 'ruleness' and not sharply distinct categories. Kathleen Sullivan, 'Foreword: The Justices of Rules and Standards' (1992–1993) 106 HarvLRev 22, fn 231.
200. Barak, *Purposive Interpretation in Law* (n 159) 198.
201. *Ibid.*
202. *Ibid.*

'standards' because 'a rule captures the background principle or policy in a form that from then on operates independently'.[203]

In the case where the text is principle-based or standard-based, the internal value principles and standards represent has not yet been assessed neither adapted to the characteristics of the legal system the text will perform in. This role is left to the interpreter who is the one called to interpret this text giving greater weight to 'the intention of the system'.[204] The text expressing a 'principle' or 'standard' sets an ideal to be reached which is shaped and influenced by the legal system in which it operates.[205]

In particular, a 'standard' tends 'to collapse decision-making back into the direct application of the background principle or policy to a fact situation'.[206] In this case, the decision-maker should therefore asses the facts of a particular situation putting emphasis on the fundamental values and purposes embodied in the 'standard'. Such values are formed within the framework in which the decision-maker operates. For example, in the case of investor-state arbitration, this process will lead to the interpretation of the principle-based or standard-based text based on the identification of how the content of particular values is shaped by the specific characteristics of investment arbitration.

However, the interpretation of 'standards' has a particularity with relation to 'principles'. A 'standard' implies a level of protection that should be accorded. For example, as will be further explained below, the level of protection the FET standard confers may be considered adequate only when it reaches the minimum protection given by international law.[207] As a consequence, the interpretation of a 'standard' requires the set of a specific level of protection which is either fulfilled or not attained.[208]

When the decision-makers consider the underlying values and policies behind a 'standard' or a 'principle', they could also be confronted with the need to balance the interests behind these components.[209] The balancing process has been described as requiring 'the explicit articulation and comparison of rights or structural provisions, modes of infringement, and government interests'.[210] In a similar context, the interpretation of rights may require the balancing of competing rights. In an investment-arbitration dispute the majority of cases involve a right – an alleged infringement of the right by the State and an alleged justification for the violation by the State. In these cases, the right of the government to regulate will be on one end of the scale, whereas the right of the investor to invest in a protective and secure environment will be on the other end of the scale. Balancing in these cases may lead to taking into account policies

203. Sullivan, 'Foreword: The Justices of Rules and Standards' (n 199) 57–58.
204. Barak refers to the process of giving greater weight to the intent of the system as interpreting the principled-based or standard-based text according to its objective purpose. Barak, *Purposive Interpretation in Law* (n 159) 198.
205. *Ibid.* 198.
206. Kennedy, 'Form and Substance in Private Law Adjudication' (n 192) 1687–1688.
207. *See* §2.02[A][2] 'Between Standards and Principles'.
208. *See* §2.02[A] 'Standards'.
209. Sullivan, 'Foreword: The Justices of Rules and Standards' (n 199) 60.
210. *Ibid.* 60–61.

and values behind the following components: how important is the right, what was the scale of the infringement, and how important is the State's reason for acting in such a way.

Based on the above, reference to each type of normative arrangement, whether 'standard', 'principle' or 'right', is linked to specific interpretational consequences. The next section, as a first step, purports to identify what kind of normative arrangements are included in the investment treaties. However, in the cases where the treaties refer to investment protection guarantees without characterising them as a 'standard', 'right' or 'principle', the legal language arbitrators use to refer to the guarantees may vary based on the interpretive needs that may arise in the context of the specific dispute.

§2.02 ARBITRAL VOCABULARY: STANDARDS OF CONDUCT–PRINCIPLES–RIGHTS

International law could be seen as an 'open-textured' legal system, consisting of 'general principles', 'specific rules', 'standards of conduct' and 'rights'.[211] Arbitral decision-making is strongly connected to the interpretation of the above-mentioned types of normative arrangements within the boundaries of arbitral discretion. The so-called professional community of treaty users that not only includes the States but also international jurists, scientists and arbitral tribunals appears to be influencing the meaning of the treaty language on an extensive level.[212]

As suggested in Part I, given the abstract nature of the guiding principles for the interpretation and application of the law as well as the vague norms on the protection of the investor and the obligations of the State, arbitral discretion becomes a reality.[213] As will be revealed in this section, the majority of investment treaties refer to investment protection guarantees directly as FET or MFN for example, without specifying what type of normative arrangement they represent, whether 'rights', 'standards' or 'principles'. In this case, the discretion of the decision-maker becomes even wider and may even lead to the use of the standard-principle-rights terminology differently by each arbitrator. Going a step further, it may also lead to the use of different interpretation methods depending on the characterisation of the legal arrangements as standards, principles or rights.

The use of vague expressions in the law 'are part of the linguistic repertoire of the competent language user, who uses them to accomplish particular communicative goals'.[214] Especially in the field of arbitration, 'discretion markers' in the legal texts are strongly connected to the 'room for interpretation' required for assuring the flexibility

211. Schachter, *International Law in Theory and Practice* (n 191) 20.
212. Tillmann Rudolf Braun, 'Part V Chapter 21: Globalization: The Driving Force in International Investment Law' in Michael Waibel and others (eds), *The Backlash Against Investment Arbitration* (Kluwer Law International 2010) 491, 497.
213. *See* §2.02[D][3] 'Legal Interpretation and Arbitral Discretion'.
214. Joanna Channell, *Vague Language* (OUP 1994) 196–197.

of the arbitral proceedings.[215] The amount of the discretion accorded to the decision-maker depends on the form of the legal norms that are to be applied.[216] The legal form a norm acquires has a double mission: on the one hand to facilitate decision-makers, improve the quality of the decisions rendered and delimit their power of choice, and on the other to provide different forms of discretion to the decision-maker.[217]

The main characteristic of vagueness in the law is that it 'leaves room for interpretation and communicative negotiation of the exact meaning of a word or expression'.[218] As will be sketched in the next section, the way arbitrators interpret 'standards', 'principles' and 'rights' reveals such a continuous negotiation process, attributing different meanings to the language used in the decision-making process.[219]

[A] Standards

This section deals with the way arbitrators use the term 'standards' in their decision-making process. After sketching their legal content, the analysis focuses on how arbitral tribunals treat 'standards' in their legal analysis.

[1] Sketching Their Legal Content

The obligations of a State towards a private investor are generally referred to as the 'treatment' owed to the investor and the investment.[220] Such a treatment included in the investment treaties has been described as 'standards of treatment' that could be either general or specific.[221] Standards of treatment include: (a) fair and equitable treatment of both the investor and the investment; (b) full protection and security; (c) protection from unreasonable or discriminatory measures; (d) minimum international standard of treatment; (e) the respect of obligations made to the investors and their investments; (f) national treatment (the host State should treat the investor no less favourably than it treats its own national investors); (g) most favoured nation treatment (a host State would accord an investor a treatment that is no less favourable than that it accords to a third foreign investor[222]); (h) free transfer of funds (especially

215. Jan Engberg and Dorothee Heller, 'Vagueness and Indeterminacy in Law' in Bhatia and others (eds) *Legal Discourse Across Cultures and Systems* (n 58) 164.
216. Sullivan, 'Foreword: The Justices of Rules and Standards' (n 199) 57.
217. *Ibid.*
218. Jan Engberg and Dorothee Heller, 'Vagueness and Indeterminacy in Law' in Bhatia and others (eds) *Legal Discourse Across Cultures and Systems* (n 58) 148.
219. On a different note, that of harmonising the terminology of national arbitration laws especially when translated into various languages and legal orders, *see* the conference organised in 1995 in Seoul on the topic 'Globalization and Harmonization of the Basic Notions in International Arbitration' (1997) 13 Int'lConstrLRev 144.
220. Salacuse, *The Law of Investment Treaties* (n 69) 131.
221. *Ibid.* 131.
222. The overwhelming majority of IIAs include a MFN provision alongside NT, mostly in a single provision; *See* UNCTAD Report, 'Most-Favoured Nation Treatment' (United Nations 2010).

when arbitral tribunals deal with EU investment disputes); (i) compensation for expropriation.[223]

Normative arrangements in investment arbitration are considered to have developed as standards rather than rules due to various reasons. The main explanation is, on the one hand, the absence of a political consensus on the degree of protection to be accorded by the States and, on the other hand, the fear of under-inclusiveness meaning that set rules may fail to consider all the facts under which the rule will be applicable.[224]

The main difference between a 'rule' and a 'standard' is that in the first case, the 'work' involved when forming its content is undertaken before the individual acts whereas in the second instance it is undertaken after the individual acts.[225] As a consequence, the content of a 'rule' is more predictable than that of a 'standard'. However, 'standards' present flexibility as being able to adapt to changes and seem to be more appropriate when the cases the law seeks to govern are unpredictable.[226] From a cost-benefit perspective, 'standards' are typically less costly to create since their formulation entails low political and administrating costs.[227] On the contrary, rules not only require preparatory work but are also more costly for individuals in their effort to predict and interpret their consequences.[228]

It should also be noted that the choice between 'rules' and 'standards' can be seen not only from a legal form perspective but also from the way the substantive issues they respond to are interpreted. In this context, a legal norm[229] is a 'rule' 'when it binds a decision-maker to respond in a determinate way to the presence of delimited triggering facts'.[230] The trigger of the rule can be described as empirical and the response as determined whereas the trigger of a standard is evaluative and the response guided.[231]

223. Salacuse, *The Law of Investment Treaties* (n 69) 131.
224. Federico Ortino, 'Refining the Content and Role of Investment "Rules" and "Standards": A New Approach to International Investment Treaty-Making' (2012) Society of International Economic Law (SIEL), 3rd Biennial Global Conference 3 <http://ssrn.com/abstract=2181426> (accessed 21 Mar. 2018).
225. Louis Kaplow, 'Rules Versus Standards: An Economic Analysis' (1992) 42 DukeLJ. 557, 560; *See* analytically §2.01 'Normative Functions of Legal Language'; Eric Posner, 'Standards, Rules, and Social Norms', 21 HarvJL&PubPol'y (1997–1998) 101; Friedrich Rosenfeld, 'The Trend from Standards to Rules in International Investment Law and Its Impact upon the Interpretive Power of Arbitral Tribunals' (2014) 108 The Effectiveness of International Law 191–193.
226. Ortino, 'Refining the Content and Role of Investment "Rules" and "Standards": A New Approach to International Investment Treaty-Making' (n 224) 3.
227. Joel Trachtman, 'The Domain of WTO Dispute Resolution' (1999) 40 HarvIntlLJ 333, 351–353.
228. Kaplow, 'Rules Versus Standards: An Economic Analysis' (n 225) 557.
229. The term 'norm' is used as a synonym for the term legal directive and normative arrangement. Schlag points out: 'It is possible to look at positive law (constitutions, statutes, judicial opinions, and administrative orders) as a series of directives. The formula for a legal directive is "if this, then that." A directive thus has two parts: a "trigger" that identifies some phenomenon and a "response" that requires or authorizes a legal consequence when that phenomenon is present. [...] directives can be general or specific, conditional or absolute, narrow or broad, weak or strong. They can also be rules or standards.' Schlag, 'Rules and Standards' (n 193) 2.
230. Sullivan, 'Foreword: The Justices of Rules and Standards' (n 199) 57.
231. Schlag, 'Rules and Standards' (n 193) 2.

The *Chemtura* tribunal refers to the rigid character of 'rules' and as a corollary to the importance of the existence of 'standards' when treating the issue of expropriation:

> The determination of whether there has been a 'substantial deprivation' is a fact-sensitive exercise to be conducted in the light of the circumstances of each case. [...] One important feature of fact-sensitive assessments is that they cannot be conducted on the basis of rigid binary rules. It would make little sense to state a percentage or a threshold that would have to be met for a deprivation to be 'substantial' as such *modus operandi* may not always be appropriate.[232]

'Standards' are not set and detailed and therefore, require the decision-maker to put more effort in order to identify their content. The content of a standard is strongly connected to the consequences of its application.[233] Its meaning depends on interpretative practices included in judgments that may well create categories able to provide future guidance.[234]

[2] Between Standards and Principles

The use of a specific legal term is important as it is strongly connected to the interpretive technique the decision-maker will employ. A legal standard covers an individual case without the need for 'specifying the content of the analysis in particular cases' whereas legal principles are depicted as a 'background idea that does not by itself "cover" an individual case, but is instead brought to bear on it as one of a number of relevant factors'.[235]

The specific meaning of the language contained in an investment treaty not only depends on the intentions of the drafters of the treaties but also on the decision-maker who is the one communicating treaty language through its interpretation. In this context, and as will be revealed through the analysis of arbitral case law, a treaty may characterise a normative arrangement as 'standard' but the decision-maker may refer to it as 'principle'. In a different case, a treaty may avoid making any legal characterisation whereas the decision-maker may refer to a legal directive as a 'standard' or as a 'principle' or even may use both concepts interchangeably.

In the *Abaclat* case the tribunal analysing the legal basis for its jurisdiction referred to the relevant provisions of the Argentina-Italy BIT. The BIT itself refers to the measures of protection of investments without characterising them as 'standards' or 'principles':

> Investments made by investors of each Contracting Party shall at all times be accorded fair and equitable treatment. Neither Party shall impair by arbitrary or

232. *Chemtura Corporation v. Canada*, UNCITRAL/NAFTA Ch. 11, Award (2 Aug. 2010) para. 249.
233. Sunstein, *Legal Reasoning and Political Conflict* (n 68) 27; Going a step further, the values embodied in legal standards i.e. their background justification, are those that confer to the facts their 'normative force with varying intensity'. Steven J Burton, *Judging in Good Faith* (CUP 1994) 52.
234. Sunstein, *Legal Reasoning and Political Conflict* (n 68) 27.
235. *Ibid.* 31.

> discriminatory measures the management, maintenance, enjoyment, transformation, cessation or disposal of investments made in its territory by the other Contracting Party's investors.[236]

However, the tribunal used the term 'standard' to characterise the means of protection of the investment contained in the BIT:

> Articles 2 to 6 contemplate various standards of investment protection and promotion, including fair and equitable treatment to investors of the other Contracting Party (Article 2(2)), national treatment standard and most-favored nation principle (Article 3), compensation for damages or losses related to certain events (Article 4), protection against nationalization and expropriation (Article 5) [...][237]

Nonetheless, in other parts it referred to the most favoured nation and most favourable treatment clause as a 'principle':

> With regard to Article 3 (and Article 10) BIT and the principles of most favored nation and most favorable treatment contemplated therein, the Additional Protocol specifies the scope of application of these principles[...].[238]

In the NAFTA context, Article 1105 which provides for FET, FPS and non-discriminatory treatment has the title 'Minimum Standard of Treatment'. In this case, the treaty itself expresses the need to treat investment protection guarantees as standards and approaches their interpretation from the attainment of a minimum level of protection perspective. Therefore, the treaty itself connects the language with specific interpretive methodology.

The *Mondev* tribunal characterises the investment protection guarantees as 'general principles of law' marking that 'the general principles referred to in Article 1105(1) and similar provisions must inevitably be interpreted and applied to the particular facts'.[239] However, some paragraphs later, when the tribunal proceeds to the interpretation of FET and FPS it refers to them as 'standards of treatment' since this is the language that the treaty used in order to promote the minimum standard of treatment methodology of interpretation.[240]

---

236. Article 2 (2) BIT Fra La Repubblica Italiana E La Repubblica Argentina Sulla Promozione E Protezione Degli Investimenti (1990).
237. *Abaclat and Others (Case formerly known as Giovanna a Beccara and others) v. The Argentine Republic*, ICSID Case No. ARB/07/5, Decision on Jurisdiction and Admissibility (4 Aug. 2011) para. 264.
238. *Ibid.* para. 265 (ii); *See also Impregilo S.P.A v. Argentine Republic*, ICSID Case No. ARB/07/17, Award (21 Jun. 2011) para. 285 (the tribunal characterised FET as at least equivalent to the international minimum standard whereas Article 2(2) of the Argentina-Italy BIT does not characterise the protection as a principle or a standard); *Hochtief AG v. Argentine Republic*, ICSID Case No. ARB/07/31, Award (19 Dec. 2016) para. 81 (the tribunal stated that 'The MFN clause stipulates a standard of treatment and defines it according to the treatment of third parties'. In the same paragraph it defines the MFN clause as 'a principle applicable to the exercise of rights and duties that are actually secured by the BIT in which the MFN clause is found').
239. *Mondev International Ltd. v. United States of* America, Case No. ARB(AF)/99/2, Award (11 Oct. 2002) para. 118.
240. *Ibid.* paras 120 et seq.

In the *Rumeli* case, the arbitral tribunal dealt with the alleged breach of the Kazakhstan-Turkey BIT. The tribunal held that Kazakhstan was liable, *inter alia*, for denying investors fair and equitable treatment. The BIT provides for FET in its preamble stating that '[...] fair and equitable treatment of investment is desirable in order to maintain a stable framework for investment and maximum effective utilisation of economic resources'.[241] The investment treaty avoids making any normative characterisation of FET either as a 'standard', 'principle' or 'right'. However, the tribunal refers to FET both as a 'standard' as well as a 'principle' just like in the *Abaclat* case. Nonetheless, in the specific situation, reference to a specific legal terminology is connected to the interpretive techniques used by the tribunal.

As a first step, the tribunal recognised that FET is not 'precisely defined' constituting a 'general point of departure in formulating an argument that the foreign investor has not been well treated by reason of discriminatory or other unfair measures being taken against its interest'.[242] The tribunal continued referring to FET as a 'standard' marking that 'the precise scope of the standard is therefore left to the determination of the tribunal which will have to decide whether in all the circumstances the conduct in issue is fair and equitable or unfair and inequitable'.[243]

What is also interesting when analysing the tribunal's language in this case is that the decision-makers stated that the FET standard contains specific principles:

> The parties rightly agree that the fair and equitable treatment standard encompasses *inter alia* the following concrete principles:
>
> - the State must act in a transparent manner;
> - the State is obliged to act in good faith;
> - the State's conduct cannot be arbitrary, grossly unfair, unjust, idiosyncratic, discriminatory, or lacking in due process;
> - the State must respect procedural propriety and due process.
>
> The case law also confirms that to comply with the standard, the State must respect the investor's reasonable and legitimate expectations.[244]

Someone may conclude by this quote that 'standards' constitute a broader concept than 'principles', since the former comprise the latter. It also seems here that the tribunal uses different principles as a means, a tool, to assert or not the breach of the broad FET standard. However, some paragraphs later, the Tribunal referred to FET as a 'principle' stating that: 'The Arbitral Tribunal therefore considers that the process that led to the decision of the Working Group lacked transparency and due process and was unfair, in contradiction with the requirements of the fair and equitable treatment

241. Agreement Between the Republic of Turkey and The Republic of Kazakhstan concerning the Reciprocal Promotion and Protection of Investments (11 Feb. 1995).
242. *Rumeli Telekom AS and Telsim Mobil Telekomunikasyon Hizmetleri AS v. Republic of Kazakhstan*, ICSID Case No. ARB/05/16, Award (29 Jul. 2008) para. 610 (citations omitted).
243. *Ibid.* para. 610 (citations omitted).
244. *Ibid.* para. 609.

principle.'[245] At this point, the tribunal referred to FET as a 'principle' because it used the above-mentioned principles encompassed in the FET to guide its interpretation.

Another argument of the tribunal which may further shed light on the vocabulary patterns used is the reference to 'the test applicable' to the obligations of the State towards the investor including FET.[246] The test applied for this purpose is the minimum standard of treatment in customary international law.[247] The tribunal used the standard of customary international law to test or, in other words, measure the acts of the State in order to conclude whether there was a breach of the FET standard. In this case the tribunal referred to FET as a 'standard' because it used the standard of customary international law for its interpretation. Customary international law standards are the ones setting the threshold which is either attained or not. It seems that FET is characterised as a standard because its interpretation and application requires the use of specific standards.

Similarly, in the *Alex Genin* case the arbitral tribunal referring to the international law rules and standards incorporated into the BIT relating to the treatment of the investment, characterises FET as a 'general principle'.[248] However, when it interprets the investment protection guarantees, it uses the term 'international law standards' to refer to FET and 'non-discriminatory and non-arbitrary treatment' of the investment.[249]

The relevant US-Estonia BIT avoids making any such characterisation. Nonetheless, it makes reference to a 'minimum standard of treatment based on customary international law' stating that:

> Article II Paragraph 3 guarantees that investment shall be granted 'fair and equitable' treatment. It also prohibits Parties from impairing, through arbitrary or discriminatory means, the management, operation, maintenance, use, enjoyment, acquisition, expansion or disposal of investment. This paragraph sets out a minimum standard of treatment based on customary international law.[250]

The BIT also refers to the standards that guarantee FET:

> Article II Paragraph 1 further bars all expropriations or nationalizations except those that are for a public purpose; carried out in a non-discriminatory manner, subject to 'prompt, adequate, and effective compensation'; subject to due process; and accorded the treatment provided in the standards of Article Il (3). (These standards guarantee fair and equitable treatment and prohibit the arbitrary and discriminatory impairment of investment in its broadest sense).[251]

245. *Ibid.* para. 618.
246. *Ibid.* para. 575.
247. *Ibid.* para. 611.
248. *Alex Genin, Eastern Credit Limited, Inc. and A.S. Baltoil v. The Republic Of Estonia*, ICISD Case No. ARB/99/2, Award (25 Jun. 2001) paras 14, 373.
249. *Ibid.* para. 316; *See also Urbaser S.A. and Consorcio de Aguas Bilbao Bizkaia, Bilbao Biskaia Ur Partzuergoa v. The Argentine Republic*, ICSID Case No. ARB/07/26, Award (8 Dec. 2016) para. 578 (the Tribunal refers to FET as a 'standard' when using the CIL minimum standard of treatment to interpret the FET protection guarantee, while in para. 872 it refers to FET as a principle).
250. Articles II(3)(a) and (b) of the US-ESTONIA BIT.
251. *Ibid.* Article II(1).

In its assessment of whether there was a violation of FET, the tribunal referred to FET as an 'international law standard'.[252] The tribunal held that while the content of the standard is not clear, the FET standard is understood to require an international minimum standard.[253] In this case, just like in the *Rumeli* award, the use of the international minimum standard for the interpretation of the FET guarantee is strongly connected to its characterisation as a 'standard'.

Based on the above considerations, practice shows that investment-arbitration tribunals use the two terms – 'standards' and 'principles' – interchangeably in specific circumstances. However, the use of the legal characterisations is strongly linked to the way arbitrators interpret the investment protection guarantees. In particular, the characterisation of FET either as a 'standard' or a 'principle' seems to derive from two main reasons: on the one hand, because of the general character of the obligation and the fact that there is no legal characterisation of it in the BIT; on the other hand, due to the use of not only specific principles but also customary international law standards in order to measure the obligations of the State. When tribunals use the term 'standard' to characterise an investment protection guarantee, they proceed to the interpretive assessment of whether a certain degree of protection is attained. In other words, the use of the legal language by arbitrators is purposive as each characterisation fulfils a specific interpretative purpose.

In this context, the use of a specific language is strongly connected to its use in practice, specifically through the analysis of the interpretive techniques employed.[254] The arbitrator becomes aware of the interpretive techniques connected to each legal term through case law. Interpretive practices included in previous judgments provide guidance as to the use of specific legal terminology. Arbitral case law reveals the purpose of using specific legal terminology in investment arbitration and guides future tribunals in their own decision-making discretion.

The purposive use of language is further enhanced by the parties' submissions. When a party refers to FET as a standard and the degree of protection to be accorded, the tribunal will use the same characterisation in order to make the specific assessment. The meaning of a specific term is formed both with a look at the past as well as in the context of the present dispute.

Such purposive language transcends traditional decision-making in private and public law disputes. According to Koh, transnational dispute resolution is non-traditional, thus breaking the traditional dichotomies between domestic and international, private and public. The development of this common use of language attributes to the arbitral decision-making process a transnational element.[255]

252. *Alex Genin*, Award (n 248) para. 366.
253. *Ibid.* para. 367.
254. A similar approach is followed by the 'linguistic turn' stream according to which the meaning of words is extracted from their use. *See* Rorty Richard (ed.) *The Linguistic Turn: Essays in Philosophical Method* (UCP 1992) 409; Armin Von Bogdandy and Ingo Venzke, 'International Judicial Institutions as Lawmakers' (2011) 12(5) GLJ 979, 985.
255. *See* §1.01 'Dispute Resolution Function: A Transnational Perspective'.

[B] Principles

The starting point for the examination of how arbitrators use the term 'principles' in investor-state arbitration is to identify their meaning in the legal scholarship. The second step is to reveal what investment tribunals consider as 'principles' and how they interpret them.

[1] Sketching Their Legal Content

Fitzmaurice gives a stark description of what a principle is:

> By a principle, or general principle, as opposed to a rule, even a general rule, of law is meant chiefly something which is not itself a rule, but which underlies a rule, and explains or provides the reason for it. A rule answers the question 'what': a principle in effect answers the question 'why'.[256]

In this context, a 'principle' is a general norm which explains a specific 'rule'.[257] 'Principles' are deeper and more general in character compared to 'rules'.[258] Their distinction can be said to be based on a 'lower and higher degree of abstraction' or on a '*lex specialis* and *lex generalis*' characterisation.[259] In this case 'principles' can guide the interpretation of a rule.[260] They can also be used as a way of justifying the application of the 'rules' to the specific case or even as a means to 'validate' the existence of the rule demonstrating its connection to wider and more general legal concepts. In other words, their context can be approached from two perspectives. On the one hand, 'principles' are the reasons, the justification behind the 'rules' also used in the process of the interpretation.[261] On the other hand, 'principles' can be introduced in a case as the sole ground for action where the particular case is not covered by rules.[262] In this last case it is possible that 'principles' may be difficult to be distinguished from 'standards'.

It has been argued by some authors that this difference between 'principles' and 'rules' should not be overstated as the difference is one of a degree rather than of kind.[263] In international law, 'principles' are sometimes understood as being equivalent to rules or that rules contain 'principles'.[264] Nonetheless, characterising the norm governing the investment-arbitration framework as a 'principle', as well as or instead

256. Gerarld Fitzmaurice, 'The General Principles of International Law Considered from the Standpoint of the Rule of Law' (1957) 92(II) Receuil des Cours 5, 7.
257. Neil MacCormick, *Legal Reasoning and Legal Theory* (OUP 1978) 152–194.
258. Martti Koskenniemi, *Sources of International Law* (Ashgate 2000) 359–402.
259. 'Fragmentation of International Law: Difficulties Arising from Diversification and Expansion of International Law' (Report of the Study Group of the International Law Commission finalised by Martti Koskenniemi, United Nations – Geneva 2006) UN Doc. A/CN/4/L.682, para. 28.
260. *Ibid.*
261. Sunstein, *Legal Reasoning and Political Conflict* (n 68) 30.
262. Antonio Cassese, *Self-Determination of Peoples: A Legal Reappraisal* (CUP 1995) 133.
263. Sunstein, *Legal Reasoning and Political Conflict* (n 68) 31.
264. Sureda, *Investment Treaty Arbitration Judging under Uncertainty* (n 162) 100.

of a 'rule', is not without importance as there is more place for the norm's interpretational evolvement than if it is characterised as a rule only. [265] Similarly, characterising a certain norm as a 'principle' or a 'right' is a matter of whether the subject is determined or not. The concept of a 'right' presupposes the determinacy of the subject of the 'right'.[266] When it comes to 'principles', their use is connected to the kind of arguments and the authority they carry.[267] Being more general than 'rules' they carry a certain weight that is not dispositive like rules which apply in an all-or-nothing fashion.[268]

Specifically, 'general principles of law' arise out of domestic law and the practice of international organisations and are found through the application of comparative law in order to establish features common to domestic legal systems.[269] The nature of general principles of law is as much a matter of choice as it is a matter of generality.[270] When applied in a particular case two fundamental and general principles may conflict one another leaving space to the decision-maker to choose one over the other in order to balance the consequences of their application with relation to the facts of the case and the international law policies.[271]

The next sections will demonstrate that reference to GPL in the decision-making process of arbitral tribunals has three main functions. First, they are used as sources of law which may or may not be distinguished from principles of international law. Second, they are used as interpretive arguments and finally they are used to signify the emergence of specialised principles of investment law and arbitration.

265. Karen Knop, *Diversity and Self-Determination in International Law* (CUP 2002) 32.
266. James Crawford, *The Creation of States in International Law* (Clarendon Press 1979) 88. Radin speaks about 'formal realisability' which describes the way a rule is applied to the facts:

> In the traditional conception of the nature of rules, a rule is self-applying to the set of particulars said to fall under it; its application is thought to be analytic. It is often said that rules are logically prior to the particular cases that fall under them. Another way of putting this is to think that somehow the applications to particulars are already present in the rule itself. [...] When a directive or command is formally realizable, its application is deductive or analytic. In other words, it deserves to be called a 'rule.' To the extent that legal directives are formally realizable they are to be implemented by mechanical jurisprudence.

Margaret Jane Radin, 'Reconsidering The Rule of Law' (1989) 69 BULRev 781, 795.
267. Knop, *Diversity and Self-Determination* (n 265) 34.
268. *Ibid.* 35.
269. *See* Christoph Schreuer, *The ICSID Convention: A Commentary* (2nd ed., CUP 2009) 610.
270. Bassiouni argues that the very generality of the concept is needed to preserve the evolutionary character of international law. M Cherif Bassiouni, 'A Functional Approach to General Principles of International Law' (1990) 11 MichJIntlL 768 <http://repository.law.umich.edu/mjil /vol11/iss3/3> (accessed 10 Jun. 2018).
271. Oscar Schachter, 'The Relation of Law, Politics and Action in the United Nations' (1963) 109 HagueRec 169, 191–193; Guido Alpa, 'General Principles of Law' (1994) 1(1) Annual Survey of International & Comparative Law; Christina Voigt, 'The Role of General Principles in International Law and Their Relationship to Treaty Law' (2008) Retfærd Årgang 31 2008 NR. 2/121 pp. 5–7.

[2] General Principles of Law and Principles of International Law

Arbitral tribunals approach general principles of law either as being part of the fundamental principles of international law or as distinct from principles of international law. As an example, the Tribunal in the *Waste Management II* case described res judicata not only as a general principle of law but also as a general principle of international law within the meaning of Article 38 (1) (c) of the ICJ Statute which identifies the sources of applicable law in the international scene.[272] Approaching the issue from a similar perspective, the *El Paso* Tribunal made reference to doctrine in order to define general principles of law and to demonstrate the difference between 'general principles of law recognised by civilised nations' and 'general principles of international law'.[273]

Similarly, the annulment committee in the *Klöckner* case interestingly pointed out the existence of a difference between principles of law and rules of law stating that:

> First, it should be asked whether the arbitrator's duty under Article 42(1) to apply 'the law of the Contracting State' is or can be fulfilled by reference to one 'basic principle,' and what is more, without making any more precise reference. This may be doubted if one considers the difference between 'rule' and 'principle' (and in particular 'basic principle') and the classic definition of law in the objective sense as a body of rules. It will also be noted in this context that Article 42(1) itself distinguishes between the concepts of 'rules of law' and 'principles of law'.[274]

Going a step further the ad hoc committee highlighted the need to separate the concept 'principles of international law' of Article 42 ICSID Convention from 'general principles of law recognised by civilized nations' of Article 38 (3) ICJ Statute pointing out at the same time the confusion of the tribunal regarding the two:

> [...] the Tribunal may have wanted to base, or thought it was basing, its decision on the, general principles of law recognized by civilized nations, as that term is used in Article 38(3) of the Statute of the International Court of Justice. It is not impossible that the Tribunal was prompted to do so by the reference in Article 42(1) in fine to the 'principles of international law as may be applicable' although these are not to be confused with 'general principles'. [275]

The ad hoc committee, after clarifying that such an interpretation is 'conjectural and cannot be accepted', analysed the function of the 'principles of international law':

---

272. *Waste Management, Inc. v. United Mexican States* (Waste Management II), Case N° ARB(AF)/00/3, Mexico's Preliminary Objection concerning the Previous Proceedings, (26 Jun. 2002) para. 39; *See also* Jonathan I Charney, 'Sources of International Law' (1998) 271 Recueil Des Cours 189, 189–891.
273. *El Paso Energy International Company v. The Argentine Republic*, ICSID Case No. ARB/03/15, Award (31 Oct. 2011) para. 622, fn 563 (The Tribunal stated: 'On this matter, and on the distinction between "general principles of law recognised by civilised nations" and "general principles of international law,"' *see*, for example, Hermann Mosler, 'General Principles of Law' in Rudolf Bernhardt (ed.), *Encyclopedia of Public International Law*, Vol. 2 (E-I) (North-Holland 1995) pp. 511–527).
274. *Klöckner Industrie-Anlagen GmbH and others v. Republic of Cameroon*, ICSID Case No. ARB/81/2, Decision on Annulment (3 May 1985) para. 68.
275. *Ibid.* para. 69.

> Article 42 of the Washington Convention certainly provides that 'in the absence of agreement between the parties, the Tribunal shall apply the law of the Contracting State party to the dispute ... and *such principles of international law as may be applicable.*' This gives these principles (perhaps omitting cases in which it should be ascertained whether the domestic law conforms to international law) a dual role, that is *complementary* (in the case of a 'lacuna' in the law of the State), or *corrective,* should the State's law not conform on all points to the principles of international law.[276]

From a linguistic perspective, the English version of the ICSID Convention in Article 42 (1) refers to 'rules of international law' whereas the French version uses the term 'principes de droit international'. Based on this observation, the ad hoc committee must be referring to the French version of ICSID. What becomes important however is to recognise the multiple functions of principles either as source of international law or as interpretive arguments. As such, in the first case the principles would require identification and further interpretation whereas in the second case they would be used as a tool to interpret the law.

[3] Interchangeability: Principles as Sources of Law and as Interpretive Arguments

Arbitral case law reveals that there is an interchangeable use of 'general principles of law' as sources of law as well as interpretive arguments.[277] The Tribunal in the *Inseysa v. El Savador* case portrayed general principles of law as 'an autonomous or direct source of International Law, along with international conventions and custom'.[278] It continued adding:

> Without attempting to define what the general principles of law are, the Tribunal notes that, in general, they have been understood as general rules on which there is international consensus to consider them as universal standards and rules of conduct that must always be applied and which, in the opinion of important commentators, are rules of law on which the legal systems of the States are based.[279]

In the *Abaclat* case, however, 'principles of international law' were used as a source of applicable law whereas in particular 'general principles of law' were used as a tool of interpretation. The Tribunal stated that the law applicable to the question of consent under Article 25 ICSID Convention is the principles of international law and

276. *Ibid.* para. 69 (emphasis in the original).
277. In *Fedax v. Venezuela,* Award (9 Mar. 1998) 5 ICSID Report 2000 para. 30 the tribunal states: 'general principles of law have all had an important and supplementary role in the consideration of this case as well as in providing the basis for the decision on jurisdiction and award on the merits'; *See CME Czech Republic B.V. v. The Czech Republic,* Final Award (14 Mar. 2003) para. 614; Vadi states that 'General principles of law are a source of law and thus imply adjudication on the basis of law'. Valentina Vadi, *Analogies in International Investment Law and Arbitration* (CUP 2015) 41.
278. *Inceysa Vallisoletana, S.L. v. Republic of El Salvador,* ICSID Case No. ARB/03126, Award (2 Aug. 2006) para. 226.
279. *Ibid.* para. 227.

not any national law.[280] The Tribunal continued using the general principle of law that a consent that is not freely given is not valid, to interpret the concept of consent of Article 8(3) and Article 25(1) ICSID Convention.[281] In this case, the general principle of law was used for the interpretation of a specific investment-arbitration concept. However, if things are viewed the other way around, the specific context of the general principle was used to interpret and apply the general meaning of 'consent'.

The *Abaclat* tribunal also made reference to the 'general principle of due process' when it dealt with the filling of the procedural gap regarding collective procedures. It particularly stated that 'adaptations made to the standard procedure must be done in consideration of the general principle of due process and must seek a balance between procedural rights and interests of each party'. [282] The 'due process principle' here was used as having an 'acceptability power' of any adaptation to the ICSID procedure in order to accommodate collective procedures.[283]

In a similar context, regarding the use of 'principles', the *Asian agricultural products* case portrayed how the latter are used not only as a source of law but also as interpretive arguments. The tribunal enumerates rules that 'should guide the Tribunal in adjudicating the interpretation issues raised'.[284] These interpretation rules include reference to custom, rules and principles of international law as well as general principles of law.

Rule D focuses on the use of international law rules and principles stating:

> In addition to the 'integral context', 'object and intent', 'spirit', 'objectives', 'comprehensive construction of the treaty as a whole', recourse to the law and principles of international law has to be considered a necessary factor providing guidance within the process of treaty interpretation.[285]

Principles of international law are used here as an interpretation tool rather than as a source of applicable law.

The tribunal also refers to additional 'canons' which complement the above-mentioned rules of interpretation and include general principles of law. These are the 'general principle of law placing the burden of proof upon the claimant' and the general principle that 'the probative force of the evidence presented is for the Tribunal to determine'.[286] Based on these rules, general principles of law are used as interpretive arguments.

Another prominent example of tribunals viewing general principles of law as interpretive arguments is the *Micula* case. The Tribunal based its reasoning on a string of investment-arbitration cases and on the Europe Cement case that held that the principle of good faith is a principle of international law that is 'applicable to the

280. *Abaclat,* Decision on Jurisdiction and Admissibility (n 237) para. 430.
281. *Ibid.* para. 437.
282. *Ibid.* para. 519.
283. *See also* the Urbaser case where the Tribunal describes due process and good faith as 'principles' which are part of the FET protection guarantee. *Urbaser,* Award (n 249) para. 621.
284. *Asian Agricultural Products Ltd. v. Sri Lanka,* ICSID Case ARB/87/3, Award (27 Jun. 1990) para. 40.
285. *Ibid.*
286. *Ibid.* para. 56.

interpretation and application of obligations under international investment agreements'.[287]

The main function of general principles of law is not only to fill gaps in the law, but also to help the interpreter in elucidating the vagueness and ambiguity of customary and treaty law.[288] The interchangeable use of the same legal directives both as sources of law as well as interpretive arguments is mainly attributed to their broad nature. This in its turn is connected to the inconsistent use of the legal vocabulary which permits attribution of multiple functions to legal directives. In this context, the multifunctioning use of legal directives enhances the emergence of a specific vocabulary used by arbitrators that is formed around the interpretive needs arising in the context of a specific dispute.

[4] Transnational Law Method for Identifying General Principles of Law as a Source of Law

General principles of law constitute the 'essence' of legal systems as a shared 'common core' of legal ideas.[289] The identification of general principles of law should be based on inductive proof and not on the hypothesis of their existence.[290] 'General principles of law' do not represent general approaches of justice but are part of the body of international law and in each case their existence and character must be proven and not just assumed.[291] Such a proof is supplied when it is based on a rigorous examination of the most fundamental representative legal systems through a comparative analysis.[292]

The comparative law analysis enables the decision-maker to apply the principles that are genuinely widely accepted and not just recognised by one specific legal system. Gaillard refers to this methodology as a 'transnational law methodology' for the identification of transnational rules such as general principles of law.[293] While it is

287. *Joan Micula and others v. Romania*, ICSID Case No. ARB/05/20, Award (11 Dec. 2013) para. 833 (the Tribunal cited the following cases: *Europe Cement Investment & Trade S.A. v. Republic of Turkey*, ICSID Case No. ARB(AF)/07/2, Award (13 Aug. 2009) para 171, citing *Amco Asia Corporation and others v. Republic of Indonesia*, ICSID Case No. ARB/81/1, Award (20 Nov. 1984); *Plama v. Bulgaria*; *Inceysa Vallisoletana S.L. v. Republic of El Salvador*, ICSID Case No. ARB/03/26, Award (2 Aug. 2006); *Phoenix Action Ltd v. Czech Republic*, ICSID Case No. ARB/06/5, Award (15 Apr. 2009).
288. Vadi, *Analogies in International Investment Law and Arbitration* (n 277) 40; *See also* Wolfgang Friedmann, 'The Uses of "General Principles" in the Development of International Law' (1963) 57 AJIL 279.
289. Frances Freeman Jalet, 'The Quest for the General Principles of Law Recognised by Civilised Nations' (1963) 10 UCLA 1041, 1044; Rudolf B Sclesinger, 'Research on General Principles of Law Recognised by Civilised Nations' (1957) 51(4) AJIL 734, 739.
290. Schreuer, *The ICSID Convention: A Commentary* (n 269) 610; Christoph Schreuer, 'The Relevance of Public International Law in International Commercial Arbitration: Investment Dispute' <http://www.univie.ac.at/intlaw/wordpress/pdf/81_csunpublpaper_1.pdf> (accessed 24 Feb. 2018).
291. *Ibid.*
292. *Ibid. See also* Rudolf Schlesinger, *The Common Core of Legal Systems, an Emerging Subject of Comparative Study* (A.W. Sijthoff 1961).
293. Gaillard, 'Transnational Law' (n 97) 62 et seq.

difficult to say that there is a universal transnational law methodology for identifying the general principles of international law, such principles should find general acceptance in the main legal systems.[294] In the field of investment arbitration, identification of such general principles of law is assisted by lists compiling common principles such as that of UNIDROIT,[295] by international treaties which reflect an extensive consensus on various issues, by arbitral case law constituting persuasive precedents, and by the doctrine developed in the field.[296] Accordingly, arbitrators may identify general principles of law through reference to the jurisprudence of international courts and tribunals with the objective of clarifying the law or to avoid lacuna and *non liquet*.[297]

The *El Paso* Tribunal described the methodology of identifying general principles of international law. It particularly referred to two conditions for principles of domestic law to be applied as general principles of international law:

> It is first of all necessary that they exist and are uniformly applied in the *great majority* of States; secondly, and this is the most characterising condition, they must be perceived as obligatory or necessary also from the point of view of international law, *i.e.* as upholding values and prescribing behaviour that States consider as pursued or prescribed or at least as necessary also at the international level.[298]

The Tribunal further emphasised on the role of case law by adding that: 'general principles' are rules largely applied in foro domestico, in private or public, substantive or procedural matters, provided that, after adaptation, they are suitable for application on the level of public international law.[299]

Similarly, the *Klöckner* Tribunal applied the French principle of the 'duty of full disclosure to a partner in a contract' as a 'general principle' stating that it is not only a principle of French law but also 'the case under the other national codes which we

294. Harold Cooke Gutteridge, 'Comparative Law and the Law of Nations' (1944) 21(1) BYCL 5.
295. *See*, Piero Bernardini, 'UNIDROIT Principles and International Investment Arbitration' (2014) 19(4) Uniform Law Review 561, 564; For example, *El Paso Energy International Company v. Argentine Republic*, ICSID Case No. ARB/03/15, Award (31 Oct. 2011) para. 623 (The Tribunal states: 'That there is a general principle on the preclusion of wrongfulness in certain situations can hardly be doubted, as is confirmed by the UNIDROIT Principles on International Commercial Contracts, a sort of international restatement of the law of contracts reflecting rules and principles applied by the majority of national legal systems'); Similarly, the *Chevron* Tribunal finds that: 'Finally, the "loss of chance" principle does not have wide acceptance across legal systems such that it can be considered a "general principle of law recognized by civilized nations." At most it can be said that the "loss of chance" principle is applied in exceptional situations where there exists a "harm whose existence cannot be disputed but which it is difficult to quantify," as noted in the commentary to the UNIDROIT Principles cited by the Respondent.' *Chevron Corporation and Texaco Petroleum Company v. Ecuador*, UNCITRAL PCA Case No. 2009-23, Partial Award (30 Mar. 2010) para. 382.
296. Gaillard, 'Transnational Law' (n 97) 62 et seq.
297. Vadi, *Analogies in International Investment Law and Arbitration* (n 277) 129.
298. *El Paso Energy International Company v. The Argentine Republic*, ICSID Case No. ARB/03/15, Award (31 Oct. 2011) para. 622. The Tribunal cites and translates from Italian: B Conforti, *Diritto Internazionale. Manuali per l'Università Napoli*, Editoriale Scientifica, 2006, writes on pp. 40–41.
299. *Ibid.* para. 622.

know of'.[300] The ad hoc committee annulled the award criticising the absence of any authority of these general principles applied.[301]

The *WDF* tribunal took a cautious approach when connecting public policy to concepts like '*bones mores*', or in other words good and right practices, highlighting the necessity to resort to comparative law but also to arbitral case law. On this basis, the tribunal's argumentation leads to connotations of 'general principles of law'. The tribunal notes:

> Arbitral tribunals have more often based their decisions on universal values in using various formulations such as 'good morals', 'bonas mores', 'ethics of international trade' or 'transnational public policy' [...]. But it has been rightly stressed that Tribunals must be very cautious in this respect and must carefully check the objective existence of a particular transnational public policy rule in identifying it through international conventions, comparative law and arbitral awards [...].[302]

The *WDF* tribunal further enhanced the 'general principle' approach when identifying how domestic laws and international conventions deal with the issue of bribery stating that 'bribery or influence peddling, as well as both active and passive corruption, are sanctioned by criminal law in most, if not all, countries'.[303] The Tribunal justified this 'general condemnation' by referring to a number of international and regional conventions aiming at combating corruption as well as to domestic court decisions on whether bribery is contrary to public policy, and arbitral awards dealing with corruption.[304]

Another example of how arbitral tribunals identify principles universally or generally accepted in the international sphere is the *Waste Management II* and *Micula* case. In both cases the tribunals relied largely on domestic and international case law in order to ascertain the res judicata and good faith principles respectively. In particular, the *Waste Management II* Tribunal recognised res judicata as a general principle of international law.[305] In making this determination, the Tribunal relied on Bin Cheng's work and the decisions cited therein,[306] as well as on several international

300. *Klöckner, Annulment* (n 274) para. 66.
301. The Ad hoc Committee held that the Tribunal had failed to apply the law and had based its decision on a 'general equity' rather than on 'positive law'; *See also* Vadi, *Analogies in International Investment Law and Arbitration* (n 277) 125.
302. *World Duty Free Company Limited v. the Republic of Kenya*, ICSID Case No. Arb/00/7, Award (4 Oct. 2006) para. 141.
303. *Ibid.* para. 142.
304. *Ibid.* paras 143–149.
305. *Waste Management, Inc. v. United Mexican States* (Waste Management II), Case N° ARB(AF)/00/3, Mexico's Preliminary Objection concerning the Previous Proceedings (26 Jun. 2002) fn 38.
306. *Ibid.* fn 38. The Tribunal clearly states that it relies on Bin Cheng's work (Bin Cheng, *General Principles of Law as Applied by International Courts and Tribunals* (CUP 1953; repr. Grotius, Cambridge, 1987) pp. 336–372) and the decisions cited therein which are: Smelter Arbitral Tribunal Final Award (1941) 3 UNRIAA, p. 1905, at pp. 1950–1951. *See also* P.C.A.: Pious Fund Case (1902) 1 H.C.R., p. 1; Fran.-Ven. M.C.C. (1902): Fabiani Case, Ralston's Report, p. 81; P.C.A.: Orinoco Steamship Co. Case (1910) 1 H.C.R., p. 226. PCIJ: Jaworzina Frontier (1923) Adv.Op., B. 8, p. 38; Monastery of St. Naoum (1924) Adv.Op., B. 9, pp. 21, 22; Polish Postal

court decisions, arbitral decisions and domestic court judgments.[307] Similarly, the *Micula* Tribunal made reference to Bin Cheng's work and investment-arbitration decisions when ascertaining the content of good faith as a general principle of law.[308]

The above analysis reveals that reference to general principles of law is strongly connected to the methodology of identifying such principles through comparative law analysis. Reference to such principles by investment-arbitration tribunals is not without consequences since it implies the need to certify their existence through a specific methodology. However, tribunals tend to ascertain the existence of general principles of law largely based on international case law rather than on a thorough comparative analysis of the universal principles of the legal systems. One may make reference to general principles of law emerging from a 'universal jurisprudence' as formed by international decision-makers:

> The reference then, to general principles in the Statute of the International Court is not to those portions of the law which various nations have in common-a common core-but to a universal jurisprudence which delves deeper than mere collating of legal rules and institutions, and whose roots spread out to nourish the legal societies of all humanity. There is no need to undertake a quest for that which forms the basis of all law. It is discoverable through the normal processes of judicial decision making followed by every judge.[309]

The Tribunal, after identifying the general principles of law, is faced with the task of interpreting those principles in the light of the investment-arbitration framework within which they are employed. This is the topic examined in the next section.

[5] General Principles of Investment Law and Arbitration

From a language perspective, the term 'general principles of law' has two meanings. According to its first meaning, it signifies that a principle has a general context, while in its second meaning it refers to a principle found generally in various legal systems.[310] In the first case, what is expressed through this terminology is the place of the rule within a legal system based on its level of generality, while in the second case, the emphasis is put on the source or, in other words, on the identification of the principle

Service in Danzig (1925) Adv.Op., B. 11, p. 24; Société Commerciale de Belgique Case (1939) A/B. 78, p. 174. ICJ: Haya de la Torre Case (1951) ICJ Reports 1951, p. 71, at pp. 77. 80, 82.

307. *Waste Management, Inc. v. United Mexican States* (Waste Management II), Case No ARB(AF)/00/3 (Mexico's Preliminary Objection concerning the Previous Proceedings, 26 Jun. 2002) paras 40–45. The Tribunal itself relies on: Compagnie Générale de l'Orénoque (1905) Ralston's Report, p. 244 at p. 355, quoting *Southern Pacific Railroad Co. v. United States*, 168 Sup. Ct. Rep. 355 (1897), at p. 377; on the SS Newchang case, (In the Matter of the S.S. Newchang, Claim No. 21, reprinted in (1922) 16 AJIL 323 at p. 324); on the PCIJ case in Polish Postal Service in Danzig PCIJ, Ser. B, No. 11 (1925) at pp. 28–30 before coming to the conclusion that res judicata is a general principle of law.
308. *Joan Micula and others v. Romania*, ICSID Case No. ARB/05/20, Award (11 Dec. 2013) at para. 833.
309. Frances Freeman Jalet, The Quest for the General Principles of Law Recognised by Civilised Nations (n 289), 1041, 1086.
310. Gaillard, 'Transnational Law' (n 97) 67.

within the different legal systems.[311] The previous section dealt with general principles of law as a source of law. This section analyses the specific way 'general principles of law' are interpreted in the investment-arbitration framework leaning towards the first meaning of the term.

Despite the fact that general principles of law are a source of law that is recognised by State practice, they are 'essentially independent'.[312] Such so-called independence permits each general principle of law to follow its own trajectory and acquire a specialised meaning when applied and interpreted in the context of a specific legal framework.

When the *Abaclat* tribunal was called to answer the question whether it could fill in the gap created by the absence of a mass proceeding in arbitration through the design of specific rules, it observed that:

> This question cannot (and should not) be answered in the abstract. Not only would this imply creating general principles thereby relying on a terminology, which is as diverse and varied as the currently existing forms and modalities of collective proceedings, but it would also go beyond the powers of the Tribunal to fill a specific gap regarding the conduct of specific proceedings.[313]

Even though the tribunal dealt with a procedural law issue, it is interesting to point out that the decision-maker recognised the varied and broad nature of the concept 'general principles' and concluded that the creation of 'general principles' is not suitable for filling a specific gap of the ICSID framework. The suitable solution is the creation of specific principles that will apply only to the specific case.

Despite the refusal of the *Abaclat* Tribunal to form general principles of law, the practice of the arbitral tribunals reveals a specialised interpretation of general principles of law.[314] Gaillard interestingly marks that general principles of law are general because they are widely accepted and not because they lack specificity.[315] Such principles include '*pacta sunt servanda*',[316] 'unjust enrichment',[317] 'res judicata',[318]

311. *Ibid.*
312. E Lauterpacht (ed.), *International Law – The Collected Papers of Hersch Lauterpacht, vol I* (CUP 1970) 91 in Vadi, *Analogies in International Investment Law and Arbitration* (n 277) 41.
313. *Abaclat,* Decision on Jurisdiction and Admissibility (n 237) para. 527.
314. Emmanuel Gaillard, *Legal Theory of International Arbitration* (Nijhoff 2010) 54.
315. *Ibid.* 55.
316. Kryvoi Yaraslau, 'Counterclaims in investor-state arbitration' (2011) LSE Law, Society and Economy Working Papers 8/2011 London School of Economics and Political Science Law Department 24 <http://ssrn.com/abstract=1891935> (accessed 28 Feb. 2018) citing *Klöckner Industrie-Anlagen GmbH and others v. United Republic of Cameroon and Société Camerounaise des Engrais*, ICSID Case No. ARB/81/2, Award (21 Oct. 1983); The principle of '*pacta sunt servanda*' has been described as being 'held in common by international and private law, but in both cases the same problem has arisen, namely, how far a supervening change in circumstances may, nevertheless, be treated as releasing the parties to an agreement from any further obligation to fulfil their promises'. Gutteridge, 'Comparative Law and the Law of Nations' (n 294) 6.
317. *Amco Asia Corporation and others v. Republic of Indonesia*, ICSID Case No. ARB/81/1, Resubmitted Case: Award (5 Jun. 1990) paras 154–156.
318. *Amco Asia Corporation and others v. Republic of Indonesia*, ICSID Case No. ARB/81/1, Resubmitted Case: Decision on Jurisdiction (10 May 1988) paras 16 et seq.; The tribunal in *Amco v. Indonesia* states that it is bound by res judicata as a general principle of international

and general principles of contract law.[319] These general principles may at first sight seem to be just 'general principles of international law' without any specific characteristic that could justify their characterisation as 'investor-state arbitration general principles'. A closer study, however, of the arbitral practice reveals that arbitrators adapt the general principles of law they use to the specific treaty nature of a dispute between a State and a private party through their interpretation process. As such, the meaning of these principles is ascertained in the light of the legal framework in which they are employed.

A stark illustration of a general principle of law which has acquired a specialised context in investment-arbitration decision-making is the 'principle of good faith'. The 'principle of good faith' is taken into account in the context of the exercise of rights and prescribes the prohibition of exercising a right in a way that would cause malicious injury to someone else.[320] 'Good faith' has both a substantive and procedural perspective. The former is connected to the substantive rights and obligations of the parties and the latter to the way the arbitral proceeding is conducted.[321] From an abstract point of view, 'good faith' is understood as 'a moral principle and is reflective of all good senses such as honesty, good conscience, fairness, equity, reasonableness, equitable dealing or fair dealing'.[322] The Malicorp Tribunal eloquently states that:

> the safeguarding of good faith is one of the fundamental principles of international law and the law of investments. As in domestic law, the principle fulfils a complementary function; it allows for lacunae in the applicable laws to be filled, and for that law to be clarified by the specific application of existing principles.[323]

---

law, *Amco Asia Corporation and others v. Republic of Indonesia*, ICSID Case No. ARB/81/1, Resubmitted Decision on Jurisdiction (10 May 1988) at para. 26 "The principle of res judicata is a general principle of law. It is a principle known both to international law and to Indonesian law. It is also generally acknowledged that (unless an instrument shall provide otherwise), nullification may be total or partial (except in the case of corruption of the arbitrator, such corruption tainting the entire award)'; Emmanuel Gaillard as well describes the use of general principles of international law by arbitrators as fundamental. *See*, Emmanuel Gaillard and Yas Banifatemi, 'The Meaning of "and" in Art. 42(1), Second Sentence, of the Washington Convention: The Role of International Law in the ICSID Choice of Law Process' (2003) 18 ICSID Rev. 375, 411.

319. *Amco Asia*, Resubmitted Case: Award (n 317) paras 180–183.
320. Bin Cheng, *General Principles of Law as Applied by International Courts and Tribunals* (CUP 1953) 121; Jose Ponce and Ricardo Cevallos, 'Good Faith in Investment Arbitration' (2016) 5 TDM.
321. Emily Sipiorski 'Evidence and the Principle of Good Faith in Investment Arbitration: Finding Meaning in Public International Law' in Dário Moura Vicente (ed.) *Towards a Universal Justice? Putting International Courts and Jurisdictions into Perspective* (Brill 2016) 352; An illustration of the procedural perspective is the case of *Methanex Corporation v. United States of America*, UNCITRAL, Final Award of the Tribunal on Jurisdiction and Merits (3 Aug. 2005) para. 54. The tribunal stated: 'the Disputing Parties each owed in this arbitration a general legal duty to the other and to the Tribunal to conduct themselves in good faith during these arbitration proceedings and to respect the equality of arms between them, the principles of "equal treatment" and procedural fairness'.
322. Munir Maniruzzaman, 'The Concept of Good Faith in International Investment Disputes – The Arbitrator's Dilemma' (2012) 89 Amicus Curiae 16, 16.
323. *Malicorp Limited v. The Arab Republic of Egypt*, ICSID Case No. ARB/08/18, Award (7 Feb. 2011) para. 116.

While 'good faith' in this broad sense acts as an interpretive principle, in another context and under a different factual situation it may acquire a specialised meaning.[324] From the principle of good faith emanate more specific principles such as good faith in the conclusion, interpretation, and performance of contracts, and interpretation against a party, which unilaterally drafted a contract.[325] The important role played by this general principle lies in the fact that it connects the exercise of the investor's rights with a specific obligation not to harm the interests of the State.[326] 'Good faith' also becomes relevant in the context of the interpretation of FET, as a defence that the state's conduct was in good faith and as an issue of whether the investment was made in good faith.[327]

The specialisation of the 'general principle of good faith' can also be demonstrated through its connection to the protection of the investor's legitimate expectations which is not generally provided for in the investment treaties. The *Thunderbird* tribunal relied on investment case law and the 'principle of good faith' in order to conclude that the concept of 'legitimate expectation' within the NAFTA framework relates to a situation where 'a failure by the NAFTA Party to honour those expectations could cause the investor (or investment) to suffer damages'.[328] The concept of 'legitimate expectation' had been characterised as 'the normative and more defined expression of the good faith obligation of the host states'.[329]

Similarly, the *Abaclat* tribunal referred to the 'general principle of good faith' as a fundamental principle of both international law and investment law stating that '[t]he theory of abuse of rights is an expression of the more general principle of good faith. The principle of good faith is a fundamental principle of international law, as well as

324. Munir Maniruzzaman, 'The Concept of Good Faith in International Investment Disputes – The Arbitrator's Dilemma' (n 322) 16, 17; *See also* Bernardo Cremades, 'Good Faith in International Arbitration' (2012) 27(4) AmULRev 783.
325. Gaillard, *Legal Theory of International Arbitration* (n 314) 54.
326. Yaraslau, *Counterclaims in Investor-State Arbitration* (n 316) 23.
327. *See* generally Sanja Đajić, 'Mapping the Good Faith Principle in International Investment Arbitration: Assessment of its Substantive and Procedural Value' (2012) 46 Zbornik Radova 207; Zachary Douglas, 'The Plea of Illegality in Investment Arbitration' 29(1) ICSID Rev (2014) 155, 169; *MTD Equity Sdn. Bhd. and MTD Chile S.A. v. Republic of Chile*, ICSID Case No. ARB/01/7, Award (25 May 2004) para. 109 (The Tribunal held: '[a]s defined by Judge Schwebel, "fair and equitable treatment" is "a broad and widely-accepted standard encompassing such fundamental standards as good faith, due process, nondiscrimination, and proportionality"'); *Tecnicas Medioambientales Tecmed v. United Mexican States*, ICSID Case No. ARB (AF)/00/2, Award (29 May 2003) para. 153 (citations omitted) (The Tribunal held: 'the commitment of fair and equitable treatment included in Article 4(1) of the Agreement is an expression and part of the bona fide principle recognized in international law, although bad faith from the State is not required for its violation'); *S.D. Myers, Inc. v. Government of Canada*, UNCITRAL, Partial Award (13 Nov. 2000) para. 134 (The Tribunal stated that 'Article 1105 of the NAFTA requires the Parties to treat investors of another Party in accordance with international law, including fair and equitable treatment. Article 1105 imports into the NAFTA the international law requirements of due process, economic rights, obligations of good faith and natural justice.').
328. *International Thunderbird Gaming Corporation v. United Mexican States*, UNCITRAL/NAFTA Chapter 11, Award (26 Jan. 2006) para. 147 (citations omitted).
329. Đajić, 'Mapping the Good Faith Principle in International Investment Arbitration' (n 327) 214.

investment law.[330] Likewise, the *Malicorp* tribunal described 'good faith' as 'one of the fundamental principles of international law and the law of investments'.[331]

Based on the above analysis, a general principle of law identified through the transnational law methodology, when interpreted in the context of investment arbitration, may further become a specialised general principle of law. As a result, in investment arbitration both meanings of the term 'general principles of law' may make their appearance in the decision-making process. Thus, from an interpretive methodology perspective, specialised principles of investment arbitration should be interpreted with reference to the specialised regime that further developed them.

In this respect, although general principles of law traditionally arise out of the comparative analysis of domestic laws, specialised general principles of law are further shaped through case-by-case interpretation in arbitral decision-making. This reflects the fact that the practice of international law actors such as international organisations and the international business community, but also investment-arbitration tribunals has led to the development of general principles of law.[332]

[C] Rights

The legal relationship between the State and the investor is expressed in investment treaties and dispute resolution provisions using the term 'rights' or 'obligations'.[333] The section analysing the standards of investment protection approached the issue from an 'obligation' owed by the State to the investor point of view.[334] This section takes a rights' approach rather than an obligations' approach focusing on the rights that arise from the investment treaties for the foreign investors.

These rights have been described as having a mixed or hybrid character since they are 'created' in the public domain arising out of a state-to-state relationship but are enforced through a private dispute resolution mechanism.[335] After sketching their legal content, this part proceeds to an analysis of how substantive rights are treated in the context of investor-state arbitration.

330. Abaclat, *Decision on Jurisdiction and Admissibility* (n 237) para. 646.
331. *Malicorp Limited v. The Arab Republic of Egypt*, ICSID Case No. ARB/08/18, Award (7 Feb. 2011) para. 116.
332. Grant Hanessian, 'General Principles of Law in the Iran-U.S. Claims Tribunal' (1989) 27 ColumJTransnatlL. 309, 351.
333. Martins Paparinskis, 'Investment Treaty Arbitration and the (New) Law of State Responsibility' (2013) 24(2) EJIL 617, 626.
334. *See* §2.02[A] 'Standards' and §2.02[B] 'Principles'.
335. Zachary Douglas, 'The Hybrid Foundations of Investment Treaty Arbitration' (2003) 74 BYIL 151, 153.

[1] Sketching Their Legal Content

Investment treaties could be described as an 'economic' bill of rights granting substantive protections and procedural rights to foreign investors.[336] In this context, modern investment treaties confer to investors substantial rights along with enforcement procedures. This has contributed to a fundamental change in international law since the individual is assigned individual rights through an international treaty and hence acquires 'the status of a partial subject of international law'.[337] These rights may be general, included in most of the investment treaties, or specific, identified on a case-by-case analysis.

The general guarantees through which the substantive protection of the investor is expressed include compensation for expropriation, the guarantees of an MFN clause, the national treatment of the investment, the full protection and security of the investment, guarantees that the State will honour its obligations, prohibition against discriminatory or unreasonable measures, guarantees for fair and equitable treatment and assurance that the investment will not be treated less favourably than the protection accorded under international law.[338]

Fair and equitable treatment and full protection and security have been described as 'non-contingent' protection rights since they afford absolute protection that does not depend on the range of protection afforded to others.[339] On the contrary, MFN and national treatment as well as non-discrimination are 'contingent' rights in the sense that '[t]he extent of the protection which they afford is dependent upon that which the host State metes out to others, who stand in the requisite legal relationship to the protected investor'.[340]

Investment treaties also provide for specific rights to be accorded to the investors. The two broad categories of specific rights are 'monetary transfers' and 'operational conditions'.[341] These rights include the remittance abroad of profits and dividends, the right of access to public services and resources, the right to enter into contracts, publication of laws and regulations affecting investment as well as the right to obtain the needed permits.[342] Specific rights are connected to carrying out the investment in practice. They are accorded mostly based on two considerations: on the one hand due

336. Susan Franck, 'The Nature and Enforcement of Investor Rights under Investment Treaties: Do Investment Treaties have a Bright Future?' (2005) 12 UCDJInternl'L&P 47, 48.
337. Braun, 'Part V Chapter 21: Globalization: The Driving Force in International Investment Law' (n 212) 495.
338. *See generally* Rudolf Dolzer and Margrete Stevens, *Bilateral Investment Treaties* (Nijhoff 1995) 330; August Reinisch (ed.), *Standards of Investment Protection* (OUP 2008) 29, 59, 111, 131; Rudolf Dolzer and Christoph Schreuer, *Principles of International Investment Law* (2nd ed., OUP 2012) 130.
339. Herman Walker, 'Modern Treaties of Friendship, Commerce and Navigation' (1957–1958) 42 MinnLR 805, 810–811.
340. Campbell McLachlan, Laurence Shore, and Matthew Weiniger, *International Investment Arbitration: Substantive Principles* (OUP 2008) 11.
341. Jeswald Salacuse and Nicholas Sullivan, 'Do BITS Really Work?: An Evaluation of Bilateral Investment Treaties and Their Grand Bargain' (2005) 46 HarvIntlLJ 67, 85–86.
342. Giorgio Sacerdoti, 'Bilateral Investment Treaties and Multilateral Instruments on Investment Protection' (1997) 269 Recueil des Cours 251, 340.

to the peculiarity of foreign investments in comparison to national investment and on the other hand because of the need to carry out business activities.[343] Remittance of profits abroad for example is a particular feature of an investment made by a foreign party whereas the right to contract is an essential ingredient of business activities.[344]

An illustration of how such specific rights appear into investment treaties can be found in the Italy-Russia BIT. Article 2 (7) deals with the employment of personnel by foreign investors providing that 'in conformity with their legislation on the entry and stay of foreigners, [the signatory States] shall permit to the citizens of the other Party who perform working activities in connection with an investment governed by this agreement, as well to their dependents, to enter, stay and leave its territory'.[345]

The nature of these rights, however, is a controversial topic that has led to debate. One approach to the issue supports the derivative nature of investors' rights under international investment agreements while another approach contends that these rights have a direct nature.[346] The International Court of Justice ruled in the *LaGrand* case that a treaty between two States can create individual rights whether these rights are classified as human rights or not.[347] The international court's approach is connected to the 'direct rights' view.[348]

The arbitral tribunals on the other hand have supported both approaches in their awards. The direct rights approach views the obligation of the State to resolve the disputes arising with the private investor through arbitration, as creating an individual right directly owed to the investor.[349] The investment treaty bestows on the private party an 'arbitral right' which cannot be unilaterally withdrawn except through the

343. *Ibid.* 340.
344. For 'monetary transfers' in particular *see* Mohamed Khalil, 'Treatment of Foreign Investment in Bilateral Investment Treaties' (1992) 7 ICSID Rev Foreign Inv LJ 339.
345. Russia-Italy BIT (1996).
346. Anastasios Gourgourinis, 'The Nature of Investor's Rights under Investment Treaties: A Rejoinder to Martins Paparinskis' (2013) EJIL <http://www.ejiltalk.org/the-nature-of-investors-rights-under-investment-treaties-a-rejoinder-tomartins-paparinskis/> (accessed 4 Mar. 2018); Paparinskis, 'Investment Treaty Arbitration and the (New) Law of State Responsibility' (n 333).
347. James Crawford, 'The ILC's Articles on Responsibility of States for Internationally Wrongful Acts: A Retrospect' (2002) 96(4) AJIL 874, 887 citing *LaGrand Case (Ger. v. U.S.)* ICJ, Merits (27 Jun. 2001).
348. The question of whether an investment treaty confers direct rights to investors is also connected to the issue of the waiver of the investor's right to arbitration. Accepting the direct nature approach would give the investor the ability to waive its right to arbitration the same way an individual would be able to do. Conversely, in the case the investor derives the right from the right of the State-party to the treaty, then the waiver is not possible as the right is not the investor's to give away; *See* Salacuse, *The Law of Investment Treaties* (n 69) 390–392 citing *EUREKO B.V. v. Republic of Poland* UNCITRAL, Partial award (19 Aug. 2005) para. 175.
349. *See* for example *Hochtief AG v. Argentina*, Decision on Jurisdiction, ICSID Case No. ARB/07/31 (24 Oct. 2011) paras 62, 66. In replying to whether dispute settlement is an 'activity in connection with the investment', the tribunal held that arbitration is a right which the investor has. It particularly stated: 'Indeed, the ("procedural") right to enforce another ("substantive") right is one component of the bundles of rights and duties that make up the legal concept of what property is.'

termination of the BIT process.[350] The principle of good faith and estoppel would also act against the withdrawal of such consent.

The investment Tribunal in the *SGS v. Philippines* case stated that modern international law treaties may confer direct rights to individuals with the aim of protecting their private interest. In particular, the Tribunal put emphasis on the ICSID Convention when stating that:

> To some extent, diplomatic protection is intervening as a residual mechanism to be resorted to in the absence of other arrangements recognizing the direct right of action by individuals. It is precisely this kind of arrangement that has come to prevail under international law, particularly in respect of foreign investments, the paramount example being that of the 1965 Convention.[351]

The alternative approach considers the obligations of the States towards the investor to be owed to the contracting States but the States confer to the individuals the right to enforce such obligations before an international tribunal.[352] This delegation of procedural rights to the private party has led to the characterisation of the rights as 'delegated rights', in the sense that States have delegated their own rights to their nationals.[353] Investment treaties have also been conceptualised through the agency theory viewing the investors as an agent who has been delegated by the agreement of the host and home State the right to bring a claim in front of an international tribunal.[354]

This model that views investor's rights as 'beneficiaries' of rights created for third persons is also supported by arbitral tribunals. Referring to the right of access to ICSID arbitration, the *Wintershall* tribunal noted:

---

350. Thomas Wälde, 'Investment Arbitration under the Energy Charter Treaty – From Dispute Settlement to Treaty Implementation' (1996) 12(6) ArbIntl 429, 435; Geneviève Burdeau, 'Nouvelles perspectives pour l'arbitrage le contentieux economique interessant l'Etat' (1995) 1 RevArb 3, 12 et seq.
351. *SGS Société Générale de Surveillance SA v. Philippines*, ICSID Case No. ARB/02/6, Decision on Jurisdiction (29 Jan. 2004) para. 45 (citations omitted).
352. Douglas, 'The Hybrid Foundations of Investment Treaty Arbitration' (n 335) 163. A discussion as to the derivative versus direct nature of the rights under the NAFTA can be found in *Archer Daniels Midland Company v. The United Mexican States*, ICSID CASE No. ARB(AF)/04/05, Award, para. 169 (The tribunal stated: 'The derivative theory [...] supports the proposition that investment treaties provide a set of obligations which require the State to treat investments of qualified investors in accordance with the standards of the treaty; but these obligations are only owed to the State of the investor's nationality. If a breach of any of these standards occurs, the investor may bring the host State to an international arbitration in order to request compensation, but the investor will be in reality stepping into the shoes and asserting the rights of the home State. [...] However, the proper interpretation of the NAFTA does not substantiate that investors have individual rights as alleged by the Claimants.'
353. Paparinskis, 'Investment Treaty Arbitration and the (New) Law of State Responsibility' (n 333) 625.
354. *Ibid*; *See also ATA Contruction v. The Hashemite Kingdomof Jordan*, ICSID Case No. ARB/08/2, Award (18 May 2010) para. 117. The tribunal held: 'At this juncture, the Tribunal observes that the right to arbitration is a distinct "investment" within the meaning of the BIT because Article I(2)(a)(ii) defines an investment *inter alia* as "claims to [...] any other rights to legitimate performance having financial value related to an investment."'

> It is a general principle of the law of treaties that a third beneficiary of a right under it must comply with the conditions for the exercise of the right provided for in the treaty or established in conformity with the treaty. On the analogy of Article 36(2) of the Vienna Convention on the Law of Treaties of 1969 (the 'Vienna Convention'), the 'secondary right-holder' under a bilateral treaty (the investor) who is conferred certain rights, being in no different position from 'the third State' (mentioned in Article 36) – must comply with the conditions stipulated for the exercise of the rights provided for in the treaty concerned, which in the instant case is the 'basic' treaty.[355.]

Another example of the derivative approach can be found in the *Loewen* case. The tribunal first described the public international law nature of the investment-treaty rights distinguishing them from private law claims:

> NAFTA claims [stem] from a corner of public international law in which, by treaty, the power of States under that law to take international measures for the correction of wrongs done to its nationals has been replaced by an ad hoc definition of certain kinds of wrong, coupled with specialist means of compensation. These means are both distinct from and exclusive of the remedies for wrongful acts under private law [...].[356]

The *Loewen* tribunal continued the description of the rights accorded to the investor putting emphasis on their derivative nature. In particular, it stated that:

> [t]here is no warrant for transferring rules derived from private law into a field of international law where claimants are permitted for convenience to enforce what are in origin the rights of Party states. If the effects of a change of ownership are to be ascertained we must do so, not by inapt analogies with private law rules, but from the words of Chapter Eleven, read in the context of the Treaty as a whole, and of the purpose which it sets out to achieve.[357]

A third recent approach to investor rights proposes the reconceptualisation of investment treaties through the triangular framework of public international law,

---

355. *Wintershall AG v. Argentina*, ICSID Case No. ARB/04/14, Award (8 Dec. 2008) para. 114; Paparinskis comments on the VCLT analogy issue:

> The appropriateness of the argument may have to be qualified by special characteristics less obviously present in investment law: in particular, the emphasis that VCLT Articles 34 and 36 place on the consent of third states as a precondition for the creation of rights. On the one hand, investors, unlike states (or international organisations) are not international law-makers. The VCLT regime deals with the grant of rights to entities that could in principle participate in the creation of rights themselves [...].

Paparinskis, 'Investment Treaty Arbitration and the (New) Law of State Responsibility' (n 333) 624.

356. The *Loewen Group, Inc. and Raymond L. Loewen v. United States of America*, Case No. ARB(AF)/9813, Award (26 Jun. 2003) para. 233.
357. *Ibid.* para. 233; *See also American Manufacturing and Trading, Inc. v. Republic of Zaire*, Case No. ARB/93/1, Award (21 Feb. 1997) para. 6.06 where the tribunal described the investor as a 'beneficiary' of BIT rights; *Archer Daniels Midland Company and Tate & Lyle Ingredients Americas, Inc. v. The United Mexican States*, ICSID Case No. ARB(AF)/04/05, Award (21 Nov. 2007) para. 171 where the tribunal held that '[...] the proper interpretation of the NAFTA does not substantiate that investors have individual rights as alleged by the Claimants[...]'.

third-party beneficiary doctrines and public law.[358] In this context, public international law accommodates the fact that investment treaties constitute international agreements between two States. The third-party beneficiary paradigm treats the issue of enforceable rights being granted to private parties created by treaties between two States.[359] Lastly, the public law model demonstrates the departure from traditional contract law due to the fact that a sovereign bestows rights to a non-sovereign party.

As investment treaties are interstate agreements, it remains a matter of interpretation whether the primary obligations contained in these treaties such as FET are directly owed to private investors or to the other contracting State.[360] Whatever approach regarding the nature of these rights is accepted, what is most critical is to reveal how 'rights' are approached in practice and what are the consequences of using such a legal term in the interpretation process.

[2] Substantive Rights and Standards

Investment treaties may present individual characteristics but they also have a common core of substantive protection rights which have originated mainly from the rights provided in treaties of friendship, navigation and commerce.[361] These substantive guarantees are not only characterised as substantive rights but as protection standards and principles as well.[362] FET for example is referred to as a principle, a standard and a right.[363] Such characterisations are not free of practical consequences. As discussed above, from an interpretative task perspective, arbitrators make purposive use of the legal terminology in order to express the interpretation process they follow. Reference to the term 'rights' in this case, may express the need to delimit appropriate boundaries of various rights.

Prime illustrations of the need to balance rights can be found in the cases connected to the Argentine economic crisis. The *CMS* tribunal refers to the substantive protection of the investor using the term 'rights': 'These rights relate mainly to fair and equitable treatment and full security and protection, arbitrariness and discrimination,

358. Anthea Roberts, 'Triangular Treaties: The Nature and Limits of Investment Treaty Rights' (2015) 56(2) HarvIntlLJ 353, 353.
359. *Ibid.*
360. Crawford, 'The ILC's Articles on Responsibility of States for Internationally Wrongful Acts' (n 347) 887.
361. Susan Franck, 'The Legitimacy Crisis in Investment Arbitration: Privatizing Public International Law Through Inconsistent Decisions' (2005) 73 FordhamLRev 1521, 1526–1527.
362. For example, Salacuse and Sullivan, 'Do BITS Really Work?' (n 341) 83 dividing the 'general standards of treatment of most BITs into six component parts'; Similarly, the Tribunal in *Telenor v. Hungary*, ICSID Case No. ARB/04/15, Award (13 Sep. 2006) para. 92 also characterises the protections as 'rights'. It states: 'In the absence of language or context to suggest the contrary, the ordinary meaning of "investments shall be accorded treatment no less favourable than that accorded to investments made by investors of any third State" is that the investor's substantive rights in respect of the investments are to be treated no less favourably than under a BIT between the host State and a third State, and there is no warrant for construing the above phrase as importing procedural fights as well'.
363. *See* §2.02[A] 'Standards'.

observance of obligations and indirect expropriation without compensation.'[364] The functionality of such vocabulary is twofold. On the one hand, the tribunal pointed out that the balance between the 'right of the host State to adopt its economic policies' and the 'rights of investors under a system of guarantees and protection' is a 'difficult balance' which 'the Convention was careful to preserve'.[365] On the other hand, the tribunal makes a distinction between the acts directly influencing the 'investor's rights under binding legal commitments' and 'other acts which relate to questions of public policy' in order to establish the jurisdiction of the Centre.[366] General economic measures of public policy are distinguished from industry-specific measures that affect the rights of the investor.[367] In this last case, the tribunal's argument concerning the kind of acts influencing the investor makes no reference to substantive protection standards but to substantive rights. The decision-maker used the term 'rights' instead of the term 'standards' or 'principles' in order to signify the need to proceed to a balancing of the investor's rights and that of the host State.[368]

This need to comprehend the interpretive functionality of legal terminology is more evident when it comes to the substantive guarantee of compensation for expropriation. Approaching the issue from a rights' perspective brings to the surface the need to find a balance between the investor's right to protection of property and the right of the State to regulate on the basis of public interest. Using the term 'standards', for example, in such a case would reveal the need to assess whether a certain level of protection is attained rather than the need to balance economic reality for example with the right of the investor to be accorded FET.[369] However, when it comes to the issue of expropriation, balancing rather than assessing standards becomes necessary.

In this context, arbitral tribunals have employed the proportionality test in indirect expropriation cases in order to find the right balance between the private interests of the investor and the public interest of the State.[370] Many tribunals have cited the *Tecmed* award[371] which is considered to be the first award to have thoroughly elaborated on the balance of rights issue setting out a framework for the application of the proportionality test. The tribunal concluded that the non-renewal of the licence restricted the claimant's property rights disproportionally, thus constituting an indirect

364. *CMS Gas Transmission Company v. The Republic of Argentina*, Case No. ARB/01/8, Decision of the Tribunal on Objections to Jurisdiction (17 Jul. 2003) para. 114.
365. *Ibid.* para. 28.
366. *Ibid.* para. 109.
367. *Ibid.* paras 23 et seq.
368. *See also AES Corp v. The Argentine Republic*, ICSID Case No. ARB/02/17, Decision on Jurisdiction (26 Apr. 2005) para. 57 where the Tribunal made reference to the issue of whether the 'delicate balance between the respective rights of the host State and those of the investor were respected in substance'.
369. *See* §2.02[A] 'Standards'.
370. *See LG&E Energy Corp., LG&E Capital Corp., LG&E International Inc v. Argentine Republic*, ICSID Case No. ARB/02/1, Decision on Liability (3 Oct. 2006) para. 158; *Total S.A. v. Argentine Republic (Total v. Argentina)*, ICSID Case No. ARB/04/1, Decision on Liability (27 Dec. 2010) para. 309; *Suez, Sociedad General de Aguas de Barcelona S.A., and InterAgua Servicios Integrales del Agua S.A. v. Argentina, (InterAgua v. Argentina)*, ICSID Case No. ARB/03/17, Decision on Liability (30 Jul. 2010) paras 147–48.
371. *Tecmed*, Award (n 147).

expropriation.[372] The recent case of *Total* also dealt with such a balancing but not only in the context of indirect expropriation but also under the FET analysis.[373]

Similarly, the *LG&E* tribunal used the term 'rights' when balancing between the State's and investor's rights. The tribunal focused on the need to distinguish 'between a regulatory measure, which is an ordinary expression of the exercise of the State's police power that entails a decrease in assets or rights, and a de facto expropriation that deprives those assets and rights of any real substance'.[374]

What remains crucial is to stress the importance of identifying and addressing the need to balance rights in the context of investment-arbitration disputes. The investment-arbitration legal framework has been criticised of being 'shockingly unsuited to the task of balancing private rights against public goods'.[375] It has also been noted that investment arbitration should be more sensitive to vital State interests.[376] The *Saluka* Tribunal verifies such considerations stating:

> The protection of foreign investments is not the sole aim of the Treaty, but rather a necessary element alongside the overall aim of encouraging foreign investment and extending and intensifying the parties' economic relations. That in turn calls for a balanced approach to the interpretation of the Treaty's substantive provisions for the protection of investments, since an interpretation which exaggerates the protection to be accorded to foreign investments may serve to dissuade host States from admitting foreign investments and so undermine the overall aim of extending and intensifying the parties' mutual economic relations.[377]

Going a step further, a line of arguments explaining the legitimacy, reasonableness and necessity of a public measure restricting a private right constitutes a transparent analytical structure that enhances the tribunal's 'adjudicative legitimacy'.[378] This has the capacity to ease the acceptance of the arbitral review of State powers and private interests. On this basis there is a strong relationship between legal reasoning such as proportionality analysis and the legitimacy of arbitral decision-making powers.[379] As such, recognising the importance of using the term 'rights' is strongly connected with the acknowledgment of the importance of balancing private and public interests in the investment-arbitration context.

---

372. *Ibid.* para. 122.
373. Erlend Leonhardsen, 'Looking for Legitimacy: Exploring Proportionality Analysis in Investment Treaty Arbitration' (2011) 3(1) JIDS 95, 135.
374. *LG&E Energy Corp., LG&E Capital Corp., LG&E International Inc v. Argentine Republic*, ICSID Case No. ARB/02/1, Decision on Liability (3 Oct. 2006) para. 194.
375. Howard Mann, 'International Institute for Sustainable Development and World Wildlife Fund, 'Private Rights, Public Problems: A Guide to NAFTA's Controversial Chapter on Investor Rights' (2001) 46 <http://www.iisd.org/pdf/trade_citizensguide.pdf> (2 Sep. 2018).
376. Guillermo Aguilar-Alvarez and William Park, 'The New Face of Investment Arbitration: NAFTA Chapter 11' (2003) 28 YaleJIL 365, 399.
377. *Saluka Investments BV (The Netherlands) v. Czech Republic*, UNCITRAL, Partial Award (17 Mar. 2006) para. 300.
378. Caroline Henckels, 'Indirect Expropriation and the Right to Regulate: Revisiting Proportionality Analysis and the Standard of Review in Investor-State Arbitration' (2012) 15 JIntlEconL 223, 228.
379. *See* Erlend Leonhardsen, 'Looking for Legitimacy' (n 373).

[3] Substantive Rights as a Source of Substantive Law

The meaning of the notion substantive rights is conceptually distinguished from the notion of substantive or applicable law. Investment treaties include the general and specific substantive rights for the protection of the investor as pictured in the previous section.[380] Substantive law is a broader concept describing the law applicable to the merits of the disputes which maybe international law, domestic law, *lex mercatoria* or decision based on *ex aequo et bono*.[381]

This distinction may seem straightforward but it is a necessary preliminary step for approaching the issue of whether substantive rights contained into investment treaties could constitute a source of substantive law, applicable beyond the parties of the investment treaty. The importance of such a wide application rests in the possible development of a 'multilateral international investment regime built on sources of law other than treaties'.[382] The substantive rights contained in investment treaties have been considered to create a 'new system of international rights and obligations for the signatories' having become in practice an important source of international law in the investment-arbitration field.[383] The substantive framework of guarantees is viewed as largely displacing customary international law, influencing the development of new customary international law as well as displacing domestic law in certain circumstances.[384]

The use of substantive rights as a source of substantive law further reflects the wider interpretive issue of balancing private and public interests. At the heart of such a development remains the balancing of the protection of the investors and their investment on the one hand, and the sovereign rights of the State on the other. The further issue that arises is whether the investor has not only rights but also obligations which can form part of the balancing process. Such obligations may include, apart from the respect of the laws of the host State, the environmental impact assessment of

380. *See* the analysis of 'rights': §2.02[C][1] 'Sketching Their Legal Content'.
381. Monique Sasson deals with the substantive definition of investment arbitration rights. Monique Sasson, *Substantive Law in Investment Treaty Arbitration. The Unsettled Relationship Between International Law and Municipal Law* (Kluwer Law International 2010) 206.
382. Salacuse and Sullivan, 'Do BITS Really Work?' (n 341) 83.
383. Franck, *The Nature and Enforcement of Investor Rights under Investment Treaties* (n 336) 53.
384. Salacuse and Sullivan, 'Do BITS Really Work?' (n 341) 70; An inference of this nature can also be drawn from the dissenting opinion in the *Diallo* case. Judge Al-Khasawneh and Yusuf argue that there is 'a wide discrepancy between the customary international law standard and the standard contained in most investment treaties, with the customary law standard (if at all represented by what is contained in Barcelona Traction) being significantly lower than the one existing in the realm of investment treaties. The least that can be said about the state of customary international law given this discrepancy is that it is unsatisfactory'. Ahmadou Sadio Diallo (*Republic of Guinea v. Democratic Republic of the Congo*), Joint dissenting opinion of Judges Al-Khasawneh and Yusuf, 702, 703 <http://www.icj-cij.org/files/case-related/103/103-20101130-JUD-01-02-EN.pdf> (accessed 10 Sept. 2018); Thomas Schultz and Cédric Dupont, 'Investment Arbitration: Promoting the Rule of Law or Over-empowering Investors? A Quantitative Empirical Study' (2015) 25(4) EJIL 1161; Gas Van Harten, 'Five Justifications for Investment Treaties: A Critical Discussion' (2010) 2 Trade L and Development 19, 31–32.

proposed investments and disclosure requirements linked to anticorruption obligations.[385]

An additional interpretational task that may surface is the balancing of rights arising from the investment treaties and the rights arising from other legal systems.[386] In this context, further consideration should be made regarding the accommodation of public interests connected to the protection of the environment and public health.[387] These concerns are better expressed through the rights terminology. Consequently, if the substantive protection guarantees included in treaties are to become a proper source of substantive law, the sincerity of the legal language ought to be respected in order to properly guide the interpretation process.

385. Aaron Cosbey, 'Investment and Sustainable Development: A Guide to the Use and Potential of International Investment Agreements' (2004) International Institute for Sustainable Development, 38 <https://www.iisd.org/pdf/2004/investment_invest_and_sd.pdf l> (accessed 15 Mar. 2018).

386. McLachlan and others, *International Investment Arbitration: Substantive Principles* (n 340) 81.

387. Aaron Cosbey, 'Investment and Sustainable Development: A Guide to the Use and Potential of International Investment Agreements' (n 385) 46.

Conclusion to Part II

This part analysed the legal decision-making process of arbitral tribunals from the perspective of 'Language'. It analytically reconstructed the arguments of the arbitral decisions in order to reveal the language arbitrators use when interpreting the law. The analysis demonstrated that arbitral tribunals have developed a common language adapted to the interpretation needs that may arise in the context of the specific dispute and based on the characteristics of investment arbitration.

As initially canvassed in Chapter 2, the terminology used to describe a normative arrangement is connected to specific interpretational consequences. The analysis of case law revealed that arbitrators treat the concepts of 'rights', 'standards' and 'principles' in an idiosyncratic way. Especially in those situations where investment treaties and arbitration rules avoid such characterisations, the arbitrators' discretion on how to address the normative arrangements in the decision-making process becomes even wider. As an example, the decision-makers may characterise FET interchangeably as a 'standard', 'right' or 'principle'.

This diversification lies in the fact that arbitrators make purposive use of language connecting the way they refer to the investment protection guarantee with the interpretive technique used. When tribunals use the term 'standard' to characterise an investment protection guarantee, they proceed to the assessment of whether a certain degree of protection is attained. Similarly, the use of the term 'principle', in particular 'general principle of law', is connected on the one hand to the transnational comparative methodology of identifying general principles through various legal systems and on the other hand to the interpretation of these principles as specialised principles of investment arbitration. The term 'right' is used when the interpretation process includes the need to balance private and public rights and interests.

The diversification of the use of these terms further demonstrates the cyclical and dynamic nature of the interpretation language. An arbitral tribunal resolving a particular dispute will turn for guidance to case law in order to identify the purpose of using a specific legal terminology. The purposive use is further enhanced by the parties' submissions. When a party will refer to FET as a 'standard' and to the degree of protection to be accorded, the tribunal will use the same characterisation in order to make the specific assessment. As a consequence, the meaning of a specific term is formed both with a look at the legal precedents as well as in the context of the present dispute.

Without wanting to overburden the language with objectives it cannot meet, juridical language has been described as constituting 'the basis of a real autonomy of thought and practice, the expression of the whole operation of the juridical field'.[388] The analysis of legal decision-making from a language perspective reveals that arbitrators have developed a common use of language which is formed based on the interpretational needs that arise in the context of the specific dispute and the experience of case law. Such language is non-traditional and dynamic; non-traditional as it is adapted to the specificities and needs of investment arbitration and dynamic as it is formed and transformed through the practice of arbitral tribunals.

Nevertheless, while the analysis of language as sketched in this part becomes more of an esoteric issue of legal decision-making, the analysis of 'Rhetoric' as effectuated in the next part is exoteric purporting to analyse the functions of an arbitral award's reasoning.

388. Pierre Bourdieu, 'The Force of Law: Toward a Sociology of the Juridical Field' (1987) 38 HLJ 814, 820.

Part III Rhetoric

'Will you [...] pray now, [not believe except] in – this Chaos, and the Clouds, and the Tongue – these three' said Socrates to his student Strepsiades who approached him to be taught how 'not [to] deliver important opinions but only to pervert the right for [his] own advantage'.

-Aristophanes-[389]

389. Aristophanes, *The Clouds*, line 392 <http://www.perseus.tufts.edu/hopper/text? doc=Perseus:text: 1999.01.0241:card=392&highlight=tongue> (accessed 3 Oct. 2018).

Introduction to Part III

While the 'Language' approach focused on the legal vocabulary of arbitral tribunals, the 'Rhetoric' approach emphasises on how the arbitrators externalise their legal decision-making process through the reasoning of their awards. Rhetoric appears to be strongly connected to an audience-oriented legal argumentation scheme.[390] The role of rhetoric in the interpretation process lies in the objective of convincing a specific audience about the interpretive statement.[391] Drawing on this approach, the legal arguments of arbitral awards will be analytically reconstructed so as to reveal the functions of the reasoning process for specific audiences and for the investment-arbitration framework in general.[392]

Aim of this part is neither to argue in favour of extremely lengthy awards nor to encourage the writing of reasons for the sake of reasons. It does not aim either at getting into the discussion of the types of deductive reasoning, inductive reasoning, and reasoning by analogy. What is purported is to analyse the dynamics and functions of the reasoning process and discover what these can reveal about the legal decision-making process of arbitrators. The part will reveal that arbitrators approach the issue of reasoning based on the special needs and characteristics of investment arbitration.

This part includes two chapters: Chapter 3 and Chapter 4. The first section of Chapter 3 focuses on whether the reasoning obligation, as pictured in investment treaties and rules, is sufficient to provide guidance on the quantity and quality of

---

390. Chaim Perelman, *Le Champ de l argumentation* (Presses Universitaires de Bruxelles 1970); *See* sections III [C] 'Legal Argumentation in Judicial Decision-Making: Logic–Rhetoric–Dialectic' and III [D] 'Legal Argumentation in Arbitral Decision-Making: Language–Rhetoric–Dialogue'.
391. Iain Scobbie, 'Rhetoric, Persuasion, and Interpretation in International Law' in Andrea Bianchi, Daniel Peat, and Matthew Windsor (eds) *Interpretation in International Law* (n 59) 64 (the author further adds: legal argument [...] by its nature [...] aims at securing the assent or adhesion of those to whom the argument is addressed rather than demonstrating the truth of the proposition or interpretation advanced).
392. As analysed above, legal arguments contained in judicial reasoning do not always follow the simple model of applying the law to the facts which results in blurring the types of legal arguments used by the decision-maker when interpreting and applying the law. This is exactly why the analytical reconstruction of the tribunals' arguments is important in order to reveal how these arguments are used from a rhetorical perspective. *See* Part Introduction section III[D] 'Legal Argumentation in Arbitral Decision-Making: Language–Rhetoric–Dialogue'.

reasoning an award should contain. The second section engages with the dynamics of reasons in the decision-making process. These dynamics touch upon the concepts of 'acceptability', 'audience' and 'legitimacy'. Chapter 4 elucidates the functions of reasons in the awards of arbitral tribunal through the analysis of case law. These are divided into a persuasion-oriented function and a development-oriented function.

CHAPTER 3

The Dynamics of Reasoning

§3.01 THE AMORPHOUS REASONING REQUIREMENT FOR INVESTMENT-ARBITRATION AWARDS

The majority of legal systems, whether civil or common law, provide for the reasoning of the judicial decisions.[393] The German Civil code for example requires that the decision should contain the facts, the operative provisions and the reasons upon which it is based.[394] Similarly, in the investment-arbitration scene, treaties and institutional rules (ICSID, UNCITRAL, ECT, NAFTA) contain specific provisions that require reasons for the awards of the arbitrators.[395] In particular, UNCITRAL and NAFTA follow a 'presumptive approach' towards the reasoning requirement as they favour but do not require reasoned awards when the parties agree that no reasons are necessary.[396]

The ICSID Convention as well as the ICSID arbitration rules refer clearly to the reasoning of an award and the annulment of an award due to failure to state reasons.[397] Article 48 (3) of the Convention further states that the award should deal with every

393. In the common law system, it was common practice for courts to render unreasoned awards except for specialised areas of law such as maritime arbitration. The modern trend is to give reasons for the decisions. Marta Infantino, 'International Arbitral Awards' Reasons: Surveying the State-of-the-Art in Commercial and Investment International Dispute Settlements' (2014) 5 JIDS 175, 175; *See also* Jerzy Stelmach and Bartosz Brozek, *Methods of Legal Reasoning* (Springer 2006) (the authors analyse the four methods used in legal practice, legal dogmatics and legal theory: logic, analysis, argumentation and hermeneutics).

394. 313(1) Code of Civil procedure. *See* MacCormick and Summers, *Interpreting Statutes: A Comparative Study* (n 179).

395. ECT for example provides in Annex D para 4 (a) that: 'The final report shall deal with every substantial issue raised before the panel and necessary to the resolution of the dispute and shall state the reasons for the panel's conclusions'.

396. UNCITRAL Article 32(3), NAFTA Article 2016 (2); Thomas Carbonneau, 'Rendering Arbitral Awards with Reasons: The Elaboration of a Common Law of International Transactions' (1984) 23 ColumJTransnat'lL 579–614, 598.

397. ICSID Articles 48 (3), 52 (1)(e).

question submitted to the tribunal and state the reasons upon which it is based.[398] Moreover, the failure to state the reasons on which the award is based constitutes a ground for annulment.[399]

Outside the ICSID annulment system, the lack or inadequacy of reasons is treated in the domestic judicial systems. National judicial control over the arbitral awards does not go so far as to evaluate the tribunal's analysis of the facts or law but is mainly restricted to procedural and public policy issues. Although failure to state reasons is not typically included in the grounds under which a domestic court may refuse enforcement, in certain legal systems it may fall under the public policy ground.[400]

Even though these rules provide for the justification requirement of the awards, they do not establish standards of soundness and acceptability of the arguments contained in the reasoning.[401] The requirement to provide reasons for the awards is clearly stated. However, there is no clarity and precision as to the specific components of this requirement.[402] A dispute resolution framework providing a blur view of how and on what basis the decisions are rendered may be a hindering factor for the confidence in investment arbitration.[403] In contrast, clarity and predictability are two components that provide certainty and surety, two dynamics that define the choice of the dispute settlement regime.

From a quantity perspective, when it comes to the issue of whether the tribunals should address in their reasoning all the arguments, pieces of evidence and authorities in the record, the *Enron* ad hoc Committee makes it clear that '[a] tribunal has a duty to deal with each of the questions [...] submitted to it, but is not required to comment on all arguments of the parties in relation to each of those questions'.[404] Based on this way of thinking the decision of the tribunal cannot be annulled on the basis that the tribunal could have provided a more detailed evaluation of the factual and legal issues raised by the parties.[405]

Out of the cadre of the ICSID annulment system and in the context of a NAFTA arbitration, Mexico initiated set aside procedure of the *Metaclad v. Mexico* award in the British Columbia Supreme Court. After reviewing the ICSID jurisprudence for guidance

398. ICSID Rule 47 (1)(i).
399. ICSID Article 52 (1) (e), ICSID Arbitration Rule 50 (1)(c)(iii).
400. Infantino, 'International Arbitral Awards' Reasons' (n 393) 189; In France, the reasoning of arbitral awards constitutes a matter of public policy. However, this is not the case for international awards subject to a foreign law. *See* Alan Scot Rau, 'Integrity in Private Judging' (1997) 38 TLR 485, 538.
401. Fauchald notes that '[t]hese general statements do not give tribunals much guidance on how to approach interpretive issues.' Ole Kristian Fauchald, 'The Legal Reasoning of ICSID Tribunals – An Empirical Analysis' (2008) 19 EJIL 301, 305; For an analysis on the soundness and acceptability of legal arguments *see* §2.02[A] 'Acceptability'.
402. Arbitrator J comments that: 'Well reasoned means that arbitrators have set out thorough reasoning instead of just saying that this is unfair and unjust. [...] A lot of the reasoning now in treaty awards is commoditised cut and pasted, it does not show a lot of independent thinking and writing of the tribunals and that's what I look for when I will cite awards'.
403. *See* generally Guillermo Aguilar-Alvarez and Michael Reisman, *The Reason's Requirement in International Investment Arbitration* (Nijhoff 2008).
404. *Enron Creditors Recovery Corp. Ponderosa Assets, L.P. v. The Argentine Republic*, ICSID Case No. ARB/01/3, Decision on Annulment (30 Jul. 2010) para. 222.
405. *Ibid.* para. 222.

regarding the reasoning requirement in Article 53 (1) ICSID Additional Facility Rules, the court adopted a low standard of reasoning noting that 'it is not reasonable to require the tribunal to answer each and every argument which is made in connection with the questions which the tribunal must decide'.[406]

A question that may also arise connected to the tribunal's decision-making function is whether the arbitrator can argue its own story based on elements the parties did not refer to such as 'authorities' deriving from case law. The Tribunal in the *Glamis* case makes reference to such a scenario when describing how the 'awareness of the context of the NAFTA ch. 11 system' aids the arbitrator in its case specific mandate to resolve the particular dispute. The tribunal states:

> In terms of its case-specific mandate, a tribunal should decide the matter before it on the basis of the authorities submitted to it, and to the degree that the parties to the dispute do not raise what the tribunal regards to be a particularly relevant authority, the tribunal should bring such an authority to the attention of the parties and provide them an opportunity to comment. But, regardless of whether the particular line of reasoning was argued to the tribunal, it is our view that the tribunal should indicate its reasons for departing from a major trend of previous reasoning.[407]

In a similar context, the ad hoc Committee in the *Caratube v. Kazakhstan* case notes that the tribunal does not violate the parties' right to be heard in the case it grounds its decision on legal reasoning that is not specifically put forward by the parties, on the condition that the arguments of the tribunal can be fitted within the legal framework argued during the procedure and thus concern issues on which the parties could reasonably be expected to comment.[408]

The concerns that surface here are not only a matter of quantity but also an issue of quality. It would be a rather bold and unfair statement to say that the reasoning of arbitral awards is non-existent, since international arbitrators almost always provide

406. Aguilar-Alvarez and Reisman, *The Reason's Requirement in International Investment Arbitration* (n 403) 13 citing *United Mexican States v. Metaclad* (2001) BCSC 1529.

407. *Glamis Gold, Ltd. v. The United States of America*, UNCITRAL/NAFTA Ch. 11, Award (8 Jun. 2009) para. 8 (citations omitted); *See also* the *Alapli* case where the Annulment Committee held that: 'On the one hand, Article 48(1) provides that any and every question that is decided by a tribunal must be approved by a majority of its members. On the other hand, Article 48(3) stipulates that, 'in its award, a tribunal needs to deal with, either directly or indirectly, all the parties' heads of claim ("questions", "chefs de conclusions" or "las pretensiones sometidas ... al Tribunal"). To meet this obligation it is for the Tribunal to determine the questions which are material to resolve the dispute between the parties and put these to a vote." *Alapli Elektrik B.V. v. Republic of Turkey*, ICSID Case No. ARB/08/13, Decision on Annulment (10 Jul. 2014) para. 129; *EDF International S.A., SAUR International S.A. and León Participaciones Argentinas S.A. v. Argentine Republic*, ICSID Case No. ARB/03/23, Decision on Annulment (5 Feb. 2016) paras 197–198 (the Tribunal stated: 'A tribunal is required to answer each "question" put to it and must therefore give sufficient reasons to meet the "minimum requirement" referred to by the Wena committee in respect of each question. It is not, however, required to deal explicitly with every detail of every argument advanced by the parties or to refer to every authority which they invoke').

408. *Caratube International Oil Company LLP v. The Republic of Kazakhstan*, ICSID Case No. ARB/08/12, Decision on Annulment (21 Feb. 2014) para. 94.

some reasons for their decision.[409] Nevertheless, an award may be supported by reasons which are unclear and incoherent. Whether such a quality of reasoning is considered sufficient to explain the decision-making process is a question connected to the standard of reasoning applied in each case. Consequently, and especially since the requirement of reasoning could provide the basis of the annulment of an award, it is essential to determine the criterion for the acceptable standard of reasoning that, if met, will not lead to the annulment of the award.

Since investment rules and treaties do not offer an unequivocal view regarding the scope of reasoning and the reasoning process that shall be followed, the arbitral tribunals follow diverse approaches when it comes to establishing the reasoning standard of an award.[410] The next sections aim to elucidate the two components that influence the reasoning standard which are the dynamics of reasoning and the functions of reasoning.

§3.02 DYNAMICS OF REASONS IN THE INVESTMENT-ARBITRATION FRAMEWORK

The legal and functional nature of arbitral awards is similar to that of court decisions. In this sense, the main considerations that justify the need to render reasoned awards are *mutatis mutandis,* as exist for the reasoning of judicial decisions.[411] In investment arbitration the dynamics of a reasoned award are closely linked to the specific features of the investor-state dispute resolution framework such as the public policy interests concerned and the need to provide a legitimate private decision-making process.

[A] Acceptability

Legal reasoning can be described as the combination of intellectual tasks containing:

> [...] the interpretation and selection of relevant facts; the identification or derivation of applicable legal rules; the explicit or implicit consideration of equities or other broader policies; and the intermediation of laws, facts, and policies to reach an outcome.[412]

409. Tai-Heng Cheng and Robert Trisotto, 'Reasons and Reasoning in Investment Treaty Arbitration' (2008–2009) 32(2) Suffolk Transnational Law Review 409, 414.

410. *See* §4.01 'Persuasion-Oriented Function: Reasoning as a Rhetorical Technique'; Haddad Michael, 'Adequacy of Reasons in Arbitral Awards' (2008) 5 MacquarieJBusL 353–367 (The author examines the obligation of the arbitrator to give reasons and whether it is a judicial or legislative duty).

411. Lord Tom Bingham, 'Reasons and Reasons for Reasons: Differences Between a Court Judgment and an Arbitration Award' (1988) 4 Arb. Int'l 141, 146; Peter Gillies and Niloufer Selvadurai, 'Reasoned Awards: How Extensive Must the Reasoning Be?' (2008) 74 Arbitration 125, 126; W T Blackstone, 'Criteria of Adequacy for Judicial Reasoning' (1971) (53) Logique et Analyse 14, 233.

412. Cheng and Trisotto, 'Reasons and Reasoning in Investment Treaty Arbitration' (n 409) 410; Bruce Anderson, 'Current Views on Legal Reasoning: The Problem of Communication'(1997) 15(2) Method: Journal of Lonergan Studies 151 (The author describes the wide nature of legal

Despite the broad content of such a definition, it is clear that the reasoning of a judgment plays a protagonist role in externalising the decision-making process followed in the context of the resolution of a dispute. Through reasoning, the decision-maker translates the legal decision-making process into a language that opens the way for its acceptability by a specific audience.

In general terms, acceptability can be achieved by understanding.[413] Understanding in its turn can be achieved through two routes. The first route is that of engaging into a process of arguing where questions, answers and explanations go back and forth ultimately inducing the understanding of an argument.[414] Whether the argument is also acceptable is a question linked to the persuasive power of the arguments put forward.[415] In the second path, an arguing process cannot be effectuated as it is addressed to a non-interactive audience.[416] Therefore, both the understanding and acceptability of the argument are dependent upon the rhetorical techniques employed in order to achieve persuasion rather than on the exchange of arguments. A stark illustration of this last case is the understanding and acceptability of a legal decision by parties who have no way of challenging the substantive validity of legal arguments in front of a judicial authority and thus limited possibility of arguing and asking for explanations. In this instance, the acceptability and understanding of the legal arguments depend on the rhetorical methods employed in the legal reasoning of the decision in order to persuade the audience.[417] Taking the analysis a step further, not only acceptability but also the normative influence of an award is connected to persuasion. In particular, such normative influence is dependent either upon the cumulative effect of a consistent line

reasoning as comprising fourteen elements: sensible experience and imaginative representations, What-questions, direct insights, formulations, Is-questions, reflective insights, judgments of fact, What-is-to-be-done-questions, practical insights, plans, What-should-be-done-questions, practical reflective insights, judgments of value, decisions, and implementations).

413. According to Habermas's communicative action theory, actors should, as a first step, understand each other in order for their interpretive claims to be acceptable. Ingo Veznke, *How Interpretation Makes International Law: On Semantic Change and Normative Twists* (CUP 2012) 218 citing Jürgen Habermas, *The Theory of Communicative Action* (Beacon Press 1987), Ch. V.

414. Thomas Risse, 'Let's Argue!': Communicative Action in World Politics' (2000) 54 IO 1, 3 et seq.

415. Persuasion for the purposes of this study does not involve manipulation or coercion employing means such as distorting the truth, brainwashing, propaganda or misstatements. Rather is focuses on the act or process followed in order 'to move by argument, entreaty, or expostulation to a belief, position, or course of action'. Cory Clements, 'Perception and Persuasion in Legal Argumentation: Using Informal Fallacies and Cognitive Biases to Win the War of Words' (2013) *BYULRev* 319, 328–329.

416. *See* Kraus distinguishing between a text which constitutes a monologue and a rhetorical text that may have the character of a solo performance. In the latter situation the audience exists but may be passive, silent or distant in space or time. Manfred Kraus, 'Arguing or reasoning? Argumentation in rhetorical context' (2013) OSSA Conference Archive Paper 97, 5 <http://scholar.uwindsor.ca/cgi/viewcontent.cgi?article=2067& context=ossaarc hive accessed> (17 Jan. 2018).

417. For a rhetorical analysis of the arbitration laws and treaties *see*: Anna Trosborg, 'Rhetorical Strategies in Arbitration Law' in Bhatia and others (eds) *Legal Discourse Across Cultures and Systems* (n 58) 199.

of cases on a specific issue or on the inherent persuasiveness of the reasoning arguments.[418]

Persuasion, understanding and rhetoric are interconnected concepts since '[w]herever there is persuasion, there is rhetoric, and wherever there is rhetoric, there is meaning'.[419] Rhetorical argumentation can be seen both from a truth and a choice perspective.[420] In the first case, the theme of reasoning and argumentation about the truth, also known as 'theoretical' or 'epistemic reasoning', is whether a proposition is true or false. Argumentation that aims at revealing the truth of a statement is an absolute process where no choice is involved. As an example, whether the diagonal is commensurable is not a matter of choice.[421] In the second case, the theme of rhetorical argumentation, also called 'practical reasoning', is a proposal to make a deliberate choice, action or take a specific decision.[422] Since there is no expression of a proposition in this case, the issue is not whether the argumentation is true or false but how the argument can lead to making one choice over another.

On a similar note, Habermans makes a separation between arguing about the truth and arguing about actions, opposing what is true to what is right:

> [t]he warrants we appeal to in action-related discussions will not be propositions that we hold to be true but *norms of action* that we hold to be 'right.' This rightness [...] is a different kind of validity claim (*Gültigkeitsbedingung*) from truth.[423]

Nonetheless in both cases the common goal is to persuade either about the truth or about the rightness of an argument.

MacCormick interestingly marks that 'law has nothing to do with truth, only with what can be proved according to the law's processes and standards of proof, applied to whatever evidence the law characterizes as relevant and admissible'.[424] Consequently, when it comes to decision-making in the context of a specific dispute, the theme of argumentation is practical rather than theoretical since it involves the justification of a certain decision taken by the decision-maker. However, in investment arbitration where there are no means to check whether the argument is right or wrong though an appeal mechanism, the understanding and acceptability of the arguments are both linked to the means of persuading a specific audience.[425]

---

418. Jan Paulsson, 'Awards – and Awards' in Andrea Bjorklund, Ian Laird, and Sergey Ripinsky (eds), *Investment Treaty Law. Current Issues III* (BIICL 2009) 97, 102.
419. Orsinger, *The Role of Reasoning and Persuasion in Legal Argumentation* (n 38) 71.
420. Christian Kock, 'Defining Rhetorical Argumentation' (2013) 46(4) Ph&Rh 437, 444–445.
421. Aristotle, *Eudemian Ethics,* 1226(a).
422. Kock, 'Defining Rhetorical Argumentation' (n 420) 450.
423. *Ibid.* 437, 445 citing Jürgen Habermas, *Theorie des kommunikativen Handelns* (Suhrkamp 1981).
424. Neil MacCormick, *The Rule of Law and the Arguable Character of Law* (OUP 2005) 15.
425. Interestingly, Arbitrator C connects the abstract concept of justice with 'getting it right'. The arbitrator states that 'when you are sitting as a decision-maker you are trying to get it right [...] to me getting it right is to apply the terms of the Treaty to the facts that are found and to reach the conclusion which is justified; if you adopt a correct methodological approach and analyse it on that base you would expect to have a justifiable a decision'. *See* Annex 'Interview Questions.'

Persuasion goals however may lead to connotations of strategic behaviour.[426] The decision-maker for example may form the reasoning of an arbitral award in such a way in order to persuade the audience to which it is addressed. At this point someone may question the legitimacy of persuasion goals since this may imply that reasoning is not a means to an end but the end itself. Reisman and Aguilar find a common thread between the persuasion goal and the consequences of the arbitral award. They argue that investment-arbitration awards are so strongly linked to and have effects on national political economies 'that their acceptability depends on their persuasiveness, that is, the extent to which they manifest a good faith application of the law'.[427] Persuasion goals in this context draw their legitimacy from their legitimising functions. Since the acceptability of arbitral awards fosters the legitimacy of the private dispute resolution process, persuasion goals become the means through which acceptability and legitimacy are attained. Reversing the way of thinking, it is difficult to conceive that non-legitimate goals – if we hypothetically accept that persuasion is not a legitimate goal – could foster legitimacy.

These perspectives on acceptability and persuasion bring to the fore two important questions and object of the analysis of the next sections: Which is the audience that will or will not accept an arbitral decision and how does legitimacy and acceptability depend on the perceptions of this audience in practice?

[B] Internal Audience

The acceptability of the arguments from a specific audience is of a high normative importance since it is connected to the belief that the justification of the decision is valid. A legal argument in this context may be described as 'a justification that motivates other to accept a speech act's claim to validity'.[428]

Reasoning has a double direction addressing two types of audiences, an internal and an external audience.[429] The reasoning of an award primarily has an internal direction by explaining to the parties of the specific dispute why they have won or lost. Rendering an award with reasons is part of the services arbitrators provide to parties. The process of reasoning connects the decision to criteria that are external to the decision-maker attributing perceptions of fairness and rationality to the whole

426. Infantino, *International Arbitral Awards' Reasons* (n 393) 191–194.

427. Aguilar-Alvarez and Reisman, *The Reason's Requirement in International Investment Arbitration* (n 406) 29.

428. Veznke, *How Interpretation Makes International Law: On Semantic Change and Normative Twists* (n 413) 218 citing Jürgen Habermas, *The Theory of Communicative Action* (Beacon Press 1987) Ch. V.

429. For Pelerman and Olbrechts-Tyteca there are three different types of audiences: the parties in dispute, the legal professionals, and the public opinion. Feteris, *Fundamentals of Legal Argumentation* (n 47) 53 citing Chaïm Perelman and Lucie Olbrechts-Tyteca, *La Nouvelle Rhetorique. Traite de l'Argumentation* (6th ed., Université de Bruxelles 2008); *See also* Chaïm Perelman, *Le Champ de l'argumentation; Justice et Raison* (2nd ed., Editions de l'Université de Bruxelles 1972); Alonso Tordesillas, 'Chaïm Perelman: Justice, Argumentation and Ancient Rhetoric' (1990) 4(1) Argumentation 109.

decision-making process.[430] Especially when it comes to private dispute resolution, the power of the arbitrator can be considered 'authoritative' when it justifies to those who are affected by such power the way it is exercised.[431] This is also a way of documenting the fairness of the decision's outcome.[432] The State and the investor expect not only the impartial application of the law but also the 'idiosyncratic intellectual process' which has been applied to be presented in the reasoning of the award.[433] The tribunal should ensure that the reasoning presents, in a balanced and fair way, the claims of the parties and the arguments connected to these claims.[434]

This is a way to delimit the scope of discretion of arbitrators within acceptable boundaries and protect the parties against arbitrariness by the private judges.[435] The proper consideration of the concerns of both of the parties as well as the balancing between competing public and private interests can be effectively represented through a well articulated reasoning. As Lord Hewart once stated 'justice should not only be done, but should manifestly and undoubtedly be seen to be done'.[436]

Especially when it comes to the acceptance of the award by the losing parties, adequate reasoning may reduce the possibility of challenge, enhancing at the same time the award's enforceability.[437]Arbitral case law has demonstrated such a correlation between a poorly reasoned award and its challenge in litigation proceedings.[438] A well-known example is the *Wena* case.[439] The lack of adequate reasons in both the tribunal's award and the ad hoc Committee's decision led to domestic court proceedings and also to an application for the interpretation of the original award.[440] Wena, which was the winning party, had to re-litigate the case in multiple fora since it was

430. David Dyzenhaus and Michael Taggart, 'Reasoned Decisions and Legal Theory' in Douglas Edlin (ed.), *Common Law Theory* (CUP 2007) 148; *See also* Jerzy Wróblewski, 'Legal Decision and its Justification' (1971) 53 Logique et Analyse 14, 409 (assessing the legal decision's great social significance).
431. Dyzenhaus and Taggart make reference specifically to the authority of public judges. They further mark that '[i]t is a short theoretical, if not historical, step from [...] presumed reasonableness to demonstrated or justified reasonableness'. *Ibid.* 152.
432. McArthur further states that 'in the long run, the need for arbitration to be fair cannot be sacrificed on the altar of finality'. John McArthur, 'Growing Pains: Building Arbitration's Legitimacy Through Everyday Arbitral Decisionmaking' (2010) Lenox Institute of Water Technology 43–44. <http://works.bepress.com/john_mcarthur/3/> (accessed 3 Jun. 2018).
433. Reisman, *The Quest for World Order and Human Dignity in the Twenty-First Century* (n 142) 173.
434. George Berman, 'Writing the award-An arbitrator's perspective' in Grant Hanessian and Lawrence W Newman (eds) *International Arbitration Checklists* (2nd ed., Juris 2009) 171, 176.
435. Cheng and Trisotto, 'Reasons and Reasoning in Investment Treaty Arbitration' (n 409) 409.
436. *R. v. Sussex Justices*, (1924) Ex parte McCarthy 1KB256.
437. Pierre Lalive, 'On the Reasoning of International Arbitral Awards' (2010) 1(1) JIDS 55, 56.
438. George Stephanov Georgiev, 'The Award in *Saluka Investments v. Czech Republic*' in Aguilar-Alvarez and Reisman, *The Reason's Requirement in International Investment Arbitration* (n 406) 149, 152.
439. *Wena Hotels Ltd v. Arab Republic of Egypt*, ICSID Case No. ARB/98/4, Proceeding on Jurisdiction, (25 May 1999); *Wena Hotels Ltd v. Arab Republic of Egypt*, ICISD Case No. ARB/98/4, Proceeding on the Merits (8 Dec. 2000); *Wena Hotels Ltd v. Arab Republic of Egypt*, ICSID Case No. ARB/98/4, Annulment Proceeding (28 Jan. 2002).
440. Infantino, *International Arbitral Awards' Reasons* (n 393) 187.

considered that the inadequate reasoning of the award did not treat substantive subsidiary issues.[441]

A well-reasoned award may also constitute the basis for the settlement of the dispute between the parties. In the *Saluka* case the arbitral award on liability was so well reasoned with regard to the amount of damages that could have been awarded in the next stage, enabling the parties to resolve the dispute amicably after eight years of domestic litigation and arbitration proceedings.[442]

Based on the above considerations, from the 'internal audience' perspective, the reasoning process is important for both parties. The private litigant acquires an explanation of why the promised treatment of the investment rights was altered, being able to revise any future investment moves in the same State appropriately. On the other hand, the State can measure the impact of investment arbitration on its regulatory sphere and adjust its policies accordingly. Despite the lack of a formal doctrine of precedent, States pay due regard to the reasoning of arbitral awards.[443] A stark illustration is the introduction by the United States of a more restrictive wording in recent BITs due to arbitral tribunals' broad interpretation practices of FET and indirect expropriation.[444]

[C] External Audience

Reasoning has not only esoteric consequences for the parties but also affects external recipients – mainly everyone who will read the award once published or will be affected by it. Latter audience may include decision-makers of future disputes as well as the legal and social community.

In this context, reasoned awards serve as a guidance to future parties to a dispute shaping common expectations as well as expected standards of behaviour.[445] They also constitute a source of reference for future tribunals since arbitral case law plays an important role when interpreting the broad protection guarantees included in the investment treaties.[446] The interest in the outcome of investment disputes may also involve legitimate interests of third parties such as States, international institutions or NGOs due to the political and economic interests involved in investor-state disputes. The importance of taking into account such interests is highlighted even more through the acceptance of *amicus curiae* submissions from non-parties when matters of public interest arise.[447]

441. Julie Maupin, '*The Awards in Wena Hotels Limited v. Arab Republic of Egypt*' in Aguilar-Alvarez and Reisman, *The Reason's Requirement in International Investment Arbitration* (n 406) 231, 259–60.
442. George Stephanov Georgiev, 'The Award in Saluka Investments v. Czech Republic' (n 438) 149, 188.
443. For precedent in Investment arbitration *see* §6.03 'Precedent Arguments'.
444. For example, Kingsbury and Schill, 'Investor-State Arbitration as Governance' (n 148) 46 citing Article 10.5(2)(a) Dominican Republic – Central America – United States Free Trade Agreement.
445. Rau, 'Integrity in Private Judging' (n 400) 536.
446. *See* §6.03 'Precedent Arguments'.
447. *See* §6.01[D] 'Expanding the Dialogue Through Third Parties'.

The significance of a reasoned award mainly lies in the nature of the consequences an investment-arbitration award entails which are not limited to the parties of the dispute. Unlike commercial arbitration, an award rendered within the context of the investment dispute resolution may affect not only the litigants but also public works and therefore, the lives of millions of people in the host States. Investment arbitration is requested to give answers to important issues and complex questions. The specificities of this system are strongly connected to the involvement of the State's development and public interest.[448] Since the scale of investment awards is usually very large, the amount of damages may influence the State's economic and foreign policies such as the allocation of public funds and as a result the population.[449] In this context, the citizens of the host State should be able to understand why the issue was decided in a certain way.[450] With all these interests at stake, investment arbitrators have been described as being part of a somehow 'public process of decision-making'.[451] It is true that these are the consequences of the outcome of the award and not the reasoning as such but civil society through NGOs, think tanks and environmental organisations show great interest in the reasoning and the way investment awards are decided criticising the transparency and predictability of the dispute resolution framework.[452]

The regulatory effects of arbitral awards on States in combination with the absence of political intergovernmental institutions in which tribunals are embedded emphasises the need for high-quality reasoning.[453] It is interesting to note at this point that drafting adequate reasons for a broader audience may entail a very different task compared to that of giving explanations to the parties of why they have won or lost.[454] This happens because the same text will have different effects on different audiences.[455] Arguing from a rhetorical perspective in different contexts requires being aware of the various expectations of the audiences and their complexity as well as the need for accuracy and adaptation of the arguments used.[456] Particularly, in investment-arbitration cases touching upon environmental issues, the decision-maker should be attentive to the wider audience's reaction on specific issues since hidden premises in

448. Lalive, 'On the reasoning of International Arbitral Awards' (n 437) 57.
449. Toby Landau, 'Reasons for Reasons: The Tribunal's Duty in Investor-State Arbitration' in Albert Jan van den Berg (ed.) *50 Years of the New York Convention: ICCA International Arbitration Conference* (Kluwer Law International 2009) 187, 196.
450. Cheng and Trisotto comment that '[t]his aspiration is compelling, particularly because it appeals to an idealized notion of a liberal democracy in which an educated and responsible demos participates actively in the formulation and appraisal of state policies' in Cheng and Trisotto, 'Reasons and Reasoning in Investment Treaty Arbitration' (n 409) 433.
451. Infantino, *International Arbitral Awards' Reasons* (n 393) 185.
452. *See* §6.05 Policy Arguments.
453. Kingsbury and Schill, 'Investor-State Arbitration as Governance' (n 148) 53.
454. Landau, 'Reasons for Reasons' (n 449) 195; Jan H Dalhuisen, 'Legal Reasoning and Powers of International Arbitrators' (2015) <https://ssrn.com/abstract=2393705> (accessed 10 Sept. 2018).
455. Kraus, *Arguing or reasoning? Argumentation in rhetorical context* (n 416) 8–9; Arbitrator E states that 'when you read somebody else's award, you reach a conclusion but it doesn't mean you are right – it doesn't mean they are wrong either – you just see something differently'. *See* Annex 'Interview Questions'.
456. *Ibid.*

the legal decision-making process may lead to possible misguidance and social outcry.[457] Nonetheless, a balance should always be reached between providing dispute resolution services to the parties of the dispute and fulfilling the wishes of players not directly involved in the dispute.[458]

[D] Legitimacy

Tracing the issue of legitimacy in investment arbitration back to its roots, the transnational characteristics of the dispute resolution framework have largely influenced the emergence of legitimacy concerns. The interaction of States, private investors, international institutions, domestic courts and international tribunals, national and international laws, and public and private interests creates the image of a decentralised and non-hierarchical dispute resolution framework. This private structure of dispute resolution does not have the safeguards of a State judicial system such as court hierarchy, review mechanisms of both procedural and substantive issues and the principle of separation of powers that guaranties impartiality. The investor-state arbitration process has been criticised as functioning without the appropriate checks and balances and the decisions rendered as deriving from 'unelected, unrepresentative, and unaccountable individuals'.[459]

This has led to the legitimacy concerns from both external and internal audiences.[460] As a result, the legitimacy debate is so large as to include discussions about the nature, theory and philosophy of arbitration, interpretational inconsistencies in case law, method of appointment of arbitrators and professional ethics.[461]

The relevant viewpoint of legitimacy in this context is oriented towards the question of the validity of a private ad hoc body resolving disputes that involve State measures of public interest.[462] An international adjudicative body's legitimacy depends on the perceived justification of its authority.[463] Such justificatory factors include perceptions of fairness and impartiality, consistent interpretation and application of the norms, and last but not least, democratic norms and transparency.[464] Based on the above approach and focusing on the legitimising elements that can be found in the

457. On the social aspects of decision-making *see* §6.05 [B][2] 'Emerging Social Policy Concerns'.
458. Arbitrator H notes the following: 'I wonder whether one way forward might be the way that the ICJ deals with it – they have press releases for the general public – anybody can read and understand what is that we speak about what have we decided and then if you have to read the whole judgment, technical staff, you can'. *See* Annex 'Interview Questions'.
459. *See* Landau, 'Reasons for Reasons' (n 449) 196. For the legitimacy debate *see generally*: David Caron, 'Investor State Arbitration: Strategic and Tactical Perspectives on Legitimacy' (2008) 32 SuffolkTransnat'lLJ 513.
460. *See* §3.02[B] 'Internal Audience' and §3.02[C] 'External audience'.
461. Stephan Schill, 'Conceptions of Legitimacy of International Arbitration' in David Caron and others, *Practising Virtue* (n 3) 106–107.
462. *See* Chen Tai-Heng noting that arbitration is a privately sponsored system whose existence and growth 'depends on the global community believing that it is legitimate' in Tai-Heng Cheng, 'Precedent and Control in Investment Treaty Arbitration' (2006) 30 FordhamIntlLJ 1014, 1026.
463. Nienke Grossman, 'Legitimacy and International Adjudicative Bodies' (2009–2010) 41 GeoWashIntlLRev 107, 115.
464. *Ibid.*

application and interpretation of the law, legitimacy in investment arbitration depends 'at least in part, on the legality and rationality of its design, its processes, and the technical quality and persuasiveness of the reasons tribunals give in explaining and justifying their decisions'.[465] As a consequence, inadequacy in reasons affects the equity and appropriateness of arbitration as a dispute resolution mechanism questioning its very own legitimacy.[466]

The 'outward show of legal argument' through the reasoning of the award is part of the so-called social legitimacy of an adjudication process.[467] Reasoning is an element of the legitimacy of the award anticipated and demanded by the direct participants in a decision-making process and by the community they are part of.[468] Taking the discussion a step further, legal argumentation is strongly connected to the legitimacy of the outcome of the decision-making process.[469] The acceptability of the decision, primarily by the parties but also by the external viewers of the dispute resolution framework, becomes an important factor expressing the validity of the legal argument contained in the decision. As a corollary, the validity and legitimacy of the argument can confer legitimacy to the outcome of the decision-making process.[470] In this context, there is a chain effect where a valid and acceptable argument is connected to the validity of the award which in its turn leads to a – perceived – legitimate decision-making process.

Legitimacy concerns encompass the way investment arbitration appears not only to the inside players but also to the outside viewers of the field. It is connected to both the dispute resolution function and to its image from an outward perspective. In this last case, if the image is 'false, actually and philosophically false, no technicians, however proficient, can make the policy that is based on it sound'.[471] Making the reasoning accessible to non-disputant parties as well reflects 'a quality of publicness in

465. Kingsbury and Schill make reference to Max Weber's analysis on legitimacy of laws and institutions which may be derived from three sources: tradition, charismatic leadership or bureaucratic rationality. Kingsbury and Schill, 'Investor-State Arbitration as Governance' (n 148) 41.
466. Rocio Digon, '*The Decision on Liability in LG&E v. Argentina*' in Aguilar-Alvarez and Reisman, *The Reason's Requirement in International Investment Arbitration* (n 406) 117, 148.
467. Ingo Veznke, 'The Role of International Courts as Interpreters and Developers of the Law Working Out the Jurisgenerative Practice of Interpretation' (2011) Loyola of Los Angeles International and Comparative Law Review, Forthcoming, 7 <http://ssrn.com/abstract=1868423> (accessed 3 Nov. 2018).
468. Reisman, *The Quest for World Order and Human Dignity in the Twenty-First Century* (n 142) 173.
469. Veznke, *How Interpretation Makes International Law: On Semantic Change and Normative Twists* (n 413) 217.
470. Veznke makes reference to Habermas's concept of 'communicative action' which 'wishes to tap into the rationality that is nested in intersubjective communicative practice, and it sees in processes of argumentation themselves, to the extent that they show certain qualities, a source of legitimation'. Veznke, *How Interpretation Makes International Law: On Semantic Change and Normative Twists* (n 413) 217.
471. Devashish Krishan, 'Thinking About BITs and BIT Arbitration: The Legitimacy Crisis That Never Was' in Todd Weiler and others (eds), *New Directions in International Economic Law* (Brill 2011) 107.

law' and enhances the 'non-electoral legitimacy' of arbitral tribunals.[472] In the sense that arbitral tribunals treat issues of public law involving the State's actions, a legitimate decision-making power becomes an element valued in all democratic societies.

472. Kingsbury and Schill, 'Investor-State Arbitration as Governance' (n 148) 45.

CHAPTER 4

The Functions of Reasoning

§4.01 PERSUASION-ORIENTED FUNCTION: REASONING AS A RHETORICAL TECHNIQUE

The connection between rhetoric, persuasion and legal reasoning can be well illustrated in arbitral case law. It has been mentioned that '[c]ategorization, narrative, and rhetorics [are] the stuff of everyday life in the law'.[473] Aristotle defines rhetoric as 'an ability, in each [particular] case, to see the available means of persuasion'.[474] In rhetorical argumentation, the premises of the arguments need only be acceptable to the audience that is intended to be convinced.[475] An important clarification at this point is that the legal reasoning process is not viewed as a mere weapon of intellectual coercion or deceitfulness but as a means of reasonable persuasion under the compelling force of acceptable arguments.[476] In this context, legal reasoning may be seen as a means to persuade the reader of the existence of a specific (interpretation and application of the law) process followed in order to reach to a certain conclusion and not necessarily of the correctness of an argument.[477]

An arbitral award typically contains the facts of the case, the claims and defences of the parties, the procedural and substantive rules applied, a brief account of the phases of the arbitral proceedings including the hearings, the legal and factual findings of the tribunal, the type of proof supporting the conclusions reached and, last but not least, a summary of the conclusions.[478] The question that arises here is whether the focus on persuasion and rhetorical arguments may result in a selective reference to the above elements in an award. Keeping in mind that the reasoning requirement is

473. Anthony Amsterdam and Jerome Bruner, *Minding the Law* (HUP 2002) 2.
474. Aristotle, *On Rhetoric* (George Kennedy tr, OUP 1991) 36.
475. Van Eemeren and Grootendorst, *A Systematic Theory of Argumentation* (n 18) 43.
476. *See* MacCormick, *Rhetoric and the Rule of Law: A Theory of Legal Reasoning* (n 172) 17 et seq.
477. *See* n 415.
478. Infantino, *International Arbitral Awards' Reasons* (n 393) 182.

actually a reasoning standard and not a vague requirement, the consequences of such a selective reference should be carefully assessed.[479]

Cheng and Trisotto present a very interesting formula that sketches the four types of reasoning an award may include and the consequences of applying a high or low reasoning standard in the investment-arbitration context.[480] According to the first hypothetical scenario of reasoning, the interpretation and application of the law are both correct but the reasoning is incoherent, preventing the reader to follow the line of reasoning. In this case, the award would be annulled as not permitting the reader to follow the tribunal's reasoning from point A to point B and eventually to the conclusion. In the second formula, the tribunal correctly and coherently states the facts and the outcome but does not make reference to the interpretation of the law.[481] The emphasis a low reasoning standard puts on the coherency of reasoning will not lead to the annulment of the award when there is no reference to the process of legal interpretation. Based on the third type of reasoning, the tribunal states the law correctly and reaches a right outcome but the facts are missing. In this case, a low reasoning standard would not entail annulment since the reasoning connected to the facts could be inferred from the award. Last but not least, in the fourth reasoning formula, the reasoning is coherent and the law is stated correctly but the facts are stated wrongly and as a result the outcome is wrong. Under a low reasoning standard, the award would survive annulment due to the fact that despite the wrong outcome, it is coherent enough to permit the reader to follow it.

Even though the practice of arbitral tribunal does not always fall under the predictions of each of the above formulas, what will be revealed in the next two parts is the emphasis that tribunals put on the consistency rather than correctness or totality of reasoning.

[A] High Rhetoric Standards

In the annulment decision *Klöckner v. Cameroon,*[482] the Committee referred to the quantity and quality of reasons that should accompany an award in order to avoid annulment. In particular, the annulment Committee assessed whether an award: (a) simply and clearly fails to state reasons, (b) presents contradictory reasons, (c) uses dubious or hypothetical reasons or reasons lacking relevance, or (d) provides inadequate reasons due to misconception or distortion.[483] If one of these cases occurs, the quantity and quality criteria of the reasoning standard are not met and therefore, the award could be annulled based on Article 52 (1) (e) due to failure to state reasons.

479. Cheng and Trisotto, 'Reasons and Reasoning in Investment Treaty Arbitration' (n 409) 424.
480. *Ibid.* 428 et seq.
481. For example, *WENA* decision in §4.01[B] 'Low Rhetoric Standards'.
482. *Klöckner,* Annulment (n 274).
483. *Ibid.* para. 114. The Tribunal also stated that the failure to deal with 'every question submitted to the Tribunal' is sanctioned either as a failure to state reasons under Article 52 (1) (e) or as the failure to deal with 'every question submitted to the Tribunal' which is considered to be a 'serious departure from a fundamental rule of procedure' under Article 52(l)(d) para. 115.

In case (a), and according to the Committee in case (b) as well,[484] the failure to state reasons is interpreted as a lack of reasons. Thus, there is no need to set any standards that the reasoning of the award should meet as it is considered that the reasoning does not exist. Under these circumstances the award can be annulled due to absence of reasons. Proposing standards of reasoning implies that a certain kind of reasoning exists but the standards of reasoning are not met. The high or low standard of reasoning will indicate if the deficiency in the legal reasoning will lead to the annulment of the award or not. The reasons requirement in this case constitutes in reality a reasoning standard.[485]

The Committee's approach in the *Klöckner* case, sets a high reasoning standard as it instructs that the reasons are the basis of the tribunal's decision and therefore, they should be 'sufficient' and 'relevant'.[486] In other words, the reasons should be 'reasonably capable of justifying the result reached by the tribunal'.[487] Thus, the reasons required are not 'purely formal or apparent' but should have such 'substance' that allows 'the reader to follow the arbitral tribunal's reasoning, on facts and on law'.[488] As a consequence, the central point of legal reasoning becomes the persuasion of the reader that the conclusion of the decision was reached through the particular application of the interpreted law to the facts of the case.

The application of this standard is clearer when the Committee addresses the complaint for absence and inadequacy of reasons. The Committee states that there would be a failure to state reasons 'if no reasoning or explanation whatsoever, or no "sufficiently relevant" or "reasonably acceptable" reasoning could be found for some conclusion or decision in the Award'.[489] However, 'such would not be the case if the Tribunal, having justified its finding or a particular decision in a certain way, even if subject to criticism, did not address this or that particular argument (subject to what will be said below on failure to deal with questions submitted to the Tribunal)'.[490]

The Committee goes to the next level addressing the matter of annulment and appeal as a means to control the legal reasoning. It distinguishes between 'relevant', 'sufficiently relevant' and 'apparently relevant' reasons creating a scale from the most power-awarding notion to the least power-awarding notion. In this context, demanding from a tribunal to form 'relevant' reasons would be like attributing to the Committee the authority to operate as an appeal mechanism and 'review the arbitrators' findings of fact or law'.[491] On the other hand, providing 'apparently relevant' reasons deprives the substance of the legality control of Article 52.[492] The annulment Committee preferred the middle position, 'sufficiently relevant reasons', as the reasoning standard

484. The Annulment Committee interestingly noted that, in principle, 'contradiction of reasons' constitutes a failure to state reasons 'for the very simple reason that two genuinely contradictory reasons cancel each other out'. *Ibid.* para. 116.
485. Cheng and Trisotto, 'Reasons and Reasoning in Investment Treaty Arbitration' (n 409) 424.
486. *Klöckner*, Annulment (n 274) paras 118, 119.
487. *Ibid.* para. 120.
488. *Ibid.* para. 119.
489. *Ibid.* para. 130.
490. *Ibid.* para. 130.
491. *Ibid.* paras 119, 128.
492. *Ibid.* para. 120.

for the arbitral award in order to avoid the risk of stepping into the appeal field. Future ad hoc committees that dealt with the same matter of reasoning followed a rather different path than the one chosen by *Klöckner*.

[B] Low Rhetoric Standards

The majority of the case law concludes that finality of the investor-state dispute resolution system is promoted with a low reasoning standard.[493] Arbitral tribunals focus on the coherency of reasons and their capability to explain to the reader how the components of the reasoning process lead to the tribunal's conclusion in a logical way. Taking the analysis a step further, the question that arises is how to justify the conclusions of judgments that do not logically follow from the premises described in the reasoning.

Some years after *Klöckner*, the annulment Committee in the *MINE v. Guinea*[494] case, set the basis for a low threshold of reasoning. The Committee took the view that an award is sufficiently reasoned when it is coherent.[495] Particularly, it highlighted the fact that the tribunals should not examine the 'adequacy' of reasons as this would be equivalent to a review of the substance of the decision and as a result, it would be similar to an appeal.[496] The reasons requirement is considered to be fulfilled when 'the award enables one to follow how the tribunal proceeded from Point A to Point B and eventually to its conclusion, even if it made an error of fact or of law'.[497] The ad hoc Committee acknowledged the fact that statement of reasons is an essential component of the arbitration process, but it concluded that an incorrect application of law does not constitute a basis for annulling the decision.

On a similar basis, the ad hoc Committee in the *Soufraki* case used the term 'sufficient' when referring to the appropriate reasoning standard. The Committee mentioned that in cases where the tribunal provides 'insufficient' or 'inadequate' reasons its decision can be annulled as these kinds of reasons do not provide a 'reasonable' basis for the solution arrived at'.[498] The annulment Committee did not support the view that the requirement of adequate reasoning leads to a review of the substance of the decision stating that inadequate reasons should be distinguished from wrong reasons.[499] Based on these arguments it concluded that the tribunal had set out all the factual and legal premises of its award as well as the course of its reasoning 'enabl[ing] one to easily understand how the Tribunal reached its conclusion'. [500]

493. Cheng and Trisotto, 'Reasons and Reasoning in Investment Treaty Arbitration' (n 409) 417.
494. *Maritime International Nominees Establishment v. Republic of Guinea*, ICSID Case No. ARB/84/4 Decision on Annulment (22 Dec. 1989) (hereinafter *MINE*).
495. Cheng and Trisotto, 'Reasons and Reasoning in Investment Treaty Arbitration' (n 409) 417.
496. *MINE*, Decision on Annulment (n 494) para. 5.08.
497. *Ibid.* para. 5.09.
498. *Hussein Nuaman Soufraki v. United Arab Emirates*, ICSID Case No. ARB/02/7, Decision on Annulment (5 Jun. 2007) paras 122,123.
499. *Ibid.* para. 123.
500. *Ibid.* paras 132–134.

On the contrary, in the *Mitchell v. Congo* case, the failure of the tribunal to state the facts led the ad hoc Committee to annul the decision despite the application of the low reasoning standard. According to the Committee the tribunal's reasoning on what it considers an investment was 'incomplete and obscure', affecting the coherence of the tribunal's reasoning.[501] On that basis, it concluded that 'the Award is tainted by a failure to state reasons, in the sense that the inadequacy of reasons is such that it seriously affects the coherence of the reasoning as to the existence of an investment'.[502]

Similarly, in the very recent case of *TECO v. Guatemala*, the ad hoc Committee largely upheld the tribunal's award but annulled sections of it on the loss of value claim and historical damages because it found that the tribunal's reasoning was 'not clear at all' and that it 'struggled to understand' it.[503] In a different context, the reasoning in the *Mondev*[504] award was criticised as failing to explain how it perceived the content of the international law minimum standard of treatment in the context of the applicable standard for denial of justice.[505]

In the aforementioned decisions the committees make reference to the importance of 'explaining', 'understanding' and 'following' the tribunal's reasoning. As analysed above, understanding can be achieved both through an interactive argumentation process and through the persuasive power of the arguments used.[506] The understanding of a tribunal's reasoning is based on persuasion rather than direct communication with the reader; persuasion that there exists a specific process followed in order to move from an argument to a certain decision. Based on these considerations it should be noted that understanding the logical line of the award's reasoning does not necessarily mean acceptance of the correctness of the reasoning.

This strand of thinking reveals an emphasis on the persuasive effect of the reasoning requiring exactly this movement pictured in the committees' decisions: the arguer moving the listener from belief X to belief Y.[507] In these cases, it is important to check whether the conclusion of an award 'follows logically from formulations of legal norms N1, N2 ... Nn whose validity has to be presupposed together with empirical statements A1, A2 ... An'.[508] In the case where there is no such logical coherence, the conclusion is not justifiable and the ad hoc committee will annul the tribunal's award. Leaving aside this task of choosing between annulling or upholding the tribunal's award, one could reasonably wonder whether the reviewing committee can infer the

---

501. *Mr Patrick Mitchell v. the Democratic Republic of Congo*, ICSID Case No. ARB/99/7, Decision on Annulment (1 Nov. 2006) para. 40.
502. *Ibid.* para. 40.
503. *TECO Guatemala Holdings LLC v. Republic of Guatemala*, ICSID Case No. ARB/10/23, CAFTA-DR, Decision on Annulment (5 Apr. 2016) para. 128.
504. *Mondev*, Award (n 239) para. 94.
505. Julien Cantegriel, 'The Final Award in *Mondev International v. United States of America*', in Aguilar-Alvarez and Reisman (ed.), *The Reason's Requirement in International Investment Arbitration* (n 406) 41.
506. *See* §3.02[A] 'Acceptability'.
507. Clements, *Perception and Persuasion in Legal Argumentation: Using Informal Fallacies and Cognitive Biases to Win the War of Words* (n 415) 329.
508. Alexy, *A Theory of Legal Argumentation* (n 52) 2.

logical coherence of the tribunal's arguments. Robert Alexy refers to such a possibility describing the following process:

> [...] it could be shown either that the transition from N1, N2 ... Nn and A1, A2 ... An [to the conclusion] is permissible (even where the conclusion does not follow logically from N1, N2 ... Nn and A1, A2 ... An) or that in addition with the presupposedly valid norms and the proven empirical statements, further propositions with a normative content N1., N2. ... Nn. can be adduced such as [the conclusion] follows logically from N1, N2 ... Nn together with N1., N2. ... Nn. and A1, A2 ... An.[509]

For Alexy, the rules that could effectuate such a justification process are the 'canons of interpretation'.[510] In the field of investment arbitration, the ad hoc committees have tried to infer the logical coherence of the reasoning taking into account the tribunal's implicit considerations.

An example is the annulment Committee's decision in the *WENA Hotels v. Arab Republic Egypt* where a minimum standard of reasoning was also adopted. The ad hoc Committee cited the *MINE v. Guinea* annulment decision noting that this minimum requirement of reasoning implies that the tribunal has the duty to 'identify, and to let the parties know, the factual and legal premises leading the tribunal to its decision. If such sequence of reasons has been given by the tribunal, there is no room left for a request for annulment under Article 52(1)(e).[511] In this case, the Committee proceeded to a teleological interpretation of Article 48(3) and Article 52(l)(e) concluding to the importance of persuasion. It specifies that the purpose of these provisions is:

> to ensure that the Parties will be able to understand the tribunal's reasoning. This goal does not require that each reason be stated expressly. The tribunal's reasons may be implicit in the considerations and conclusions contained in the award, provided they can be reasonably inferred from the terms used in the decision'.[512]

The *WENA* decision is an example of reasoning which failed to identify the rule upon which the decision was based. The tribunal benchmarked the interest rate to Egyptian bonds without making any reference to the legal rule providing for such a decision[513] The ad hoc Committee adopting the low reasoning standard inferred reasons into the tribunal's award noting:

> [i]t must be assumed that [the tribunal] took such decision in order to award damages corresponding to an 'adequate and effective compensation' as provided for in Article 5 of the IPPA. The reasons underlying the Tribunal's decision in this respect are thus stated sufficiently.[514]

Based on the above line of reasoning, the Tribunal's decision survived annulment since the application of the low reasoning standard permitted the ad hoc Committee to

509. *Ibid.*
510. *Ibid.* 3.
511. *WENA*, Annulment (n 439) para. 79.
512. *Ibid.* para. 81.
513. *WENA*, Award (n 439) para. 128.
514. *WENA*, Annulment (n 439) para. 96.

extract the implicit reasons underlying the decision.[515] However, the reasoning standard expressed in the *WENA* annulment decision is considered to be ambiguous as it can be interpreted in two ways.[516] On the one hand, it may have the meaning that the award will survive annulment in the case the committee can infer the reasons of the tribunal's award. On the other hand, it may mean that the award will survive annulment if the committee concludes from its own analysis that the tribunal reached the correct conclusion even for the wrong reasons. This last interpretation of the *WENA* argument can be found in the *CMS* annulment decision where the tribunal concluded that the tribunal had failed to state its reasons in finding a breach of the umbrella clause contained in the BIT.[517]

A similar approach of focusing on how to 'save' a problematic reasoning can be found in the *CDC v. Seychelles* case where the ad hoc Committee held: 'In construing awards, as in construing statutes and legal instruments generally, one necessarily should construe the language in issue, whenever possible, in a way that results in consistency [...].'[518] An analogous strand of thinking can be found in the *Rumeli v. Kazakhstan* annulment decision. The ad hoc Committee mentioned that the reasoning does not need to be explicit but it should be understood from the rest of the award:

> [I]f reasons are not stated but are evident and a logical consequence of what is stated in an award, an ad hoc committee should be able to so hold. Conversely, if such reasons do not necessarily follow or flow from the award's reasoning, an ad hoc committee should not construct reasons in order to justify the decision of the tribunal.[519]

The practice of the ad hoc committees demonstrates that the majority of the case law gives priority to the persuasive effect of the reasoning of the award rather than to the correct reasoning.[520] In the case that the reader can follow the reasoning of the tribunal from one point to another, the reasoning standard is met and the award avoids annulment. As a consequence, the 'objective' presentation of the decision-making steps, in certain cases, gives its place to persuasion about the specific judicial opinion.[521]

515. Cheng and Trisotto, 'Reasons and Reasoning in Investment Treaty Arbitration' (n 409) 429.
516. Aguilar-Alvarez and Reisman, *The Reason's Requirement in International Investment Arbitration* (n 406) 21.
517. *Ibid.* 21.
518. *CDC Group plc v. Republic of Seychelles*, ICSID Case No. ARB/02/14, Decision on Annulment (29 Jun. 2005) para. 8.
519. *Rumeli Telekom A.S. and Telsim Mobil Telekomunikasyon Hizmetleri A.S. v. Republic of Kazakhstan*, ICSID Case No. ARB/05/16, Decision on Annulment (25 Mar. 2010) para. 83.
520. Arbitrator H mentioned that 'in the reasoning when you are alone [...] you can be as detailed as you want because you don't have to compromise with anybody; but when you are three you do have to compromise [...] that also explains why the reasoning is perhaps not what it should be in terms of what you see on the paper as there have been compromises'. *See* Annex 'Interview Questions'.
521. Referring to the reasoning of judicial decisions, Edward further marks that '[...] the primary rhetorical task of a judicial opinion is to persuade. The opinion is the judge's defense of the decision the judge has already made. Thus, the judge's written opinion is a *post hoc* persuasive document, much as the advocate's briefs are persuasive documents. In both kinds of documents, the writer bolsters the justification for the preferred result by using all available

An issue that arises at this point is whether the only focus of reasoning should be the persuasion of an audience and thus the avoidance of annulment or whether there are other functions that reasoned awards can and do fulfil. This is what the next section purports to address.

§4.02 DEVELOPMENT-ORIENTED FUNCTION: REASONING AS A MEANS FOR NORMATIVE DEVELOPMENT

Based on the above analysis, the awards' reasoning is oriented towards the persuasion of the audience that the conclusion of the award was reached through the specific process of interpretation and application of the law followed by the tribunal.[522] This is an attitude corresponding to any rhetoric structure under which '[...] arguments are not fully laid out the table in all their parts for logical examination, since such a procedure would quickly bore and tire a non-expert audience'.[523] Such a rhetorical practice can keep the attention of the audience awake preventing them from deviating from the argumentative core to peripheral information.[524]

The focus of the reasoning process on persuasion may lead someone to the conclusion that describing the legal interpretation process followed for the resolution of the dispute is not a priority for reasoning. This conclusion could be enhanced by the lack of an appeal mechanism through which errors of law can be reviewed. However, this is not the case since the process of interpretation preserves its importance even in the absence of an appeals facility for it is connected to the development of the content of investment protection guarantees.

Thirty years ago, Professor Carbonneau dealt with the issue of rendering arbitral awards with reasons highlighting that reasoned awards are indispensable for the development of a 'common law of international transactions'.[525] Arbitral tribunals have been described as 'major agencies' in the evolution of international investment law.[526] The task of tribunals to decide a specific dispute includes the assignment of a 'contemporary meaning' to broad investment-treaty terms avoiding in this way the application of 'anachronism[s] from the past'.[527] Lauterpacht refers to 'judicial legislation' by international court decisions as an indirect, yet significant contribution towards the development of the law of nations.[528]

Using a broader description of the role of investment tribunals in shaping the law is likely to have a larger explanatory power and avoid connotations of attributing

forms of reasoning, not merely the forms the writer personally finds determinative'. Linda Edwards, 'The Convergence of Analogical and Dialectic Imaginations in Legal Discourse' (1996) 20 LegalStudF 7, fn 19.

522. *See* §4.01 'Persuasion-Oriented Function: Reasoning as a Rhetorical Technique'.
523. Kraus, *Arguing or Reasoning? Argumentation in Rhetorical Context* (n 416) 8.
524. *Ibid.*
525. Carbonneau, *Rendering Arbitral Awards with Reasons* (n 396) 614.
526. Aguilar-Alvarez and Reisman, *The Reason's Requirement in International Investment Arbitration* (n 406) 29.
527. *Ibid.*
528. Hersch Lauterpacht, *The Development of International Law by the Permanent Court of International Justice* (Longmans 1934) 45.

tribunals the power to make law without a traditional political and legal justificatory basis. In this sense, normative development through arbitral decisions refers to the development of the meaning of vague legal rules through the process of interpretation.[529]

The question however still remains: where does the authority of the tribunals to develop the content of the investment protection guarantees derive from? As analysed in Part II, investment-arbitration tribunals are called to interpret rather broad protection guarantees contained in the investment treaties such as FET or requirements of non-discrimination.[530] The mandate of the arbitrator to decide, avoiding *non liquet,* would be difficult to perform 'unless international adjudicators were free to device new solutions within the interstices of established norms which are too general or too abstract to yield a definite answer'.[531]

The generalised treaty language gives discretion to the arbitrator to form the content of such guarantees through their interpretation and application to the specific dispute, the whole process being illustrated through the award's reasoning. Arbitral case law plays the important role of a 'vehicle', transmitting the detailed interpretation and application of the general protection guarantees of the investment treaties.[532] Especially since due consideration paid to arbitral case law – despite the absence of a formal doctrine of stare decisis – has led to the emergence of an evolving jurisprudence, legal interpretation and reasoning constitute the means to develop the law.[533] As such, the legal decision-making process acquires a normative character. Awards accompanied by reasons constitute an appropriate means for fulfilling the so-called normative potential of transnational arbitration and as such contribute to the development of a new type of law – that of transnational law. [534]

Accepting this development oriented function of the award's reasoning takes us to the next questions: is there any mechanism for reviewing such normative development? And how do tribunals treat the issue of interpretation of the law in the absence of the fear of an appeals facility?

529. *See also* §6.03[D][4] 'Dialogue with International Legal Orders: Reciprocal Communication' discussing about the development of international law through investment arbitration awards.
530. *See* Part II 'Language'.
531. Jan Paulsson, 'International Arbitration and the Generation of Legal Norms: Treaty Arbitration and International Law' (2006) 3(5) TDM 11.
532. Landau, 'Reasons for Reasons' (n 449) 200.
533. Ortino states that an internally consistent decision will be able to 'positively contribute to the development of a set of legal principles and standards for the protection and promotion of foreign investment'. Federico Ortino, 'Legal Reasoning of International Investment Tribunals: A Typology of Egregious Failures' (2012) 3(1) JIDS 31, 47; The application of the language and dialogue approach have revealed that arbitral tribunals have developed the content of specialised principles of investment arbitration and have reshaped Customary International Law to meet the needs of investment arbitration *see* Part II 'Language' and Part IV 'Dialogue'.
534. Carbonneau, *Rendering Arbitral Awards with Reasons* (n 396) 681. *See* sections §2.02 [B][5] 'General Principles of Investment Law and Arbitration' and §6.04 'Customary Law Arguments'.

[A] Errors of Law

Investment-treaty arbitration conducted under UNCITRAL arbitration rules can be subject to limited procedural review by the courts of the seat.[535] The ICSID Convention also offers one level of review of the awards unlike other arbitration bodies like AAA or ICC that under specific circumstances permit the parties to form an appeal in front of a national court.[536] Thus, it aims at promoting finality and ensuring the quick resolution of the dispute. Article 53(1) ICSID states that the tribunal's decision is not subject to appeal. In other words, no review can be realised on the merits of the decision regarding the facts or the law. The case law, regardless of proposing a low or high reasoning standard, confirms this position. The annulment committees state clearly that they have no intention to determine the correct interpretation of law or facts.[537]

The matter of choosing between a high or low reasoning standard is delicate as it could affect the character of the ICSID annulment system. When the ICSID annulment committees are confronted with the duty to decide if the tribunal has based the decision on reasons, it is essential that it will not, unintentionally, be transformed into a Court of Appeal. Sir Franklin Breman eloquently pictures such a dilemma noting that the examination of the tribunal's legal reasoning takes place:

> [...] not in order to determine its 'correct' interpretation (as the Committee rightly says, that would amount to appeal, not annulment), but in order to bring out the elements that on any analysis must necessarily have formed part of a properly-conducted interpretative process.[538]

In this way, by not deciding whether the interpretation given by the arbitral tribunal is correct or not, the annulment committee avoids the danger of reviewing the award on the merits. However, such an approach reflects the need to reveal the elements that form part of properly conducted process of interpretation.

Nonetheless, despite the fear of turning into an appeal mechanism, ad hoc committees have thoroughly mentioned the importance of legal interpretation. The *Lucchetti* case is a very interesting example treating the issue of the adequacy of reasoning when it comes to treaty interpretation. The majority of the ad hoc Committee found that the Tribunal's reasoning 'does not give a full picture of the various elements which should be taken into account for treaty interpretation under the Vienna Convention'.[539] However, the fact that the tribunal made reference to the various

535. Landau, 'Reasons for Reasons' (n 449) 201.
536. Sylvia Schatz, 'The effect of the Annulment Decisions in *Amco v. Indonesia* and *Klöckner v. Cameroon* on the Future of the International Centre for the Settlement of Investment Disputes' (1988) 3(2) AmUIntlLRev 481, 515.
537. For example, *Lucchetti*, Annulment-Dissent (n 143) para. 7.
538. *Ibid.* para. 17.
539. *Industria Nacional de Alimentos, S.A. and Indalsa Perú, S.A. (Lucchetti) v. The Republic of Peru*, ICSID Case No. ARB/03/4, Decision on Annulment (5 Sep. 2007) para. 129; Arbitrator H and G confirmed the fact that the reasoning of the award does not include the whole deliberation and thinking process of the arbitrator. According to the arbitrators interviewed,

standards as adopted in the case law and as pictured in the doctrine satisfied the committee which concluded that it:

> [...] cannot find in the Tribunal's reasoning any contradiction or lack of precision such as to leave a doubt about the legal or factual elements upon which the Tribunal based its conclusion. Moreover, the Committee is satisfied that the Tribunal examined all Lucchetti's arguments and finds that it dealt with them in the Award to such an extent and in such a manner as could reasonably be required.[540]

Sir Franklin Berman dissented on the issue forming a noteworthy line of arguments in order to conclude that the award should be annulled. Starting from the distinction between the standard of reasoning in the jurisdictional phase and that of the merits phase, he argued that if in the first case the tribunal declines jurisdiction without giving adequate explanations for its reasons, this could lead to the annulment of the award, at least on the basis of a failure to state reasons.[541] The decisive factor here is not whether the tribunal 'failed to describe what rules of treaty interpretation it was applying' but whether it 'adequately explained what [it was] doing in the interpretative process'.[542]

The *CMS* annulment decision also brought to the surface the issue of how to deal with an incorrect interpretation of the law by the tribunal. In this case, the ad hoc committee highlighted the fact that the annulment review of the award was not an appeal drawing analogies from the reasoning of the *MINE* and *WENA* ad hoc Committees.[543] However, it stated that it did not agree with the Tribunal's interpretation of the umbrella clause. The ad hoc Committee, after referring to possible interpretations of the umbrella clause, described the unsuccessful attempt of inferring the reasoning of the tribunal noting:

> [i]t is quite unclear how the Tribunal arrived to its conclusion that CMS could enforce the obligation of Argentina to TGN. It could have done so by the above interpretation of Article II(2)(c), but in that case one would have expected a discussion of the issue of interpretation referred to above. Or it could have decided that CMS had an Argentine law right to compliance with the obligations, yet CMS claims no such right; and Argentine law appears not to recognize it.[544]

Based on the above argument, the ad hoc committee concluded that in the specific circumstances:

> [t]here is a significant lacuna in the Award, which makes it impossible for the reader to follow the reasoning on this point. It is not the case that answers to the question raised 'can be reasonably inferred from the terms used in the decision';

---

what is referred to is usually the most essential issues for reaching the final decision and not the entire process of interpreting the law. *See* Annex 'Interview Questions'.

540. *Ibid.* para. 129.
541. *Lucchetti,* Annulment-Dissent (n 143) para. 4.
542. *Ibid.* para. 6.
543. *CMS Gas Transmission Co. v. Argentine Republic,* ICSID Case No. ARB/01/8, Decision on Annulment (25 Sep. 2007) paras 45, 124–127.
544. *Ibid.* para. 96 (citations omitted).

> they cannot. Accordingly, the Tribunal's finding on Article II(2)(c) must be annulled for failure to state reasons. [545]

Based on this line of reasoning, the ad hoc Committee annulled in part the Tribunal's award. The *CMS* annulment decision has been described as a 'quasi-appeal' since the problem the ad hoc committee saw was that the tribunal's plausible literal reasoning of the treaty was incorrect.[546]

In a similar context, the annulment Committee in the award *Amco Asia v. Indonesia* assessed whether the failure to refer to the law applied constituted a ground for annulment. The *Amco* Committee departed from the high reasoning standard of the *Klöckner* annulment decision but at the same time did not require such a low standard as the *MINE* Committee. On the contrary, it supported the middle position of 'sufficiently pertinent reasons' describing the reasoning requirement in the following terms:

> [T]here must be a reasonable connection between the bases invoked by a tribunal and the conclusions reached by it. The phrase 'sufficiently pertinent reasons' appears to this ad hoc Committee to be a simple and useful clarification of the term 'reasons' used in the Convention.[547]

In this case, despite the fact that the committee did not apply a high reasoning standard, failure to state the law applied to the facts of the case led to the annulment of the award. Due to the failure to identify the legal rule under which the shortfall of the investment was calculated, the tribunal was considered to have reached a wrong outcome.[548]

The above-mentioned perspectives of arbitral tribunals have brought to the fore the procedural rather than substantive nature of the reasoning requirement. Reasoning is viewed as a procedural standard which ensures the transparency and readability of the decision-making process in a language the audience can understand. Nonetheless, arbitrators also flirt with a substantive review of the arbitral reasoning when acknowledging the importance of a correct legal interpretation and application of the law to facts. On that basis, while the arbitral bodies draw a line between annulment and appeal, their practice shows that it is important to understand the existence of an incorrect interpretation of law and facts, even if at the end the majority of the ad hoc committees overlook their findings in order to remain within the limits of annulment.

545. *Ibid.* para. 97 (citations omitted).
546. Aguilar-Alvarez and Reisman, *The Reason's Requirement in International Investment Arbitration* (n 406) 25.
547. *Amco Asia Crop. v. the Republic of Indonesia*, ICSID Case No. ARB/81/1, Decision on Annulment (16 May 1986) para. 43.
548. Cheng and Trisotto, 'Reasons and Reasoning in Investment Treaty Arbitration' (n 409) 421, 428, fn 104; *Maritime International Nominees Establishment v. Republic of Guinea*, ICSID Case No. ARB/84/4, Decision on Annulment (29 Dec. 1989) paras 5.07–5.13; *Hussein Nuaman Soufraki v. The United Arab Emirates*, Decision on Annulment ICSID Case No. ARB/02/7 (5 Jun. 2007) paras 101–128; *Duke Energy International Peru Investments No. 1 Ltd. v. Republic of Peru*, ICSID Case No. ARB/03/28, Decision on Annulment (1 Mar. 2011) paras 228–229.

Such an approach further illustrates the similarities between an annulment process and an appellate review procedure by a court.[549] In practice, the line between a procedure for appeal and a procedure for annulment becomes quite blurred. Even though, prima facie, the test for annulment differs from the test for appellate review, the content is nearly the same.[550] The ad hoc committees examine the reasoning process and the interpretation of the facts and law in order to conclude that a legal reasoning is 'consistent', 'reasonable' or 'relevant', the same way an appeal mechanism would do. Whether they support a high or low reasoning standard, the ad hoc committees follow a certain process, like the one that judges would follow in an appeal procedure in order to characterise an interpretation as 'correct' or not. Nevertheless, most of the annulment committees choose to avoid this characterisation, as it would exceed the limits of annulment. However, the fact that they do not go as far as to prescribe consequences to an incorrect interpretation of the law does not mean that errors of law are welcomed in investment-arbitration decision-making.

Arbitral case law as described in this section reveals that arbitrators approach the issue of errors of law with caution, albeit with great interest in pointing out their existence. Nine out of ten arbitrators interviewed highlighted the importance of a correct legal interpretation for the integrity of the legal decision-making process.[551] Recently, the importance of dealing with errors of law has been well emphasised in the proposals for the creation of a standing appeal body in CETA[552] and the EU proposal of creating a standing investment court within the framework of TTIP and other EU investment treaties.[553] Even though these discussions are not new, they have brought to the surface the pressing need for consistency and predictability in legal decision-making especially on issues of law.[554] In this context, the acceptability of a final decision mostly from the external audience can also be seen as depending on a large extent on the justification of the interpretation of the legal rules applied.[555]

549. Schatz, *The effect of the Annulment Decisions in Amco v. Indonesia* and *Klöckner v. Cameroon on the Future of the International Centre for the Settlement of Investment Disputes* (n 536) 514.
550. *Ibid.*
551. Only Arbitrator A had a different view noting that 'because there is no opportunity to correct errors of law, sometimes the interpretation or application issues may not be so essential'. *See* Annex 'Interview Questions'.
552. European Commission Press Release, 'CETA: EU and Canada agree on new approach on investment in trade agreement' (29 Feb. 2016) <http://europa.eu/rapid/press-release_IP-16-399_en.htm> (accessed 21 Apr. 2018).
553. European Commission Press Release, 'Investment Court System for TTIP and other EU trade and investment negotiations' (16 Sep. 2015) <http://europa.eu/rapid/press-release_IP-15-5651_ en.htm> (accessed 21 Apr. 2018).
554. The United States has inserted in several IIAs provisions for the potential establishment of a standing appeals body. The Chile-US FTA established such a possibility provided the State parties would enter into a separate multilateral agreement (Article 10.19(10)). The Dominican Republic-Central America-US FTA (CAFTA) (2004) required the establishment of a negotiating group for the development of an appellate body (Annex 10-F); An alternative solution is a system of preliminary rulings, within which tribunals would be able to refer questions of law to a specific central body. *See* Christoph Schreuer, 'Preliminary Rulings in Investment Arbitration' in Karl Sauvant (ed.), *Appeals Mechanism in International Investment Disputes* (OUP 2008).
555. Feteris, *Fundamentals of Legal Argumentation* (n 47) 6.

Arbitrator I eloquently puts the discussion on a different basis stating that errors of law do exist but they are not common: 'Are they errors of law or are they decisions on the application of law that many people could disagree with? It is a difficult distinction. The pure errors of law are limited in number. The question, for those who think about optimizing the system of arbitration, is do the number of those errors justify adding a dimension of appeal that would have negative impact in other ways for the arbitration process. That is the real question.' Arbitrator J contributes to the discussion by emphasising on the relative meaning of the concepts 'right and wrong': 'An arbitrator or a judge in any national court system has to make its own personal decision on what is right or wrong in applying the law to the facts. [...] Even where you have an appellate mechanism, there is no pure right or wrong however many levels of instance you have. It is very important for each individual tribunal to do its best to do what it thinks is the right application of law to facts.'[556]

What becomes evident from the above analysis is the need to profit from the inherent predisposition of a review on the substance of the awards. Even though the committees will not annul an award due to incorrect interpretation of the law they generally will review and comment on the interpretation process. This should act as an impetus for arbitral tribunals to provide a coherent interpretation of the investment protection guarantees and thus promote the uniform development of the law without endangering the effectiveness of investment arbitration. Clearly, an excessively long decision addressing each and every point that may not be of any consequence to the resolution of the dispute, would not be in the interest of the parties and would cause undue delay to the issuing of the decision. Nonetheless, a high level of clarity in the reasoning of arbitral awards, especially when it comes to issues of interpretation, provides an assurance that the decision is grounded in the law.[557] After all, the decision-maker, whether judge or arbitrator, should not only decide disputes 'by the rational application of principle and authority, and not his or her own personal view of the justice of the case', but should also be seen to decide this way.[558]

556. *See* Annex 'Interview Questions'.
557. Ortino, 'Legal Reasoning of International Investment Tribunals' (n 533) 34.
558. Landau, 'Reasons for Reasons' (n 449) 188 citing Lord Bingham, 'Reasons and Reasons for Reasons: Differences Between a Court Judgment and an Arbitral Award' (1988).

Conclusion to Part III

This part analysed the legal decision-making process of arbitral tribunals through the perspective of 'Rhetoric' and the way arbitral awards are reasoned. What is revealed is that arbitral tribunals approach the issue of reasoning in a specialised way, based on the characteristics and needs of investment arbitration.

The first section of Chapter 3 focused on how investment rules and treaties approach the issues of reasoning. It concluded that while they clearly refer to the requirement to provide reasons, they do not clarify the reasoning standards that an award should meet. This creates a blurred view on the quantity and quality of an award's reasoning leading to various approaches formed by the arbitral tribunals in practice.

The second section of the chapter presented the dynamics of the reasoning requirement and its importance for the parties as well as the investment-arbitration framework as a whole. Reasoning plays a significant role since it limits arbitral discretion and sets the decision-making power within specific limits. It is also connected to the acceptability of the award by a specific audience. The internal audience includes the parties of the dispute which are offered an explanation of why they won or lost and as a result acquire the ability to plan their post-award strategies such as enforcement or annulment of the decision. However, the interest in the outcome of investment disputes is not only party related but may also involve legitimate interests of third parties such as States, international institutions or NGOs.

The public nature of the issues treated enhances the need for an acceptable and transparent dispute resolution process. The acceptability of the award from the above-mentioned audience fosters in its turn legitimacy in the investment-arbitration framework. The legitimacy of an adjudicatory body also depends on the consistent interpretation and application of the law as well as on the persuasiveness of the justifications of the award. Reasoning is capable of expressing the validity and legitimacy of the award's arguments and outcome and as a result the acceptability and legitimacy of the decision-making process. Legitimacy in this context encompasses the way investment arbitration appears not only to the inside players but also to the outside viewers of the field.

Apart from the dynamics of reasoning, this part analysed the functions of an award's reasoning as revealed through arbitral case law. In particular, Chapter 4 identified two functions of reasoning. The first function is the persuasion-oriented function. The debate over a high or low reasoning standard illustrates the different approaches of the arbitral tribunals and annulment committees regarding the tribunal's discretion to express its reasoning in certain ways. It is undoubtedly accepted that reasons must exist. However, the issue of characterising the existent reasons as 'adequate', 'clear', 'sufficient', or 'coherent' ends up being a matter of persuasion. It turns out that the reasoning of arbitral awards primarily aims at persuading the parties, the ad hoc committees, and the reader in general that the components of the reasoning process lead to the tribunal's conclusion in a logical manner.

However, in investment arbitration, the role of reasoning is not only about how well parties understand the awards when reading them but also how arbitrators decide on the legal points, and how law is interpreted and applied. The development function of reasoning illustrates clearly this concern. Apart from persuasion, reasoning has the important normative function of developing the content of vague investment protection guarantees and, even more, their consistent development through the de facto use of precedent by future tribunals. The interpretation of abstract legal norms requires thorough legal argumentation and this is confirmed by the importance of the interpretation process despite the absence of an appeals mechanism.

The analysis of the way arbitral tribunals externalise their decision-making process through reasoning revealed that legal interpretation is a process strongly linked to the characteristics of investment arbitration. Specificities such as legitimacy concerns, the vague reasoning requirement and the importance of correct legal interpretation despite the lack of an appeals facility have all led to the gradual development of a dynamic and normative decision-making process.

However, an additional element that requires attention when analysing legal decision-making is the fact that arbitrators consider various national and international legal orders when deciding on a specific dispute. The way tribunals deal with such a challenge is examined in the next part which analyses the legal decision-making process from the perspective of 'Dialogue'.

PART IV Dialogue

Interpretation should be informed by an actor's sense about its place in a grand normative pluriverse.[559]

559. Venzke, *How Interpretation Makes International Law* (n 56) 198.

Introduction to Part IV

This part approaches the legal decision-making process of arbitrators through the perspective of 'Dialogue'.[560] It proposes a novel 'dialogical network' approach for identifying the methodology arbitrators use to interpret the law.[561] Specifically, it analyses how arbitral tribunals use certain types of arguments to interpret the law, and the role of dialogue between these arguments.

This part does not purport to present a comprehensive taxonomy of modern interpretations nor attempts to refer to all the representatives and variants of the principal types of interpretation. Instead, it aims to analyse the legal arguments of arbitral tribunals using a proposed 'dialogical network' approach. In the dialogue context the interpretation process is viewed as one combined operation where each argument may contribute to the overall interpretation process.

This part proposes that arbitral tribunals make use of five main arguments when interpreting the law as revealed through the arbitral case law analysis. Each of these arguments focuses respectively on narrative techniques, the VCLT, precedent, policy and customary international law. The Narrative arguments are connected to how the submissions of the parties and the 'stories' told by them influence the way the arbitrator will interpret a legal concept. The Convention argumentation scheme refers to how arbitrators use the VCLT to interpret investment treaties. The Precedent-based arguments reveal the way arbitral tribunals communicate with international and domestic judicial systems in order to draw analogies and guidance from their peers on interpretational issues. The Policy-based arguments are linked to the consideration of policies contained in the investment treaties, as well as policies not clearly referred to in treaty texts but extracted from the specificities of the investment-arbitration framework. Lastly, the Customary Law based arguments refer to the use of customary international law in the interpretation process. These arguments interact between them forming networks which eventually constitute the synthesis of the legal decision-making process.

560. On the Dialogue perspective *see* Part Introduction section III[D] 'Legal Argumentation in Arbitral Decision-Making: Language–Rhetoric–Dialogue'.
561. *See* §5.01'Dialogical Networks'.

This part is comprised of Chapters 5 and 6. Chapter 5 develops the theoretical framework of the 'dialogical network' of arguments approach in order to analyse the legal decision-making process through the prism of 'Dialogue'. In particular, this chapter delimits and defines the concept 'dialogical network' of arguments. Chapter 6 brings theory into practice analysing how each of these five argument types is used by arbitral tribunals and the dialogical networks that can be formed between them.

CHAPTER 5

Dialogical Network: Theory

§5.01 DIALOGICAL NETWORKS

The interpretation arguments employed by arbitral tribunals (narrative techniques, the VCLT, precedent, policy and customary international law)[562] rarely operate alone but interact with one another forming a dialogical relationship. The outcome of such a dialogical process is the 'synthesis' of an integral legal interpretation method. The arbitrator will interpret a legal concept based on the synthesis of some or all of the arguments. Within this background, multiple arguments may interact in order to interpret a legal concept.[563]

The 'dialogical network' of arguments is symptomatic of the distinct nature of investment arbitration and an appeal to an investment-arbitration legal framework growing into an organic whole. This methodological technique permits the analysis of legal interpretation in the context of elements underlying the investment-arbitration framework but not yet translated into positive legal rules of interpretation. Such elements are the use of precedent, customary international law and policy.[564] This

562. *See* Chapter 6 'Dialogical Network-Practice'.

563. For the assessment of the arguments *see* §5.02 'Assessing Legal Arguments'; The synthesis of the interpretive arguments can also be viewed as a syllogistic type of reasoning. For Aristotle, a 'syllogism' is connected to a structure of deductive logic consisting of two statements – called 'premises' – and a third one deriving logically from the first two – the conclusion. The tripartite description of a syllogism refers to the existence of a major premise (broad statement of law), a minor premise (application of law to specific facts) and a conclusion (logical consequence of the major and minor premises). However, forming a 'syllogism' is not only a matter of pure logic but also an issue of methodology and choices. Huhn Wilson, 'The Use and Limits of Syllogistic Reasoning in Briefing Cases' (2001) 42(3) SantaClaraLRev 813; Orsinger, *The Role of Reasoning and Persuasion in Legal Argumentation* (n 38) 13.

564. General Principles of Law could also constitute part of the dialogical network of arguments since they are used as interpretive arguments by arbitrators. However, for reasons of structure, their role and nature is analysed in the 'Language' Part. *See* §2.02[B] 'Principles'; *See also* Maksymilian Del Mar, 'The Role and Value of Coherence in Theories of Legal Reasoning' (2017) 30(4) Ratio Juris 491 (the author refers to the multifaceted nature of reasoning stating: we

emphasises the fact that the decision-making process is an issue of dispute resolution but it is also governed by aims associated with its particular nature and needs.

[A] Dialogue

In the legal field, the concept 'dialogue' has been used in different contexts. One of these is to picture the judicial review process as an interaction between courts and legislators.[565] Another type of dialogue is the so-called dialogue des juges.[566] The dialogue between the judiciaries has two forms, the horizontal and the vertical dialogue. The former pictures the communication between judicial bodies that are on the same level without a sense of hierarchy between the courts. This happens when international judicial bodies interact between them or national courts communicate with other national courts. The vertical dialogue is effectuated between courts that are mainly in a hierarchical relationship with one another. Such a dialogue is realised for example between the Supreme Court and the national courts. It may also be realised between courts that are of a different level but there is no clear hierarchical relationship between them such as between international and national courts.

In the context of this study, the term 'dialogical' is preferred over the term 'dialectical' as having a wider content. The dialectic process is mostly connected to the aim of exposing the other speaker's weakness of arguments in order to persuade for the validity of one's own arguments.[567] The term 'dialogical' is better situated to describe the dialogues formed in the context of a decision-making process since it does not only focus on the aim to persuade through defeating the interlocutor's arguments.

As with the 'Language' and 'Rhetoric Parts of the book, the 'Dialogue' analysis is also connected to a decision-making process which takes place within a transnational legal environment.[568] The multifaceted investment-arbitration framework is shaped by a variety of actors including 'individual or corporate claimants and sovereign respondents as parties, arbitrators as decision-makers, party counsel and expert witnesses as decision-shapers, arbitral institutions as administrators, and non-governmental organisations as public interest representatives'.[569] These interconnected relationships are expressed through a 'transnational' terminology. As already mentioned, a transnational legal process is a process of interaction between public and private actors, in national and international fora, to interpret, enforce, and ultimately internalise, rules of international law.[570] Interaction, interpretation and internalisation constitute the main

cannot build a theory of legal reasoning around one mode of justification, or more broadly, one mode of expression or communication – our theory, instead, must try to balance the pluralism of modes of justification, expression and communication in legal reasoning).

565. *See* Peter Hogg and Alison Bushell, 'Charter Dialogue Between Courts and Legislatures, (Or Perhaps the Charter of Rights Isn't Such a Bad Thing after All)' (1997) 35(1) OsgoodeHallLJ 75.
566. *See* William Burke-White, 'International Legal Pluralism' (2003) 25 MichJIntlL 963.
567. *See* Part Introduction [III][C] 'Legal Argumentation in Judicial Decision-Making: Logic – Rhetoric – Dialectic'.
568. *See* Part II 'Language' and Part III 'Rhetoric'.
569. Bekker, 'Recalibrating the Investment Treaty Arbitration System Through Non-Compartmentalized Legal Thinking' (n 77) 55.
570. *See* section §1.01 'Dispute Resolution Function: A Transnational Perspective'.

components of such a transnational environment especially when it comes to the issue of compliance with international law: 'Those seeking to embed certain norms into national conduct seek to trigger *interactions* that yield legal *interpretations* that are then *internalized* into the domestic law of even resistant nation states'.[571]

In this context, the participants of the dialogue are numerous and of different nature. 'Dialogue' for the purposes of this study is not restricted to its classic meaning of a two-person exchange but covers all of the cases from an n-participant conversation to a two-participant interaction. In this setting, it does not only take two to tango or put in the context of this analysis, it does not only take two to dialogue.[572] As will be analysed below, the dialogue may be effectuated between the parties of the dispute, between the parties and the arbitral tribunal, between national and international legal systems, between national and international judges and arbitrators or even between policies.[573]

The 'Dialogue' in investment arbitration does not have the form of questions posed by one participant and answers expected by the other. In other words, it does not operate around declarative and interrogative phrases. Rather it constitutes a conversation that aims to draw analogies, provide guidance and ideas, fill in gaps and even draw delimitations based on interpretational needs. The exchange of knowledge and opinions may either take place simultaneously, as happens, for example, when the parties communicate with each other through their memorials and counter-memorials or may be effectuated in different time frames, as for example, when arbitrators refer to judicial decisions through their citation practices. A corollary of these characteristics is that the dialogue constitutes a cross-fertilisation between the participants, a reciprocal communication, rather than constituting a one-way contact.

[B] Networks

The 'dialogical network' approach, as the words themselves signify, analyses the legal decision-making process through the use of dialogue networks. Network analysis is a technique mostly used in computer science[574] and sociological studies.[575] In the legal field, the network analysis is used to picture the citation practices of judicial bodies.[576] It has also been used for modelling a legislation corpus in which two or more legal

571. *Ibid.*
572. On multiparty dialogues *see* Jinping Yuan and others, 'Multi-party Dialogue Games for Dialectical Argumentation' (2012) 7(10) JC 25, 64.
573. These dialogues are pictured through the five interpretive syllogisms. *See* Part IV 'Dialogue'.
574. For example, Jon Kleinberg, 'Authoritative Sources in a Hyperlinked Environment' (1999) 46(5) JACM 604.
575. For example, Richard Nobles and David Schiff, *Observing Law Through Systems Theory* (Hart 2012); Network analysis is also used in the sociolegal analysis of the law and social systems. This is not going to be the focus of the dialogue network approach which aims at presenting the relationship between decision-making, policies, precedents, customs, international and national legal orders.
576. Yonatan Lupu and Erik Voeten, 'Precedent in International Courts: A Network Analysis of Case Citations by the European Court of Human Rights' (2012) 42 BrJPoliticalSci 413; *See also* A Le Quinio, *Recherche sur la circulation des solutions juridiques: le recours au droit comparé par les*

documents, belonging to the same or different types, may be linked to others by more than one relationship.[577]

Network analysis illustrates and measures relationships such as those between people, groups or information, through the use of 'nodes' and 'links'.[578] Each 'node' represents a party to the relationship, for example a person or information, whereas 'links' map the relationship between the nodes. Aim of this technique is to create a measure that demonstrates the centrality of certain elements over others. The relationships created among the nodes are used to develop 'quantitative indicators of interest regarding, for instance, the centrality or prestige of the nodes within a network'.[579]

In the legal interpretation process, each argument represents one 'node'. The relationships created between the nodes are depicted with 'links'. The network analysis aims at offering a qualitative approach to legal decision-making process of arbitrators rather than a quantitative measurement of the interpretive techniques used in investment arbitration. Figure 5.1 sketches the 'dialogical network' approach proposed by this study.

juridictions constitutionnelles (Fondation Varenne 2011) 179–187; M Claes and M de Visser, 'Are You Networked Yet? On Dialogues in European Judicial Networks' (2012) 8 Utrecht LR 100.

577. Marios Koniaris, Ioannis Anagnostopoulos, and Yiannis Vassiliou, 'Network Analysis in the Legal Domain: A Complex Model for European Union Legal Sources' in Rinke Hoekstra (ed.), *Legal Knowledge and Information Systems* (IOS Press BV 2014) 143.

578. James Fowler and others, 'Network Analysis and the Law: Measuring the Legal Importance of Supreme Court Precedents' (2007) 15(3) Political Analysis 324, 325; *See also* Salacuse stating that the term 'network' suggests the existence of a 'structural connection between the constituent parts of the network', Jeswald Salacuse, 'The Emerging Global Regime for Investments' (2015) 51(2) HarvIntlLJ 427, 430. In the dialogical network theory proposed in this book, the structural connections can be found between the various interpretation arguments that synthesise the interpretation of the law.

579. *Ibid.*

Figure 5.1 Dialogical Network of Interpretive Arguments

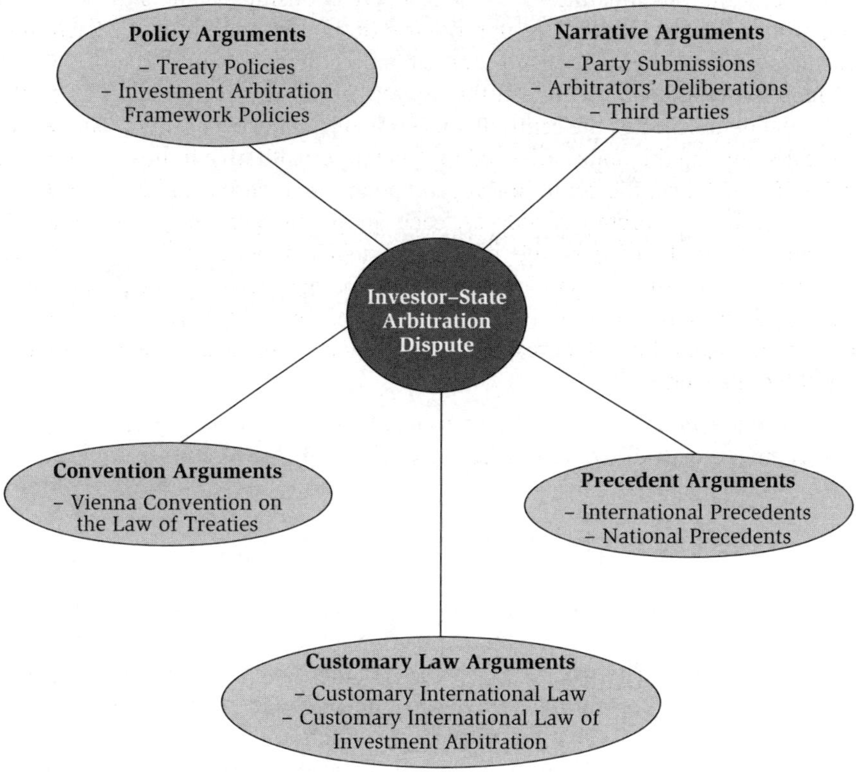

Centre Circle: Investor-State Dispute.
Outer Circles: Legal arguments used for the interpretation process.
Links: Dialogue between the legal arguments within the specific dispute.

Dialogue networks of interpretive arguments

1. Narrative Arguments

- Dialogue between the parties through their submissions
- Dialogue between the parties and the arbitrators
- Dialogue between the members of the tribunal
- Dialogue between the parties, the arbitrators and third parties

2. Convention Arguments

- Dialogue with the Vienna Convention on the Law of Treaties

3. Precedent Arguments

- Dialogue between the arbitrators and international legal orders
- Dialogue between the arbitrators and national legal orders

4. Policy Arguments

- Dialogue with treaty policies
  - Economic policies
  - Political policies
- Dialogue with the investment-arbitration framework policies
  - Legal policies (consistency, predictability, transparency, rule of law)
  - Social policies (environmental concerns, sustainable development)

5. Customary Law Arguments

- Dialogue with Customary International Law
- Dialogue with Customary International Law of Investment Arbitration

§5.02 ASSESSING LEGAL ARGUMENTS

As analysed above, the five legal arguments (narrative techniques, the VCLT, precedent, policy, and customary international law) used in the decision-making process operate in a 'dialogical network'.[580] The product of this dialogue constitutes a synthesis of legal arguments representing the chosen interpretation of a legal concept. The practical issue is how will the arbitrator choose which of the five types of arguments will be used to interpret a legal term. A dialogue between the legal arguments could be pictured as an exchange of interpretation criteria which constitute the arguments' 'thesis'. The interaction between the 'thesis' of the arguments may take the following forms: The 'thesis' of argument n1 may be compatible with the 'thesis' of argument n3, and n5 but not compatible with the 'thesis' of argument n2 and n4. The latter arguments constitute in this case an 'antithesis' to the 'thesis' of argument n1, n3 and n5. Seen form a reversed perspective, arguments n1, n3 and n5 also form an antithesis to argument n2 and n4. As a result, 'thesis' and 'antithesis' alternate according to the spectrum through which one observes the dialogical process.

In the case where one legal argument operates as complementary to another legal argument, enhancing it or adding to it, that does not seem to constitute a problem as both these interpretation arguments will constitute a part of the 'synthesis'. However, one can also logically imagine the case where one argument may be in contrast with

580. *See* §5.01'Dialogical Networks'.

another leading to completely different interpretations. How can the rival arguments be tested and which one will prevail over the other? Is it purely a matter of quantity where the 'synthesis' that will be created will simply include only the arguments that agree with one another (the 'thesis') or is there a need to justify why the antithetical syllogism is side-lined?

The 'dialogical network' methodology introduces a way of assessing and comparing interpretive arguments. However, the effectiveness of comparing pairs of arguments is questioned due to the multiple scenarios that could arise. For instance, even if the customary law argument dominates in relation to its antithetical policy-based argument, the latter argument can be 'restored' when combined with a precedent-based argument dominating in relation to a customary law argument. A practical example here would be the interpretation of the FET guarantee. If the decision-maker employs the customary international law minimum standard of treatment to interpret the FET guarantee, then the protection accorded to the investor will be no more than what customary international law prescribes. However, if the tribunal makes reference to the case law approaching FET from an evolutionary rather than a static perspective, the protection to be accorded to the investor will surpass the minimum standard of customary international law. Going a step further the Tribunal may enhance the precedent argument with the use of policy-based arguments such as the need to ensure a stable framework for the investor. A stark illustration of how such a use of arguments appears in practice is the *Enron* case.[581]

The *Enron* dispute arose when in response to its financial crisis, Argentina took various measures affecting TGS, a gas transportation company in which the claimant participated. The *Enron* tribunal dealt with claims arising out of specific tax assessments that were allegedly imposed by Argentina to TGS and the alleged refusal of the State to allow tariff adjustments in accordance with the US Producer Price Index.

The tribunal dealt with the claim concerning the breach of the FET guarantee established under Article II(2)(a) of the Treaty on various counts: failing to act in good faith, abusing its rights, repudiating assurances given, altering regulatory approvals and conditions, and failure to provide a stable and predictable legal environment.[582] The tribunal arrived at its conclusion employing Narrative arguments, the Vienna Convention-based arguments, Precedent arguments, Policy arguments and Customary International Law arguments.

The parties argued on the autonomous or not nature of the FET standard. The dialogue between the parties at this stage revealed concerns regarding the evolutive interpretation of international customary law concepts in the process of adapting these concepts to the investment-arbitration framework. On the one hand, the claimant argued that the FET standard has 'acquired a specific meaning in light of decisions and treaties, including a treatment compatible with expectations of foreign investors, the observance of arrangements on which the investor has relied to make the investment

581. *Enron Corporation and Ponderosa Assets, L.P. v. Argentine Republic*, ICSID Case No. ARB/01/3, Award (22 May 2007) para. 240.
582. *Ibid.* para. 251.

and the maintenance of a stable legal and business framework'.[583] On the other hand, the respondent answered to this claim noting that the FET standard is not different from the customary international law minimum standard and as such it is not left to the tribunals to delimit its meaning or even less, legislate on the issue.[584] As a result, the respondent noted that the FET standard 'does not entail any treatment additional to or beyond that required by customary law'.[585]

The tribunal's position was closer to the claimant's. The tribunal, at first, noted that the FET standard is unclear and not precise.[586] The reason is that neither international law is clear and precise on 'the treatment due to foreign citizens, traders and investors or with respect to the fact that the pertinent standards have gradually evolved over the centuries'.[587] In this context, 'customary international law, treaties of friendship, commerce and navigation, and more recently bilateral investment treaties, have all contributed to [the development of these standards]'.[588]

The tribunal described the evolution that has taken place as to the content of the FET standard through the use of Precedent-based arguments. It stated that such a development is the product of judicial and arbitral case law as well as the formulation of general principles of law capable of guiding and disciplining the evaluation of the State conduct:

> The evolution that has taken place is for the most part the outcome of a case by case determination by courts and tribunals, as evidenced among many other investment treaty and NAFTA decisions by the TECMED, the OEPC and the Pope & Talbot cases. This explains that, like with the international minimum standard, there is a fragmentary and gradual development. Such development however partly hinges on the gradual formulation – both in cases and legal writings – of 'general principles of law' (as understood under Article 38(1)(c) of the ICJ Statute) able to guide and 'discipline' the evaluation of state conduct under investment treaty standards.[589]

The tribunal continued describing the need to adapt the content of the concept of FET in the framework of the specific treaty applied. Since in the specific circumstance the international minimum standard of customary international law is unclear and not sufficiently elaborate it is difficult to equate with it the FET standard.[590] As a result, in this case, the FET standard may be more precise than the international minimum standard of customary international law:

> But in other more vague circumstances, the fair and equitable standard may be more precise than its customary international law forefathers. This is why the Tribunal concludes that the fair and equitable standard, at least in the context of

583. *Ibid.* para. 252 (citations omitted).
584. *Ibid.* para. 252.
585. *Ibid.* para. 252.
586. *Ibid.* para. 256.
587. *Ibid.* para. 256.
588. *Ibid.* para. 256 (citations omitted).
589. *Ibid.* para. 257 (citations omitted).
590. *Ibid.* para. 258.

> the Treaty applicable to this case, can also require a treatment additional to, or beyond that of, customary law.[591]

Against this background, the tribunal employed the Vienna Convention arguments along with Policy arguments in order to interpret the specific meaning of the FET standard under the particular Treaty. Since the FET standard is contained in Article II(2)(a) of the Treaty, the tribunal referred to the interpretation rule of Article 31 of the Vienna Convention.[592] The tribunal focused on the treaty's preamble in order to demonstrate the link between the FET standard and the legal and economic policies: 'fair and equitable treatment of investment is desirable in order to maintain a stable framework for the investment and maximum effective use of economic resources'.[593]

Subsequently, the tribunal employed Precedent arguments to reveal the role of case law in the development of the FET standard in international law:

> Thus, the Tribunal concludes that a key element of fair and equitable treatment is the requirement of a 'stable framework for the investment', which has been prescribed by a number of decisions. Indeed, this interpretation has been considered 'an emerging standard of fair and equitable treatment in international law'.[594]

Reference to arbitral case law continues in order to draw the line between legal stability and the '[...] freezing of the legal system or the disappearance of the regulatory power of the State'.[595]

Based on this analysis, the tribunal found that a facet of the FET standard is the protection of the investor's expectations. The connection of the FET standard to the expectations of the investor as well as the determination of the content of the term 'expectations' are both effectuated through Precedent-based arguments since the interpretation of the treaty according to the Convention does not offer the tools for such a task. In this context, the tribunal found that:

> The protection of the 'expectations that were taken into account by the foreign investor to make the investment' has likewise been identified as a facet of the standard. The Tecmed approach has been consistently adopted by subsequent decisions. Tecmed described such expectations as 'basic', while in the context of NAFTA, tribunals have qualified them as 'reasonable and justifiable'. What seems to be essential, however, is that these expectations derived from the conditions that were offered by the State to the investor at the time of the investment and that such conditions were relied upon by the investor when deciding to invest.[596]

The tribunal continued delimiting the context of the FET standard based on arbitral case law excluding the principle of good faith as an essential element of FET.[597]

591. *Ibid.*
592. *Ibid.* para. 259.
593. *Ibid.*
594. *Ibid.* para. 260 (citations omitted).
595. *Ibid.* para. 261.
596. *Ibid.* para. 262 (citations omitted).
597. *Ibid.* para. 263.

The tribunal observed that the respondent may be right in pointing out that the scenario of the *Enron* case is different from the factual scenarios of recent decisions.[598] However, this does not lead to the conclusion that Argentina's acts do not violate treaty obligations. On the contrary, the tribunal concluded that since the stable legal framework that 'allured' the investor in making the investment, does no longer exist, 'there is here an objective breach of the fair and equitable treatment due under the Treaty'.[599]

This analysis of the legal arguments used in the *Enron* case reveals the way the Tribunal employed arguments based on Precedent, the Vienna Convention, Policy and Customary International Law in order to interpret the FET protection guarantee.

What still remains necessary, however, is to examine the criteria based on which the tribunal may choose one interpretation argument over the other. [600] The binary relations between the interpretive arguments lead to the assessment of the strength of each conflicting argument concluding to their relative strength only in the context of their relationship. In an attempt to surpass the limited results arising from such a binary relationship, what is important is the introduction of stable criteria against which each argument will be tested. Such criteria determining which legal arguments will finally underpin the interpretation of a legal concept may be the following: whether the argument supports or enhances the reasoning of the tribunal; whether a specific argument has to be addressed as part of the parties' submissions; whether interpretation arguments that are contrary to the main reasoning of the tribunal should be addressed as a way for the tribunal to distinguish itself from them. A less evident criterion is the adaptation test which signifies whether the interpretation arguments used are adapted to the specificities of investment arbitration.[601] A prominent example is the integration of national or international legal concepts into the arbitral decision-making process through the use of precedent arguments. Arbitral tribunals make reference to national and international judicial precedents seeking guidance on how to use the concept of 'proportionality' when considering indirect expropriation. However, the concept of 'proportionality' will in the end be used bearing in mind that investment-arbitration disputes deal with the need to balance public and private interests.[602]

598. *Ibid.* para. 267.
599. *Ibid.* para. 268.
600. Prakken describes the methodology for addressing conflicting legal arguments dividing them into three classes: 'arguments with which a dispute can be "won," respectively, "lost" and arguments which leave the dispute undecided [...] these classes are denoted with the terms justified, overruled and defensible arguments'. Prakken, *Logical Tools for Modelling Legal Argument* (n 53) 152.
601. *See* §5.04 'Legal Pluralism and Adaptation'; Burton, *Judging in Good Faith* (n 233) 57 (The author states that: Each legal reason can justify changing the weight of another reason in the congeries, but only by shifting an increment of additional weight onto itself or giving up some. The weight of one reason depends on the justifications for the other reasons invoked by the circumstances. Giving one reason too little weight hence may be checked by the need to give another too much and vice versa. A judge in good faith seeks to give each and every relevant legal reason a proportional share within the frame fixed by the judicial duty to uphold the law).
602. *See* the analysis in §6.03[D][3] 'Dialogue with International Judges'.

§5.03 FROM LEGAL TRANSPLANTS TO LEGAL DIALOGUES

The spread of international courts and tribunals has led to the development of judicial practices that are not expressly referred to in national and international laws.[603] Such practices may include: '(a) the recognition of the jurisdiction and implementation of decisions by judges belonging to supranational systems; (b) the dialogue between courts for solving transnational cases; (c) the resort to foreign or global law; and (d) in the cross-citation between courts belonging to different judicial systems'.[604]

These kind of techniques employed by international dispute resolution bodies present common characteristics such as: '(a) the spontaneous and discretionary nature of these techniques; (b) the need to solve conflicts, potential or actual, between different judicial systems; and (c) the inadequacy of normative criteria for solving these contrasts'.[605]

In line with the development of such techniques, arbitrators form dialogical networks in order to communicate with national and international legal orders. These legal dialogues may have common features with the theory of legal transplants developed in the field of comparative law. However, they also have specific characteristics that distinguish them from legal transplantation. The latter is described as a process of diffusion of the law from the country of origin to a country of reception leading to connotations of law creating.[606] The diffusion of law, also referred to as 'borrowing', constitutes a source of development and change for the receiving countries.[607]

In particular, 'legal transplantation' has been described as one-way legal transfer from an advanced legal system to another:

> [A] bipolar relationship between two countries involving a direct one-way transfer of legal rules or institutions through the agency of governments involving formal enactment or adoption at a particular moment of time (a reception date) without major change. [I]t is commonly assumed that the standard case involves transfer from an advanced (parent) civil or common law system to a less developed one, in order to bring about technological change ('to modernize') by filling in gaps or replacing prior local law.[608]

---

603. Elisa D'Alterio, 'From judicial comity to legal comity: A judicial solution to global disorder?' (2011) 9 Int'lJConstL 394, 395.
604. *Ibid.*
605. The author connects this practice with the phenomenon of judicial comity aiming at regulating the relations between judicial systems within the global legal space, Elisa D'Alterio, *From Judicial Comity to Legal Comity* (n 603) 395.
606. *See* generally Alan Watson, *Legal Transplants: An Approach to Comparative Law* (2nd ed., University of Georgia Press 1993); *See also* Daniel Berkowitz and others, 'Economic Development, Legality, and the Transplant Effect' (2003) 47 EurEconRev 165 (analysing the relationship between legal transplants and economic development).
607. Sheldon Bernard Lyke, 'Brown Abroad: An Empirical Analysis of Foreign Judicial Citation and the Metaphor of Cosmopolitan Conversation' (2012) 45 VandJTransnatL 83, 125.
608. William Twining, 'Social Science and Diffusion of Law' (2005) 32 JL&Soc'y 203, 207 (emphasis omitted).

Transferring legal rules or institutions from one legal order to another is a process with normative, political and social consequences which are often disregarded.[609] Some authors have proposed a more nuanced approach to judicial borrowing[610] using the terms 'legal transposition'[611] or 'legal translation'[612] which are more flexible and encompass the transformation process of the concept when entering into the legal system of the receptive country.

The use of legal transplants fulfils the function of filling systematic lacunae in legal systems and enhancing the legitimacy of judicial decisions.[613] Legal transplant theories address in essence issues of 'horizontal judicial borrowing' between national legal systems.[614] 'Vertical legal borrowing' between a national and international legal system requires a specialised analysis as it is called to cover different needs in a different background.[615] In a similar context, the borrowing between international legal regimes also requires a specialised approach. The judicial borrowing process implies a specific reform process where the rules borrowed undergo a local interpretation or 'translation' process by the receiving culture.[616]

Legal concepts and ideas acquire their certain meaning and shape when they enter into a specific environment and when used by the participants of this environment. The dialogical network approach focuses on the legal reasoning process of the decision-makers rather than on law creating through borrowing rules from analogous legal cultures. Going a step further, it does not describe a communication between legal concepts *in abstracto* but emphasises on both the environment and the actors of the dialogical process in order to demonstrate the adaptation process that such a dialogue process entails.[617] The environment of investment arbitration is characterised by interactions between private and public entities, public interests and emerging legal

609. *See* Máximo Langer, 'From Legal Transplants to Legal Translations: The Globalization of Plea Bargaining and the Americanization Thesis in Criminal Procedure' (2004) 45 HarvIntlLJ 1, at 29–35 (referring to the inadequacy of the transplant theory when analysing the movement of laws and ideas).
610. Analogical reasoning has been described as the essence of judicial borrowing. When analogous issues arise, adjudicators can find similar solutions and learn from each another. Vadi, *Analogies in International Investment Law and Arbitration* (n 277) 88.
611. Esin Örücü, 'Law as Transposition' (2002) 51(2) ICLQ 205.
612. Langer, 'From Legal Transplants to Legal Translations: The Globalization of Plea Bargaining and the Americanization Thesis in Criminal Procedure' (n 609).
613. Valentina Vadi, 'Critical Comparisons: The Role of Comparative Law in Investment Treaty Arbitration' (2010) 39 DJILP 89; Cuniberti Gilles, 'Enhancing Judicial Reputation Through Legal Transplants – Estoppel Travels to France' (2012) 60 AmJCompL 2, 383.
614. Teerawat Wongkaew 'The Transplantation of Legitimate Expectations in Investment Treaty Arbitration' in Shaheeza Lalani and Rodrigo Polanco Lazo (eds) *The Role of the State in Investor-State Arbitration*, (Brill/Nijhoff 2014) 73.
615. *See* Jonathan Wiener, 'Something Borrowed for Something Blue: Legal Transplants and the Evolution of Global Environmental Law' (2001) 27 Ecology LQ 1295, 1297 (discussing the different needs of horizontal and vertical legal borrowing).
616. Palmer describes such a process as 'creative convergence' which leads to the construction of autonomous law out of borrowed elements. Vernon Valentine Palmer, 'From Lerotholi to Lando: Some Examples of Comparative Law Methodology' (2004) 4(2) Global Jurist Frontiers 16.
617. *See* §5.04 'Legal Pluralism and Adaptation'.

and social policy concerns.[618] These transnational characteristics of investment arbitration constitute the driving force for such a dialogical communication.

The arbitrator confronted not only with treaty interpretation issues but also with the interpretation and use of customary international law, precedents and policies, has formed communication networks with national and international judicial legal systems and adjudication bodies. In an attempt to avoid the danger of basing this analysis on a strict legalistic attitude[619] which may ignore investment arbitration's context and characteristics, the dialogical approach is connected to the functions and policies of investment arbitration.

In addition, the decision-makers are the centre of the dialogue process since they constitute the means for realising such a dialogue. The role of the parties' and their counsel is also taken into account.[620] What should also be kept in mind is that the dialogue process differs from legal transplantation on an additional basis. It entails a twofold relationship where both legal frameworks take advantage of the interaction with one other. As an example, the way arbitral tribunals interpret investment law may also be a source of guidance for national and international judges.[621] In this context, legal decision-making depicts a constant process of interacting with national or international legal concepts. The adaptation of the legal concepts and ideas in the legal and political culture of investment arbitration is an evidence of the success of legal transfer.[622] The dialogical network approach demonstrates this adaptation process.

§5.04 LEGAL PLURALISM AND ADAPTATION

Dialogue presupposes knowledge; knowledge of the other interlocutor; knowledge of the specific characteristics of each interlocutor's environment; knowledge of the function of the dialogue; knowledge of what results are anticipated.

The investment-arbitration framework has formed a dialogical relationship with both domestic laws and case law as well as with international laws and the jurisprudence of international courts. As will be demonstrated in the next chapter, this relationship is well pictured in the interpretive arguments tribunals use. A more systematic approach to such interactions is necessary in order to define their specific roles when determining rights and obligations that involve the interpretation and application of both national and international laws. Especially in situations where the investment-arbitration framework does not provide for definitions of rights or guidance as to the interpretation and application of domestic law concepts, the interaction between national judges and arbitrators encompasses a methodologically appropriate

618. *See* §1.01 'Dispute Resolution Function: A Transnational Perspective'.
619. *See* Otto Kahn-Freund, 'On Uses and Misuses of Comparative Law' (1974) 37 ModLRev 1 (referring to the abuse of the comparative law approach when used for practical purposes).
620. *See* §6.01[B] 'Dialogue Between the Parties and the Tribunal'.
621. *See* §6.03[D][4] 'Reciprocal Communication' and §6.03[E][3] 'Reciprocal Communication'.
622. David Nelken, 'Towards a Sociology of Legal Adaptation' in David Nelken and Johannes Feest (eds) *Adapting Legal Cultures* (Hart 2001) 7, 9.

solution. The investor's entitlement to protection under the investment treaties presupposes the existence of a right, which if not possible to be defined under international law, could be defined under the existing rules of national law rather than under rules created ad hoc by the tribunal.[623] If the latter scenario prevailed, it could foster uncertainty and unpredictability and present the danger of resorting to 'vague and undefined interests' rather than rights.[624]

The international investment-arbitration framework, dealing specifically with the resolution of investor-state disputes, constitutes a specialised regime within the cadre of international law thus participating in the dialogue network formatted between the specialised international judicial bodies. The interaction of international courts and tribunals could be pictured in the awareness of international judicial decisions and frequent cross-referencing practices of the judicial bodies.[625] These practices form a judicial dialogue that permits the fruitful communication between the international judges and arbitrators. It also constitutes a way of addressing the social policies of the investment-arbitration system.[626] Environmental and human rights concerns within the context of investor-state disputes could be better addressed with reference to tools such as the judgments of the ECtHR.[627] Equally, domestic legal orders also put the basis for a communication with the investment-arbitration framework. However, even though current practice demonstrates a use of domestic law principles and national case law, there is no clear methodology of how exactly they should be applied in the investment-arbitration context.

The dialogue with national and international legal orders, gives the opportunity to the decision-makers to make use of the experiences of national and international adjudicative bodies. An interaction of this type does not operate as a restrain to arbitral decision-making but rather as a means to provide a type of soft-law guidelines and fill in lacunae of the investor-state arbitration framework regarding the interpretation and eventually application of vague and broad legal concepts. The extent of the impact of public law depends on the 'interpretative leeway' the arbitral procedure and the investment-treaty leave.[628] Consequently, the dialogue approach does not constitute a

623. Sasson, *Substantive Law in Investment Treaty Arbitration* (n 381) 206.
624. *Ibid.* 206.
625. Alain Pellet, 'The Case Law of the ICJ in Investment Arbitration' (2013) 28(2) ICSID Rev 223.
626. *See* §6.05 'Policy Arguments'.
627. *See*, for example, *Mondev International Ltd. v. United States of America*, ICSID Case No. ARB(AF)/99/2, Award (11 Oct. 2002) paras 138 and 141–144; *Saipem S.p.A. v. The People's Republic of Bangladesh*, ICSID Case No. ARB/05/07, Jurisdiction (30 Jun. 2009) para. 130; *Técnicas Medioambientales Tecmed, S.A. v. The United Mexican States*, ICSID Case No. ARB (AF)/00/2, Award (29 May 2003) para. 122; For a discussion on the dialogue between arbitral tribunals and, national and international judges as pictured in arbitral case law *see* §6.03 'Precedent Arguments'.
628. Stephan Schill, 'The Sixth Path: Reforming Investment Law from Within' (2014) Fourth Biennial Global Conference of the Society of International Economic Law (SIEL) Working Paper. No. 2014/02, 16 (The author describes the delimitation of comparative public law approach in terms of 'what the law should be' and 'what the law is': To the extent the applicable rules leave no room for doubt, the ambit of comparative public law will be limited to *a de lege ferenda* perspective. To the extent, however, there is interpretative leeway, as is often the case, comparative public law can be used as a method to determine the *lex lata*).

means to reform the procedural, jurisdictional and substantive regulatory framework of investment arbitration.

Caution must be borne as to the choice of regimes that take part in this type of interaction with investment arbitration. Creating 'faux amis' may lead to the use of similar or identical concepts out of context generating results that do not align with the object and purpose of the investment treaty at issue.[629] The analogies drawn from interstate international relations should be treated with care given the fact that investor-state arbitration deals with the assessment of State behaviour towards a private party. The scene seems more clear when it comes to the interaction with 'judicial review relating to governmental conduct – be it international judicial review (as carried out by the WTO dispute panels and Appellate Body, by the European – or Inter-American Human Rights Courts or the European Court of Justice) or national administrative courts judging the disputes of individual citizens' over alleged abuse by public bodies of their governmental powers'.[630] Another factor influencing the dialogue process is the background of arbitrators. Arbitrators will tend to draw insights from the legal orders they are more familiar with.[631] As a result, in order to avoid the criticisms of 'selectiveness and euro-centric bias' it is important to choose the comparative legal orders with caution.[632]

The channels of communication developed between the decision-makers encompass the concerns of preserving a specialised framework's diversity by adapting the dialogue to the needs of each framework. In the inter-judicial dialogue context, the process of adaptation is enshrined in the concept of 'legal pluralism'. Legal pluralism on an international level is all about interaction and recognition. In particular, it 'recognizes the value of diversity in the choices, traditions, and approaches of international actors when those actors create rules, procedures, and even courts [...] operat[ing] within what David Held terms "a framework of universal law"'.[633] A pluralist approach to the needs of a hybrid legal framework such as investment arbitration should not 'erase the reality of that hybridity'.[634]

629. John Gaffney, 'Going to Pieces Without Falling Apart: Wälde's Defence "Specialisation" in the Interpretation of Investment Treaties' (2012) 9 TDM 55, 61; *See also* Paulsson stating that: 'There is a danger associated with the fact that all decisions of all courts or tribunals have in principle equal status as concerns their *potential* for normative influence. One must be aware of the perils of conflating the learning to be derived from the great variety of courts and tribunals which coexist in the modern world.' Jan Paulsson, 'International Arbitration and the Generation of Legal Norms' (n 531) 13.

630. *International Thunderbird Gaming Corporation v. The United Mexican States*, UNCITRAL/ NAFTA Chapter 11, Separate Opinion of Thomas Wälde (1 Dec. 2005) para. 13 (citations omitted); *See also* Stephan W Schill, 'Deference in Investment Treaty Arbitration: Reconceptualising the Standard of Review' (2012) 3(3) JIDS 277.

631. *See* Vadi, 'Critical Comparisons: The Role of Comparative Law in Investment Treaty Arbitration' (n 613) p. 84; *See also* Anthea Roberts referring to how the different interests of States, investors and NGOs and the different backgrounds of the lawyers who shape and critique the system as arbitrators affect the comparisons tribunals invoke. Anthea Roberts, 'Clash of Paradigms' (n 76) 45, <http://ssrn.com/abstract=2033167> (accessed 30 Aug. 2018).

632. Stephan W Schill, 'The Sixth Path: Reforming Investment Law from Within.' (n 628), 19.

633. Burke-White, *International Legal Pluralism* (n 566) 978.

634. Paul Schiff Berman, 'Global Legal Pluralism' (2007) 80 SCalLRev 1155, 1192; Paulsson makes reference to a three-dimensional pluralism. The first dimension is the *horizontal* which

In this vein, dialogue in investment-arbitration decision-making on the one hand preserves the specificities of the investment-arbitration framework and on the other carves the way for mutual recognition amongst arbitration and other legal orders. Such a dialogue is formed in the absence of a hierarchical relationship founded on coercive powers.[635] This is evident through the way tribunals use interpretive arguments. The next chapter analyses how interpretive arguments are adapted to the specific interpretation needs that may arise in the investment-arbitration context.

In particular, recourse to Convention-based arguments reveals that arbitrators use the VCLT but they seem to have developed an adapted methodology of interpretation.[636] In this context, even though arbitral tribunals interact with general international law for guidance regarding the interpretation of treaties, arbitral tribunals do not blindly follow the Conventional rules. Moreover, in an investment-arbitration case the interpretive issues that arise do not only concern treaties but also the interpretation of concepts and principles not necessarily contained in treaties. An example is when the need to interpret other sources of law arises, such as customary international law. The VCLT is limited to the interpretation of treaties and, as such, may not provide the appropriate guidance on how to approach customary international law. Tribunals are also confronted with the need to fill in lacunae. Thus arbitrators are confronted with the need to have recourse to interpretive syllogisms other than the convention-based one.

Similarly, the use of Precedent-based arguments depicts the principal role of case law in the decision-making of arbitral tribunals. Arbitrators refer not only to investment-arbitration case law but also to national and international jurisprudence. Equally, legal issues arising in comparative public law regimes such as administrative, constitutional and international aim at introducing solutions for investors, States and the civil society. In this last case, the tribunals do not blindly follow 'foreign' jurisprudence but attempt to avoid the danger of 'faux amis' by selecting carefully their points of reference based on the submissions of the parties and the relevance of the case law. As such comparative analysis generates interpretations adapted to the changing circumstance in investment law and arbitration responding at the same time to the needs and demands of the community.[637] Zumbansen, in particular, describes the emergence of a transnational legal order as a next step in the theory of comparative law.[638]

The policies and functions of investor-state arbitration that may not clearly be pictured in investment treaties but stem from the nature of the dispute resolution

accounts for the cooperation of territorially sovereign legal systems; the second dimension is the *vertical* and accounts for non-State systems engaging in governance; the third dimension is the *depth* which refers to legal orders overlapping and partially overlaying each other. Jan Paulsson, 'Arbitration in Three Dimensions' (2011) 60(2) ICLQ 291. Cf Emmanuel Gaillard, *Aspects Philosophiques du Droit de l'Arbitrage International* (Nijhoff 2008).

635. *Ibid.* 1197.

636. *See* §6.02 Convention Arguments.

637. Vadi, *Analogies in International Investment Law and Arbitration* (n 277) 15.

638. *Ibid.* 44 citing Peer Zumbansen, 'Transnational Comparisons: Theory and Practice of Comparative Law as a Critique of Global Governance', in Maurice Adams and Jacco Bomhoff (eds), *Practice and Theory in Comparative Law* (CUP 2012) 186, 200.

mechanism should also not be disregarded. The policies in the decision-making process are revealed through the Policy arguments employed by the tribunals. Such policies do not only contain policies of the investment treaties but also policies behind the need to balance States' and investors' interests as well as the policies of the arbitration framework, namely consistency and transparency. In this context, arbitrators use interpretive principles expressing the different policies taken into account.

Likewise, such a need for adaptation is found in the use of Customary International Law by arbitrators. As will be demonstrated below, the decision-makers proceed to an evolutionary interpretation of Customary International Law in order to cope with the developing needs of the investor-state arbitration framework.[639]

Last but not least, the dialogical networks formed by the arbitral decision-makers are formed into the confines of a specific dispute. The Narrative arguments perform a constraining role keeping the dialogues adapted and connected to the specific dispute and the submissions of the parties.

A stark illustration of the above-mentioned adaptation process can be found in the *CMS* case. The tribunal acknowledges the need to determine the 'meaning and extent' of the decisions referred to by the parties in order to determine whether they fit in the context of the investment dispute.[640] Since the investment treaties did not address the issue of whether shareholders can advance claims independently from those of the corporation concerned, both the parties and the tribunal recognised the need to have recourse to analogous cases. The tribunal dealt, at first, with the status of the shareholder's rights under general international law as pictured through the ICJ Barcelona Traction decision. Agreeing with the interpretation of the award as given by the counsel of the claimant, the tribunal concluded that the Barcelona Traction decision was not relative to the specific arbitration case since it was concerned only with the exercise of diplomatic protection. [641] However, the tribunal added that the ICJ decision 'marks the beginning of a fundamental change of the applicable concepts under international law and State practice'. [642]

Departing form the Barcelona traction findings, the tribunal refers to the 'changing scenario' wanting the minority and non-controlling shareholders to be admitted to claim in their own right.[643] This scenario is supported by the practice of specialised international regimes such as the decisions of the Iran-United States Tribunal and the rules and decisions of the United Nations Compensation Commission as well as contemporary practice relating to lump-sum agreements.[644] Moreover, the tribunal refers to the relationship between general international law and *lex specialis* marking that the prevalent nature of *lex specialis* results in considering it as the general rule as far as foreign investments are concerned.[645] The tribunal continues its investment-arbitration oriented approach stating that '[t]o the extent that customary international

639. *See* §6.04 'Customary Law Arguments'.
640. *CMS*, Decision on jurisdiction (n 364) para. 43.
641. *Ibid.* (n 364) paras 43–44.
642. *Ibid.* paras 43–44.
643. *Ibid.* para. 47.
644. *Ibid.*
645. *Ibid.* para. 48 (citations omitted).

law or generally the traditional law of international claims might have followed a different approach – a proposition that is open to debate – then that approach can be considered the exception'.[646]

The above analysis reveals that it is necessary for the dialogues formed between arbitrators and national and international legal orders to be adapted to the specificities of the investment-arbitration framework as well as the interpretive needs that may arise in the context of resolving a specific dispute. Bringing theory into the practice of arbitral decision-making, the next sections purport to thoroughly picture how exactly each legal argument is used in the arbitral decision-making process.

646. *Ibid.*

CHAPTER 6
Dialogical Network: Practice

§6.01 NARRATIVE ARGUMENTS

The Narrative-based arguments play their own particular role in the process of interpretation and eventually application of the law by the arbitrators.[647] These arguments reveal in what way arbitrators make reference to the factual and legal claims advanced by the parties when interpreting the law.

The dialogical network formed around the 'node' of the narrative arguments can be analysed into three strands of dialogue. The first type embodies the dialogue between the parties involved in the dispute. The 'story' told by the claimant in its submissions is juxtaposed to the one told by the respondent. Each party, or better the counsel of each party, portrays and interprets the facts and law in a specific way. Of course each 'story' is supported by the appropriate evidence. The dialogue formed between these two stories reveals their common points and differences assisting the decision-makers in reaching a full picture of the dispute while forming their own perspective of the story.

The interlocutors in the second type of dialogue are the arbitrators and the parties. The dialogue is performed between the stories told by the parties on the one hand and the arbitrators' views on how the facts and law should be interpreted on the other. The story of the arbitrators is either a revised form of the stories of the parties or a third different version.

Strongly connected to the above-mentioned types of dialogues is the third type of dialogue formed amongst the members of the arbitral tribunal.[648] The tribunal concludes with a specific story in the process of deliberation between the arbitrators. The

647. For the relationship between law and narrative *see generally* Robert Cover, 'Foreword: nomos and narrative' (1983) 97(1) HarvLRev 4.
648. *Estudio v. Puma Judgment of the Spanish Supreme Court* 102/2017 at p. 8 <https://internationalarbitrationblog.mccarthyblogs.com/wp-content/uploads/sites/50/2017/03/

arbitrators may either unanimously reach the same conclusions or there may be a dissenting opinion on certain issues.

The role of the decision-maker in the legal process is adapted according to the level of dialogue effectuated. In the first level of the dialogue, where the parties face an argumentation challenge, using written submissions as their armoury, the arbitrator has the role of the third objective observer, informed about the claims, counterclaims and strategies of the parties. The decision-making tasks are fully activated in the second and third dialogue levels where the arbitrators administer oral hearings and make a decision about the dispute on the basis of the claims, evidence and arguments presented in the argumentation challenge phase.

The significance of the use of narrative arguments in the decision-making process is double. First, it constrains the legal decision-making process into the confines of the specific factual dispute between the parties. The parties make reference to those factual circumstances that are relevant to the terms of the norms relied upon. The arbitrators will decide the dispute *in concreto* based on the facts presented and the legal framework relevant to those facts. In this context, the Narrative arguments restrain the interpretation process guaranteeing that any legal interpretation is connected to the facts of the case and the submissions of the parties. Conversely, the interpretation process restrains, at least in theory, the use of the narrative arguments since the facts referred to in the legal interpretation process should be those connected to the specific legal rules interpreted. On a second note, the use of narrative arguments reveals the interrelation between dialogue and persuasion. Viewing law as an argumentative discipline highlights the role of rhetoric since the interlocutors of a dialogue process aim at advancing an arguably sound legal and factual proposition.[649]

[A] Dialogue Between the Parties

In the investment-arbitration scene, the exchange of factual and legal arguments between the parties is well illustrated in both the arbitration rules and case law. The ICSID Arbitration Rules, setting the legal framework for the arbitration procedure, picture, in theoretical terms, the dialogue between the 'stories' of the claimant and the respondent. Within the context of the written procedure and in the specific time limits, the requesting party files a memorial containing a statement of the relevant facts, a statement of law and the submissions. The other party gives its answer to the claimant by filing a counter-memorial.[650] The pleading contains an admission or denial of the facts stated in the claimant's pleading, any additional facts, observations concerning

TSupremo-Civil-15-feb-2017.pdf> (accessed 4 Jul. 2018) (The Court held that collegiality is an important principle of international arbitration stressing on the importance of dialogue between arbitrators).

649. MacCormick, *Rhetoric and the Rule of Law: A Theory of Legal Reasoning* (n 172) 14–22; The role of facts in decision-making is just as important when it comes to weighing legal reasons. As an example, judges have been described as weighing concrete reasons by combining facts with standards rather than by taking into account abstract facts and standards. Burton, *Judging in Good Faith* (n 233) 54.

650. For the written procedure *see* Rule 31 ICSID Arbitration Rules.

the statement of law in the claimant's memorial, a statement of law in answer thereto and the submissions.[651] Where the parties agree or the Tribunal considers it necessary, this dialogue continues in the form of a reply by the requesting party on the defences previously raised by the responded and a rejoinder memorial by the respondent answering to the claimant's last responses. [652]

A similar procedural framework favouring both the dialogue between the parties and between each party and the tribunal can be found under the UNCITRAL framework. The claimant communicates its written statement of the claim, including the facts of the case, the legal arguments and the relief sought, to the respondent as well as to the members of the tribunal.[653] As a response to the claimant's positions, the other party communicates to the claimant and the arbitrators a written statement of defence.[654] The latter constitutes a reply to the facts of the case and the legal arguments as presented by the claimant, accompanied by any evidence relied upon.[655] The parties have the opportunity to amend or supplement the claim or defence.[656] Any type of dialogue formed in this context acquires transparency given the fact that any communication between one party and the arbitral tribunal should also be communicated by that party to all others.[657]

In investment arbitration, the written submissions of the parties are considered to be the most important component of the case presentation playing a significant role in the outcome of the dispute.[658] This procedure is characterised by both common law and civil law elements. While the common law elements of witness cross-examination and expanded document discovery are introduced, the importance of written submissions indicates an inclination towards the civil law pleading traditions.[659] From a practical perspective, oral hearings have a complementary function regarding the factual and legal issues already presented in the written submissions.[660]

Within this context, each party constructs its own narrative. The 'stories' of the parties present the facts of the case, the relevant legal norms and the connection of the facts to the legal principles. The careful exploration, organisation and presentation of the facts constitute the starting point of the dialogue between each party's 'story'. In order to assess each 'story', a first reading of the facts and supportive evidence presented frequently in a chronological order, offers useful insight into incentives and

651. Rule 31 (3) ICSID Arbitration Rules.
652. Rule 31 (1) ICSID Arbitration Rules.
653. UNCITRAL Arbitration Rules Article 20 (1).
654. *Ibid.* Article 21 (1).
655. *Ibid.* Article 21 (2).
656. *Ibid.* Article 22.
657. *Ibid.* Article 17 (4).
658. Mark Clodfelter, 'Written Proceedings in International Investment Arbitration' in Chiara Giorgetti (ed.) *Litigating International Investment Disputes: A Practitioner's Guide* (Nijhoff, 2014) 207.
659. *Ibid.*
660. Despite the equal interest in both phases, practice shows that arbitration practitioners put emphasis on the written submission phase. Clodfelter, 'Written Proceedings in International Investment Arbitration' (n 658) 207; *See also* Article 17 UNCITRAL Arbitration Rules; Rule 29 ICSID Arbitration Rules (Normal Procedures).

helps spotting evidentiary gaps.[661] The facts also play a significant role in shaping the decision-maker's opinion on the correct interpretation of the law.[662]

When it comes to the appropriate legal norms triggered by the facts, the parties' counsel face the challenge of choosing from an array of statutes, case law, literature and customary law principles. Given the fact that the process of connecting legal norms to the facts of the case is a continuous process, that evolves as relevant facts are explored and organised, legal principles acquire an importance from an early stage. In this context, a party may select an arbitrator who is familiar with the interpretation and application of a certain legal system.[663]

In other words, and laconically put, the dialogical process between the parties' stories usually takes the following form of thesis and antithesis:

> [...] claimant will file statement of claim, respondent submits its statement of defense, claimant presents a reply and respondent concludes with a rejoinder. In addition, the parties may request the right to file simultaneous or successive post-hearing briefs.[664]

Each party interprets the legal arguments advanced by the other in terms of a position and counter-position. Koskenniemi sets out a very interesting argumentative discourse structure which takes the form of:

Ax(-y) / By(-x);

A-x(y) / B-y(x).

He describes this structure in the following terms:

> Arguments proceed by arranging themselves first into contradiction which is then negated into its contrary. The initial positions of A and B ((x) and (y)) are first presented as contradicting (x = -y; y = -x). Because both remain vulnerable to the criticism from their opposite, they must move into another level to accommodate each other there. Here A comes to espouse B's initial point (y) and B comes to adopt A's first view (x). The arguments are both internally inconsistent and indeterminate. Neither set of arguments can be given preference as *they are ultimately the same*. The fact that they are presented by different States remains their only difference.[665]

Even though Koskenniemi refers to a public law dispute between two States, what also may come to surface for investment arbitration as well, is the reversibility of the parties' arguments. The parties may put emphasis on the same interests and concepts in order to conclude to different points. One example is when the host State puts forward the argument of individualism and the state's freedom to support its sovereignty when it comes to expropriation. At the same time, the private party may

661. Guillermo Aguilar-Alvarez, 'Written Advocacy' in Albert Jan van den Berg (ed.), *Arbitration Advocacy in Changing Times* (Kluwer Law International 2011) 55, 57.
662. Rudolf Bernhardt, 'Interpretation in International Law' in Rudolf Bernhardt (ed.) *Encyclopedia of Public International Law*, vol. 2 (n 273) 1417.
663. Aguilar-Alvarez, 'Written Advocacy' (n 661) 59.
664. *Ibid.* 55.
665. Koskenniemi, *From Apology to Utopia* (n 41) 510–511.

argue its right to compensation basing its arguments on the same points of individualism and good faith.[666] The task of the decision-maker in this setting becomes more complicated. What arises is the need for balancing the same interests but viewed from a different perspective.

In this context, the role of the arbitrator is twofold. The first task is the assessment of the 'internal validity' of the claim viewed in the absence of a counterargument.[667] The second task is an evaluation of the 'dialectical validity' of the claimant's 'story' and whether it predominates when compared to its counter-syllogism.[668]

Reference to each party's 'story' would be incomplete without reference to the genuine authors of these narratives – the counsel. The *Enron* tribunal clearly refers to the counsel's contribution to the formation of the arbitrator's own story:

> The Tribunal is again grateful to counsel for the parties for having undertaken a thorough explanation of their views on the issue of expropriation, invoking in support of their respective views a wealth of decisions, opinions of writers and other authorities that allow understanding the parties' arguments in all their meaning and differences.[669]

Counsel have the complicated task of considering the involvement of various national and international legal systems.[670] In combination with the specialised dispute resolution procedure and the interaction between public and private interests, they face different challenges than those appearing in other dispute resolution scenes. This transnational legal architecture of the investment-arbitration framework influences the expectations from the investment-arbitration counsel.[671] Drawing on the consensual nature of both the appointment of the arbitrators and the counsel they have both been described as 'agents of the parties' whose relationship should be collaborative.[672]

The role of the counsel has been characterised as 'a formative, if not the key formative, influence on investment jurisprudence'.[673] As eloquently put, good advocates 'know their case cold' but successful advocates will know the other party's case better.[674] Even though the submissions of the parties are rarely publically available, those chosen by the counsel's interpretation styles as pictured in the arbitral award delineate 'the intellectual construct, composed of factual narratives and legal argument, within which tribunals make their decision'.[675] 'Ideal' legal representation in

666. *Ibid.* 509 et seq.
667. Henry Prakken, 'A Formal Model of Adjudication Dialogues' (2008) 16(3) AI&L 305, 308.
668. *Ibid.*
669. *Enron* (n 581) para. 240.
670. *See* Doak Bishop and Edward G Kehoe (eds) *The Art of Advocacy in International Arbitration* (2nd ed., Juris 2010).
671. Donald Francis Donovan, 'The Transnational Advocate' in Albert Jan van den Berg (ed.), *Arbitration Advocacy in Changing Times*, ICCA Congress Series, vol. 15 (Kluwer Law International 2011) 4–5.
672. *Ibid.* 5.
673. Thomas Wälde, 'Interpreting Investment Treaties: Experiences and Examples' in Christina Binder and others (eds) *International Investment Law for the 21st Century: Essays in Honour of Christoph Schreuer* (OUP 2009) 726.
674. Aguilar-Alvarez, 'Written Advocacy' (n 661) 57.
675. Wälde, 'Interpreting Investment Treaties' (n 673) 726.

investment disputes has been described as having the following transnational characteristics:

> [It will include expertise connected to] 'both public international law, international arbitration and comparative public/administrative law. It will go beyond rules and concepts that may be academically known and researchable, to include the much more arcane areas of the advocacy and politics of investment arbitration e.g., arbitrator and chair selection; proclivities of appointment institutions; and personal, professional, institutional and philosophical linkages and preferences'.[676]

Reality reveals that the quality of advocacy in investment arbitration differs from one case to another.[677] Inexperienced pleaders may aim at leading the other party to a quick settlement rather than the substantive arguing of the case before the tribunal.[678] Landau also points out that oral presentations are not always used as a means to 'advance the debate' by creating a 'road map' on 'how to get from here to the award' but often repeat the arguments of the written submissions, thus failing to persuade and connect with the tribunal.[679]

In cases where a party is not effectively represented, the question that arises as to whether the tribunal has a duty to restore the ability of the party to present its case. In the context of judicial proceedings, there are two main views.[680] According to the principle of presumed equality of the parties, in the adversarial proceedings each party must be given the opportunity to present its case rendering irrelevant the fact whether this occurs or not.[681] There is also the opposing view that the responsibility of the decision-maker to ensure the equality of arms requires intervention from the court in one way or another. In the field of investment arbitration, the case law is not clear on the issue. Nevertheless, what becomes important is the need for legal expertise of the counsel.[682] The tribunal's engagement in a dialogue with them may reveal, in a non-biased way, the absence of such legal expertise.

[B] Dialogue Between the Parties and the Tribunal

MacCormick well remarks that there are two kind of narratives or stories: the first is the one put forward by the parties in their submissions and the second one is the 'story of the trial' where arguments are tested, witnesses are called and proof is provided.[683]

676. Thomas Wälde, 'Equality of Arms' in Investment Arbitration: Procedural Challenges' in Katia Yanacca Small (ed.), *Arbitration under International Investment Agreements – A Guide to the Key Issues* (OUP 2012) 161, 177.
677. *See* Pierre Lalive, 'Threats to International Investment Arbitration' (1986) 1(1) ICSID Rev 26.
678. Paulsson, 'Awards-and Awards' (n 418) 102–103.
679. Toby Landau, 'Luncheon Address: Advocacy in International Arbitration' (2011) 5 WAMR 351, 459.
680. Wälde, 'Equality of Arms' in Investment Arbitration' (n 676) 179.
681. Arbitrator B mentions that in the case where a party is not represented by an arbitrator, to some extent, he/she will have to make the case for the unrepresented party in order to have a form of adversarial proceedings. *See* Annex 'Interview Questions'.
682. Wälde, 'Equality of Arms' in Investment Arbitration' (n 676) 180.
683. MacCormick, *Rhetoric and the Rule of Law: A Theory of Legal Reasoning* (n 172) 228.

In a litigation proceeding the judge's role in the argumentation phase, where the parties exchange arguments and counter-arguments, is to supervise the respect of the procedural rules by the parties, to decide on the admissibility of evidence, to allocate the burden of proof and regulate turntaking.[684] In investment arbitration, the oral procedure resumes the dialogical spirit of the written submission phase giving to the arbitrators, this time, the role of the interlocutor. During the hearing, the tribunal may ask questions to each party in order to request explanations.[685] It may also require the parties to produce documents, witnesses and experts.[686] In contrast to mediators who promote 'integrative, collaborative interactive reasoning', both arbitrators and parties actively argue.[687] The explicit arguments of the arbitrators are found in the arbitral award.[688]

The dialogue continues in the post-award phase with the negative or positive reaction of the parties to the award. The response of the parties to the decision-maker and its award may be positive from the winning party when trying to enforce the award and negative from the losing party in the event it decides to challenge the award or refuse its enforcement. In an attempt to continue the dialogue on a social and epistemic basis, the post-award phase opens the road for a dialogue between the award and its commentary and 'social' assessment by NGOs, international and European organisations, national and international literature, blogs and social media.

The description of the relevant facts and the process of pleading and providing admissible evidence have an inevitable narrative character.[689] Steven Barton describes a 'case' as a 'short story of an incident'.[690] The parties' stories connect a certain interpretation and presentation of the facts of the case to legal norms and their consequences. Such stories, however, are also framed based on certain party-oriented policies. The facts and the law are interpreted in a certain way that favours the economic or other expectations of each party.

As eloquently described, persuasion is the purpose of the 'trial communication'.[691] Against this background, the parties translate their idiosyncratic views into a language that is adapted to the dispute resolution environment. The parties during the written and oral procedures create strands of various arguments in order to persuade

684. Prakken, 'A Formal Model of Adjudication Dialogues' (n 667) 307; *See* Sir Robert Jennings, 'The Differences Between Conducting a Case in the ICJ and in Ad Hoc Arbitration Tribunal – An Inside View' in Liber Amicorum Judge Shigeru Oda (Brill 2002) 893–909.
685. Rule 32 (3) ICSID Arbitration Rules; Arbitrator A supports that 'if the parties have not argued a point well then it's a problem because the case may go in a certain direction simply because the parties didn't make the right arguments'. *See* Annex 'Interview Questions'.
686. Rule 34 (2) ICSID Arbitration Rules.
687. Walker and Daniels, *Argument and Alternative Dispute Resolution Systems* (n 58) 698.
688. *Ibid.* Arbitrator J describes the role of party submissions stating: 'We start as arbitrators by reading the parties submission and going to the awards that they prioritise, so rightly or wrongly that can set the framework for analysis.'
689. MacCormick, *Rhetoric and the Rule of Law: A Theory of Legal Reasoning* (n 172) 40.
690. Steven Burton, *An Introduction to Law and Legal Reasoning* (Little, Brown & Co 1985) 11.
691. Clements, *Perception and Persuasion in Legal Argumentation: Using Informal Fallacies and Cognitive Biases to Win the War of Words* (n 415) 329.

the decision-maker about their soundness and acceptability.[692] Duncan Kennedy describes a persuasive legal argument as the combination of 'argument bites' that are formed in connection to the facts of the case.[693] The decision-maker has the triple role of the interlocutor, the narrator and the creator of the 'synthesis'.

Going a step further, the arbitrator will employ his/her own rhetoric skills when reasoning the award.[694] The *Enron* tribunal provides a fine illustration of how arbitrators may form their story with reference to the party's prevailing contribution to it: 'The Tribunal is grateful to counsel for the parties for the detailed arguments with which they have assisted the Tribunal in the examination of this claim. The Tribunal finds the Claimants' arguments [...] persuasive.'[695] However, the tribunal commented on the narrative techniques of the parties and in particular those of the claimant who claimed simultaneously direct and an indirect expropriation. It asserted that a given measure cannot qualify at the same time both as a direct and indirect expropriation given the fact that their nature and extent is different.[696] However, the claim was not rejected for that particular reason since the measure complained of was 'completely substantiated'.[697]

This type of dialogue opens the door for 'rhetoric' in the decision-making of arbitral tribunals which aims to persuade about the veracity of the arguments advanced. The question that arises here is to what extent arbitrators are influenced by the rhetorical techniques each party employs when presenting their case. Arbitrator H and A mentioned that an experienced arbitrator is well able to distinguish such rhetorical techniques and focus on the substantive issues of the parties' submissions.[698] In the

692. It has also been mentioned that 'tribunals should be particularly vigilant to ensure that they test thoroughly the legal case advanced and should not hesitate to introduce a focus on the legal issues during the course of an oral hearing where appropriate'. Judith Gill, 'The Development of Legal Argument in Arbitration' in David Caron and others, *Practising Virtue* (n 3) 407; Arbitrator H commented on how he/she recognises any rhetorical techniques counsel use: 'I am very proactive myself, so if I see an argument that I find for example very attractive, I will try to fight for result at the hearing – I will ask the counsel – what about this, what about that, what about what your opponent says – and obviously a good counsel would be prepared for this sort of thing and will be able to even persuade me more and if I cannot manage to unsettle them; then that's a very good point in their paper]'. *See* Annex 'Interview Questions'.
693. Duncan Kennedy, *A Critique of Adjudication* (HUP 1997) 137 et seq; *See also* Jean d'Aspremont arguing that: 'international lawyers, while trying to give meaning to legal rules (content-determination) or while engaging in the identification of rules (law-ascertainment), necessarily commit themselves to certain techniques, rhetoric, and traditions that are provided by the normative universe of international law'. Jean d'Aspremont, 'The Multidimensional Process of Interpretation' in Andrea Bianchi, Daniel Peat, and Matthew Windsor (eds) *Interpretation in International Law* (n 59) 112 et seq.
694. *See* Part III 'Rhetoric'.
695. *Enron*, Award (n 581) para. 127.
696. *Ibid.* para. 250.
697. *Ibid.* para. 250.
698. *See* Annex 'Interview Questions'. Additionally, Arbitrator J stated that 'A good advocate will always use effective rhetorical techniques that get your attention but only if they are using rhetoric to illustrate what is the law.' Arbitrator I stated that 'It depends on the arbitrator, there are some that are less subject to advocacy than others. [...] Skilled advocate use techniques all the time. My sense is that you cannot make a bad case good and you cannot make a good case ultimately bad but you can change the impact of those cases that are not so clear.'

context of the *Thunderbird* dispute, Thomas Wälde, in his separate opinion remarks that:

> It is therefore particularly important for a tribunal not to get influenced, directly or indirectly, by 'insinuations' meant to colour and influence the arbitrators' perception and activate a conscious or subconscious bias, but to make the decision purely on grounds that have been subject to a full and fair hearing by both parties. Cards should be placed, 'face up', on the table rather than be waved around, with hints and suggestions.[699]

Despite the fact that the presentation of the case by the parties is considered to be close to rhetoric, the effectiveness of rhetoric 'is likely to be that which rests on a clear understanding of the implicit logic of the process'.[700] In light of the emphasis placed on legal argumentation through dialogue, law appears to be 'something arguable, sometimes, but not always, conclusively, always at least persuasively'.[701]

Nonetheless, there are checks and balances to these rhetorical techniques that can assure a decision-making process based on the interpretation of the law by an objective decision-maker and not only on persuasion. The resolution of a particular dispute also requires its legal evaluation based on criteria outside of the dispute between the parties. Criteria such as rules and case law ensure the resolution of the dispute in such a way that is 'fair, functional, and consistent with moral values and meanings'.[702] In addition, they minimise the rhetoric focus, placing significance on the legal aspect of decision-making as a stable and predictable process.

[C] Dialogue Between the Arbitrators of the Tribunal

The dialogue between the arbitrators and the parties described above helps the decision-makers to reach a conclusion regarding the interpretation and application of the law. A large part of the arbitrators' knowledge and comprehension of the dispute comes from the evidence and arguments that are presented by the parties in the arbitration hearings.[703] However, the conclusions themselves need to be justified through arguments and by balancing the possibilities arising.[704]

---

699. *International Thunderbird*, Separate Opinion of Thomas Wälde (n 630) para. 20.
700. MacCormick, *Rhetoric and the Rule of Law: A Theory of Legal Reasoning* (n 172) 43.
701. *Ibid.* 15.
702. Edwards, 'The Convergence of Analogical and Dialectic Imaginations in Legal Discourse' (n 521) 9–11.
703. Frank Elkouri and Edna Elkouri, *How Arbitration Works* (4th ed., Bureau of National Affairs Washington 1985) 237.
704. MacCormick, *Rhetoric and the Rule of Law: A Theory of Legal Reasoning* (n 172) 42; Arbitrator H describes his/her role in the decision-making process: 'in the hearing, interestingly, I try to forget everything that I have learned and I listen to [the parties'] story – so it's the same story but called by the advocates verbally in a different way; and then the hearing goes on; you hear witnesses and then you hear the submissions on the law; and then you go away and you have a transcript and the first thing I do after the hearing is to read the transcript. When you are in the hearing and you have things going on and you listen, a lot of it sinks in and then that's what you see in writing again'. *See* Annex 'Interview Questions'.

In the deliberation phase the dialogue takes place between the arbitrators through their opinions expressed regarding the dispute.[705] Deliberation amongst the members of the tribunal may take various forms such as:

> [...] the exchange of written memoranda; the exchange of written memoranda and then an oral deliberation or deliberations; oral deliberations to determine tentative views and then an exchange of written memoranda; or a series of written memoranda, draft opinions, and oral deliberations.[706]

After the closure of the proceedings, the arbitrators deliberate without the presence of the parties in order to render the award. During this private session, the decision-makers discuss the merits of the presentation of each party aiming at a consensus on the outcome of the dispute. What should also be noted at this point is the role of each arbitrator to advance the dialogue in a certain way. Parties but also arbitrators have the perception that party-appointed arbitrators participate in the dialogue having a specific perspective and are expected to 'translate' into the dialogue the arguments of the parties that appointed them.[707] This way they may assist the other members of the tribunal with understanding the view of the party that appointed them.[708] In a similar vein, the presiding arbitrator is perceived as a 'moderator' and the final decision-maker in the dialogue.[709]

After the completion of the deliberations, the presiding arbitrator is the one who usually drafts the award incorporating the comments of each arbitrator. The arguments of the other members of the tribunal are put forward when commenting upon the draft award. In the context of this dialogue, the award may be redrafted several times before the arbitrators agree on the final version. Of course, aim of each discussion is not only to reach to a consensus but the fruitful exchange of opinions that advance knowledge. The arbitrator that has a different view on questions of law or fact issues a dissenting opinion, which may not have legal force, but may acquire persuasive force in future cases.[710]

The private character of the deliberation phase makes it difficult to comprehend in detail the practical side of how each decision-maker engages in a discussion with the other. Nonetheless, the *CME Czech Republic B.V. v. Czech Republic* case sheds some light on this process.[711] In this dispute, the Czech Republic sought to set aside the

705. *See generally* Bernhard Berger and Michael Schneider (eds) *Inside the Black Box: How Arbitral Tribunals Operate and Reach Their Decisions* (Juris 2013).
706. Richard Mosk, 'Deliberations of Arbitrators' in David Caron and others, *Practising Virtue* (n 3) 495.
707. Lawrence Newman and David Zaslowsky, 'The Party-Appointed Arbitrator Dialectic' (2009) 242(20) International Litigation 2.
708. Chiara Giorgetti, 'Who Decides Who Decides in International Investment Arbitration?' (2013) 35 UPaJIntlL 431, 473; For the issue of how impartiality is ensured in this context *see* Rogers, 'The Vocation of International Arbitrators' (n 134) 957.
709. Newman and Zaslowsky, *The Party-Appointed Arbitrator Dialectic* (n 707) 2. Laurent Lévy, 'The Chairman's Role in the Arbitral Tribunal's Dynamics' in Bernard Hanotiau and Alexis Mourre (eds), *Dossier IX: Players' Interaction in International Arbitration* (Dossiers of the ICC Institute of World Business Law 2012) 67–85.
710. *See generally* Paulsson, 'Awards-and Awards' (n 418) 99–102.
711. *See* Christopher Dugan and others, *Investor-State Arbitration* (OUP 2012) 180.

tribunal's award in the national court of the place of arbitration, in Stockholm. Amongst other reasons, the Czech Republic argued that the arbitrator it had appointed was excluded from participating in the deliberations in violation of UNCITRAL and Swedish law. After depicting the communications between the arbitrators in the process of deliberation, the Court of Appeal found that Hándl, the respondent-appointed arbitrator, had received due time to submit comments to the draft award as well as all essential communications between the arbitrators:

> It has been testified that essentially all significant issues were discussed at the meeting. Both Schwebel [claimant-appointed arbitrator] and Kühn [chairman] have stated that Hándl [respondent-appointed arbitrator] was the one who spoke most. The focal point of the deliberations must be deemed to have been the list of questions, the answers thereto, and the discussions between the arbitrators in Düsseldorf [...].[712]

Diving into the adyta of arbitral deliberations is a difficult task that requires thorough empirical research. It could be useful, however, to attempt to draw some analogies from the way the judges frame the case in the civil and common law procedures. English decision-makers present both similarities and differences in comparison to their German colleagues. The common feature in both systems is the task of the decision-makers to narrow the case down to a point where a decision can be reached.[713] Their differences lie in the way the case is framed by the decision-maker. In the English system, the case gains its judicial profile largely based on the skills of the barrister and the detailed judgment is framed with 'facts, particulars and precedents'.[714] The German decision-maker will deal separately with the facts and the law where the latter '[...] may be characterised as positivistic and idealistic, but sometimes remote from the very facts of the decided case'.[715] As described:

> [...] in the English system the judges spend time, care and skill largely in opening up a case from a summarized form to a more detailed state of factual accuracy in a time-consuming oral hearing, which ends with an elaborate account of the facts and reasons in the judgment. [...] the German judgments rarely show ambitions to elaborate facts and to draw a decision from the very facts in detail. On the contrary, there is a tendency to rely mainly on the statute law and to attempt logical statements in order to justify the decision of the court. The German tendency of justification by > statutory arguments < leads to the significance of substantive law in civil litigation.[716]

712. *Czech Republic v. CME Czech Republic B.V.*, Challenge of arbitral award-Svea Court of Appeal Judgment, Case No. T 8735-01 (15 May 2003) 87 et seq.
713. Oskar Hartwieg, *Tatsachen und Normarbeit im Rechtsvergleich* (Mohr Siebeck 2003) 86; *See also* Basil Markesinis, 'Judicial Style and Judicial Reasoning in England and Germany' (2000) 59(2) The Cambridge Law Journal, 294-309 (the author offers insights into judicial thinking and the differences between legal systems when one places judgments from two different systems next to one another and compares their style of reasoning as well as the way they resolve substantive issues).
714. *Ibid.* 86.
715. *Ibid.*
716. *Ibid.* 90.

In investment arbitration the decision-makers give great importance to the submissions of the parties as they delimit the power of the tribunal to decide on a specific dispute. The Tribunal's mandate cannot go beyond the limits framed by the parties in their submissions. In the *Generation Ukraine* case the arbitral tribunal specifies this task in the following words:

> The task of the Arbitral Tribunal, however, is not to rule on every allegation, but rather to determine whether the claims for relief are founded or not. It is, therefore, constrained only to deal with those arguments which it finds to be decisive with respect to the relief sought.[717]

The award is the final 'product' of the arbitration procedure written by the arbitrators-authors. Each author chooses to write its award in a personalised way.[718] Typically, arbitrators choose to tell their story by referring to the claimant's and respondent's stories and finally by presenting their story in the form of 'stichomythia'. The 'stichomythia' style expresses a 'dialogue in which two characters speak alternate lines of verse, used as a stylistic device in ancient Greek drama'.[719] An example of this narrative style can be found in the *Bosh* award where the tribunal grouped the particular issues treated in the decision. After presenting the facts of the dispute it used the following style in order to address the issue of applicable law, jurisdiction, admissibility and attribution: (1) Position of the Claimant (2) Position of the Respondent (3) Determination of the Tribunal.[720]

What comes up as a necessity at this point is the unbiased and objective assessment of the arguments of each party from a holistic perspective based on both the factual and legal points advanced. The dialogical network of the narrative arguments formed depicts the interaction between the arguments of the parties and the arguments of the arbitrators regarding both the facts and the law as a unity.

[D] Expanding the Dialogue Through Third Parties

Third-party participation in arbitral proceedings raises questions of the evolving role of *amicus curiae*, or third-party intervention in the arbitration procedure. Arbitral tribunals have well defined the role of an *amicus curiae* focusing on the fact that they are not considered as parties to the proceedings:

> The traditional role of an amicus curiae in an adversary proceeding is to help the decision maker arrive at its decision by providing the decision maker with

717. *Generation Ukraine, Inc. v. Ukraine*, ICSID Case No. ARB/00/9, ICSID, Award (16 Sep. 2003) para. 5.2.
718. Despite the fact that the structure of arbitral awards varies, the generic features they contain are the following: (1) Introduction / The parties / (2) Procedural History/ Summary of procedure (3) Summary of facts and Parties' Contentions/ Factual Background (4) Analysis of issues/ Considerations/ Applicable law/ Legal Considerations (5) Decision. Vázquez-Orta, 'Authoritative Intervention in Legal Discourse' (n 58) 96.
719. Oxford dictionaries <www.oxforddictionnaries.com> (accessed 10 May 2018).
720. *Bosh International, Inc and B&P Ltd Foreign Investments Enterprise v. Ukraine*, ICSID Case No. ARB/08/11, Award (25 Oct. 2012).

arguments, perspectives and expertise that the litigating parties may not provide. In short, a request to act as amicus curiae is an offer of assistance – an offer that the decision maker is free to accept or reject. An amicus curiae is a volunteer, a friend of the court, not a party.[721]

The participation of *amicus curiae* usually has the form of written submissions addressed to the decision-maker.[722] Especially in the dialogue context, what seems a logical consequence is to investigate what position third parties have, if any, in this world of dialogical networks. In this setting, new dialogues may be formed with the submission of *amicus curiae* briefs between the parties to the dispute, the arbitrators and the third parties.

The ICSID arbitration rules regulate two types of *amicus* participation, through written submissions ((Rule 37(2)) and the attendance of the hearings ((Rule 32(2)). The participation of third parties in the hearings is subject to any objection of the parties to the dispute. Furthermore, ICSID tribunals have the discretion to accept written submissions from interested third parties. The tribunal may allow a non-disputing party submission after opening a dialogue with both parties in order to consult them on the issue.[723] As a further step, the tribunal should also open a dialogue with the content of the third-party submissions in order to consider, *inter alia*, whether it will assist the tribunal to determine any factual or legal issue by conveying a perspective, particular knowledge or insight that is different from that of the parties to the dispute.[724] Such a communication, however, is framed with safeguards limiting the third parties mostly to written submissions without permitting them to enhance their arguments with discovery of documents and evidence-taking that would affect the efficiency and speed of the proceedings.

The dialogue also expands to the communication of the disputing parties with the third parties. The tribunal should ensure that both parties have an opportunity to present their observations on non-disputing party submissions.[725] This dialogue opportunity ensures that the parties are able to comment on, discuss and even respond to what has been pronounced in the third-party submissions ensuring at the same time that the parties remain the main actors of the arbitral proceedings.

The NAFTA Free Trade Commission issued a statement on non-disputing party participation in order to ensure the interests of fairness and the orderly conduct of the arbitration proceedings.[726] The guidelines towards the tribunal on its discretion to

721. *Suez, Sociedad General de Aguas de Barcelona, S.A. and Vivendi Universal, S.A. v. Argentine Republic, (formerly Aguas Argentinas, S.A., Suez, Sociedad General de Aguas de Barcelona, S.A. and Vivendi Universal, S.A. v. Argentine Republic*, ICSID Case No. ARB/03/19, Order in Response to Transparency and Amicus Curiae Petition (19 May 2005) para. 13; Schreuer, *The ICSID Convention: A Commentary* (n 269) 705.
722. Lance Bartholomeusz, 'The Amicus Curiae Before International Courts and Tribunals' (2005) 5 NSAIL 209, 211.
723. Rule 37 (2) ICSID Arbitration Rules.
724. Rule 37 (2) (a) ICSID Arbitration Rules. The Tribunals should further consider whether: '(b) the non-disputing party submission would address matter within the scope of the dispute; (c) the non-disputing party has a significant interest in the proceeding'.
725. Rule 37 (2) ICSID Arbitration Rules.
726. Statement of the Free Trade Commission on non-disputing party participation <http://www.state.gov/documents/organization/38791.pdf> (accessed 8 Nov. 2018).

accept written submissions by third parties constitutes at the same time the delimitation of the dialogue networks formed in this procedure.[727] In general terms, the criteria on which the tribunal will accept third-party written submissions are the same as in the ICSID framework.[728] Additionally, the third party should specifically identify which issues of fact and law in the arbitration are addressed in the written submission.[729] The traces of the dialogue between each party and the non-disputing party can be found in the process of identifying the legal and factual issues the third party will comment on. These issues, having already been specifically addressed by each party will constitute the starting point based on which the third party will launch a discussion with the party-views presented therein. As a response, the disputing parties may comment in writing on the non-disputing party submission.[730] However, the dialogue is limited, consistent with the fact that *amici* do not have the status of a party to the dispute. In this spirit, the non-disputing party that filed the submission is not entitled to make further submissions in the arbitration.[731]

However limited, the dialogue strands that can be formed with the participation of *amicus curiae* submissions play a special role in the de-fragmentation of international law through the interaction between investment law and human rights or EU law. There are calls that international investment law and its interpretation are consistent with international law, including human rights, multilateral environmental treaties and WTO law.[732] The lack of awareness that the international scene requires coordinating features may lead to national systems increasingly becoming subject to conflicting instructions from different supranational legal frameworks.[733] The *amici* participating in an arbitral procedure may inform the decision-maker of the different legal regimes that are associated with the particular dispute introducing once more a dynamic and non-statist transnational decision-making aspect. This constitutes a means of ensuring that the international system of laws develops as a whole in which each of its branches informs the other rather than as a rigid and fractured discipline.[734]

727. *See* Barnali Choudhury, 'Recapturing Public Power: Is Investment Arbitration's Engagement of the Public Interest Contributing to the Democratic Deficit?' (2008) 41 VandJTransnatL 775, 809.
728. *See* part B (6) of the Statement (n 726).
729. *See* part B (2) (g) of the Statement.
730. *See* part B (8) of the Statement.
731. *See* part B (9) of the Statement; A stark illustration of an *amicus* submission is the case of *Chevron v. Ecuador.* The Tribunal replied to the *amici*, which was 'The International Institute for Sustainable Development (IISD)' that after consulting the Parties, both in writing and during the oral hearings on jurisdiction, and after considering the Petition submitted and the comments of the Parties, it has decided not to permit the participation of the Petitioners in the proceedings as *amici curiae*, 'Letter to Amici from Permanent Court of Arbitration' (26 Apr. 2011) <https://www.italaw.com/cases/257> (accessed 2 Jul. 2018), *Chevron Corporation and Texaco Petroleum Corporation v. The Republic of Ecuador*, UNCITRAL, PCA Case No. 2009-23.
732. Anne van Aaken, 'Fragmentation of International Law: The Case of International Investment Protection' (2008) USGL&Econ Working Paper No. 2008-01, vol XVII 91, 92.
733. Eugenia Levine, 'Amicus Curiae in International Investment Arbitration: The Implications of an Increase in Third-Party Participation' (2011) 29 BerkeleyJIntlL 200, 218.
734. *Ibid.* 219.

§6.02 CONVENTION ARGUMENTS

The Vienna Convention on the Law of Treaties constitutes the main point of reference when decision-makers interpret international treaties. Article 31(1) VCLT provides that international treaties must be interpreted in 'good faith in accordance with the ordinary meaning to be given to the terms of the treaty in their context and in the light of its object and purpose'. Treaty interpretation in this context includes the following approaches: the textual approach (ordinary-plain meaning of the text), the contextual approach, the teleological approach, the relevant rules of international law applicable to the parties and the negotiating history. This process may be followed in practice step-by-step but there is also another view that considers the application of Article 31 as 'one integrated 'rule' (singular) rather than a number of rules to be applied in sequence'.[735] Some tribunals highlight the customary international law nature of these rules[736] and others also make reference to the supplementary rules of interpretation as pictured in Article 32 VCLT.[737] The supplementary means of interpretation clearly referred to in Article 32 are the preparatory work of the treaty and the circumstances of its conclusion, which usually include (written) minutes of negotiation proceedings and interpretive statements by the drafting committee.[738] Nonetheless, decision-makers rely on further supplementary means such as testimonials of former negotiators of investment treaties.[739]

The so-called principles or rules of treaty interpretation of the VCLT have been portrayed as 'principles of logic and good sense valuable only as guides to assist in appreciating the meaning which the parties may have intended to attach to the

735. Wälde, 'Interpreting Investment Treaties' (n 673) 751; *See also* Ulf Linderfalk, 'Is the Hierarchical Structure of Arts 31 and 32 of the Vienna Convention Real or Not? Interpreting the Rules of Interpretation' (2007) 54 NILR 133.
736. *Camuzzi International S.A. v. The Argentine Republic*, ICSID Case No. ARB/03/2, Decision on objection to jurisdiction (11 May 2005) paras 133, 134 (citations omitted); *Aguas Del Tunari v. Republic of Bolivia*, ICSID Case No. ARB/02/3, Decision on Objection to Jurisdiction (21 Oct. 2005) para. 88.
737. Makane Mbengue, 'Rules of Interpretation (Art. 32 of the Vienna Convention on the Law of Treaties)' (2016) 31(2) ICSID Rev 388; *Maritime International Nominees Establishment v. Republic of Guinea*, ICSID Case No. ARB/84/4, Decision on Annulment (14 Dec. 1989), para. 5.10; *Noble Ventures v. Romania*, ICSID Case No. ARB/01/11, Award (12 Oct. 2005) para. 50 (The Tribunal stated: 'Accordingly, treaties have to be interpreted in good faith in accordance with the ordinary meaning to be given to the terms of the treaty in their context and in the light of the object and purpose of the Treaty, while recourse may be had to supplementary means of interpretation, including the preparatory work and the circumstances of its conclusion, only in order to confirm the meaning resulting from the application of the aforementioned methods of interpretation. Reference should also be made to the principle of effectiveness (effet utile), which, too plays an important role in interpreting treaties'
738. Luigi Sbolci, 'Supplementary Means of Interpretation', in E Cannizzaro (ed.) *The Law of Treaties Beyond the Vienna Convention* (OUP 2011) 144–163.
739. Makane Mbengue, 'Rules of Interpretation (Art. 32 of the Vienna Convention on the Law of Treaties)' (n 737) 388, 396 (The author refers to the *Sempra Energy v. Argentina* case where the Tribunal stated that 'the opinion of those who were responsible for the drafting and negotiation of a State's bilateral treaties [is not] irrelevant, in that it serves, precisely, to establish the original intention', *Sempra Energy International v. Argentine Republic*, ICSID Case No. ARB/02/16, Decision on Objections to Jurisdiction (11 May 2005) para. 145).

expressions that they employed in a document'.[740] In particular, they have been described as being 'neither rules, nor principles in the classical sense of 'something [...] which underlies a rule, and explains or provides the reason for it'.[741] Continuing the negative definition, they are neither 'merely maxims with equal and opposite force'.[742] Rather '[t]hey underlie the interpretation of the rule, not the rule itself [helping] answer why a rule is to be given one meaning and not another'.[743] Consistent with this line of reasoning, the VCLT interpretive rules are general propositions that are better viewed as 'over-arching argumentative structures' that acquire substance once more specific arguments are introduced.[744] In arbitral decision-making, the issue that arises is twofold: How do investment-arbitration tribunals use the VCLT interpretation principles and are the latter effective to treat all interpretational issues that arise in the context of an investment arbitration?

[A] The Use of the VCLT by Investment-Arbitration Tribunals

The use of the VCLT by arbitral tribunals is a topic that, at first sight, may seem to entail a straightforward analysis concluding with the fact that arbitrators distinctively use these principles for the interpretation of investment treaties. If only the answer was so simple. The issues that may arise go far beyond such an analysis. Based on this way of thinking, the present section deals with the following questions: Does the fact that certain arbitral tribunals do not clearly refer to the methodology of the VCLT mean that they disregard the Convention? Reversely, does the fact that arbitrators refer to the VCLT in their awards mean that they actually use these interpretive rules in their reasoning?

The first question is whether the lack of description of the treaty interpretation rules applied by the tribunal can be translated as a disregard to the recognised international rules of treaty interpretation. The ad hoc Committee in the *Lucchetti* case noted that although the interpretation given by the tribunal 'does not reflect all relevant aspects of treaty interpretation according to the Vienna Convention, the Committee has no basis for concluding that the tribunal disregarded any significant element of the well-known and widely-recognised international rules of treaty interpretation'.[745] Based on this argument it concluded that although the tribunal's reasoning was 'summary and somewhat simplified in relation to the Vienna Convention' it did not

740. 'Draft Articles on the Law of Treaties with commentaries 1966' (n 150) para. 4.
741. Isabelle Van Damme, 'Jurisdiction, Applicable Law, and Interpretation' in Daniel Bethlehem and others (eds), *The Oxford Handbook of International Trade Law* (OUP 2009) 322 (citations omitted).
742. Van Damme, *Treaty Interpretation by the WTO Appellate Body* (n 180) 381.
743. Van Damme, 'Jurisdiction, Applicable Law, and Interpretation' (n 741) 322 (citations omitted).
744. Iain Scobbie, 'Rhetoric, Persuasion, and Interpretation in International Law' in Andrea Bianchi, Daniel Peat, and Matthew Windsor (eds) *Interpretation in International Law* (n 59) 75 (e.g., such specific arguments may be 'the adverse party's prior practice, its interpretative views expressed in official statements to international organizations or conferences, or in diplomatic *démarches*, or even in statements to the press').
745. *Lucchetti* Annulment (n 539) para. 116; *See also* Anthea Roberts, 'Power and Persuasion in Investment Treaty Arbitration: The Dual Role of States' (2010) 104 AJIL, 179.

constitute an excess of the tribunal's powers according to Article 52(1)(b) of the Convention.[746]

What is interesting in the context of the same case is the dissenting opinion of Sir Franklin Berman who made the distinction between 'supposing that the tribunal must have applied the proper rules of treaty interpretation' and 'adequately explaining what the tribunal did in the interpretative process in order to conclude to a specific interpretive outcome on the basis of which it declined jurisdiction'.[747] According to his analysis, the tribunal did not 'diligently and systematically apply the Vienna Convention rules at all, let alone with the particular care the situation would seem to have dictated'.[748] In this respect, the award was considered not to meet the accepted standard of reasoning. As a result, what remains important is to analyse what practice reveals for the interpretation practice of the tribunal. Sometimes, action goes beyond words:

> But to suppose that the Tribunal must have applied the proper rules of treaty interpretation is not, to my way of thinking, the end of the matter. The real question [...] is whether they adequately explained what they were doing in the interpretative process [...]. And the only way to answer that question, given that the Tribunal (somewhat surprisingly, I think) did neglect to tell us what they were doing, is to look to what the Tribunal actually did as evidence of what rules they were applying.[749]

Based on the above considerations, there is no certainty that a decision will disclose all the elements taken into account and the weight placed on them by the decision-maker.[750] The majority of the arbitrators interviewed also confirmed the fact that arbitral awards do not reveal the whole process of interpretation followed.[751] So, how do arbitral tribunals use the VCLT principles of interpretation?

The drafters of the VCLT never claimed to have restrained the interpretive power of the decision-maker by cataloguing all the possible methods of interpretation.[752] Consequently, the VCLT is not considered to include an exhaustive list of interpretive techniques as there is no mention for example of *lex specialis* or *lex posterior* even though they are used in the interpretation process.[753] The International Law Commission did not include a list of interpretation principles as it maintained that 'recourse to many of these principles is discretionary rather than obligatory and the interpretation of documents is to some extent an art, not an exact science'.[754] As a result, the VCLT

746. *Ibid.* para. 116.
747. *Ibid.* para. 6.
748. Lucchetti, *Annulment-Dissent* (n 143) para. 12.
749. *Ibid.* para. 6.
750. Van Damme, 'Jurisdiction, Applicable Law, and Interpretation' (n 741) 322.
751. Arbitrator A was the only one considering that the reasoning depicts the whole interpretation and application of the law process followed. *See* Annex 'Interview Questions'; *See also* §4.02[A]'Errors of Law'.
752. Van Damme, *Treaty Interpretation by the WTO Appellate Body* (n 180) 381.
753. Koskenniemi, 'Fragmentation of International Law' (n 259) para. 427.
754. Wälde, 'Interpreting Investment Treaties' (n 673) 729 citing 'Draft Articles on the Law of Treaties (1966), Commentary to the (then) Article 27'.

is present in the legal decision-making of investment tribunals but without a reverential devotion[755] to what it provides regarding the interpretation of the treaties.

As Wälde expressively put it:

> Confusion, rather than clarity, prevails in today's practice of investment arbitration, notwithstanding increasing references to the Vienna Rules. Styles of traditional, pre-Vienna public international law mingle freely with styles of reasoning from commercial arbitration, with each player inclined to resort to familiar habits in his or her domestic law and maxims of (usually) pseudo-Latin origin that seem to fit the strategy, that is, retracing from the desired outcome to the expected reasoning.[756]

Practice reveals that the VCLT is used by investment tribunals for the interpretation of investment treaties but not consistently.[757] Some investments tribunals pay lip service to the VCLT commencing their analysis with reference to these rules of interpretation.[758] While the lip service of these rules is omnipresent, what is lacking is the systematic application of Articles 31 to 33 of the Vienna Convention.[759] The reality of international arbitration reveals that these rules constitute a type of 'clause de style' in arbitral awards, either as 'routinely and briefly referred to' or as 'solemnly reproduced verbatim'.[760]

A prominent example is the *Maffezini* case where the Tribunal resorted to the VCLT in the absence of other 'specified rules of interpretation'. It held that 'Like all

755. *See Aguas Del Tunari v. Republic of Bolivia*, ICSID Case No. ARB/02/3 para. 116.
756. *Ibid.* 725 (citations omitted).
757. Several awards have used the VCLT to base their reasoning; *See* C H Schreuer, 'Diversity and Harmonization of Treaty Interpretation in Investment Arbitration', 3(2) Transnational Dispute Settlement (2006) 1; As an illustration: *CSOB v. Slovakia*, ICSID Case No. ARB/97/4, Jurisdiction 1 (24 May 1999) para. 57; *Fireman's Fund v. Mexico*, ICSID Case No. ARB(AF)/02/1, Award (17 Jul. 2006) paras 94–95, *Técnicas v. Mexico*, ICSID Case No. ARB (AF)/00/2, Award (29 May 2003) paras 121 and 155; *ADF v. US*, ICSID Case No. ARB (AF)/00/1 (9 Jan. 2003) para. 149; *MTD v. Chile*, ICSID Case No. ARB/01/7, Award (25 May 2004) paras 112–113, *Siemens v. Argentina*, ICSID Case No. ARB/02/8, Award (17 Jan. 2017) paras 80–81; *Plama v. Bulgaria*, ICSID Case No. ARB/03/24, Jurisdiction (27 Aug. 2008) paras 117, 147, 158, 160, 188, 194, and 196.
758. In the *Jan de Nul* award the Tribunal refers to Article 31 VCLT when treating the State's consent to arbitration. However, regarding the interpretation of FET the tribunal does not invoke the VCLT but interprets the guarantee by referring to case law. *Jan de Nul NV and Dredging International NV v. Arab Republic of Egypt*, ICSID Case No. ARB/04/13, Award (6 Nov. 2008) para 139; Andrea Saldarriaga, 'Investment Awards and the Rules of Interpretation of the Vienna Convention: Making Room for Improvement' (2013) 28(1) ICSID Rev 97, 204; Similarly, Arbitrator I mentioned that: 'The VCLT seems to be a frequent step in a tribunal's analysis but I am not sure how determinative of their analysis it may be.'
759. Wälde, 'Interpreting Investment Treaties' (n 673) 729 (citations omitted). The author further adds that the VCLT rules '[...] provide rather a structure of analysis, with ample room for selective use of the many interpretation maxims, for emphasizing this or that opposite element' at 730; *See also* the *Asian Agricultural* case where the Tribunal held that it will rely on the VCLT for the interpretation of the BIT but it went on making reference to '[t]he other rules that should guide the Tribunal in adjudicating the interpretation issues raised' found in case law such as the need to follow precedents, *Asian Agricultural Products Ltd. v. Sri Lanka*, ICSID Case No. ARB/87/3, Award (27 Jun. 1990) paras 38 et seq.
760. Mahnoush Arsanjani and Michael Reisman, 'Interpreting Treaties for the Benefit of Third Parties: The "Salvors Doctrine" and the Use of Legislative History in Investment Treaties' (2010) 104 AJIL 597, 598–599; *See*, for example, the *Rumeli* case where the tribunal refers to the

other provisions of the BIT and in the absence of other specified applicable rules of interpretation, Article X must be interpreted in the manner prescribed by Article 31 of the Vienna Convention on the Law of Treaties.'[761] In some other cases, the decision-maker will use the methodology spelled out in the VCLT but in a different order, giving to each step of interpretation a different value and meaning.[762] Fauchald researched the extent to which ICSID tribunals follow the general rules on treaty interpretation of the VCLT. The author concluded that 'only in exceptional decisions did tribunals integrate the VCLT into their reasoning beyond general references'.[763] The specificity of the investment-arbitration framework and treaties has led the arbitrators to follow interpretational paths that are not identical with the interpretational guidelines included in the VCLT.[764] This view was expressed in the *Aguas del Tunari* case where the Tribunal held that rather than approaching the Vienna Convention interpretive canons as reflecting a general pattern, the interpreter should focus upon the specific case which may, or may not, be representative of such general pattern. It adds that:

> [t]he Vienna Convention's directive to look to the ordinary meaning of a word in its context and in light of the object and purpose of the treaty is intended to (1) to

'accepted rules of treaty interpretation' when interpreting the FPS guarantee but does not specify these rules. The tribunal interprets the guarantee with reference to case law. *Rumeli*, Award (n 242) para. 668.

761. *Emilio Agustín Maffezini v. The Kingdom of Spain*, ICSID Case No. ARB/97/7, Award (13 Nov. 2000) para. 27.
762. The ILC notes that: 'Although the Convention does not require the interpreter to apply its process in the order listed in articles 31–32, in fact that order is intuitively likely to represent an effective sequence in which to approach the task. But there is no reason to separate these techniques too sharply from each other'. Koskenniemi, 'Fragmentation of International Law' (n 259) para. 428.
763. Fauchald, 'The Legal Reasoning of ICSID Tribunals – An Empirical Analysis (n 401) 314 (citations omitted). The analysis includes 98 decisions by ICSID tribunals in the period between 1 Jan. 1998 and 31 Dec. 2006; Bekker also mentions that 'arbitrators [...] are not working with these key provisions of international law in approaching questions of methodology for resolving investment disputes governed by public international law'. Bekker, 'Recalibrating the Investment Treaty Arbitration System Through Non-Compartmentalized Legal Thinking' (n 77) 12; *Mondev International Ltd. v. US*, ICSID Case No. ARB(AF)/99/2, Award (11 Oct. 2002) para. 43 (the tribunal stated: 'In the Tribunal's view, there is no principle either of extensive or restrictive interpretation of jurisdictional provisions in treaties. In the end, the question is what the relevant provisions mean, interpreted in accordance with the applicable rules of interpretation of treaties. These are set out in Arts 31–33 of the Vienna Convention on the Law of Treaties, which for this purpose can be taken to reflect the position under customary international law'); *Noble Venture Inc v. Romania*, ICSID Case No. ARB/01/11, Award (12 Oct. 2005) para. 55 (The Tribunal states: 'In consequence, as with any other exception to established general rules of law, the identification of a provision as an "umbrella clause" can as a consequence proceed only from a strict, if not indeed restrictive, interpretation of its terms and, more generally, in accordance with the well known customary rules codified under Article 31 of the Vienna Convention of the Law of Treaties (1969).'); *Philippe Gruslin v. Malaysia*, ICSID Case No. ARB/99/3, Award (27 Nov. 2000) para. 26.1 (The Tribunal states that ' [i]f its meaning is found to be clear, the Tribunal will not reduce its reach by reference to general consideration of assumptions derived from extrinsic sources of the sort relied upon by the Respondent in its materials and arguments').
764. Arbitrator H mentions that '[i]f you compare it to a tree, then the VCLT is a trunk and then you are in a branch that is more specifically investor to state arbitration [...] and then you have smaller branches of human rights for example, if that's applicable; that's how I see it, branching out]'.*See* Annex 'Interview Questions'.

> find the intent of the parties in the specific instrument, (2) to respect the possibility that the parties have used the instrument to address issues of mutual concern in innovative ways, and (3) to not forcibly conform the specific aims of a treaty to general assumptions about the intent of states, assumptions which necessarily are based on assessments of past practice.[765]

The arbitrators do refer to and rely on the Vienna Convention of the law of treaties but also show the need to adapt the interpretation of legal concepts to the interpretational needs that arise in the context of the specific dispute. As such, the main categories of interpretative arguments are the wording of the text, the context, the object and purpose, customary international law, general principles of law, analogies and *a contrario* arguments, agreements between the parties, case law, State practice, preparatory work, legal doctrine and reasonable results (Article 32 (b) VCLT).[766] Despite the lack of a de jure doctrine of precedent, the majority of interpretative arguments used by ICSID Tribunals derive from the investment-arbitration case law giving a clear preference to decisions of ICSID tribunals.[767] Although judicial decisions are approached as a subsidiary source of interpretation, the citation practice of ICSID tribunals resembles that of common law judges giving priority to the case law.[768]

Based on these considerations, the tribunals seem to be oscillating between a traditional public international law attachment to the VCLT and the limits of the value of these interpretation principles in the investment-arbitration practice. In this context, identifying the interpretive statements of the investment awards referring to the VCLT does not necessarily mean that this is the way arbitral tribunals interpret the legal concepts contained in the treaties. As such, reference to the VCLT may be a starting point but it is still 'difficult to find a tribunal which formally and properly applied the Vienna Rules step by step'.[769]

In general, international courts and tribunals resort to the VCLT interpretive principles for diverse reasons. They are used as a source of 'guidance and justification,

765. *Aguas del Tunari SA v. Bolivia*, ICSID Case No. ARB/02/3, Decision on Respondent's Objections to Jurisdiction (21 Oct. 2005) para. 91.
766. Fauchald, 'The Legal Reasoning of ICSID Tribunals – An Empirical Analysis' (n 401) 301, 308, fn 35.
767. *Ibid.* 356; Commission provided an empirical study reviewing 207 publicly available investment-treaty decisions and awards issued from 1972 until 2006. He states that 'citations to supposedly subsidiary sources, such as judicial decisions, including arbitral awards, predominates' Jeffery Commission, 'Precedent in Investment Treaty Arbitration: The Empirical Backing' (2007) 4(5) TDM 1, 5; *See* §6.03 'Precedent Arguments'.
768. *See Enron Corporation and Ponderosa Assets, L.P. v. The Argentine Republic*, ICSID Case No. ARB/01/3, Decision on Jurisdiction (14 Jan. 2004) para. 40; Commission, 'Precedent in Investment Treaty Arbitration: The Empirical Backing' (n 767) 5; *See also* the view of Mbengue that 'previous awards or academic writings are not supplementary means of interpretation in the sense of Article 32 but remain mere sources of inspiration, comfort or reference to arbitrators'. [...] Pursuant to Art. 38 of the Statute of the ICJ, the function of judicial decisions is the 'determination of the rules of law'. It follows that these decisions may help the Court in identifying the content of customary international rules, general principles of law, and other international rules. It goes without saying that this function is distinct from that of supplementary means of interpretation under Article 32, which serve as aids to the interpretation of a specific text.' Makane Mbengue, 'Rules of Interpretation (Art. 32 of the Vienna Convention on the Law of Treaties)' (n 737) 388, 399.
769. Wälde, 'Interpreting Investment Treaties' (n 673) 730, 746.

as tools to build credibility and to exercise and assert their judicial function (sometimes in an institutional context), as instruments to achieve accountability, as techniques to order and structure their reasoning process, and as aids to making their decisions acceptable and comprehensible'.[770] The use of these principles in arbitral decision-making plays a significant role in justifying a legitimate judicial function in the field of public international law. These well-recognised and universally adopted rules of interpretation confer to investment-arbitration tribunals a place in the long interpretive tradition of international courts and tribunals. However, the convention-based arguments are better described as a means to an end rather than as the end itself. As will be revealed through the use of the rest of the interpretive arguments, arbitral legal decision-making goes some steps further since the interpretation of treaties is not the only interpretive task of the arbitrator. The need to interpret other sources of law such as precedents, customary international law and even policies underlies the questioning of the effectiveness of the VCLT when treating these issues.

[B] Effectiveness of the VCLT in the Investor-State Arbitration Disputes

One may question in the first place the suitability of the rules provided in the VCLT for the interpretation of a treaty in the cadre of a dispute between a State and a private party. The VCLT addresses interpretation issues of a treaty when a dispute arises between two state parties to a treaty.[771] Over-emphasising the state-to-state relationship as integrated into the investment treaties to the detriment of the State-investor relationship oversimplifies the interaction between the public and private elements of the investor-state arbitration framework. The interpretive tools of the VCLT are formed around the former relationship. In the investment-arbitration framework, there are two equally important elements of legal decision-making: the international commitment of States when signing the international treaties, and the implementation of these treaties which may require the balance between public and private interests.

Based on the above considerations, the existence of private investors in a dispute resolution framework regulated by treaties between States may influence the way the decision-makers take into consideration the rules of the VCLT when interpreting legal concepts.[772] The VCLT remains an important and useful tool for the interpretation of investment treaties underlying the public international law feature of the investment-arbitration framework. However, the need to take into account the involvement of a

770. Van Damme, *Treaty Interpretation by the WTO Appellate Body* (n 180) 381.

771. At this point, it is interesting to note that many parties to the ICSID Convention are not at the same time parties to the VCLT. One may of course justify their application based on the customary nature of the VCLT interpretation rules as stressed out by arbitral tribunals. For example, *Camuzzi International,* Decision on objection to jurisdiction (n 737) para. 133.

772. Arbitrator F confirms that 'the problem is that the way these tools were designed were for the interpretation of treaties and for the interpretation of substantive private international law – they are not totally adequate'. *See* Annex 'Interview Questions'.

private party in the whole procedure has become a reality entrenched within the very own nature of investor-state arbitration.[773]

An important preliminary issue that arises at this point is whether the meaning of 'international law' has the same context in investment arbitration as it is described in the ICJ Statute. The sources of international law are clearly expressed in Article 38 ICJ Statute that describes the law to be applied by the ICJ when deciding on a case. These sources are the international conventions, international custom which reflects general practice accepted as law, general principles of law and lastly judicial decisions and teachings as subsidiary means for the determination of rules of law.[774]

The report of ICSID Executive Directors mentions that the term 'international law' has the sense given to it by Article 38 of the ICJ Statute 'allowance being made for the fact that Article 38 was designed to apply to inter-State disputes'.[775] The nature of investment disputes where the parties are a private investor and a State is different from the nature of international disputes dealing with State sovereignty and disputes between States. The limitations of traditional public international law treaties for addressing the needs of specialised areas of international law such as investment law, is connected to the traditionally conceived contract-like nature of treaties. The implications of such a conception is the 'contractarian structure' displayed by treaty rules despite the fact that international relations become less and less characterised by bilateral 'contractarian structures'.[776] What seems to be crucial is to respond to the necessity of 'adapt[ing] the law of treaties to recent developments, the most salient of which is [...] the opening up of international actors'.[777] The International Law Commission comments on the effectiveness of the Vienna Convention marking the following:

> In general, the VCLT gives insufficient recognition to special types of treaties and the special rules that might go to interpret and apply them. More work here seems

773. Arbitrator H interestingly marks that 'the way that investment arbitration is developing, that difference between state to state and investor to state would be more pronounced than it was at the beginning of investor to state jurisprudence'. *See* Annex 'Interview Questions'.
774. Article 38 ICJ Statute provides:

    1. The Court, whose function is to decide in accordance with international law such disputes as are submitted to it, shall apply:
        a. international conventions, whether general or particular, establishing rules expressly recognized by the contesting states;
        b. international custom, as evidence of a general practice accepted as law;
        c. the general principles of law recognized by civilized nations;
        d. subject to the provisions of Article 59, judicial decisions and the teachings of the most highly qualified publicists of the various nations, as subsidiary means for the determination of rules of law.
    2. This provision shall not prejudice the power of the Court to decide a case *ex aequo et bono*, if the parties agree thereto. Statute of the International Court of Justice, <http://www.icj-cij.org/en/statute> (accessed 4 Jul. 2018).

775. Report of Executive Directors on the ICSID Convention, para. 40 <https://icsid.worldbank.org/ICSID/FrontServlet?requestType=ICSIDPublicationsRH&actionVal=ViewAnnouncePDF&AnnouncementType=archive&AnnounceNo=26_Rules_en.pdf> (accessed 3 Apr. 2018).
776. Jan Klabbers, 'Re-inventing the Law of Treaties: The Contribution of the EC Courts' (1999) 30 NYIL 45, 47.
777. *Ibid.*

> necessary. It is proposed to give guidelines on how the Vienna Convention provisions might give recognition to the wide variation of treaty types and normative implications of such types and whether it might be possible to set up informal guidelines on how to deal with treaty conflicts.[778]

These considerations confirm the fact that the interpretation process has particular features in 'different areas of law, institutional settings, and dispute settlement systems'.[779] Abi-Saab has remarked that:

> [...] each of [these treaty regimes] constitutes a legal universe quite different from the others. The difference can be explained not only by the disparity in the structure, mandate, and composition, but also, and perhaps mainly, by the 'judicial policy' of each forum, which is also a function of its environment.[780]

Therefore, while public international law and in particular Article 31 Vienna Convention continues to provide the main interpretation guidance, it is important to bear in mind that investment treaties deal with a considerably different context from the one envisaged by traditional public international law. At the heart of such treaties is the right of a private party to resolve the dispute with a foreign State through arbitration, something 'fundamentally different from traditional international public law, which is based on solving disputes between sovereign States and where private parties have no standing'.[781] Moreover, what should not be neglected is the fact that the VCLT was adopted in 1969 and the investment treaties existing at that time where very limited. The interpretation of 3,000 treaties that exist up-to-date present common features that could justify their interpretation in a way not clearly envisaged by the VCLT.

Adding to the above points, the principles of treaty interpretation of the VCLT are not of a substantive nature requiring their further assessment and interpretation.[782] The traditional treaty interpretation methods often turn out to be too vague and as a result offer limited guidance in the interpretation of vague legal concepts. Taking as an example the FET standard, an interpretation according to its ordinary meaning will replace the terms 'fair and equitable' with vague definitions such as 'just,' 'even-handed,' 'unbiased,' or 'legitimate,' without clarifying its normative content.[783] The Vienna Convention does not make the connection between the principles of interpretation and their application in different contexts characterised by 'the subject matter of the treaty, the character of the institution interpreting the text, and the audience for whom the text is interpreted'.[784]

---

778. Koskenniemi, 'Fragmentation of International Law' (n 259) para. 251.
779. Isabelle Van Damme, 'Jurisdiction, Applicable Law, and Interpretation' (n 741) 337.
780. Abi-Saab, *The Appellate Body and Treaty Interpretation* (n 155) 460.
781. *International Thunderbird*, Separate Opinion of Thomas Wälde (n 630) para. 13.
782. Van Damme, *Treaty Interpretation by the WTO Appellate Body* (n 180) 381; Arbitrator H stated that the VCLT constitutes a 'starting point, a skeleton [but it is not sufficient] because the wording is extremely broad and so further guidance is needed; I will look to the sources of international law pointed out loud by the ICJ; I [also] find other decisions from arbitrators in other treaty cases'.
783. Schill, 'The Sixth Path: Reforming Investment Law from Within' (n 628) 15.
784. Van Damme, *Treaty Interpretation by the WTO Appellate Body* (n 180) 643.

Going a step further, the suitability of the VCLT interpretation principles depends on an array of considerations that have to be appreciated by the interpreter of the specific text.[785] Such considerations vary from 'the particular arrangement of the words and sentences, their relation to each other and to other parts of the document' to 'the general nature and subject-matter of the document and the circumstances in which it was drawn up'.[786] However, even in the case that these principles may appear to apply, 'their application is not automatic but depends on the conviction of the interpreter that it is appropriate in the particular circumstances of the case'.[787] In this context, the discretionary use of these principles reveals a non-obligatory interpretation process attributing to it an artistic rather than a purely scientific character.[788]

It is also important to note that, in an investment-arbitration dispute, the decision-maker may confront not only issues requiring the interpretation of treaties but also the interpretation of customary international law, as well as the interpretation of precedent, and the evaluation of policies.[789] How the interpretation of the latter sources can be realised is neither evident nor an easy task. What becomes critical at this point is to highlight a fact often neglected; that the interpretive task of the arbitrator is not restricted to treaty interpretation. How does theory keep up with arbitral reality in practice? Do interpretations of the arbitral tribunals follow the beaten track methodology of the VCLT or do arbitrators demonstrate more creativity in order to accommodate the needs of the investment-arbitration framework?

Based on these considerations, the legal interpretation may deviate from the general rules of treaty interpretation. As such, the 'Dialogue' approach does not restrict the interpretation process of investment-arbitration tribunals to the analysis of the VCLT but refers to other interpretive arguments that arise in practice such as precedent.

§6.03 PRECEDENT ARGUMENTS

Maybe the dialogue between judges flows more easily than between politicians. Judges share common values and attitudes; they may be more interested in the intrinsic value of legal concepts, in the quality of the legal argument, than in their precise origin.[790]

785. When asked whether he/she uses the Vienna convention when interpreting the law, arbitrator G answered: 'I use it as far as it helps. The Vienna Convention is a set of principles rather than tools.' *See* Annex 'Interview Questions'.
786. 'Draft Articles on the Law of Treaties with commentaries 1966' (n 150) para. 4.
787. *Ibid.*
788. *Ibid.* For an analysis of the artistic nature of interpretation *see* §1.02[D][2] 'The Science and Art of Legal Interpretation'.
789. Arbitrator D stated that the VCLT for the interpretation of the law is sometimes sufficient since 'it is not usually the case that the only thing you have to decide is a matter of interpreting a Treaty. Usually there are matters of substance as well which looking at the Vienna Convention, I think, do not tell you how to answer'.; Similarly, Arbitrator J stated: 'I consider the VCLT sufficient for interpreting treaty language, but to look at customary international law, I would look at decisions of other tribunals and commentators to which I give qualitative credence'.
790. Christiaan Timmermans, 'The European Union's Judicial System' (2004) 41(2) CMLRev 393, 399.

The precedent-based arguments reveal the use of case law in the decision-making of arbitral tribunals.[791] They are connected to the way arbitrators use previous decisions, the functions of this practice and its importance for the decision-making process. Such interpretive arguments further describe the communications and exchange of ideas between private and public decision-makers. The dialogue links represent the 'travel-ling' of legal principles, case law and general 'legal mentality' from one legal order to another. Arbitrators communicate with other arbitrators and judges contributing to the establishment of 'a transnational discourse and act[ing] as merchants of law'.[792] Such transnational dialogue is the corollary of the coexistence of legal orders which may at time overlap and diverge reflecting legal pluralism.[793]

The proliferation of international courts and tribunals has led to the growth of 'transnational judicial interaction' which includes 'the citation of foreign decisions, negotiated divisions of judicial responsibility in complex cross-border litigation, and the enforcement of foreign judgments'.[794] The relationships created amongst judges, especially through cross-citation practices, are considered to develop a 'sense of transnational judicial solidarity' that may eventually lead to the emergence of a 'transnational or supranational body of law: a set of principles informed by and building on one another, textually and culturally differentiated as necessary but acknowledging the promise of universality'.[795] The exchange of ideas and legal concepts between various legal orders, and investment law and arbitration contributes to the transnational identity of investment-arbitration tribunals analogous to other international dispute resolution mechanisms such as the ECtHR and the CJEU.[796] Participation in such a form of judicial borrowing positions arbitral tribunal within 'a cosmopolitan network of international courts and tribunals'.[797]

[A] A Doctrine of Precedent?

Article 59 of the ICJ Statute,[798] which can be extended so as to conclude other international courts and 'even more so ad hoc tribunals', reveals the absence of any formal rule of precedent in the form of 'stare decisis' in international law.[799] The issue

791. The use of the phrases jurisprudence, case law and prior awards refer to earlier cases without implying a binding or persuasive force.
792. Sabino Cassese, 'Beyond Legal Comparison' (2012) AnnuarioDirComp 387, 388.
793. Valentina Vadi, 'The Migration of Constitutional Ideas to Regional and International Economic Law: The Case of Proportionality' (2015) 35(3) NJILB 557, 564; *See* Part Introduction section III[D] 'Legal Argumentation in Arbitral Decision-Making: Language–Rhetoric–Dialogue'.
794. Robert Ahdieh, 'Between Dialogue and Decree: International Review of National Courts' (2004) 79 NYULRev 2019, 2032.
795. Laurence Helfer and Anne-Marie Slaughter, 'Toward a Theory of Effective Supranational Adjudication' (1997) 107 YaleLJ 273, 373.
796. Vadi, *Analogies in International Investment Law and Arbitration* (n 277) 130.
797. *Ibid.*
798. Article 59 Statute ICJ: 'The decision of the Court has no binding force except between the parties and in respect of that particular case'
799. Thomas Wälde, *International Investment Law: An Overview of Key Concepts and Methodology*, Report of the 2004 Research Seminar on International Investment Law, Hague Academy of International Law (October 2005) 64.

of precedent may appear to be more problematic in the international scene due to the fragmentation of the adjudicatory function.[800] Even more, the investment arbitration's institutional setting differs from that of WTO and other international courts.[801] The field of investment-treaty arbitration cannot be characterised as unitary in the sense that the tribunals do not sit under the same source of jurisdiction.[802]

Since there is no formal rule regarding the form precedent has in investment arbitration, the practice of citing prior awards and decisions by arbitrators has led to the division of scholars into two main streams of 'verdicts'. On the one hand, there are studies concluding that an arbitrator's use of previous awards leads to the existence of a system of precedent characterised as 'jurisprudence constante'.[803] In this context, prior decisions have a persuasive authority, meaning that arbitrators can follow prior awards if they are convinced by the strength of the award's reasoning.[804] Persuasive authority has the potential to persuade without constraining the decision-making power of the adjudicator.[805] *Jurisprudence constante* figures an appealing answer towards a theory of precedent in investment arbitration. As in the French tradition, where the code has the first role, in investment-arbitration tribunals will start by analysing the language of the treaty in question. The next step will be to 'get acquainted' with the decisions of other tribunals that have treated the same or similar questions. These decisions will be 'viewed as persuasive to the extent they are well reasoned'.[806] It is important to clarify that the doctrine of *jurisprudence constante* in the French Law has two meanings: it refers to the decisions of high courts that are followed by lower courts for practical reasons even though they are not binding; and to decisions of lower or equal courts that can be seen as a model for a particular case.[807] The latter

800. Giorgio Sacerdoti, 'Precedent in the Settlement of International Economic Disputes: The WTO and Investment Arbitration Models', Bocconi Legal Studies Research Paper No. 1931560, 1.
801. *Ibid.* 15.
802. Christoph Schreuer and Matthew Weiniger, 'A Doctrine of Precedent', in Peter Muchlinski, Federico Ortino, and Christoph Schreuer (eds) *The Oxford Handbook of International Investment Law* (OUP 2008) 1189.
803. For example, Valentina Vadi, 'Towards Arbitral Path Coherence & Judicial Borrowing: Persuasive Precedent in Investment Arbitration' (2008) 5(3) TDM 14; *See also* Patrick Dumberry, 'The Role and Relevance of Awards in the Formation, Identification and Evolution of Customary Rules in International Investment Law' (2016) 33(3) JIntlArb 269, 269–287; Andrea K Bjorklund, 'The Emerging Civilization of Investment Arbitration' (2009) 113 PennStLRev 1269, 1273.
804. *Jurisprudence constante* may be in some respects weaker than *persuasive precedent* since any precedential effect requires a line of consistent decisions. It may also be more rigid than *persuasive precedent* since 'once the existence of a line of cases is established, the doctrine imposes a decisional burden on adjudicators in the form of a strong presumption in favor of consistency'. Irene Ten Cate, 'The Costs of Consistency: Precedent in Investment Treaty Arbitration' (2013) ColumJTransnatlL 29.
805. *Ibid.* 26; Arbitrator A states that 'looking at what others have done before you is a natural thing and it's useful'. *See* Annex 'Interview Questions'.
806. Andrea K Bjorklund, 'Investment Treaty Arbitral Awards as Jurisprudence Constante' in Douglas Arner, Isabella Bunn, and Colin Picker (eds) *International Economic Law: The State and Future of the Discipline* (Hart 2008) 265, 272.
807. Michel Troper and Christophe Grzegorczky, *Precedent in France*, in Neil D MacCormick and Robert S Summers (eds), *Interpreting Precedent: A Comparative Study*, (Ashgate: Dartmouth, 1997); Bjorklund, *Investment Treaty Arbitral Awards as Jurisprudence Constante* (n 806) 272;

meaning of *jurisprudence constante* is considered to correspond better to the equal authority tribunals of investor-state arbitration.

On the other hand, there have been studies that propose a system of binding precedent in investment-treaty arbitration. Arbitral awards with binding precedential value are considered to reconcile inconsistent awards and enhance the ability of arbitration to provide a predictable and equitable dispute resolution system.[808]

There is also the view that what is important in reality is not the form of precedent but the ways to promote quality in the citation of awards and effective case management of the large arbitral case law emerging.[809] The heated debate on its common law or civil law doctrinal form may have created the impression that the methodological role it plays in legal decision-making depends on its official characterisation as 'jurisprudence constante' or 'stare decisis'. The 'dialogical network' approach gives precedent its proper position in arbitral decision-making, concluding that whatever characterisation given to the function of case law, its role is essential for it constitutes a method of legal interpretation.

[B] Precedential Value of Investment Arbitration Awards

Arbitrators are viewed as doing justice within the limits of a particular case.[810] Yet precedent plays its own special role in arbitral decision-making. Even though there is no formal doctrine of precedent, practice shows that arbitrators bear in mind the relevant case law when deciding on a case.

As accurately mentioned by Guilluame 'the judge and the arbitrator are not machines that distribute judgments and awards; they enjoy a certain freedom in the exercise of their duties'.[811] Arbitral decision-making is not a rigid process especially in the field of investment arbitration where the arbitrator does not base decision-making strictly on the facts and contract between the parties, like in commercial arbitration. In investment arbitration, issues occur that must be resolved in the same way for the sake of the predictability of investments and the credibility of the dispute resolution

See also Charles Brower and Stephan Schill, 'Is Arbitration a Threat or a Boon to the Legitimacy of International Investment Law?'(2009) 9 ChiJIntlL 471.

808. Marie-Louise Rodgers, 'Bilateral Investment Treaties and Arbitration: An Argument and a Proposal for the ICSID's Implementation of a System of Binding Precedent' (2008) 5(3) TDM 24; *See also* Reinisch noting that the examination of how tribunals consider prior awards in practice, has led to the finding that tribunals do not deal with the doctrinal issue of why a binding system of precedent could not emerge, but have taken it 'for granted', August Reinisch, 'The Role of Precedent in ICSID Arbitration' in Klein Klausegger, and others (ed.) Austrian Arbitration Yearbook 495 (2008) 497, 14; Carbonneau interestingly states that the publication of arbitral awards and their subsequent enforcement by national courts 'may lead to the creation of a general arbitral principle of *stare decisis* possessing a transnational stature' Carbonneau, *Rendering Arbitral Awards with Reasons* (n 396) 581.
809. For example, Judith Gill, 'Is There a Special Role for Precedent in Investment Arbitration?' (2010) 25(1) ICSID Rev 87.
810. Mark Weidemaier, 'Toward a Theory of Precedent in Arbitration' (2010) 51 Wm&MaryLRev 1895, 1895; Laurent Lévy, 'L'interprétation arbitrale' (2013) Revue de l'arbitrage, 861–952.
811. Gilbert Guillaume, 'The Use of Precedent by International Judges and Arbitrators' (2011) 2(1) JIDS 5.

mechanism.[812] In this setting, integrity in legal decision-making acquires great significance. Dworkin highlights the fact that it is important for human institutions and their laws to exhibit a kind of integrity; '[e]ven though the law cannot stand still, it is a matter of fairness that the decisions issued at one point in time be capable of rational reconciliation with those issued at an earlier time'.[813]

The question of whether the decisions of arbitral tribunals would become 'precedents' in other cases was posed during the discussion on the draft articles of the ICSID Convention in 1970. Ghana's representative inquired whether 'the decisions of arbitral tribunals would become precedents in other cases, even if they were not published'.[814] Despite Article 53 Washington Convention clearly stating that the award is binding only between the parties, arbitration tribunals have relied on prior awards when examining questions such as the clause on FET and the obligation of the States to compensate damages. In this context, it has become a 'common practice' not only for governments and private investors to refer to prior investment awards that figure to favour them, but also for investment tribunals to rely upon awards of other tribunals when interpreting similar provisions of investment treaties.[815]

Investment arbitrators refer to previous awards in order to form their own legal reasoning through following a principle well established in the jurisprudence, fill in gaps in the treaty, drawing analogies and *a contrario* arguments.[816] A prominent example of the reasons behind a tribunal's reference to ICSID case law can be found in the *AES Corporation v. The Argentine Republic* decision on jurisdiction.[817] The Tribunal stated that 'it may consider decisions on jurisdiction dealing with the same or very similar issues [...] in order to compare its own position with those already adopted by its predecessors and, if it shares the views already expressed by one or more of these tribunals on a specific point of law, it is free to adopt the same solution'.[818] The Tribunal continued mentioning that another reason for considering precedents, even when the cases had been seized on a basis of another BIT, is that a tribunal 'has set a point of law which, in essence, is or will be met in other cases whatever the specificities

812. Gabrielle Kaufmann-Kohler, 'Arbitral Precedent: Dream, Necessity or Excuse? – The 2006 Freshfields Lecture' (2007) 23(3) ArbIntl 357, 376.
813. MacCormick, *Rhetoric and the Rule of Law: A Theory of Legal Reasoning* (n 172) 235 citing Ronald Dworkin, *Law's Empire* (HUP 1986) 228–32.
814. Commission, 'Precedent in Investment Treaty Arbitration: The Empirical Backing' (n 767) 1 citing 'ICSID: History', vol II, 817.
815. David Gantz, 'The Evolution of FTA Investment Provisions: From NAFTA to the United States – Chile Free Trade Agreement' (2003) 19(4) AmUIntlLRev 679, 689; *See also* Alejandro A Escobar, 'The use of ICSID precedents by ICSID and ICSID tribunals', at The British Institute of International and Comparative Law (BIICL) Annual Meeting panel, 'Used and Abused: The role of Precedent in Investment Protection Arbitration', (19 Jun. 2005) 3 <https://www.biicl.org/files/917_alejandro_escobar_-_precdent.pdf> (accessed 3 Jul. 2018).
816. Arbitrator I confirms that 'The trend is very much in favour of looking what other tribunals have done. What motivates that trend is the desire at the level of principle to contribute to a homogenous body of law that is therefore predictable, and on a more mundane level to find cover of your decision by indicating how it is the same as another arbitrator's decision.'
817. *AES Corporation v. The Argentine Republic,* ICSID Case No. ARB/02/17, Decision on Jurisdiction (26 Apr. 2005).
818. *Ibid.* para. 30.

of each dispute may be'.[819] On this basis precedents can be considered as a matter of 'comparison' and 'inspiration'.[820] Similarly, the *Enron* tribunal focused on the 'correctness' of the ICSID decisions as a justification for referring to them despite not being 'a primary source of rules': 'The citations of and references to those decisions respond to the fact that the Tribunal in examining the claim and arguments of this case under international law, believes that in essence the conclusions and reasons of those decisions are correct.' [821] Likewise the *Chevron* Tribunal held that it will consider arbitral decisions and the parties' arguments based on these decisions 'if they shed any useful light on the issues that arise for decision in this case'.[822]

Arbitral practice reveals that there is a progressive emergence of rules through lines of consistent cases on some issues, while on others there are still contradictory outcomes.[823] It also still remains to be ascertained whether a consistent, well established and accepted standard jurisprudence can lead to a rule of international law, specifically to customary international law, that is respected by tribunals.[824]

[C] The Need to Interpret Precedents

The importance of precedent in the arbitral decision-making process reveals that the arbitral awards are relied upon and discussed by the parties and the tribunal, they guide the decision-maker on the interpretation of vague concepts, and they contribute to the development of investment law.[825] However, case law could not fulfil such functions if the decisions where not themselves analysed, interpreted and understood.[826]

---

819. *Ibid.* para. 31; The Tribunal added here that '[t]he same may be said for the interpretation given by a precedent decision or award to some relevant facts which are basically at the origin of two or several different disputes, keeping carefully in mind the actual specificities still featuring each case. If the present Tribunal concurs with the analysis and interpretation of these facts as they generated certain special consequences for the parties to this case as well as for those of another case, it may consider this earlier interpretation as relevant'. para. 33.
820. *Ibid.* para. 31.
821. *Enron Corp. & Ponderosa Assets, L.P. v. Argentine Republic*, ICSID Case No. ARB/01/3, Decision on Jurisdiction (14 Jan. 2004) para. 40; *See also Bayindir Insaat Turizm Ticaret Ve Sanayi A.S. v. Islamic Republic of Pakistan*, ICSID Case No. ARB/03/29, Decision on Jurisdiction (14 Nov. 2005) para. 76 (the tribunal stated that although not bound by previous decisions, it will take them into account 'whenever appropriate').
822. *Chevron Corporation and Texaco Petroleum Company v. Ecuador*, UNCITRAL PCA Case No. 2009-23, Partial Award (20 Mar. 2010) para. 164.
823. Kaufmann-Kohler, 'Arbitral Precedent: Dream, Necessity or Excuse?' (n 812) 373.
824. Wälde particularly states that investment tribunals can generate a *jurisprudence constante* equivalent to customary international law or recognised principles of law. Wälde, *International Investment Law: An Overview of Key Concepts and Methodology* (n 799) 66; For an analysis of CIL *see* §6.04 'Customary Law Arguments'.
825. Ten Cate, 'The Costs of Consistency' (n 804) 423.
826. The need to interpret precedents in this context arises in the process of legal interpretation and reasoning. For the different issue of whether international courts have the power to interpret or revise their own judgments on request of the parties *see* Chester Brown, *A Common Law of International Adjudication* (CUP 2007) 153 et seq.; *See also* the *AES v. Argentina* case where Argentina argued that 'repeating decisions taken in other cases, without making the factual and legal distinctions, may constitute an excess of power and may affect the integrity of the

The way the arbitrator interprets an award or a decision may differ from the way the parties would do it. The *CMS* tribunal pictures this process. At a first stage, the tribunal refers to the different 'meaning' that each party as well as the tribunal give to investment-arbitration case law:

> With this background in mind, it is then possible for this Tribunal to examine the meaning of a number of decisions of ICSID tribunals that have dealt with the protection of shareholders. The parties have a different reading of these ICSID cases, [...]. For the Republic of Argentina, all these cases deal with shareholder rights, underlying arrangements and factual situations different from those given in the instant case, and hence do not support jurisdiction in this case. CMS, for its part, believes that, to the contrary, in all those cases the right of shareholders, including minority shareholders, to claim independently from the corporate entity affect has been upheld.[827]

The tribunal continues referring to the differences of the factual background of each case:

> There can be no doubt that the factual setting of each case is different and that some may lend themselves more than others to illustrate points of relevance. In some cases, there has been majority shareholding or control by the investor, in others not; in some cases there has been expropriation affecting specifically the shares, in others not; in some cases, there has been no objection to jurisdiction, in others there has been.[828]

The tribunal concludes that despite the factual differences, the awards express the same trend:

> However, there can be no doubt that most, if not all, such cases are immersed in the same trend discussed above in the context of international law and the meaning of the 1965 Convention. In the present case, the Claimant has convincingly explained that notwithstanding the variety of situations in ICSID's jurisprudence noted by the Republic of Argentina, the tribunals have in all such cases been concerned not with the question of majority or control but rather whether shareholders can claim independently from the corporate entity. [...] The Tribunal can therefore conclude that there is no bar to the exercise of jurisdiction in light of the 1965 Convention and its interpretation as reflected in its drafting history, the opinion of distinguished legal writers and the jurisprudence of ICSID tribunals.[829]

---

international system for the protection of investments'. The Tribunal replied that 'Each tribunal remains sovereign and may retain, as it is confirmed by ICSID practice, a different solution for resolving the same problem; but decisions on jurisdiction dealing with the same or very similar issues may at least indicate some lines of reasoning of real interest', *AES Corporation v. The Argentine Republic,* ICSID Case No. ARB/02/17, Decision on Jurisdiction (26 Apr. 2005) paras 22, 30; Arbitrator J confirms this point by stating 'I selectively use case-law, the awards that are well reasoned and whose reasoning I agree with. I do look to other tribunals' decisions but I have to find that they are robust and I have to agree with what they say.'

827. *CMS*, Decision on jurisdiction (n 364) para. 53 (citations omitted).
828. *Ibid.* para. 54.
829. *Ibid.* paras 55–56.

The process to find the thread that may unite the multiple awards and decisions is not an easy task. It has been described as an art since it brings to the surface the creative role of the decision-maker:

> [i]nto the interpretation of precedents there may enter something like an artistic element. In his creative role the judge is, indeed, not unlike the poet who respects the inheritance of his native language in the very act of exploiting its resources for novel uses. It is to be hoped that the creativity of a poetic insight may bridge some of the contradictions that have become apparent in the practice of investment treaty tribunals.[830]

The need to interpret and understand the decisions becomes even more evident when realising that not all awards have the same weight. Paulsson eloquently remarks that not all awards have the same importance since 'while hierarchically undistinguishable, there are awards and awards, some destined to become ever brighter beacons, others to flicker and die near-instant deaths'.[831] In order to conclude to the importance of each award it is necessary to interpret the award. When prior awards are discussed, they are granted, consciously or unconsciously, weight and authority. There are, in this context, various factors that could be taken into account when interpreting an award such as the legal background of the arbitrators, the existence of dissenting opinions, and the separation between *obiter dicta* and *ratio decidendi*.[832] The citation frequency of each award is also a good way of evaluating the importance of not only arbitral case law but also the influence of the decision-maker.[833] With this background in mind, the next two parts analyse how arbitrators treat international and national precedents.

830. Andrés-Rigo Sureda, 'Precedent in Investment Treaty Arbitration' in Christoph Schreuer and others, *International Investment Law for the 21st Century* (n 673) 842 citing Lon Fuller, *Anatomy of the Law* (Penguin 1971) 136. Sureda also underlines the fact that it is necessary, for the sake of the certainty of law and its development, that tribunals explain why they choose to rely on certain awards or why they consider some decisions not relevant to the issues under consideration.
831. Jan Paulsson, 'International Arbitration and the Generation of Legal Norms' (n 531) 5; Francisco Orrego Vicuña, *International Dispute Settlement in an Evolving Global Society* (CUP 2004) 61 (making reference to the concept of 'leading cases').
832. For an analysis of the distinction *see* Joel Dahlquist, 'Beside the Point. On Obiter Dicta in Investment Treaty Arbitration' (2016) 1 ArbIntl 1; *See also* Vadi arguing that the distinction between *radio decidendi* and *obiter dicta* may not always be the indicator of an 'important' decision. Certain orbiter, such as reference to *erga omnes* in the Barcelona Traction case may have been the most often cited part of the decision. Vadi, *Analogies in International Investment Law and Arbitration* (n 277) 39; *See also* Maciej Koszowski, 'The Scope of Application of Analogical Reasoning in Precedential Law' (2016) 37 Liverpool Law Rev. 19 (analysing the issue of distinguishing, ascertaining and crystallizing the meaning of *ratio decidendi* in precedents).
833. *See* generally Commission, *Precedent in Investment Treaty Arbitration: The Empirical Backing* (n 767) 5; *See also* Gupta and Limond applying citation analysis to measure influence in investment-treaty arbitration. The data analysis led to the conclusion that some decisions had not received any citations at all, such as the final award in *SwemBalt AB v. Latvia* while other decisions have citation counts in excess of 100, such as the *Mondev*, Award (n 239). In addition, their calculation of the Arbitrator influence index based on the number of citations to decisions issued by the arbitrators and the number of appointments revealed the most influential arbitrator in investment arbitration. Rishab Gupta and Katrina Limond, 'Who is the most influential arbitrator in the world?' (GAR, 16 Jan. 2016) <http://globalarbitrationreview.com/journal/article/34478/who-influential-arbitrator-world> (accessed 20 May 2018).

[D] Dialogue with International Legal Orders

International law has its own important role in the decision-making of investment tribunals. According to Article 42(1) ICSID, in the case the parties have not agreed on the substantive law, the tribunal will apply the national law of the host State along with international law and its principles.[834] Even though not stated expressly in Article 42(1), in the case the parties have agreed on the applicable law and have chosen in particular a domestic law, international law remains applicable except if the parties have explicitly excluded its application. As a result, when there is a lacuna in the domestic law or in case where the domestic law violates international law, the tribunal is 'bound' to apply international law.[835] What should be kept in mind, however, is that international law might play a different role in the phase where the arbitrator specifies the applicable law and in the phase where the arbitrator interprets the law.

During the course of interpretation, the arbitrator may refer to precedents of international law courts as a guide to the interpretation of vague concepts. International law is the normative environment of the specialised framework of investment law and arbitration.[836] Within such a background, custom, general principles of law and international treaties inform the content of the investment protection rights and affect the judicial protection accorded to them through their open communication with the arbitral decision-maker. International jurisprudence has the function 'to resolve the conflict of opposing rights and interests by applying, in default of any specific provisions of law, the corollaries of general principles, and so to find [...] the solution of the problem'.[837]

[1] Specialised International Legal Orders

The evolution of the treaty-making mechanisms from a state-to-state game of delimiting State sovereignty to a specialised regulation procedure directed by international organisations, portrays the international law arena as a mosaic of many tesserae. The absence of an international legislature with a general lawmaking mandate has led to the development of coexisting regional, functional and historical treaty-making groups

834. 'In the absence of such agreement the Tribunal shall apply the law of the Contracting State party to the dispute (including its rules on the conflict of laws) and such rules of international law as may be applicable.' Article 42 (1) second sentence.
835. *Southern Pacific Properties (Middle East) Ltd. v. Arab Republic of Egypt*, ICSID Case No. ARB/98/4, Award (20 May 1992) para. 84.
836. McLachlan notes: 'Today, at least, if there is to be a meaningful consideration of international law in relation to the treatment of aliens, it can only be done by reference to a continuum of development from the pre-War custom into post-War treaty negotiation and application. So it remains of vital importance to consider how such treaties fit, and fall to be interpreted, within the general framework of international law' Campbell McLachlan, 'Investment Treaties and General International Law' (2008) 57 ICLQ 361, 369.
837. *Ibid.* 361 citing *Eastern Extension, Australasia and China Telegraph Co Ltd Case* (British-United States Claims Arbitral Tribunal) (1923) 114.

that inevitably interact with each other.[838] These specialised legal orders[839] reflect the related 'autonomisation of parts of global society'.[840] Investment treaties are considered to provide a special regime for the protection of investors constituting as well *lex specialis.*[841]

While such specialised regimes seek to accommodate particular circumstances that need to be addressed in a more specific way, they have developed at the same time adapted approaches to the interpretation and application of the law. Regimes such as international trade law, investment law, human rights and environmental law have created their own epistemic groups of academics and jurists, institutions creating the law, and judicial bodies interpreting and applying it. At the same time, the specific mandate of these courts to interpret the specialised instruments under which they are established is not detached from general international law.[842]

Systemic coherence of international law has been a matter of concern in the decentralised and non-hierarchical judicial bodies of international law. While on the one hand certain international courts describe themselves as 'self-contained systems'[843] or as 'autonomous judicial institutions',[844] on the other hand, judicial practice of the international courts and tribunals may lead to the emergence of a 'system of international courts and tribunals'[845] or a 'global community of courts'[846] comprising of both international and national courts. The term 'transgovernmentalism' has also been used to describe the new form of governance of international relations and the so-called judicial foreign policy of judges 'building a global community of law'.[847]

---

838. Wilfred Jenks, 'The Conflict of Law-Making Treaties' (1953) 30 BYIL 401, 403; Koskenniemi notes that 'there is no single legislative will behind international law'. Koskenniemi, 'Fragmentation of International Law' (n 259) para.
839. The concepts 'specialised legal framework', 'specialised legal order' and 'specialised legal regime' are used in a wide context to describe the specialised institutional and legal framework of the resolution of investor-state disputes under multilateral and bilateral investment treaties. The concept 'specialised decision-making process' has the meaning of a decision-making process which is adapted to the interpretive needs that may arise in the context of a specific dispute and to the idiosyncratic transnational characteristics of investment arbitration.
840. Gaffney, 'Going to Pieces Without Falling Apart' (n 629) 56.
841. Wälde, 'Interpreting Investment Treaties' (n 673) 742.
842. As an example, the ECtHR held that 'the principles underlying the Convention cannot be interpreted and applied in a vacuum. The Court must also take into account any relevant rules of international law [...], although it must remain mindful of the Convention's special character as a human rights treaty'. *Banković v. Belgium,* ECtHR, Decision as to the admissibility of Application No. 52207/99 (12 Dec. 2001) para. 57.
843. Specialised legal orders dealing with areas such as international trade law, human rights, and environmental law have been described as 'self-contained regimes'. *See* Koskenniemi, 'Fragmentation of International Law' (n 259) paras 128, 129.
844. Bruno Simma, 'Universality of International Law from the Perspective of a Practitioner' (2009) 20(2) EJIL 265, 278 citing 'The Right to Information on Consular Assistance in the Framework of the Guarantees of the Due Process of Law', IACtHR, Advisory Opinion OC-16/99 (1 Oct. 1999) para. 61.
845. Yuval Shany, *The Competing Jurisdictions of International Courts and Tribunals* (OUP 2003) 86.
846. Anne-Marie Slaughter, 'A Global Community of Courts' (2003) 44 HarvIntlLJ 191.
847. Anne-Marie Slaughter, 'The Real New World Order' (1997) 76 Foreign Affairs 183, 186.

Keeping this picture in mind, the specialised international law regimes, when accorded proper place and attention, constitute an indispensable part of the international law mosaic necessary to make sense to any observer. As the responsibility for the interpretation of international law is dispersed amongst diverse judicial and quasi-judicial bodies, the decision-makers should be aware of each other's decisions and develop 'channels of communication'.[848]

An example of a federal-type judicial communication is the OSCA Charter aiming at organising triennial meetings of the judges of the US Supreme Courts in order to promote and strengthen judicial independence, the rule of law and the appropriate constitutional treatment of the judges as an important branch of the State.[849] The communication in this case is a face-to-face oral exchange of ideas and knowledge. Another illustration is the initiative of the ICJ President Higgins (2006–2009) to set up a system of sending summaries and excerpts of the ICJ judgments to the ICTY, ICTR, ICCt, ECJ, ECtHR and the WTO Appellate body.[850] The system worked reciprocally and the judicial bodies also sent summaries of their own decisions to the ICJ highlighting important findings. Moreover, on a state-to-state level informal dialectical networks are formed such as the 'Transatlantic Business Dialogue' which brings together representatives from US and EU businesses discussing on regulatory and policy issues.[851]

The division of international law into specialised legal frameworks is not necessarily an 'evil' mutation of traditional public international law seen as the regulator of the relationships between States.[852] Fragmentation of international law can be seen from two perspectives depending on the purpose of the analysis. On the one hand, it could be connected to a panoply of complex issues linked to the conflict of treaties in the case each of the specialised regimes regulates in a different way the same relationships.[853] On the other hand, these specialised regimes may interact and communicate with each other forming dialogue links on various legal issues. The next sections take the latter perspective of interaction, treating the way international judicial bodies communicate with arbitral tribunals.

848. Rosalyn Higgins, 'Speech on the Occasion of the Opening of the Judicial Year' (2009) European Court of Human Rights Annual Report 2009, 45 <http://www.echr.coe.int/Documents/Annual_report_2009_ENG.pdf> (accessed 6 Dec. 2018).

849. Anne-Marie Slaughter, 'Government Networks: The Heart of the Liberal Democratic Order' in Gregory Fox and Brad Roth (eds) *Democratic Governance and International Law* (CUP 2000) 213.

850. Philippa Webb, *International Judicial Integration and Fragmentation* (OUP 2013) 220.

851. Hans-Ulrich Engel, 'The Transatlantic Business Dialogue: The Perspective of the European Chemical Industry' in George Bermann, Matthias Herdegen and Peter Lindseth (eds), *Transatlantic Regulatory Cooperation: Legal Problems and Political Prospects* (OUP 2000) 39.

852. The vocabulary that describes the augmentation of specialised international legal orders within the general legal system of international law varies. Notions like 'universalism' 'fragmentation', 'proliferation' are used in the literature acquiring different connotations and focus. The term 'universality' of international law is used in order to describe the existence on a global scale of an international law that is valid for and binds all States. International law is pictured as an 'all inclusive' universal body encompassing regional international law, treaty regimes creating specific legal sub-systems as well as bilateral relationships between States. *See* Simma, 'Universality of International Law from the Perspective of a Practitioner' (n 844) 267.

853. *See* generally Jan Klabbers, *Treaty Conflict and the European Union* (CUP 2009).

[2] The Role of 'Systemic Integration' in Investment Arbitration

The principle of 'systemic integration'[854] encompassed in Article 31(3)(c) VCLT is a broadly accepted principle of interpretation considered to give a response to the 'fragmentation' of the international legal order through the harmonisation of international law.[855] The question that arises here is the place of such a principle in investment-arbitration decision-making. Is the interaction between investment tribunals and other international courts based on Article 31(3)(c) VCLT or are we talking about a broader form of judicial dialogue not necessarily connected to the Vienna Convention?

Article 31(3)(c) VCLT provides that 'there shall be taken into account, together with the context [...] any relevant rules of international law applicable in the relations between the parties'. The positive aspect of the 'systemic integration' principle requires the parties to the treaty 'to refer to general principles of international law for all questions which [the treaty] does not itself resolve in express terms or in a different way'; the negative aspect expresses the fact that 'in entering into treaty obligations, the parties intend not to act inconsistently with generally recognised principles of international law or with previous treaty obligations towards third States'.[856]

Article 31(3)(c) is considered to refer to 'rules of international law' rather than broader principles and comprises all sources of international law including general principles of law, customary law and other treaties.[857] These rules must be relevant as well as applicable in the relationship between the parties. There is no specification, however, as to whether such rules are meant to apply to the parties of the treaty or to the parties to the dispute.[858]

The ICJ court describes 'systemic integration' as a rule of interpretation 'that a text emanating from a Government must, in principle, be interpreted as producing and intended to produce effects in accordance with existing law and not in violation of it'.[859] The rights and obligations the treaties establish receive their validity from general international law and exist and operate together with other treaties as well as with rules of CIL and the general principles of international law.[860] In this context, international treaties are viewed as a coherent whole constituting the normative background of a treaty under interpretation. The ILC report on fragmentation pictures Article 31(3)(c) as requiring '[...] the integration into the process of legal reasoning – including reasoning by courts and tribunals – of a sense of coherence and meaningfulness. Success or failure here is measured by how the legal world will view the outcome'.[861]

854. Campbell McLachlan, 'The Principle of Systemic Integration and Art. 31(3)(c) of the Vienna Convention' (2005) 54 ICLQ 279–320.
855. Gaffney, 'Going to Pieces Without Falling Apart' (n 629) 56.
856. McLachlan, 'The Principle of Systemic Integration and Art. 31 (3) (c) of the Vienna Convention' (n 854) 311.
857. Gaffney, 'Going to Pieces Without Falling Apart' (n 629) 57.
858. *Ibid.*
859. *Portugal v. India*, Case concerning the Right of Passage over Indian Territory, Preliminary Objections (26 Nov. 1957) ICJ Reports 1957, 142.
860. Koskenniemi, 'Fragmentation of International Law' (n 259) para. 414.
861. *Ibid.* para. 419.

The role this principle plays in the interpretation of investment treaties is rather obscure given the ad hoc nature of the arbitral tribunals and the consensual basis of their jurisdiction. Investment-arbitration tribunals have treated the issue very sporadically. What should be kept in mind, however, is the fine line between the interpretation of the investment treaty within the confines of Article 31(3)(c) as a systemic whole and the application of international law rules in the cadre of the specific dispute. In *Kardassopoulos v. Georgia*, for example, the tribunal dealt *inter alia* with the provisional application of the ECT treaty and the interpretation of its Article 45(1) in light of Article 31(3)(c) VCLT. The tribunal did not find sufficient justification to conclude to the provisional application of the treaty based on Article 31(3)(c):

> There is some uncertainty whether the provisional application of treaties constitutes a rule of international law applicable in relations between Georgia and Greece, so as to be taken into account under Article 31(3)(c) of the Vienna Convention.[862]

However, the tribunal found adequate ground to conclude to the provisional application of the treaty based on the 'intention of the negotiating States', the 'clear terms of the treaty providing for provisional application' and the 'object and purpose of the treaty'.[863]

The issue could be approached both as applicable law, especially in connection to the specific provisions of the investment treaties, as well as a process of interpretation. As a result, the requirement of Article 31(3)(c) to 'take into account' relevant rules of international law is not clear as to whether it signifies to take into consideration such rules when interpreting the treaty provisions or to apply the rules of international law in the investment-treaty cases.[864] To the complexity of the situation is added the interchangeability of the role of international treaties, customary international law and general principles of law as either sources of law or as interpretive tools as illustrated in Part II.[865] Additional issues that seem to be unresolved in this context are the exact meaning of the phrase 'relevant rules of international law' for the interpretation of investment treaties, whether Article 31(3)(c) applies only when interpretation is not possible based on Article 31(1),(2), and the exact adjudicative phase – jurisdiction or treaty application – the specific Article comes into play.[866] Based on these considerations and as will be revealed in the next sections, the dialogue formed in the investment-arbitration context differs from the systemic integration concerns approach of the Vienna Convention.

862. *Ioannis Kardassopoulos v. The Republic of Georgia*, ICSID Case No. ARB/05/18, Decision on Jurisdiction (6 Jul. 2007) para. 215.
863. *Ibid.* para. 221.
864. Thomas Wälde favours the former approach. Wälde, 'Interpreting Investment Treaties' (n 673).
865. *See* §2.02[B][3] 'Interchangeability: Principles as Sources of Law and as Interpretive Arguments'.
866. Gaffney, 'Going to Pieces Without Falling Apart' (n 629) 66–68.

[3] Dialogue with International Judges

The existence of specialised legal orders on an international level raises queries regarding the role of the dispute resolution bodies and the productive exploitation of the diversification of international law.[867] International judicial bodies, being aware of the need to get acquainted and communicate with their peers, have developed mechanisms that permit the consideration and even integration of principles and concepts developed in other legal orders. Communication between international judges through their awards is a horizontal type of dialogue since it is effectuated between interlocutors of the same international level.[868] The aim of such a communication process is not the homogenisation of differences but rather the fruitful communication and exchange of ideas in a heterogeneous environment. The dialogue stresses out the gaps of the investment-arbitration framework and satisfies the need to find guidance elsewhere depending on the similarities of the interlocutor-legal order. It also points out the differences and specificities of investment arbitration and, therefore, the need to adapt any 'foreign concept' to the particular context of investment arbitration.

The dialogue between international judges and investment arbitrators is not restricted to the obscure and complicated application of Article 31(3)(c) VCLT as seen above.[869] Rather, it encompasses the communication between specialised regimes of international law even without the need to directly refer to the VCLT in order to realise such an interaction. The driving force behind such a communication is the very own nature and needs of the investment-arbitration framework. Investment arbitration is a 'hybrid' dispute resolution mechanism decentralised through ad hoc tribunals and driving from its infancy to its adolescence.[870] While the first BIT was entered into in 1959, the vast majority – 1,857 – was signed by 2000.[871] The investment-arbitration framework is still in the process of its evolution and development.

Many unresolved issues arise that are connected to the sensitive public-private, international-domestic dichotomies.[872] In addition, the open-ended wording of investment treaties urges the arbitrator to shape the content, fill in gaps and resolve ambiguities through a dialogue with other decision-makers. Arbitrators and counsel look into the case law of specialised international legal orders for guidance when 'language and principles' arise that need to be interpreted but have already been treated in the foreign jurisprudence.[873] The awareness of the judicial views expressed in related fields inform, supplement and even test the interpretive arguments of investment tribunals. Even if one accepts that the Vienna Convention provides full

867. *See* Jonathan Charney, 'Is International Law Threatened by Multiple International Tribunals?' (1998) 271 RecDesCours 101.
868. *See* §5.03 'From Legal Transplants to Legal Dialogues'.
869. *See* §6.05[B][1][c] 'Systemic Integrity'.
870. Douglas, 'The Hybrid Foundations of Investment Treaty Arbitration' (n 335) 153.
871. UNCTAD Report 'Non-equity modes of international production and development' (2011) 100 <https://unctad.org/en/PublicationsLibrary/wir2011overview_en.pdf> (accessed 4 May 2018).
872. Roberts, 'Clash of Paradigms' (n 76) 8.
873. Thomas Wälde, 'The Specific Nature of Investment Arbitration', in Philippe Kahn and Thomas Wälde (eds) *New Aspects of International Investment Law* (Brill 2007) 109.

guidance for the interpretation of treaties, the need may arise that concepts not included in treaties, such as the principle of proportionality, need to be inserted in the investment-arbitration context in order to fulfil specific functions such as the balancing of rights. The use of interpretive arguments from other legal regimes in order to fulfil these decision-making functions does not necessarily imply that tribunals have in mind Article 31(3)(c) VCLT.

Investment tribunals through their citation practices have formed dialogues with various international judicial bodies such as the ECtHR, ICJ, WTO, ECJ and the Iran-US claims Tribunal.[874] The choice of the interlocutor-legal order which will be part of the dialogue is a delicate exercise. Each discipline will offer the solution that suits its context, functions and purposes. Comparisons with each discipline will bring to the fore differences and similarities both shaping the basis and limits of the dialogue. The choice of communicating with public international law orders has been described as locating investment arbitration 'on the public side of the public/private divide and firmly situates it within a broader corpus of international legal rules, paving the way for the introduction of public international law rules and analogies, including from trade, human rights and environment law'.[875]

The nature of the rights acquired by the investor against the State is significantly close and comparable to the rights of individuals in the context of human rights. Both frameworks deal with the sensitive balance between State regulatory powers and the protection of individuals. Tribunals take the initiative to refer to human rights concepts when there is a lacuna or where guidance is needed as to the methodologies applied in order to evaluate competing interests. Human rights considerations may be imported into the arbitral process not only through the initiative of the tribunal but also through the parties' submissions. Concepts developed by the ECtHR such as proportionality and moral damages appear in the claims of the investors.[876] As an example, in determining the content of the 'minimum standard of treatment' concept under NAFTA, the *Mondev* tribunal examined the ECtHR jurisprudence regarding the 'right to a court' in order to obtain 'guidance by analogy'.[877]

---

874. *See* generally Jeffery Commission, 'Precedent in Investment Treaty Arbitration – A Citation Analysis of a Developing Jurisprudence' (2007) 24(2) JIntlArb 129; The method of cross-referencing cases is described as 'a comparative method based on similarity, analogy and differentiation'. Vernon Valentine Palmer, 'From Lerotholi to Lando: Some Examples of Comparative Law Methodology' (n 616) 1; For the citation of the Iran-United States Claims Tribunal cases in ICSID awards *see* Christopher R Drahozal, 'The Iran – U.S. Claim Tribunal and Investment Arbitration: A Citation Analysis', 3 TDM, No. 2 (2006); Cf Thomas Carbonneau, *The Elaboration of Substantive Legal Norms and Arbitral Adjudication: The Case of the Iran-United States Claims Tribunal, in* R. Lillich, Ed. The Iran-United States Claims Tribunal 1981–1983 104, 128 (1984) (arguing that the awards of the US-Iran Claims Tribunal 'have been essentially devoid of substantive legal content and, as a result, [are] incapable of having much precedential value'.
875. Roberts, 'Clash of Paradigms' (n 76) 38; For an analysis of the method for comparative reasoning, how analogies are drawn and whether there is a suitable method for drawing them, *see* Vadi, *Analogies in International Investment Law and Arbitration* (n 277).
876. *See*, for example, *Desert Line Projects LLP v. Yemen*, ICSID Case No. ARB/05/17, Award (6 Feb. 2008) paras 9–10.
877. *Mondev*, Award (n 239) para. 144; Vadi points out that the reasoning by analogy can lead to different results depending on the selected case-comparator. As an example, the *Lauder* and

In particular, the principle of proportionality has gained an important place in the investment-arbitration decision-making process as a means to balance the State's regulatory power on the one hand and the protection of the investors on the other.[878] Investment tribunals, in considering the protection guarantees accorded by the treaties such as fair and equitable treatment, full protection and security, or compensation for expropriation, recognise the need to balance the State's and investor's interests through the application of proportionality.

In this sense, proportionality fulfils the double objective of taking into account the public interest of a State by relying on immunity justifications while on the other hand controlling abuses of State powers if they are used over an acceptable standard.[879] This legal interpretation method works in a 'more or less' fashion rather than in an 'all-or-nothing' way.[880] It mainly encompasses the philosophy of utilising the appropriate means in order to achieve the specific aim pursued.[881]

The proportionality analysis involves a three-step procedure. The first step is the application of the suitability test while as a second step comes the principle of necessity, and the final phase includes the evaluation of *stricto sensu* proportionality. The suitability phase requires the State measure to be suitable for achieving the objective pursued and presupposes a causal link between the State measure and its purpose.[882] The principle of necessity determines whether there are less restrictive but equally effective alternative measures to achieve the same goal. In the proportionality *stricto sensu* phase, the question the decision-maker is called to answer is whether the restriction of the interest is analogous to the objective of the restriction. At this stage the factors that are taken into account are diverse, from a cost-benefit analysis to the minor or major degree of interference, and the permanent or temporary nature of the interference.[883] This last step functions as a safety net in the case the first two steps are satisfied; not any restriction of rights is possible, but only a restriction satisfying the safeguards of *stricto sensu* proportionality.

CME cases were parallel proceedings over the same dispute but under different BITs. When establishing the standards for expropriation, the two tribunals reached different outcomes since the Lauder tribunal made reference to a human rights case while the CME tribunal did not. Vadi, *Analogies in International Investment Law and Arbitration* (n 277) 4, 37. *CME Czech Republic B.V. v. Czech Republic*, Final Award (14 Mar. 2003); Ronald S. *Lauder v. Czech Republic* UNCITRAL Final Award, (3 Sep. 2001) para. 200.

878. *See generally* Kingsbury and Schill, 'Investor-State Arbitration as Governance' (n 148).
879. Stephan Schill, 'Cross-Regime Harmonization through Proportionality Analysis: The Case of International Investment Law, the Law of State Immunity and Human Rights' (2012) 27(1) ICSID Rev 87, 108.
880. Dworkin, *Taking Rights Seriously* (n 174) 24.
881. Nicholas Emiliou, *The Principle of Proportionality in European Law: A Comparative Study* (Kluwer Academic Publishers 1996) 23–24; For the debate on the legitimacy of transplanting proportionality into international investment arbitration *see*: Valentina Vadi who argues that 'Transplanting proportionality into international investment law and arbitration would be legitimate if proportionality was part of the applicable law, as a general principle of law, or reflected state practice, which is an element of customary international law, or as a matter of treaty interpretation.' Vadi, *Analogies in International Investment Law and Arbitration* (n 277) 195.
882. Jan Jans, 'Proportionality Revisited' (2000) 27 LIEI 239, 240.
883. Kingsbury and Schill, 'Investor-State Arbitration as Governance' (n 148) 30.

Proportionality is integrated and developed in investment arbitration through the dialogue with international and domestic legal orders and judicial bodies. In the *Técnicas Medioambientales Tecmed SA* case, the tribunal relied on the ECtHR jurisprudence,[884] referring to Article 1 of Protocol 1 in order to draw guidance for the use of the proportionality analysis in determining whether a legitimate regulation turned in fact into indirect expropriation.[885] The Tribunal applied the proportionality test through the determination of the reasonableness of the State measures in relation to their pursued objectives, as well as the deprivation of economic rights, and the legitimate expectations of the person suffering such deprivation.[886] The tribunal concluded that the non-renewal of the license was a measure that restricted the investor's property rights in a disproportionate manner constituting as a result an indirect expropriation.

Some years later, the *Azurix* tribunal relied on *Techmed's* analysis of the ECtHR case law in order to conclude that a measure resulting in expropriation must pursue a 'legitimate aim in the public interest' employing means that are reasonably proportional to the State's objective.[887]Similarly, the tribunal in the *Occidental Petroleum* case proceeded to a very broad dialogue engaging arguments from ICSID case law, domestic jurisprudence, European case law, the case law of the ECtHR as well as WTO decisions in order to form its interpretive syllogism regarding the application of the proportionality principle:

> On the application of proportionality generally in the context of administrative action, the most developed body of jurisprudence is in Europe. It is very well-established law in a number of European countries that there is a principle of proportionality which requires that administrative measures must not be any more drastic than is necessary for achieving the desired end. The principle has been adopted and applied countless times by the European Court of Justice in Luxembourg, and by the European Court of Human Rights in Strasbourg. [...] Against that background, the Tribunal observes that there is a growing body of arbitral law, particularly in the context of ICSID arbitrations, which holds that the principle of proportionality is applicable to potential breaches of bilateral investment treaty obligations.[888]

However, the three-step methodology of the proportionality analysis cannot always be distinguished in arbitral case law. The proportionality analysis of arbitral tribunals also includes concepts such as 'reasonableness', 'appropriateness' and 'fairness'. Additionally, arbitral tribunals also evaluate the legitimacy of the purpose of the State measure. However, the threshold is rather low to pass as common public

884. The tribunal relied on the following cases: *In the case of Matos e Silva, Lda., and Others v. Portugal,* ECtHR, Judgment (16 Sep. 1996); *In the case of Mellacher and Others v. Austria,* ECtHR, Judgment (19 Dec. 1989); *In the case of Pressos Compañía Naviera and Others v. Belgium,* ECtHR, Judgment (20 Nov. 1995); *In the case of James and Other v. The United Kingdom s,* ECtHR, Judgment (21 Feb. 1986).
885. *Tecmed,* Award (n 147) para. 122 (citations omitted).
886. *Ibid.*
887. *Azurix v. Argentine Republic,* ICSID Case No. ARB/01/12, Award (23 Jun. 2006) para. 311.
888. *Occidental Petroleum Corporation and Occidental Exploration and Production Company v. The Republic of Ecuador,* ICSID Case No. ARB/06/11, Award (5 Oct. 2012) paras 402–404 (citations omitted).

purposes are considered to be legitimate.[889] This application of proportionality reveals the tribunal's attempt to 'fit' the proportionality concept in the context of investment arbitration. A stark illustration is the *Total* case where the tribunal used the proportionality test in order to balance competing interests in the context of the application of the FET standard. Along with proportionality, there is reference to standards of 'reasonableness', 'appropriateness' and 'fairness' which are also connected to the balancing of interests exercise.[890] In this context, the tribunal dealt with the balancing of public-private interests taking into account the reasonableness of the investor's legitimate expectation, reasonableness of the normative changes challenged, appropriateness of the normative changes challenged and fairness of the conduct of the host country towards an investor.[891]

From a similar perspective, proportionality analysis figures in *El Paso,* employed for the distinction between indirect expropriations and general regulation, and as part of the FET standard. The tribunal also makes reference to the principle of non-discrimination as a combined with the proportionality test. In this context, discriminatory or disproportionate general regulations could be characterised as expropriatory if there is a sufficient interference with the investor's rights.[892]

The balancing of interests procedure depends on the cultural, social and value-driven characteristics of a specific institution, its hermeneutics, its regulations and the objectives of the specific legal regime.[893] The diversity of the use of proportionality analysis across different legal systems leads to thoughts about its adaptation when applied in the investment-arbitration framework.[894] Arbitral case law demonstrates that arbitrators have made efforts to adapt the proportionality methodology when adding to the proportionality analysis concepts such as 'reasonableness', 'fairness' and 'non-discrimination'. However, these concepts are of a general content and acquire their specific meaning in practice. As such, arbitral tribunals have, on the one hand, acknowledged the importance of their use in the application of proportionality, while, on the other hand, still strive for a consistent approach to their interpretation. In this

889. Kingsbury and Schill, 'Investor-State Arbitration as Governance' (n 148) 29; *See generally* Gebhard Bücheler, *Proportionality in Investor-State Arbitration* (OUP 2015).
890. *See also* Vadi, 'The Migration of Constitutional Ideas to Regional and International Economic Law' (n 793) 583.
891. *Total SA v. The Argentine Republic,* ICSID Case No. ARB/04/1, Decision on Liability (27 Dec. 2010) para. 123 (citations omitted); *See also Urbaser* Award (n 249) para. 529 (where the Tribunal made reference to the concept of 'reasonableness' when interpreting the FET standard and determining the investor's legitimate expectations).
892. *El Paso Energy International Company v. The Argentine Republic,* ICSID Case No. ARB/03/15, Award (31 Oct. 2011) paras 243, 246. The 'sufficiency' of the interference was defined with reference to the Pope & Talbot award: 'the test is whether that interference is sufficiently restrictive to support a conclusion that the property has been "taken" from the owner'.
893. Kingsbury and Schill, 'Investor-State Arbitration as Governance' (n 148) 28.
894. Wälde also highlights this with regards to the application of general legal principles such as 'good faith' and 'legitimate expectation' noting that these 'should take into account the specific functions of investment treaties and the structural weakness of foreign investors. That means allocating the risk of, for example, ambiguity rather to the host State than to the investor and of requiring a higher-level of good faith from the host State. That has indeed been the recurrent theme of a series of recent arbitral jurisprudence applying the good faith and legitimate expectations principle'. Wälde, 'The Specific Nature of Investment Arbitration' (n 873) 117.

vein, the functions of the arbitrators become broader requiring the decision-maker's engagement in attributing to each 'imported' concept the appropriate weight keeping in mind the special needs and characteristics of the investment-arbitration context.

The use of proportionality analysis by investment tribunals is used to delimit the interaction between substantive investment protection standards on the one hand and jurisdictional and enforcement immunity on the other.[895] This is a logical consequence of the evolution of international investment law and the law of State immunity towards an investor-state relationship governed by a rule of law-based framework.[896] Even though there are controversial views on whether proportionality constitutes a general principle of international law and, as such, constitutes part of the international law applicable to the dispute,[897] arbitral practice reveals that it helps the tribunals to properly fulfil not only their hermeneutic functions but also their function related to the fair resolution of conflicts between private interests and legitimate public interests.[898]

The human rights law discipline,[899] as well as any chosen interlocutor,[900] may be a useful source of guidance but what should always be kept in mind is that the nature of the rights accorded by each discipline is different. It is still disputable, for example, whether investment treaties accord *erga omnes* substantive rights such as human rights treaties do.[901] Moreover, the investment treaties constitute a type of political risk management tool for the investor and this function should also be taken into account.[902]

What remains to be answered is whether such a cross-fertilisation process would lead to importing the specialised legal regimes into investment arbitration through the back door at the time when the parties consented to the dispute being resolved through investment arbitration rather than in any other international judicial context.[903] What should be primarily distinguished is the dialogue between arbitrators and judges through their citation practices as opposed to the application of the specialised framework in the investment-arbitration dispute. Taking as an example the ECHR framework, the reference to the way the ECtHR interprets specific legal concepts that also appear in the investment-arbitration framework does not automatically indicate the application of the ECHR framework to the dispute. Rather than assuming that

895. Schill, 'Cross-Regime Harmonization through Proportionality Analysis' (n 879) 118.
896. *Ibid.*
897. For example, Andreas Kulick, *Global Public Interest in International Investment Law* (CUP 2012) 168 et seq.
898. Kingsbury and Schill, 'Investor-State Arbitration as Governance' (n 148) 23.
899. *See also* Bohoslavsky and Justo proposing the conventionality control of arbitral awards through the verification of their compatibility with human rights treaties enhancing the coherence of the overall international legal system through more dialogue among judicial and quasi-judicial bodies that have a say in foreign investment issues. Juan Bohoslavsky and Juan Bautista Justo, 'The Conventionality Control of Investment Arbitrations: Enhancing Coherence Through Dialogue' (2013) 10 TDM 1.
900. In particular, the principle of proportionality is described as having itself migrated form the constitutional law sphere. *See* Vadi, *Analogies in International Investment Law and Arbitration* (n 277) 203–207.
901. Roberts, 'Clash of Paradigms' (n 76) 33.
902. Wälde, 'The Specific Nature of Investment Arbitration' (n 873) 117; *See also* §6.05[A][1] 'Political Policies'.
903. Gaffney, 'Going to Pieces Without Falling Apart' (n 629) 59.

principles of other regimes and cases 'cross-apply' to the investment-arbitration framework as a matter of law, such references are better viewed as a means to draw comparisons between legal fields with textual and functional resemblances.[904] In these cases, the function of citation practices is to contribute in shaping the content of legal norms and fill in lacunae.

[4] Reciprocal Communication

As demonstrated in the above analysis, the investment-arbitration framework profits from the dialogue with international judges especially when there is a lacuna or ambiguity in the investment treaties. In volition to accommodate the reciprocal type of communication that a dialectical approach expresses, what should be further examined is whether investment arbitrators contribute in any way to the dialogue with international legal orders.

The decisions of arbitral tribunals have effects that go beyond the dispute in hand bearing on the general legal structures such as the creation of normative expectations and development of the legal norms.[905] A consistent interpretation of the general protection guarantees contained in investment treaties promotes the development of the body of investment law. In its turn, the interpretational consensus in arbitral case law may gradually contribute to the development of a homogenous international body of rules. The process of 'cross-fertilisation' of principles by international courts when taking into consideration the practice of other international courts has led to the emergence of a 'common law of international adjudication'.[906]

The normative effect of an arbitral award in the international legal scene was mentioned many years ago by Sir Hersch Lauterpacht:

> It is in the interest of international justice that its continuity should not be confined to the jurisprudence of the Court itself. International arbitral law has produced a body of precedent which is full of instruction and authority. Numerous arbitral awards have made a distinct contribution to international law by reason of their scope, their elaboration, and the conscientiousness with which they have examined the issue before them.[907]

One example is the way tribunals shape the standard of FET stabilising normative expectations regarding the behaviour of host States. An investment tribunal would be expected by investors and host States to address the lack of due process or arbitrary and discriminatory process as breaching the standard of fair and equitable treatment.[908] Eminent jurists sitting as arbitrators have rendered a number of awards that have

904. Roberts, 'Clash of Paradigms' (n 76) 11.
905. Armin Von Bogdandy and Ingo Venzke, 'Beyond Dispute: International Judicial Institutions as Lawmakers' (2012) 12 GLJ 979, 979.
906. Chester Brown, A *Common Law of International Adjudication* (n 826) 5.
907. Sir Hersch Lauterpacht, *The Development of International Law by the International Court* (n 528) 17–18.
908. Stephan Schill, 'Fair and Equitable Treatment, the Rule of Law, and Comparative Public Law', in Stephan Schill (ed.) *International Investment Law and Comparative Public Law* (OUP 2010) 151.

contributed to the development of the law.[909] The *Enron* tribunal, stressing the role of case law in the development of the FET standard in international law, notes:

> Thus, the Tribunal concludes that a key element of fair and equitable treatment is the requirement of a 'stable framework for the investment', which has been prescribed by a number of decisions. Indeed, this interpretation has been considered 'an emerging standard of fair and equitable treatment in international law.[910]

Based on the above considerations, the dialogue between tribunals and courts and the use of concepts found in other specialised legal orders contributes in counteracting the fragmentation of international law, reinforcing at the same time international law's unity.[911] Judicial dialogues contribute to the coherence of the international legal system enhancing its legitimacy and political acceptability.[912] International legal rules are tested, argued and analysed in the context of judicial practice and eventually tailored to the conditions and environment of each specialised legal system.

Moreover, investment tribunals are considered to influence the approaches to State behaviour followed by specialised regimes such as human rights and trade law in the context of balancing public and private interests as well as influencing the development of customary international law and general principles of law.[913] In this context arbitrators have been described as contributing to the formation of a 'global administrative law'.[914] Even though the investment-arbitration framework is still in the process of its development, the 'authentic' jurisprudence developed by arbitral tribunals 'should gradually acquire more specificity and authority than authorities from more remote fields' shifting the directions of relevant analogies.[915]

[E] Dialogue with National Legal Orders

The dialogue network between judges is not created on a solely international and regional level but also on an international-national level leading to the creation of new global relationships.[916] Domestic judicial practice as well as State laws and practices influence in their own way the investment-arbitration framework.

The interaction is twofold forming a dialectical relationship both with national laws as well as with domestic jurisprudence. Arbitral tribunals make references to domestic case law mainly when issues of contract interpretation arise such as License

909. Ian Brownlie, *Principles of Public International Law* (6th ed., OUP 2003) 19.
910. *Enron*, Award (n 581) para. 260 (citations omitted).
911. Vadi, 'The Migration of Constitutional Ideas to Regional and International Economic Law' (n 793) 563.
912. Burke-White, *International Legal Pluralism* (n 566) 978.
913. Kingsbury and Schill, 'Investor-State Arbitration as Governance' (n 148) 2; *See* §6.04 'Customary Law Arguments' and §4.02 'Development-Oriented Function: Reasoning as a Means for Normative Development'.
914. *Ibid.* 2.
915. Wälde, 'The Specific Nature of Investment Arbitration' (n 873) 110.
916. Slaughter, 'The Real New World Order' (n 847) 187.

contracts. National courts also make reference to arbitral case law when confronted with issues of investment-treaty interpretation.[917]

[1] Dialogue with National Law

Despite the fact that the breach of an investment treaty is assessed according to international law – in the same way a contract claim will be assessed with reference to national law – there still remains place for interaction between the two. The applicable law governing investment disputes has been described as a 'hybrid of international and municipal law due to the private or commercial interests at the heart of this jurisdiction'.[918] Domestic law plays an important role in the arbitration of investment disputes since the protection of investors' rights under the investment treaties requires their creation and recognition under domestic law.[919]

In this sense, national legal orders may be relevant to a treaty claim when international law makes it relevant in supplying facts for applying the international standard or by incorporating the standard of compliance with "municipal law" into the applicable international standard.[920] Moreover, many concepts of international investment treaties such as 'contract', 'property rights' and 'shareholders' rights', are not clearly defined. It has been argued that the absence of such definitions in international law requires a 'renvoi' to 'municipal law' in an attempt to search for relevant definitions and 'if necessary to import rules of municipal law into an international context'.[921]

Interactions between national law and investment-arbitration can also be found in the cases where the tribunal is called to interpret the meaning of terms such as 'nationals' in order to satisfy the requirements of the ICSID Convention.[922] In this case the decision-maker will apply the nationality law of the investor's home country. When it comes to the definition of 'investment', the arbitral tribunals have followed diverse paths. Certain tribunals attempted to identify the characteristics of an 'objective' concept of investment which is not dependent upon the existence of an underlying right.[923] Other tribunals have determined these characteristics based on 'undefined international law principles' while some tribunals had recourse to national rules.[924]

Similarly, the Enron Tribunal, referring to the complementary role of international law and domestic law as expressed in the *Wena* annulment decision, applied

917. *See* below §6.03[E][3] 'Reciprocal Communication'.
918. Douglas, 'The Hybrid Foundations of Investment Treaty Arbitration' (n 335) 195.
919. *Ibid.* 199.
920. Sasson, *Substantive Law in Investment Treaty Arbitration* (n 381) 205.
921. *Ibid.* 198–200. The author refers to certain delimitations of the renvoi principle: 'The principle of renvoi does not affect the supremacy of international law. It permits the application of concepts developed for many years at a municipal level when such application does not conflict with international law and does not affect the characterisation of an act as internationally wrongful.'
922. Jeswald Salacuse, *The Three Laws of International Investment: National, Contractual, and International Frameworks for Foreign Capital* (OUP 2013) 407.
923. Sasson, *Substantive Law in Investment Treaty Arbitration* (n 381) 202.
924. *Ibid.* 202.

domestic law when interpreting the contracts-License agreement in order to determine whether liability exists under the domestic legal order.[925] In particular, the tribunal noted that domestic law is not limited to the determination of factual questions as the claimant asserted but it has a broader role. In referring to the boarder role of domestic law the tribunal stated:

> [Domestic law] has indeed a broader role, as it is evident in this very case from the pleadings and arguments of the parties that have relied heavily on the Gas Law and generally the regulatory framework of the gas industry, just as they have relied on many other rules of the Argentine legal system, including the Constitution, the Civil Code, specialized legislation and the decisions of courts.[926]

The main role of domestic law is in shaping the content of and enforcing the contractual framework of the investment transaction through regulating the negotiation processes of the contracts or by requiring governmental approval of certain contracts.[927] The regulation of the admission of foreign investments by host States is also echoed in the World Bank Guidelines on the Treatment of Foreign Direct Investment. The Guidelines mention that host States have 'the right to make regulations to govern the admission of private foreign investments' and that the investments should operate 'in full conformity with the laws and regulations of the host-state'.[928]

As such, the symbiosis of international and national laws in international dispute resolution frameworks constitutes a reality in the investment-arbitration scene. With this preliminary background in mind, the next section revels the relationship between arbitrators and national judges.

[2] Dialogue with National Judges

In the decision-making process, investment-arbitration tribunals consider the findings of national laws by national courts, tribunals or regulatory bodies.[929] Such a communication, especially with the national courts, is largely justified due to the public law aspect of investor-state arbitration which reflects the establishment of this private adjudication mechanism through a sovereign act of a State. The public nature of the disputes is interrelated to the jurisdiction that the States have accorded to the arbitral

925. *Enron*, Award (n 581) para. 207.
926. *Ibid.* para. 206.
927. Salacuse, *The Three Laws of International Investment* (n 922) 405.
928. McLachlan and others, *International Investment Arbitration: Substantive Principles* (n 340) 440–445.
929. *Ibid.* 69; Schreuer refers to five types of interaction between international and domestic courts: (1) Prior Use of Domestic Courts (prior exhaustion of local remedies), (2) Competition between Investment Tribunals and Domestic Courts, (3) Support by Domestic Courts in Investment Arbitration, (4) Interference by Domestic Courts in Investment Arbitration v. Mutual Scrutiny of Investment Tribunals and Domestic Courts. Christoph Schreuer, 'Interaction of International Tribunals and Domestic Courts in Investment Law' (2010) 4 Contemporary Issues in International Arbitration and Mediation: The Fordham Papers 71-94.

tribunals over public law.[930] Thus, this public law function of investment tribunals can be described as being analogous to a court's task to define individual environmental, economic and property rights in national public law.[931]

Comparative public reasoning as an interpretive methodology places the State obligations toward the private investor alongside the State's obligations owed to its citizens under domestic law, and to other transnational actors under international and transnational legal rules.[932] The public nature of the disputes that investment-treaty tribunals are requested to resolve raises questions on the interpretation of concepts and rights that belong to the sphere of public law.[933] Within this background, the dialogue with national judges has a double purpose. Its first aim is to guide the definition and delimitation of vague treaty concepts. A second purpose is the introduction of traditionally domestic law concepts into arbitral decision-making in order to cope with specific decision-making needs.

Reference to domestic case law can be found in multiple investment-arbitration cases. A stark illustration is the *Total v. Argentina* case where the tribunal clearly revealed the dialectical approach it followed in forming its interpretive arguments:

> In determining the scope of a right or obligation, Tribunals have often looked as a benchmark to international or comparative standards. Indeed, as is often the case for general standards applicable in any legal system (such as 'due process'), a comparative analysis of what is considered generally fair or unfair conduct by domestic public authorities in respect of private firms and investors in domestic law may also be relevant to identify the legal standards under BITs. Such an approach is justified because, factually, the situations and conduct to be evaluated under a BIT occur within the legal system and social, economic and business environment of the host State.[934]

Similarly, in the *Feldman v. Mexico* case the tribunal, in order to address the issue of transparency, referred to the decision of the British Columbia Supreme Court:

> The British Columbia Supreme Court held in its review of the Metalclad decision that Section A of Chapter 11, which establishes the obligations of host governments to foreign investors, nowhere mentions an obligation of transparency to

930. Gus Van Harten, 'The Public-Private Distinction in the International Arbitration of Individual Claims Against the State' (2009) 29 <http://ssrn.com/abstract=1461125> (accessed 9 Jan. 2018).
931. *Ibid.*
932. Julie A Maupin, 'Public and Private in International Investment Law: An integrated Systems Approach' 54(2) Virginia Journal of International Law 367, 399; Vadi, *Analogies in International Investment Law and Arbitration* (n 277) 193.
933. *See also* Federico Ortino who refers to a 'public law adjudication' Ortino, 'Legal Reasoning of International Investment Tribunals' (n 533) 28.
934. *Total*, Decision on Liability (n 891) para. 111 (citations omitted); *See also Grand River Enterprises Six Nations, Ltd., et al. v. US*, UNCITRAL, NAFTA, Decision on Objections to Jurisdiction (20 Jul. 2006), para. 77 where the Tribunal made reference to US case law to confirm that 'a person may "incur" expenses before he or she actually disburses any funds' in Vadi, *Analogies in International Investment Law and Arbitration* (n 277) 107.

such investors, and that a denial of transparency alone thus does not constitute a violation of Chapter 11 [...].[935]

Despite the fact that the *Feldman* tribunal recognised that it was not required to follow the same result as the domestic court, it found the specific aspect of the decision 'instructive'.[936] Similarly, the *Occidental v. Ecuador* tribunal noted that although domestic court decisions do not constitute binding precedent, 'the discussions contained in the decisions of the Ecuadorian tax courts and of the Supreme Court give useful guidance in understanding Ecuadorian legislation and important related concepts'.[937]

Tribunals have also taken into account the reasoning of domestic courts for the interpretation of the MFN clause and the dispute settlement arrangements. Enhancing its syllogism with reference to the United States Supreme Court Decision,[938] the *Maffezzini* tribunal concluded that even though the treaty did not expressly refer to dispute settlement arrangements, the latter are 'inextricably related' to the protection of the investor.[939]

Nonetheless, what should be kept in mind is that reference to the decisions of national courts treating questions of domestic law connected to the investor's rights presupposes that the findings are untainted by a procedural irregularity such as lack of 'due process'.[940] The assessment of a court decision is not an easy exercise and has its own limits but 'it is more of an affront to judicial comity to completely ignore the prior decisions of competent courts and tribunals than to subject such decisions to a level of

935. *Marvin Roy Feldman Karpa v. United Mexican States*, ICSID Case No. ARB(AF)/99/1, Award (16 Dec. 2002) para. 133.
936. *Ibid.* para. 133.
937. *Occidental Exploration and Production Co v. Republic of Ecuador*, LCIA Case No. UN3467, UNCITRAL, Award (1 Jul. 2004) para. 137; *See also*, *Amco v. Indonesia*, ICSID Case No. ARB/81/1, Award (20 Nov. 1984) para. 177, where the Tribunal held that 'an international tribunal is not bound to follow the result of a national court. One of the reasons for instituting an international arbitration procedure is precisely that parties – rightly or wrongly – feel often more confident with a legal institution which is not entirely related to one of the parties. If a national judgment was binding on an international tribunal such a procedure could be rendered meaningless'. However, Schreuer notes that 'this does not preclude an international tribunal from relying on decisions of domestic courts, especially where the applicable law is the law of the domestic courts' forum State', Christoph Schreuer, 'Interaction of International Tribunals and Domestic Courts in Investment Law' (n 929) 71, 77.
938. *Magno Santovincenzo v. James F. Egan*, United States Supreme Court, Decision (23 Nov. 1931) 284 US Reports, 30; Similarly, the US Supreme Court's decision in *Penn Central Transportation Co. v. New York City'* (26 Jun. 1978) influenced the three factors established for the distinction between indirect expropriation and legitimate, non-compensable regulation in the new annex to the 2004 US Model BIT. These factors are: the degree of interference with property rights; the character of the government measure; and the interference of the measure with reasonable and investment-backed expectations. Anthony B Sanders, 'Of All Things Made in America Why Are We Exporting the Penn Central Test?', (2010) NJILB 30, 339–381; Jonathan Bonnitcha, Lauge N Skovgaard Poulsen, and Michael Waibel, *The Political Economy of the Investment Treaty Regime* (OUP 2017) 108.
939. *Emilio Agustín Maffezini v. The Kingdom of Spain*, ICSID Case No. ARB/97/7, Decision on Jurisdiction (25 Jan. 2000) para. 55.
940. Douglas further marks that such grounds would normally defeat the res judicata effect of a judgment or award. Douglas, 'The Hybrid Foundations of Investment Treaty Arbitration' (n 335) 273–274.

scrutiny before adopting their findings'.[941] When the *Enron* Tribunal addressed the Respondent's argument regarding the state of necessity it referred to a national court decision. The Tribunal held that since the Gas Transportation Licence was governed by the Argentinian legal order, which includes the Constitution, the Civil Code, specialised legislation and the decisions of courts, it must be interpreted in its light.[942] The tribunal relied on the Supreme Court's decision in order to examine the legal validity of the emergency measures:

> The Supreme Court has held in connection with the Emergency Law presently in force that '... it is not useless to remind, as the Tribunal has done for long, that restrictions imposed by the State on the normal exercise of patrimonial rights must be reasonable, limited in time, and constitute a remedy and not a mutation in the substance or essence of the right acquired by judicial decision or contract ...'.[943]

However, the Tribunal, recognising the need for adaptation, acknowledged that the Provincia de San Luis decision of the Supreme Court is connected to the facts of the specific cases and the results may defer in the *Enron* case:

> It so happens that the domestic judicial control of the emergency decisions has for the most turned out adversely for the Respondent's justification, as in Provincia de San Luis noted above, but as judicial determinations are made on a case by case basis they have not been taken to mean that the measures as a whole might not be compatible with Argentine legislation.[944]

A different use of domestic case law can be found in the *Loewen v. US* case where the tribunal assessed the procedural fairness of the court procedure. The Tribunal examined whether the treatment Loewen was accorded at a trial level and the resultant verdict, satisfied minimum standards of international law, or fair and equitable treatment and full protection and security as referred to in Article 1105 of NAFTA. The Tribunal concluded that the methods employed by the jury and tolerated by the judge did not comply with the concept of due process and as such the courts of the State did not provide a fair trial to the foreign investor.[945] In reaching such a conclusion, the tribunal based its syllogism on the case law developed in the US and other jurisdictions regarding advocacy and the way it should be conducted.[946] In the cases such conduct amounts to injustice, 'the trial judge comes under an affirmative duty to prevent improper tactics which will result in an unfair trial'.[947] In this context, reference to

941. *Ibid.* 274.
942. *Ibid.* para. 206.
943. Judgment in the case *Provincia de San Luis*, Argentine Supreme Court (5 Mar. 2003); *Enron*, Award (n 581) para. 218.
944. *Enron*, Award (n 581) para. 227.
945. *Loewen*, Award (n 356) para. 122.
946. *Ibid.* para. 123.
947. The tribunal cites Kevin *Pappas v. Middle Earth Condominium Association*, US Court of Appeals for the Second Circuit, 963 F 2d 534 (8 May 1992); John *Koufakis v. Carvel*, US Court of Appeals for the Second Circuit, 425 F 2d 892 (24 Apr. 1970); *Loewen*, Award (n 356) para. 123.

domestic case law enhances the transnational interaction degree regarding the relevant due process standards.[948]

Communication with national judges may go a step further, introducing traditionally domestic law concepts into arbitral decision-making in order to cover the specific needs of the interpretation process. Investor's claims are frequently connected to State regulations that incorporate public interests such as the promotion of labour or human rights, the protection of public health and of the environment.[949] Public law principles such as 'proportionality' and 'legitimate expectations'[950] become relevant for employing a suitable balance of the investor's rights and public policy goals encompassed in State regulatory actions.[951] As already analysed above, investment tribunals when dealing with matters of indirect expropriation, use the principle of proportionality inspired from the ECtHR jurisprudence but adapted to the investment-arbitration framework.[952]

A similar adaptation process can be found in the use of the principle of 'legitimate expectation' in the investment-arbitration framework. The use of the 'legitimate expectations' concept, which is not directly incorporated into the investment treaties, is coupled in arbitral decision-making with concepts such as 'fairness and justice', 'stability and predictability', 'transparency', 'consistency', 'reasonableness', and 'legitimacy'.

'Legitimate expectations' are considered to be part of the principle of good faith. The latter is a principle of international customary law.[953] It has also been described as a general principle of international law and a 'guiding principle' for the application of the fair and equitable treatment standard that appears 'more or less identically' in most of the investment treaties in force.[954] The value of incorporating this concept in investment arbitration lies in its elasticity that permits standards of fairness and justice to be ensured through the balancing of the investor's interests on the one hand and the State's interests on the other.[955] An example is the *Metalclad Corporation v. United Mexican States* case, where the tribunal referred to the expectation of the investor to be treated fairly and justly in accordance with the NAFTA.[956]

---

948. Ahdieh, 'Between Dialogue and Decree: International Review of National Courts' (n 794) fn 483.
949. UNCTAD Report, *Interpretation of IIAs: What States Can Do*, IIA Issues Note No. 3 (2011), Introduction.
950. *See* Hector Mairal, 'Legitimate Expectations and Informal Administrative Representations' in Stephan Schill (ed.) *International Investment Law and Comparative Public Law* (OUP 2010).
951. Roberts, 'Clash of Paradigms' (n 76) 29.
952. *See* Benedict Kingsbury and Stephan Schill, 'Public Law Concepts to Balance Investors' Rights with State Regulatory Actions in the Public Interest – The Concept of Proportionality' in Stephan Schill (eds) *International Investment Law and Comparative Public Law* (n 950); For 'proportionality' *see* §6.03.[D][3] 'Dialogue with International Judges'.
953. *International Thunderbird*, Award (n 328) para. 147.
954. *International Thunderbird*, Separate Opinion of Thomas Wälde (n 630) para. 25.
955. Wongkaew, 'The Transplantation of Legitimate Expectations in Investment Treaty Arbitration' (n 614) 71.
956. *Metalclad Corporation v. The United Mexican States*, ICSID Case No. ARB(AF)/97/1, Award (30 Aug. 2000) para. 99.

In the context of legitimate expectations the use of reasonableness as an interpretive tool serves as a basis for evaluating the public conception of justice along with the political choices.[957] In the *Saluka* case, the tribunal stated that the protection accorded to the investor by the treaty cannot be determined based on the investor's subjective motivations and considerations but any expectation must 'rise to the level of legitimacy and reasonableness *in light of the circumstances*'.[958]

In the same spirit, the *Suez v. Argentina* tribunal employed the objective criterion of the 'reasonable investor' taking into account at the same time, the country's specific circumstances. The tribunal asked the following question:

> What would have been the legitimate and reasonable expectations of a reasonable investor [...] at the time they made their investment [...] in view of the concession's legal framework and bearing in mind that country's history and its political, economic, and social circumstances?[959]

In assessing the reasonableness of the expectations of the investor, arbitral tribunals have also considered pertinent factors such as 'political volatility', 'post-civil war', 'high regulatory risk', 'financial crisis, energy shortage and crisis'.[960]The jurisprudence of arbitral tribunals demonstrates how dialogue functions for inserting this domestic law – or according to others' international law – principle in the investment-arbitration framework and for tailoring and adapting this principle to the characteristics and needs of investor-state arbitration.[961]

In the *Thunderbird* case, Thomas Wälde issued a separate opinion describing the insertion of the concept of 'legitimate expectations' from the domestic and international legal system into investment arbitration.[962] He insisted, however, on the need to adapt this concept to the characteristics of investor-state dispute resolution and the

957. Wongkaew, 'The Transplantation of Legitimate Expectations in Investment Treaty Arbitration' (n 614) 98.
958. *Saluka, Partial Award* (n 377) para. 304 Emphasis in the original.
959. *Suez, Sociedad General de Aguas de Barcelona S.A., and InterAguas Servicios Integrales del Agua S.A. v. The Argentine Republic*, ICSID Case No. ARB/03/17, Decision on liability (30 Jul. 2010) para. 228.
960. *See* respectively *Bayindir Insaat Turizm Ticaret Ve Sanayi A.S. v. Islamic Republic of Pakistan*, ICSID Case No. ARB/03/29, Award (27 Aug. 2009) para. 194; *Toto Costruzioni Generali S.p.A. v. The Republic of Lebanon*, ICSID Case No. ARB/07/12, Award (7 Jun. 2012) para. 245; *Duke Energy Electroquil Partners & Electroquil S.A. v. Republic of Ecuador*, ICSID Case No. ARB/04/19, Award (18 Aug. 2008) para. 347; Wongkaew, 'The Transplantation of Legitimate Expectations in Investment Treaty Arbitration' (n 614) 98.
961. *See also* Wongkaew, 'The Transplantation of Legitimate Expectations in Investment Treaty Arbitration' (n 614) 69 et seq.
962. In the Thunderbird case, the Tribunal concluded that the expectations of the investor were unreasonable. The US company's gaming machines were misrepresented by Thunderbird being ultimately unlawful under Mexican law. Mexico subsequently closed down the gaming facilities. *International Thunderbird Gaming Corporation v. The United Mexican States*, Award (n 328); Bonnitcha and others, *The Political Economy of the Investment Treaty Regime* (n 938) 112.

policies pursued. The 'doctrinal structure' of the concept is derived from precedent-based arguments with reference to the way general international, international economic (including EU), ECHR, comparative contract and comparative administrative law and the relevant jurisprudence delimit the concept of 'legitimate expectations'.[963]

Even though this dialogue does not exactly delimit the content of the concept, it proposes that 'under developed systems of administrative law, a citizen – even more so an investor – should be protected against unexpected and detrimental changes of policy if the investor has carried out significant investment with a reasonable, public-authority initiated assurance in the stability of such policy'.[964] In this context, the approach emerging in national and international practice is reflected in investment arbitration but always taking into account the balance of interests between a public and private party:

> Assurance on a particular interpretation of often open-ended statute against an unexpected detrimental change of such interpretation is in this context particularly relevant. Such protection is, however, not un-conditional and ever-lasting. It leads to a balancing process between the needs for flexible public policy and the legitimate reliance on in particular investment-backed expectations. The consulted authorities are indicative of contemporary state practice and the minimum standards of comparative national and international law. The 'fair and equitable standard' can not be derived from subjective personal or cultural sentiments; it must be anchored in objective rules and principles reflecting, in an authoritative and universal or at least widespread way, the contemporary attitude of modern national and international economic law.[965]

The concept of 'legitimate expectation' is analysed, interpreted, adapted and applied against this methodological background. Alongside with this international and comparative law background, the interpretation is enhanced with reference to investment-arbitration jurisprudence which is considered to further develop the concept of 'legitimate expectations'.[966] Although these awards may not specifically delimit the principle, Wälde notes that the value of these 'authoritative precedents' lies in the establishment of 'legitimate expectations' as a subcategory of Fair and Equitable Treatment:

> The most relevant NAFTA (and ICSID) awards have translated these authoritative objectives and instruments provided by the NAFTA and similar investment treaties into an emphasis on 'transparency' and a concept of 'legitimate expectation' that takes up, but further develops the meaning of this concept in conventional international, comparative contract, administrative and European and WTO law jurisprudence. One can observe over the last years a significant growth in the role and scope of the legitimate expectation principle, from an earlier function as a subsidiary interpretative principle to reinforce a particular interpretative approach

963. *International Thunderbird*, Separate Opinion of Thomas Wälde (n 630) paras 26–30.
964. *Ibid.* para. 30 (citations omitted).
965. *Ibid.*
966. *Ibid.*

chosen, to its current role as a self-standing subcategory and independent basis for a claim under the 'fair and equitable standard' as under Art. 1105 of the NAFTA.[967]

The above analysis demonstrates that, before appearing in the investment-arbitration field, the protection of legitimate expectations was well established in many domestic legal systems, most commonly in the administration area. In addition, the concept is treated in many international judicial contexts and its content is being developed through international case law. However, given the international law environment of investor-state arbitration, arbitral tribunals seem to acknowledge that comparative legal reasoning is not an automatic transplantation process. Despite the dialogue with national and international judges, investment-arbitration tribunals have developed their own approach to the use of legitimate expectation in the interpretation process integrating in the decision-making process concepts such as 'reasonableness', 'fairness', and 'justice'.

[3] Reciprocal Communication

The public and private law elements governing the investment-arbitration framework justify the intersection of areas such as environmental law, criminal law or labour law with investment-treaty arbitration.[968] Such an interaction is not one-way. Rather it reflects a 'give and take' relationship evolving between investment law and domestic law.[969]

The role of national courts in interpreting international investment law has been growing. National courts have created a jurisprudence regarding investment-arbitration issues. Certain domestic decisions aim at delimiting the relationship between investment arbitration and the national legal order. In an appeal procedure, the Court of Appeal for Ontario dealt with an application to challenge the constitutionality of Canada agreeing in NAFTA the resolution of investor-state disputes by arbitral tribunals. One of the issues at stake was whether the competence of investment tribunals to resolve such disputes has deprived the Canadian superior courts of their authority to decide upon matters reserved to them by section 96 of the Constitution Act

967. *Ibid.* paras 30, 37 (citations omitted); *See also Urbaser*, Award (n 249) paras 615, 628 where the Tribunal connected the FET standard with the concepts of 'legitimate expectations' and 'transparency'.
968. Susan Franck, 'Book Review: The Public International Law Regime Governing International Investment, by Jose E. Alvarez, The Hague: Hague Academy of International Law, 2011, Pp. 502 (4 Oct. 2012)' (2012) Washington & Lee Legal Studies Paper No. 2012-34, 12; Burke-White and Slaughter refer to the relationship between domestic and international law noting that 'the future of international law lies in its ability to affect, influence, bolster, backstop, and even mandate specific actors in domestic politics'. William Burke-White and Anne-Marie Slaughter, 'The Future of International Law is Domestic (or, The European Way of Law)' (2006) 47(2) HarvIntlLJ 327, 350.
969. *See* Beth A Simmons and Lisa L Martin, 'International Organizations and Institutions', in W Carlsnaes and T Risse, Simmons *Handbook of International Relations* (Sage Publications 2002) 192 (referring to how international frameworks and institutions affect national behaviour).

1867.[970] Another question touched upon was whether such a competence has violated principles of judicial independence, the rule of law or the Charter of Rights and Freedoms. It was concluded that section 96 does not apply to the arbitration mechanism of NAFTA Chapter 11 for two reasons. The first one is that NAFTA has not been incorporated into the domestic law of Canada and the second was that NAFTA constitutes an international treaty and as such remains unaffected by section. 96 of the Constitution Act, 1867.[971] Domestic case law makes a clear distinction between a parliamentary approval of a treaty and the incorporation of the treaty into Canadian domestic law.[972]

The analysis of the Appeal Court touches on issues of autonomy of the investment-arbitration mechanism regarding the domestic legal order. It also deals with the relationship between national courts and investment tribunals. The Commercial Arbitration Act implementing NAFTA does not incorporate into the Canadian domestic system 'the entire investor–state adjudication process, including the tribunal's makeup, its procedures, its governing law and the defined limits within which it can act [...] only the decision it has made is incorporated into domestic law'.[973] Based on these premises investment arbitration is presented as a dispute resolution framework distinct from the domestic courts and with different powers. NAFTA tribunals deal with disputes regarding the States' international obligations to accord national treatment, MFN and FET to the foreign investors. On the other hand, according to Article 1121 NAFTA Chapter 11, a foreign investor can either choose whether to proceed to domestic courts or an investment tribunal to review the governmental action.[974]

Likewise, in the recent *BCB* case, the Caribbean court of Justice was confronted with the nature of the right to arbitrate in the context of an investment treaty. The claimant contended that the Belize-UK BIT provided for an unqualified and indefeasible right to have disputes under the BIT resolved by an arbitral tribunal. As a result, they argued, the court could not make any order restraining the continuation of the

970. Section 96 provides: 'The Governor General shall appoint the Judges of the Superior, District, and County Courts in each Province, except those of the Courts of Probate in Nova Scotia and New Brunswick.' <http://laws-lois.justice.gc.ca/eng/const/page-5.html#docCont> (accessed 4 Feb. 2018).
971. *The Council of Canadians et als v. Attorney General of Canada*, Supreme Court of Canada, C43995,Appeal (30 Nov. 2006) para. 20.
972. *Ibid.* para. 25 citing *Canada (AG) v. Ontario (AG)*, (1937) A.C. 326 (Labour Conventions).
973. *Ibid.* para. 25.
974. *Ibid.* para. 53; In a similar attempt to regulate the competing jurisdiction between national courts and investment arbitration tribunals, the Pakistani Supreme Court issued an anti-arbitration injunction against the private investor in the context of the *Société Générale de Surveillance S.A. (SGS) v. Federation of Pakistan* case. The national court restrained SGS from 'taking any step, action or measure to pursue or participate or to continue to pursue or participate in the ICSID arbitration'. *Société Générale de Surveillance S.A. v. Fed'n of Pak.*, Supreme Court of Pakistan (Appellate Jurisdiction), Civ. App. Nos. 459 & 460 of 2002, para. 84, *reprinted in* 2003 Y.B. COMM. ARB. (Int'l Council for Comm. Arb.) 1312, 1341; Julian D M Lew, 'Does National Court Involvement Undermine the International Arbitration Process?' (2009) 24(3) AmUIntlLRev 489, 513. *See also C. Liebscher*, 'Monitoring of Domestic Courts in BIT Arbitrations: A Brief Inventory of Some Issues' in Christina Binder and others (eds), *International Investment Law for the 21st Century* (n 673), 105.

arbitral proceedings.[975] The Court took an interesting systemic approach to the issue underlying its obligation to balancing the rights of individuals as well as the rights of the society as a whole: 'The exercise by one individual of his or her rights often infringes on the rights of other individuals or the society as a whole and the courts are and must remain the final arbiter of the relative distribution of those rights'.[976]

The effects of an arbitration provision in domestic law were also discussed by the court mainly with reference to domestic law jurisprudence.[977] The agreement to arbitrate that resulted from an investment treaty was approached by the court as not being a treaty itself but as having the form of a 'contract from an advertisement containing certain terms to get a reward'.[978] This type of advertisement comprises a binding unilateral offer that can be accepted by whoever performs its terms.[979] The court's way of framing the issue of the right to arbitrate:

> [...] admits of the possibility that provisions in the bilateral investment treaty could have given rise to the formation of a *contract* along the lines of reasoning adopted in *Carlill v Carbolic Smoke Ball Co.* and that it is this contractual right to arbitrate and not the treaty (albeit the terms of the contract are found in the treaty) of which the courts take notice.[980]

Similarly, when the *BCB* court dealt with the requirement of the exhaustion of local remedies as a precondition to the right to submit the dispute to arbitration, it referred to investment-arbitration jurisprudence.[981] In addition to reference to precedent the Court took into account the objective of international arbitration to avoid possible pitfalls of domestic litigation and the effectiveness of investment arbitration.[982]

In general, a number of domestic courts consider foreign judgments when treating analogous issues. While reference by domestic courts to the investment-arbitration jurisprudence as a source of interpretive guidance is mostly connected to issues that concern the delimitation of the relationship between public courts and arbitral tribunals, such a type of interaction has its own meaning and further potentials. In this sense, the dialogue with investment-arbitration tribunals helps domestic courts in better understand the functioning of the investment-arbitration framework. This

975. *The British Caribbean Bank Limited v. The Attorney General*, CCJ 4, Appeal (25 Jun. 2013) para. 14.
976. *Ibid.*
977. *Ibid.* para. 20 citing *Republic of Ecuador v. Occidental Exploration and Production Co*, QB 432, challenge to arbitral award of the LCIA court (2 Mar. 2006); *Carlill v. Carbolic Smoke Ball Co*, QB 256, Appeal (1891–1894).
978. *The British Caribbean Bank*, Appeal (n 975) para. 20.
979. *Ibid.* para. 20.
980. *Ibid.*
981. *See*, for example, *The British Caribbean Bank*, Appeal (n 975) para. 21 citing the following arbitral awards: *Mytilineos Holdings SA v. the State of Union Serbia & Montenegro and Republic of Serbia*, UNCITRAL, Partial award on jurisdiction (8 Sep. 2006); *Compania de Aguas del Aconquija SA and Vivendi Universal (formerly Compagnie General des Eaux) v. Argentine Republic*, ICSID Case No. ARB/97/3, Decision on Annulment (3 Jul. 2002).
982. *Ibid.*

understanding has the potential to result in a more conscious balancing of domestic and investment protection interests when this need arises in national jurisdictions.

Such a dialogue also gives rise to the gradual development of a 'common lexicon' that encourages the 'circular migration' of ideas from national courts to international and regional courts and then back to national courts.[983] National legal systems cannot close their eyes to the emergence of a common terrain where national, international and regional actors function and interact. Some commentators have described such a common terrain as a corollary of the globalisation of legal standards, which are also formed by private actors.[984] These global standards urge national governmental and judicial branches to conform to them especially when treating issues of international law. Evolving common standards regarding the protection of the environment or of a foreign investment may have the same impact on national courts. Creating communication codes between the national and international juridical orders will create better awareness of the changing legal environment within which domestic courts are called upon to perform. Stein emphasises on the role of the so-called transnational jurisprudence in informing national authorities about the needs of the international legal process and the desires of each State.[985] Based on these considerations, the interaction between international and national courts testifies a transnational legal process within which international legal norms 'seep into, are internalized, and become embedded in domestic legal and political processes'.[986]

§6.04 CUSTOMARY LAW ARGUMENTS

The dialogue between investment arbitrators and their international background can also be illustrated by the use of customary international law in the legal decision-making process. International custom is defined as 'evidence of a general practice accepted as law'.[987] Customary international law in investment arbitration has a double function. It may be used either as an interpretive tool in relation to treaty provisions or as a source of law directly applied by the decision-maker.[988] In the last case where it operates as a source of law, the tribunal will employ further interpretive techniques in order to interpret the legal source. A customary rule possesses its own rationale.[989] Thus the process of interpretation of customary international law is not necessarily the same as the way to interpret a treaty. Treaty and custom may appear to

983. Vadi, 'The Migration of Constitutional Ideas to Regional and International Economic Law' (n 793) 564.
984. *See* Eyal Benvenisti, 'Reclaiming Democracy: The Strategic Uses of Foreign and International Law by National Courts' (2008) 102 AJIL 241; Nico Krisch and Benedict Kingsbury, 'Introduction, Global Governance and Global Administrative Law in the International Legal Order' (2006) 17 EJIL 1.
985. Ted Stein, 'Jurisprudence and Jurists' Prudence: The Iranian-Forum Clause Decisions of the Iran-U.S. Claims Tribunal' (1984) 78(1) AJIL 32, 23.
986. Koh, 'Transnational Legal Process' (n 94) 205.
987. Wälde, 'The Specific Nature of Investment Arbitration' (n 873) 96.
988. Fauchald, 'The Legal Reasoning of ICSID Tribunals – An Empirical Analysis' (n 401) 309.
989. Alexander Orakhelashvili, *The Interpretation of Acts and Rules in Public International Law* (OUP 2008) 497.

deal with similar contexts, however, their creation and functions present differences. The challenge that arises here is twofold: first, the understanding of how investment tribunals use customary international law in the interpretation process; and second, whether investment tribunals use customary international law based on the traditional content it has acquired in the international scene or whether they adapt its content to fit into the investment-arbitration context.

[A] Interpreting Investment Protection Guarantees: A Cyclical Relationship

In the ninetieth and twentieth centuries, the concerns of investors regarding the protection of their investment from arbitrary State measures, were dealt with through the development of customary international law by western States.[990] Today the situation has changed since investor-state relations are primarily governed by bilateral and multilateral investment treaties. Due to the lack of consensus concerning the customary international law applicable to investor-state relations, capital-exporting States created international rules to protect the foreign investments of their nationals.[991] States concluded investment treaties in order to confront the gaps and limitations in the protection accorded by customary international law.[992] Such limitations for example were the precondition of exhausting local remedies in order to file an international claim or the contested nature of the 'treatment of aliens' rights.[993] Another issue of concern which could not be addressed through customary international law is the investor's right to effectuate monetary transfers from the host State.[994] Going a step further, investment protection guarantees, such as MFN treatment and national treatment as well as dispute resolution provisions should be provided for in treaties rather than in custom, since they require the express consent of the State.[995]

However, the vague content of the investment protection guarantees contained in the investment treaties has led the arbitral tribunals to interpret them with reference to their customary international law background.[996] Certain investment treaties make

990. Salacuse, *The Law of Investment Treaties* (n 69) 54.
991. Salacuse and Sullivan, 'Do BITS Really Work?' (n 341) 71.
992. McLachlan and other, *International Investment Arbitration: Substantive Principles* (n 340) 17.
993. *Ibid.*
994. Salacuse and Sullivan, 'Do BITS Really Work?' (n 341) 68.
995. Campbell McLachlan and other, *International Investment Arbitration: Substantive Principles* (n 340) 17; *See Generation Ukraine, Inc. v. Ukraine*, ICSID Case No. ARB/00/9, Award (16 Sep. 2003) para. 11.3 (The Tribunal held that '[i]t is plain that several of the BIT standards, and the prohibition against expropriation in particular, are simply a conventional codification of standards that have long existed in customary international law').
996. On this relationship Arbitrator C states that: 'the Treaty comes first and if the Treaty is clear you don't worry about [customary international law] principles; if a Treaty is uncertain in some way, then you seek to interpret the Treaty consistently with customary international law; that might not always mean consistent with the ILC, that's just their own version of it, but you do your best to find out what is customary international law. [...] Customary international law can be used to fill a lot of gaps.' For interview design *see* Annex 'Interview Questions'; *See also* Dumberry arguing that despite the large number of BITs, they 'still do not cover the whole spectrum of possible bilateral treaty relationships between States. This necessarily results in

direct reference to the connection between investment protection standards and customary international law. As an example, Article 5 US-Rwanda BIT links the minimum standard of treatment, accorded to the investor, including fair and equitable treatment and full protection and security to the customary international law minimum standard of treatment of aliens.[997] Nevertheless, tribunals resort to customary international law even where there is no express reference to it in the treaty.

The relevance of CIL may appear in the context of dealing with procedural issues such as 'abuse of process', jurisdictional issues such as exhaustion of local remedies or piercing the corporate veil, and substantive issues such as expropriation and FET.[998] As an example, due to the vagueness of the expropriation concept under Article 1110 of the NAFTA, the *Feldman* Tribunal made reference to the 'rules of customary international law' in order to conclude that 'neither NAFTA nor rules of customary international law require a State to permit grey market cigarette export'.[999] The *El Paso* Tribunal also makes reference to customary international law specifying its particular role in arbitral decision-making: 'Customary international law, which is explicitly incorporated by the BIT in its provisions, has a double role: (1) to clarify the terms of the BIT; and (2) to establish a floor for the treatment of investments.'[1000]

Be that as it may, a certain caveat should be raised at this point, which enhances the cyclical nature of the relationship between customary international law and investment arbitration. When it comes to the process of legal decision-making, relying solely on customary international law would create a vicious circle, importing through the means of interpretation the same gaps and limitations the States wished to address in the first place when concluding specific treaties on investment protection.[1001] However, arbitrators consider themselves as part of an international yet specifically investment-arbitration regime. Should the Tribunals consider the provisions of international law and customary international law to suffice, there would be no practical need to recognise the *lex specialis* nature of investment treaties in order to decide differently on an issue.

Although arbitral tribunals are expected, in certain cases, to follow the minimum standard of protection required by international law, the decision-makers interpret and

gaps in the legal protection of foreign investments', Patrick Dumberry, *The Formation and Identification of Rules of Customary International Law in International Investment Law* (CUP 2016) 1–13.

997. Article 5 para. 2 US-Rwanda BIT (2008).

998. *See* respectively *Waste Management v. Mexico II*, ICSID Case No. ARB(AF)/00/3, Decision on Jurisdiction (26 Jun. 2002) paras 48–49; *Maffezini*, jurisdiction (n 939) para. 29; *Tokios Tokelės v. Ukraine*, ICSID Case No. ARB/02/18, Decision on Jurisdiction (29 Apr. 2004) paras 53–56; *Feldman*, Award (n 935) paras 115–116; *Tecmed*, Award (n 147) paras 153–155; Fauchald, 'The Legal Reasoning of ICSID Tribunals – An Empirical Analysis' (n 401) 310.

999. *Feldman*, Award (n 935) para. 111.

1000. *El Paso Energy International Company v. The Argentine Republic*, ICSID Case No. ARB/03/15, Award (31 Oct. 2011) para. 123.

1001. *See also* Christopher M Ryan, 'Discerning the Compliance Calculus: Why States Comply With International Investment Law' (2009) 38 GaJIntl&CompL 63, 66 (2009) (arguing that international investment law has many differences from traditional or customary international law. The reason is that international investment law does not principally derive its authority from 'consistent State practice' and '*opinio juris*'. Additionally, the investment protection guarantees are directed towards private investors).

apply these standards based also on the investment-arbitration doctrine and case law. A stark illustration is the reasoning process of the *Alex Genin* tribunal, which interpreted the arbitrary or discriminatory treatment through a three-step process starting from the most general argumentation to the most specific one. At first, the arbitrators referred to international law as generally requiring that a State refrains from discriminatory treatment of aliens and their property.[1002] As a second step, the tribunal made reference to customary international law noting that it does not require a State to treat all aliens equally or as favourably as nationals.[1003] In its third phase of argumentation, the tribunal referred to the MFN clause contained in the BIT concluding that, in the particular case, discriminatory treatment is not permitted by the MFN clause, which requires that a foreign investment is treated not less favourably than the treatment of nationals.[1004] Making use of the MFN clause, which is specific to investor-state arbitration, the tribunal gave its own understanding of 'non-discrimination' in a more specific way than what is understood in general international law and at the same time formed an exception from customary international law. The tribunal's argumentation technique to start from general international law, continue with customary international law and conclude based on the investor-state framework demonstrates the need of the decision-maker to decide in connection with the specific nature of investment arbitration. In addition, it proves the fact that the provisions of investment treaties as *lex specialis* should prevail customary international law in the event they resolve an issue in a different way.[1005]

Based on the above, it is noticeable that the tribunal recognises the need to keep a connection with general international law and specifically customary international law but at the same time it uses interpretative arguments deriving specifically from the investment-arbitration framework.

[B] Towards the Emergence of Customary International Investment Law

[...] any legal system, if it is going to be effective, has to be able to evolve incrementally through practice.[1006]

Investment arbitration evolved from its customary origins in order to regulate foreign investments and balance the interests of the 'players' of the field.[1007] However, the continuously developing needs of the international investment transactions requires the development of the law in order to cope with new challenges. Since the amount of transaction costs to continuously renegotiate the investment treaties is high,[1008] the

1002. *Alex Genin,* Award (n 248) para. 368.
1003. *Ibid.* para. 368.
1004. *Ibid.*
1005. McLachlan and others, *International Investment Arbitration: Substantive Principles* (n 340) 17.
1006. Giacomo Ponzetto and Patricio Fernandez, 'Case Law Versus Statute Law: An Evolutionary Comparison' (2008) 37 JLS 379, 411.
1007. Cheng, 'Precedent and Control in Investment Treaty Arbitration' (n 462) 1022.
1008. *Ibid.*

need for investment law to keep up with the demands of the international community is addressed in practice by the private judges.

Resort to customary international law standards of protection in the process of legal decision-making leaves space for its further development through arbitral case law in order to respond to the specific interpretation needs that may arise in practice. This may lead, in the course of time, to the development of specialised investment-arbitration standards that initially originated from customary international law. Such specialised standards can be developed when the customary law interpretive arguments are adapted to the investment-arbitration framework. Such independent standards do not signify a disconnection with international law – how could it after all as the natural environment of investment arbitration is international law – but their development according to the special nature of investor-state arbitration.

Within this background, the development of the investment protection guarantees may acquire two forms. According to the first form, it may mean the development – or better ascertainment – of customary international law which is specifically applied to investment arbitration. This requires a 'research' of State practice as well as the existence of an *opinio juris.*[1009] In its second form, development signifies an evolution of a concept from a CIL standard to a distinct treaty obligation acquiring its meaning based on the specificities of the investment-arbitration framework. Despite the fact that the 'task of seeking the meaning of a treaty guarantee, such as FET, by way of treaty interpretation is fundamentally different from the task of ascertaining the content of custom',[1010] both processes may lead to the emergence of a customary international investment law as will be revealed in the following sections.

[1] State Practice and **Opinio Juris** *Revisited*

The legal framework of investment arbitration has been described as largely displacing customary international law and relevant domestic law revealing steady steps towards the emergence of a 'new customary international law of investment'.[1011] The development of new law brings to the fore questions of legitimacy of a dispute resolution body creating law. Of course when referring to customary law, its development does not stem from a democratically empowered legislation body but is connected to State practice and the *opinio iuris,* the conviction that a certain practice is binding. Professor Reisman speaks about a 'dynamic and increasingly democratic customary international law process' which does not only consist of States but also of non-State actors.[1012] In the field of investment arbitration, the concepts 'State practice' and '*opinio juris*' have themselves acquired a dynamic meaning.

1009. *See* the report of the ILC marking that the 'identification of a rule of customary international law requires an assessment of both practice and the acceptance of that practice as law ("two-element" approach)'. 'Second Report on identification of customary international law' (2014) (ILC, by Michael Wood) A/CN.4/672 para. 21.
1010. *Glamis Gold,* Award (n 407) para. 20.
1011. Salacuse and Sullivan, 'Do BITS Really Work?' (n 341) 70.
1012. Michael Reisman, 'Canute Confronts the Tide: States Versus Tribunals and the Evolution of the Minimum Standard in Customary International Law' (2015) 30(3) ICSID Rev 616, 616.

In particular, 'State practice' has been described by the International Law Commission as consisting of: 'material and detectable' acts of subjects of international law, and it is these 'instances of conduct' that may form 'a web of precedents' in which a pattern of conduct may be observed.[1013] Transcending the narrow context of 'State practice', the term 'general practice' could be more accurate as including not only States as subjects of international law but also non-State actors such as international organisations, international courts and tribunals, NGOs and private corporate entities.[1014] Article 38(1)(b) of the ICJ Statute refers to international custom as 'evidence of a general practice accepted as law' giving preference to the term 'general practice'.

A source indicating general practice with regards to the interpretation of a treaty are court decisions. Consistent national court decisions, for example, are considered 'sufficient to establish a discernible pattern' that reveals the agreement of the parties on a specific treaty interpretation and implementation.[1015] In the investment-arbitration framework, evidence of a 'general practice', including State practice and their approach to treaty implementation, can be found in the awards of arbitral tribunals. The development of the content of vague investment protection guarantees in a consistent manner by arbitral case law constitutes evidence of how these guarantees are interpreted and applied, and thus generally perceived in the investment-arbitration context.[1016] In this case, customary international law cannot be restricted to how individual States consider what is law, but also to how specialised frameworks view custom through their decision-making powers.[1017] As discussed in Part I of the book, in a transnational law scene such as investment arbitration, where there is absence of a solid State authority, decentralised liquid forms of authority gradually make their appearance.[1018] A traditional concept of authority is characterised by the domination of States and public actors who monopolise rule-settling.[1019] This approach has also affected the way the emergence of custom is ascertained. However, general practices as pictured in an arbitral award gain specific authority since arbitrators are mandated by both States and investors to apply investment protection guarantees in the confines of the specific case. The practice of future tribunals to pay due regard to arbitral case law, either by following, commenting on or even distinguishing themselves from the reasoning of an award, is exactly what gives weight and authority to arbitral case law.

1013. 'Second Report on Identification of Customary International Law' (n 1009) para. 32.
1014. *See* Arsanjani referring to the existence of non-State actors shaping international law. Mahnoush Arsanjani, 'The United Nations and International Law Making' (2012) 362 RecDesCours 9, 25.
1015. Vadi, *Analogies in International Investment Law and Arbitration* (n 277) 162 citing the Appellate Body report, Japan–Taxes on Alcoholic Beverages (1 Nov. 1996) WT/DS8/AB/R, WT/DS10/AB/R, WT/DS11/AB/R; *See also* Brownlie, *Principles of Public International Law* (n 909) 6 (arguing that State practice may also take the form of national court decisions).
1016. For a discussion on consistency *see* §6.05 [B][1][a] 'Consistency, Predictability, Legal Stability' and for a discussion on precedent *see* §6.03 'Precedent Arguments'.
1017. *See* §6.03 [D][1] 'Specialised International Legal Orders'.
1018. Larry Catá Backer, 'The Emerging Normative Structures of Transnational Law: Non-State Enterprises in Polycentric Asymmetric Global Orders' (n 87), 31 BYU Journal Public International Law 1, 38; *See* Part I 'Arbitral Decision-Making'.
1019. Ulrika Morth, *Soft Law in Governance and Regulation: An interdisciplinary Analysis* (Edward Elgar Publishing 2004) 2.

The reasoning of the *Mihaly* Tribunal can be viewed as going along these lines when emphasising on the practice of ICSID tribunals as a means to fill in the treaty gap for the definition of 'investment'. The Tribunal stated that since there was no definition of 'investment' in the ICSID Convention, the definition is left to be worked out through the subsequent practice of States 'thereby preserving its integrity and flexibility and allowing for future progressive development of international law on the topic of investment'. [1020] The tribunal continued that '[i]n the absence of a generally accepted definition of investment for the purpose of the ICSID convention, the Tribunal must examine the current and past practice of ICSID and the practice of States as evidenced in multilateral and bilateral treaties and agreements binding on States [...]'. [1021]

Similarly, the *Saluka* Tribunal held that case law is a source of customary international law in addition to State practice. However, it relied only on case law to identify principles that form part of customary international law. In particular, the Tribunal stated that 'the principle that a State does not commit an expropriation and is thus not liable to pay compensation to a dispossessed alien investor when it adopts general regulations that are "commonly accepted as within the police power of States" forms part of customary international law today'.[1022] The Tribunal based its conclusion on a cyclical reasoning: the fact that the above is a principle of customary international law derives from case law.[1023] Additionally, the fact that case law is considered as a source of customary international law is also a reasoning based on case law. The Tribunal specifically states that:

> The tribunal in ADF Group Inc. v. United States of America agreed with the position taken by a tribunal in another case (Mondev International Ltd. v. United States of America, ICSID Case No. ARB(AF)/99/2) 'that any general requirement to accord 'fair and equitable treatment' ... must be disciplined by being based upon State practice and judicial or arbitral case law or other sources of customary or general international law'. Although the foregoing case deals with 'fair and equitable' treatment, the principle quoted applies in the same way to 'deprivation'. See ADF Group Inc. v. USA, ICSID Case No. ARB(AF)/00/1, Award, 9 January 2003, para. 184.)[1024]

When it comes to the existence of an *opinio juris,* its meaning is also formed against the investment-arbitration background. The *Merrill* Tribunal made reference to the evolution of customary international law 'in accordance with the realities of the

1020. *Mihaly International Corporation v. Democratic Socialist Republic of Sri Lanka*, ICSID Case No. ARB/00/2, Award (15 Mar. 2002) para. 33.
1021. *Ibid.* para. 58.
1022. *Saluka,* Partial Award (n 377) para. 262.
1023. The Tribunal cited the following cases: *Methanex Corp. v. USA*, Final Award, (n 321) para. 410; *See also Too v. Greater Modesto Insurance Associates*, 23 Iran U.S. Cl. Trib. Rep. 378, (1989) para. 26; *S.D. Myers, Inc. v. Canada,* Partial Award (n 327) para. 281; *Lauder (USA) v. Czech Republic,* Final Award (3 Sep. 2002) para. 198 <www.investmentclaims.com> (accessed 10 May 2018); *Technicas Medioambientales Tecmed S.A. v. United Mexican States*, ICSID Case No. ARB(AF)/00/2 (29 May 2003) para. 119; *Saluka,* Partial Award (n 377) para. 262.
1024. *Saluka,* Partial Award (n 377) para. 261, fn 11.

international community' and the existence of *opinio juris* as demonstrated specifically in the area of business, trade and investment:

> A requirement that aliens be treated fairly and equitably in relation to business, trade and investment is the outcome of this changing reality and as such it has become sufficiently part of widespread and consistent practice so as to demonstrate that it is reflected today in customary international law as opinio juris. In the end, the name assigned to the standard does not really matter. What matters is that the standard protects against all such acts or behavior that might infringe a sense of fairness, equity and reasonableness.[1025]

In the context of the emergence of a 'new customary international law for foreign investment', States and investors follow a general practice 'out of the conviction that it is binding'.[1026] This binding general practice stems from the coordination between State and non-State actors[1027] thus attributing to customary international law a non-statist, transnational element. Non-State actors in this case are investment tribunals which constitute a form of 'State delegated practice'.[1028] States give their consensus to investor-state arbitration tribunals through the ratification of investment treaties which include arbitral dispute resolution provisions. After their ratification, treaties become part of the State's legal system.[1029] Going a step further, the States accept to enforce arbitral awards that may be rendered based on these treaties, with a reservation put at place when public policy issues may arise. Private parties, i.e., investors, give their own consensus to investment tribunals in two different time periods, by accepting the arbitration clause and by deciding to submit the dispute that has arisen to arbitration.

On this basis, both parties to a dispute have consented to the tribunal's issuing a binding decision on the resolution of a specific dispute through the interpretation and application of the law. The arbitral award has been described as consisting of two elements; the dispositive of the award which is the practice component, and the award's reasoning which is the *opinio juris*.[1030] The extensive reference to the reasoning of arbitral awards by both litigants in their pleadings and the tribunals in their reasoning has led to the emergence of a *jurisprudence constante* characterising a certain pattern of decision-making as legally persuasive and widely acceptable.[1031] As an example, investment protection guarantees such as FET are inserted in multiple

1025. *Merrill & Ring Forestry L.P. v. The Government of Canada*, UNCITRAL/NAFTA Chapter 11, ICSID Administered Case, Award (31 Mar. 2010) paras 193, 210 (citations omitted); *Urbaser* Award (n 1093). For a discussion on *Urbaser see* §6.04[C] 'Reciprocal Communication'.
1026. Stephan Schill, 'From Sources to Discourse: Investment Treaty Jurisprudence as the New Custom?' 16, <http://www.biicl.org/files/5630_stephan_schill.pdf> (accessed 22 Jul. 2018).
1027. Reisman, 'Canute Confronts the Tide' (n 1012) 620.
1028. *Ibid.*
1029. Salacuse and Sullivan, 'Do BITS Really Work?' (n 341) 70.
1030. Reisman, 'Canute Confronts the Tide' (n 1012) 620.
1031. For an analysis on precedent *see* §6.03 'Precedent Arguments'.

treaties of the same genre, leading to the generality of the *opinio juris* of arbitral awards.[1032]

Based on the above, the gradual formation of customary law of investment arbitration can be evidenced through the decision-making process of investment tribunals and the discourse between arbitral tribunals through precedent.[1033] In this case, precedent may on the one hand function as evidence of customary norms by indicating the existence of *opinio juris* and general international practice, and on the other hand, may indicate the emergence of a general principle of international law.[1034] The concept of customary international law has evolved from its traditional meaning in order to accommodate the new custom indentified not only through the practice of States, but also by the practices of arbitral tribunals in the context of investment-arbitration disputes.

[2] Evolutionary Interpretation of Customary International Law

The previous section revealed that the relationship between investment protection guarantees and customs of international law have a cyclical character. In order to cope with the deficiencies of customary international law, States developed an investment-treaty framework for the protection of the foreign investor and the promotion of the investments.[1035] Yet, certain treaty protection guarantees seem so closely connected to customary international law that they require for their interpretation reference to these customs. Such reference is translated as a need to further interpret customary international law. The question that arises here is how this interpretation is effectuated.[1036] There appear to be two possible ways to approach such a task: either the decision-maker interprets customary international law the way it is traditionally interpreted in general international law or the interpretation is adapted to the investment-arbitration framework. In this latter case, the approach does not propose that standards such as the FET are self-standing in the meaning of being completely disconnected from customary international law.[1037] Rather it argues for an evolutionary interpretation of such concepts as adapted to the investment-arbitration context.

1032. Reisman, 'Canute Confronts the Tide' (n 1012) 620 citing Stephen Schwebel, 'Is Neer Far from Fair and Equitable' (2011) 27(4) ArbIntl 555.

1033. Schill, 'From Sources to Discourse: Investment Treaty Jurisprudence as the New Custom?' (n 1026) 2.

1034. Vadi, *Analogies in Investment Treaty Arbitration*, 141 citing ICTY, *Prosecutor v. Zoran Kupreskic*, Case No.: IT-95-16-T, Judgment (14 Jan. 2000) para. 540; For the emergence of general principles of law *see* §2.02 [B][4]'Transnational Law Method for Identifying GPL as a Source of Law'.

1035. *See* §6.04[A] 'Interpreting Investment Protection Guarantees: A Cyclical Relationship'.

1036. Arbitrator A explained how the Vienna Convention helps in interpreting CIL noting that: 'there are other means to interpret customary law [...] but I am not a big fan of adding codifications to codifications so I rather keep some flexibility'. *See* Annex 'Interview Questions'.

1037. FET as a self-contained standard signifies that 'the standard of treatment is given its plain meaning, that is each word contained in the standard must be analysed on the basis of its own general definition. Therefore, the assessment to be carried out to determine the content of that standard which will be afforded to the foreign investor, is based on the proper meaning of the

While the case may seem to be clearer when the investment treaty itself equates the investment protection standards to the protection accorded by customary international law, the scene is blurred for the majority of cases since most of the investment treaties do not contain such a provision.[1038] In the latter scenario, despite the fact that a number of investment tribunals interpret standards such as the FET as conforming to the international minimum standard, it has been argued that 'these sparse cases do not suffice to transform that interpretation to the general approach to the meaning of the standard'.[1039]

In the NAFTA context, the Free Trade Commission issued Notes of Interpretation in 2001, which equate the protection accorded by the investment-treaty standards to the minimum standard of treatment accorded by customary international law whereby FET and FPS are included in the minimum standards, and not in addition to them.[1040] The Commission's interpretation of Article 1105 is far from favouring an autonomous treaty standard as the minimum standard of treatment to be afforded to investments is the customary international law minimum standard of treatment of aliens rather than an independent standard.[1041] The scope of Article 1105 is significantly restricted, as customary international law constitutes the framework for the assessment of the investor's protection. The same interpretation of the standard being restricted to customary international law also appears in the 2004 US Model BIT[1042] and other agreements such as the US Free Trade Agreements with Australia.[1043]

Nonetheless, such official interpretations do not clarify the content of the customary international law standard of protection and how this should be interpreted.[1044] Such uncertainty enhances even more the discretion of the arbitral tribunals to interpret the standard of protection under customary international law. A number of NAFTA Ch. 11 proceedings had already commenced at the time the Free Trade Commission Notes of Interpretation were issued. These proceedings included *Pope & Talbot*, which was in the damages phase, as well as notices of arbitration for *Modev, ADF, Waste Management, Methanex* and *UPS*.[1045] However, NAFTA Tribunals, even after the interpretation note, approached the matter more openly connecting the

---

terms "fair" and "equitable".' Marcela Klein-Bronfman, 'Fair and Equitable Treatment an Evolving Standard' (2006) 10 MaxPlankUNYB 609, 672.

1038. Jack Coe, 'Fair and Equitable Treatment in the NAFTA's Investment Chapter' (2002) 96 ASIL PROC. 17.

1039. Klein-Bronfman, 'Fair and Equitable Treatment an Evolving Standard' (n 1037) 678.

1040. 'North American Free Trade Agreement Notes of Interpretation of Certain Chapter 11 Provisions' (NAFTA Free Trade Commission 31 Jul. 2001) B, < http://www.sice.oas.org/tpd/nafta/Commission/CH11understandinge.asp > (accessed 5 Sep. 2018).

1041. Jack Coe, 'The State of Investor-State Arbitration-Some Reflections on Prof. Brower's Plea for Sensible Principles' (2005) 20(5) AmUIntlLRev 929, 942.

1042. Article 5 (2) 2004 US Model BIT.

1043. Chapter 11 US – Australia Free Trade Agreement, Article 11.5 (1).

1044. *See* Bonnitcha and others, *The Political Economy of the Investment Treaty Regime* (n 938) 113.

1045. Gabrielle Kaufmann-Kohler, 'Interpretive Powers of the Free Trade Commission and the Rule of Law' in Emmanuel Gaillard and Frédéric Bachand (eds) *Fifteen Years of NAFTA Chapter 11 Arbitration* (Juris Publishing 2001) 175, 182; *See also* Dumberry, 'The Role and Relevance of Awards in the Formation, Identification and Evolution of Customary Rules in International Investment Law' (n 803) 269.

evolutive nature of customary international law with arbitral interpretative power that does not plainly turn around the interpretative note.

A stark illustration is the *Pope and Talbot* award on damages which followed an evolutionary interpretation approach of the FET. In particular, the tribunal stated that:

> [t]here has been evolution in customary international law concepts since the 1920's. It is a facet of international law that customary international law evolves through state practice. International agreements constitute practice of states and contribute to the grounds of customary international law.[1046]

The same tribunal's partial award on the merits treats FET as a self-standing right.[1047] The elements of fairness in Article 1105 are considered as '*additive* to the requirements of international law' meaning that 'investors under NAFTA are entitled to the international law minimum *plus* the fairness elements'. [1048] The tribunal continued mentioning that even though the language of Article 1105 suggests that the fairness elements are included within international law, this interpretation 'is clouded' by the fact that the language of the Article 1105 is derived from the provisions of bilateral commercial treaties which evolved over the years into their present form.[1049] As a result, investors are entitled to such a protection 'no matter what else their entitlement is under international law' and 'compliance with the fairness elements must be ascertained free of any threshold that might be applicable to the evaluation of measures under the minimum standard of international law'.[1050]

The same year, the *Mondev* tribunal dealt with the relationship between treaty protection standards and customary international law. At first, the tribunal explained how customary international law is relevant for the case agreeing with the US party that 'when adopting provisions for fair and equitable treatment and full protection and security in NAFTA (as well as in other BITs), the intention was to incorporate principles of customary international law'.[1051] This intention of the parties to the NAFTA treaty is further demonstrated in the explanations given by the signatory governments to the legislature in the course of ratification or implementation of the treaty. The tribunal notes however that 'these official statements repeatedly refer not to "the" but to "a" minimum standard of treatment'[1052] leaving open the door for development of customary international law concepts.

The arbitral Tribunal further proceeded to identify the content of customary international law providing for FET and FPS in investment treaties. The tribunal did not apply the *Neer* requirements considered to set the traditional approach for the existence of a breach of international law. Instead, it used three arguments that purport to

1046. *Pope & Talbot Inc. v. The Government of Canada*, UNCITRAL, Award in Respect of Damages (31 May 2002) para. 59 (citations omitted).
1047. Kaufmann-Kohler, 'Interpretive Powers of the Free Trade Commission and the Rule of Law' (n 1045) 182.
1048. *Pope & Talbot, Inc. v. The Government of Canada*, UNCITRAL, NAFTA Chapter 11, Award on the Merits of Phase 2 (10 Apr. 2001) para. 110.
1049. *Ibid.* para. 111.
1050. *Ibid.*
1051. *Mondev*, Award (n 239) para. 111.
1052. *Ibid.* para. 111.

demonstrate the evolutionary nature of the customary international law standards of protection. According to the first argument, the tribunal noted that the *Neer* case concerned the physical security of the alien and not the treatment of foreign investment.[1053] The tribunal here recognised the need to take into account that the interpretation of the legal concepts is connected specifically to the investment-arbitration framework. Based on the second argument, the status of the individual in international law as well as the international protection of foreign investments is considered to have developed since the *Neer* decision.[1054] This development requires that the meaning of FET and FPS is determined based on 'the modern eye' since it appears 'unconvincing' to confine to these terms the meaning they had in the 1920s when applied to the physical security of an alien.[1055]

The third argument the Tribunal employed refers to the importance of State practice as influencing the content of CIL, a content that goes beyond the *Neer* decision. The large number of regional and bilateral investment treaties 'almost uniformly' provide for FET and 'largely provide' for FPS, thus forming a 'body of concordant practice' that necessarily influences the 'the content of rules governing the treatment of foreign investment in current international law'.[1056] Based on this line of reasoning, the Tribunal concluded that '[i]t would be surprising if this practice and the vast number of provisions it reflects were to be interpreted as meaning no more than the *Neer* Tribunal (in a very different context) meant in 1927'.[1057]

The Tribunal also referred to the NAFTA Free Trade Commission notes of interpretation (2001) which seem to have concluded differently from the *Mondev* Tribunal on the issue of interpretation of customary international law. The tribunal recognised that according to 'Article 1105(1) the terms "fair and equitable treatment" and "full protection and security" are, in the view of the NAFTA Parties, references to existing elements of the customary international law standard and are not intended to add novel elements to that standard.'[1058] The Tribunal remarks on the issue that while 'Art 1105 does not intend to supplement or add' to the standard of treatment under international law, this does not mean that 'the phrase "including fair and equitable treatment and full protection and security" adds nothing to the meaning of Article 1105(1) nor did the Free Trade Commission seek to read those words out of the article, a process which would have involved amendment rather than interpretation'.[1059]

1053. *Ibid.* paras 114, 115. Cf. *Glamis Gold,* Award (n 407) noting that the '[...] fundamentals of the *Neer* standard thus still apply today', para. 616.
1054. *Mondev,* Award (n 239) para. 116.
1055. *Ibid.* para. 116.
1056. *Ibid.* para. 117 (citations omitted).
1057. *Ibid.*
1058. *Ibid.* para. 122; Article 1105 (1) NAFTA: 'Each Party shall accord to investments of investors of another Party treatment in accordance with international law, including fair and equitable treatment and full protection and security.'; *See also* the analysis of Todd Weiler: Todd Weiler, *The Interpretation of International Investment Law Equality, Discrimination and Minimum Standards of Treatment in Historical Context* (Brill 2013).
1059. *Mondev,* Award (n 239) para. 122.

Based on the above syllogism, the tribunal recognises that it may not apply its own 'idiosyncratic standards' and proceeds to a 'reasonable, evolutionary interpretation of Art 1105'.[1060] Such an interpretation is considered to be consistent with the travaux and with normal principles of interpretation.[1061] Likewise, the *Technicas* tribunal argued for an evolutionary interpretation of CIL in the context of investment-treaty arbitration noting that the dispute will be resolved by resorting *inter alia* to 'customary international law, not as frozen in time, but in their evolution'.[1062]

A similar evolutive approach was followed by the *Siemens* tribunal, which made reference to the NAFTA case law and held that the content of the minimum standard is not limited to the content of customary law as it was presented in the arbitral decisions of the 1920s.[1063] The international standard of treatment has evolved along with the evolution of customary international law.[1064] The tribunal observed that the recent NAFTA awards do not require bad faith or malicious intention as a condition for the failure to treat investments in an equitable and fair way marking the evolution of customary international law in this matter.[1065] Arbitral case law and the purpose of the treaty, which is the promotion and protection of investments constitute the basis of the tribunal's reasoning when referring to customary international law.[1066] In this context, there is an intention of applying an independent standard but not disconnected from its original and natural environment which is international law. As Professor Schreuer noted in his legal opinion:

> An interpretation that is in accordance with the BIT's object and purpose would also have to give some independent meaning to the fair and equitable treatment standard. An interpretation that reduces its meaning to standards that are contained already in customary international law would deprive it of any independent meaning and would make the provision redundant. The application of the general principles of international law is already mandated by Article 10, paragraph 5 of the BIT. If Article 2(1) of the BIT providing for fair and equitable treatment is to have an independent meaning it must be in addition to the general principles of international law.[1067]

A dynamic approach of the fair and equitable treatment standard was also adopted in the more recent *Merrill & Ring* award. In this case the fair and equitable treatment standard was further connected to a sense of fairness, equity and reasonableness. The tribunal first recognised that the approach it is following constitutes an established view in other arbitration cases:

1060. *Ibid.* para. 123.
1061. *Ibid.* paras 119, 123.
1062. *Tecmed*, Award (n 147) para. 116. The tribunal cites the *Mondev*, Award (n 239).
1063. *Siemens AG v. Argentina* ICSID Case No. ARB/02/8, Award (17 Jan. 2007) para. 295 citing: *Mondev*, Award (n 239), *ADF Group, Inc. v. United States of America*, ICSID Case No. ARB(AF)/00/1, Award (9 Jan. 2003) and *Waste Management, Inc. v. United Mexican States*, ICSID Case No. ARB(AF)/98/2, Award (2 Jun. 2002).
1064. *Siemens*, Award (n 1063) para. 295.
1065. *Ibid.* para. 299.
1066. *Ibid.* paras 300, 295.
1067. *Ibid.* para. 284.

> Mondev and ADF, while accepting that fair and equitable treatment had to be understood within customary international law, favored a dynamic interpretation of the content of this source, the first in conjunction with the role of investment treaties and the second, it appears, more generally on state practice, judicial and arbitral case law or other sources of customary or general international law. This evolutionary approach was also endorsed by Waste Management II and Gami.[1068]

Interestingly, the tribunal did not specifically mention the interpretation tools of the Vienna Convention but formed its argument based on arbitral precedent.[1069] The tribunal further commented on the Free Trade Commission interpretation noting that the fact that it is binding 'does not mean that that interpretation necessarily reflects the present state of customary and international law'.[1070] Moreover, it is mentioned that 'the FTC Interpretation seems in some respect to be closer to an amendment of the treaty, than a strict interpretation'.[1071] The tribunal concluded that it recognises the evolutionary nature of customary international law 'which provides scope for the interpretation of Article 1105(1), even in the light of the Free Trade Commission 2001 interpretation'.[1072]

What is further noteworthy is how the tribunal described the development of customary international law over time through a double track of evolution.[1073] The *Neer* approach along with similar case law dealing with due process, denial of justice and physical mistreatment constituted the first track evolution of the minimum standard of treatment. The second track of evolution was linked to the treatment of aliens in relation to business, trade and investments. In this last case, the standard of protection was more liberal as the States support their citizens' claims within the field of diplomatic protection with 'an open mind' without requiring 'outrageous' treatment.[1074] In parallel with this second track evolution, 'diplomatic protection gradually gave way to specialised regimes for the protection of foreign investments and other matters'.[1075] In this context, 'the customary law standard has led to and resulted in establishing the fair and equitable treatment standard as different stages of the same evolutionary process'.[1076]

Based on the above considerations, the idiosyncratic characteristics of the investment treaties do not justify either 'the blind transposition of customary international law rules into treaty cases [or] their wholesale exclusion'.[1077] Investment

1068. *Merrill*, Award (n 1025) para. 190 (citations omitted).
1069. Schill mentions that '[...] most investment treaty tribunals deduce the meaning of fair and equitable treatment from the case law more generally without paying much attention to the investment treaty that was at issue in those cases.' Schill, 'From Sources to Discourse: Investment Treaty Jurisprudence as the New Custom?' (n 1026) 9.
1070. *Merrill*, Award (n 1025) para. 192 (citations omitted).
1071. *Ibid.* para. 192.
1072. *Ibid.*
1073. *Ibid.* paras 201, 205.
1074. *Ibid.* para. 205.
1075. *Ibid.*
1076. *Ibid.* para. 209.
1077. Campbell Mclachlan, 'Fragmentation and Custom in Investment Treaty Law', BIICL Investment Treaty Forum (2007) 1 <http://www.victoria.ac.nz/law/about/staff/campbell-mclachlan/publications-campbell-mclachlan> (accessed 30 Sep. 2018).

protection standards such as the fair and equitable treatment, which have their origin in customary international law, led arbitral tribunals to turn to customary international law in order to interpret them. Nonetheless, the evolutionary interpretation of these standards reveals the need to interpret customary international law bearing in mind the investor-state dispute resolution environment.

The emergence of such an interpretive approach is a corollary of the adaptation process within which the evolutionary interpretation of legal concepts becomes possible. With the democratic evolution of the international community's expectations regarding fair and equitable treatment, arbitral tribunals may not be traditional lawmakers but play an essential role in shaping customary law.[1078] A legal concept derived from customary international law, when integrated and adapted according to the characteristic of the arbitration framework, is interpreted in terms of the concept's content as acquired through the practice of arbitral tribunals and as evolved over time. In this context the dialogue with customary international law is used progressively:

> [...] by modernizing a treaty's meaning in light of subsequent, more modern terms of international law and other treaties. That would mean not 'backwards interpretation' in light of earlier customary international law, but 'forwards interpretation' using, for example, subsequent investment treaties, customary law as it evolves under the impact of modern concurrent treaty practice, and developments in relevant but outside areas of international law, for example, trade, environment, climate change, and human rights.[1079]

Following an evolutionary interpretation approach that depicts the development of the concept as used in the field of investment arbitration seems logically connected to the *lex specialis* nature of the investment-arbitration framework. If investment treaties provided the same protection standards as customary international law, then the only reason for creating investment arbitration would be to create enforcement mechanisms for the already existing customary international law standards. However, investment arbitration is more than procedural rules. It has developed a broad range of substantive protection guarantees ensuring the protection of foreign investors and the promotion of investments.

At the same time, this evolution could acquire such a specific meaning when applied in the investment-arbitration context that could lead to the standard evolving to a specific treaty obligation. This becomes possible due to the *lex generalis-lex specialis* nature of general international law and investment arbitration. The fact that a customary international law standard can develop into a treaty standard does not signify that it cuts every connection with its broader international environment and customary international law origins. Their relationship should stay as a *lex generalis-lex specialis* requiring resort to customary international law when the treaty and investment-arbitration case law has no answers on how to treat a specific issue.

1078. Reisman, 'Canute Confronts the Tide' (n 1012) 633.
1079. Wälde, 'Interpreting Investment Treaties' (n 673) 748.

[C] Reciprocal Communication

The dialogue formed through the use of customary international law interpretive arguments may go in both directions. The previous section discussed the issue of how general customary international law constitutes the basis for the development of a specialised customary international investment law. The practice of arbitral tribunals revealed the process of adapting the interpretation of the customary international law standards to the specific nature of investment-arbitration disputes. This section will focus on the reverse action, which is whether the investment treaties and the practice of investment tribunals are able to influence the way general customary international law is perceived and is developing.

The majority of investment treaties have a common core including investor protection guarantees and dispute resolution provisions. Additionally, the language used to express these protection guarantees is often identical. As such, despite any textual differences, investment treaties have been described as forming 'a single international regime for investment'.[1080] However, the literature is divided as to whether this common core of protection may elevate these protection guarantees to the status of customary international law. Some commentators have described customary international law dealing with the protection of the foreign investor as being reshaped in order to accommodate the legal principles established in the numerous concordant BITs.[1081] Despite the fact that a treaty is binding only for the parties to it based on reciprocity, BITs in particular are the 'contemporary exemplar' of rules that 'become generalised through the conclusion of other similar conventions containing identical or similar provisions'.[1082] International investment law and arbitration are also a piece of customary international law. BITs especially are considered a source of customary international law.[1083]

Other commentators have argued that each investment treaty is different, with different goals and perspectives. Thus they should be viewed simply as constituting a

1080. Salacuse, 'The Emerging Global Regime for Investments' (n 578) 427, 432–433, (The author also states that the common treaty language accounts for reference by tribunals and counsel to arbitral case law when interpreting one treaty, such as NAFTA, in order to interpret a similar provision in a totally unrelated treaty, such as a BIT between Chile and Malaysia); Jeswald Salacuse, 'The Treatification of International Investment Law' (2007) 13 Law & Bus. REV. AM. 155, 165–166 (discussing the impact of international custom on the creation of BITs as well as the impact of BITs on the development of international custom); Jose Alvarez, *The Public International Law Regime Governing International Investment* (Brill/Nijhoff 2011) (discussing the evolution of investment treaties and the emergence of an investor-State *jurisprudence constante*).

1081. Stephen Schwebel, 'The Influence of Bilateral Investment Treaties on Customary International Law', (2004) 98 ASIL PROC 27, 27; Andreas Lowenfeld, 'Investment Agreements and International Law' (2003) 42 ColumJTransnatlL 123; José Alvarez, 'A BIT on Custom' (2009) 42 New York University Journal of International Law and Policy 17.

1082. *Ibid.* 29 citing the 'Report of the International Law Commission covering the work of its Twelfth session' (1960) 2 Yearbook of the International Law Commission 145, UN Doc. A/4425.

1083. *See* Bernard Kishoiyian, 'The Utility of Bilateral Investment Treaties in the Formulation of Customary International Law' (1994) 14 NJILB 327.

lex specialis that regulate investments.[1084] This was the reasoning of the *ADM* Tribunal which stated that 'Section A of Chapter Eleven offers a form of *lex specialis* to supplement the under-developed standards of customary international law relating to the treatment of aliens and property.'[1085] The Tribunal added that '[t]he customary international law that the ILC Articles codify do not apply to matters which are specifically governed by *lex specialis* – i.e., Chapter Eleven of the NAFTA in the present case'.[1086]

Based on a different reasoning, the *Camuzzi* Tribunal, held that 'there is no obstacle in international law to the expression of the will of States through treaties being at the same time an expression of practice and of the *opinio juris* necessary for the birth of a customary rule if the conditions for it are met'.[1087] The Tribunal further agreed with the CMS Tribunal which held that the system of treaties on protection gives rise to a *lex specialis* which '[...] can now be considered the general rule, certainly in respect of foreign investments and international claims'.[1088] Despite this reasoning the *Camuzzi* Tribunal concluded that the emergence of a general rule 'does not necessarily mean that it refers to the emergence of a customary rule' without explaining whether the missing element was the *opinio juris*.[1089]

This discussion evolves around the issue of whether investment treaties may gain the status of customary international law leading to their respect even in the absence of a written treaty.[1090] However, apart from the language and similarities of investment protection guarantees contained into investment treaties, the role of arbitral tribunals in shaping the rules of customary international law is also an important factor often disregarded. As already discussed, with non-State actors gaining an active role in the transnational scene, the concepts of 'general practice' and '*opinio juris*' have been revisited in order to accommodate both public and private interests.[1091] Investor-state tribunals, through their decision-making functions, influence the development of:

> [...] a body of global administrative law that guides State behavior, through influencing both customary international law and approaches taken in other

1084. Muthucumaraswamy Sornarajah, *The International Law on Foreign Investment* (2nd ed., CUP, 2004) 4 (arguing that the treaty formulations are different. As such, the 'treaty balances' are also different and the same provision in one treaty does not necessarily generate the same interpretation in another treaty. Consequently, this is against treaties generating customary international law); Irene Ten Cate, 'The Costs of Consistency' (n 804), 418; Kishoiyian, 'The Utility of Bilateral Investment Treaties in the Formulation of Customary International Law' (n 1083) 327; Eustace Chikere Azubuike, 'The Place of Treaties in International Investment' (2013) 19(1) Annual Survey of International & Comparative Law 155, 168.
1085. *Archer Daniels Midland Company and Tate & Lyle Ingredients Americas, Inc. v. The United Mexican States*, ICSID Case No. ARB(AF)/04/05, Award (21 Nov. 2007) para. 116.
1086. *Ibid.* para. 117.
1087. *Camuzzi International S.A. v. The Argentine Republic*, ICSID Case No. ARB/03/2, Decision on Jurisdiction (11 May 2015) para. 144.
1088. *Ibid.* para. 145.
1089. *Ibid.* para. 145.
1090. *See* Bonnitcha, Poulsen and Wailbel stating that in the case investment treaties influenced the way customary international law develops, investment treaties would have implications for all States, even those that have not signed investment treaties. Bonnitcha and others, *The Political Economy of the Investment Treaty Regime* (n 938) 199.
1091. *See* §6.04[B][1] 'State Practice and Opinio Juris Revisited'.

sub-fields such as trade law or human rights, and through their approaches to balancing different investor and public interests, in ways that affect public policy and the future conduct of States and investors alike.[1092]

Investment tribunals have acknowledged their power to influence the development of customary international law standards when interpreting their vague content in the context of investment-arbitration cases. In the *Urbaser v. Argentina* case, the dispute arose out of a concession contract for water and sewage services granted by Argentina to a company established by the Spanish corporation 'Urbaser'. The claimant alleged violation of the fair and equitable standard of treatment because Argentina adopted measures such as the pesification of tariffs, which negatively influenced its investment. When interpreting the fair and equitable treatment standard of protection, the Tribunal initially recognised that the customary international law minimum standard of treatment is ambiguous 'when the legal foundation of such standard is not identified simultaneously'. [1093] This is because 'such term makes sense only when put in relation to the body of law capable of demonstrating the standard itself'.[1094] After stating that the interpretation of the fair and equitable treatment requirement cannot be left to the exclusive discretion of each tribunal, the *Urbaser* Tribunal held that the elements of the standard should be determined in a general way so that they can apply in future investment cases in general.[1095] Going a step further, the Tribunal concluded that the fair and equitable treatment standard: 'must be objective, not based on personal opinions of the arbitrators or personal expectations of a party. Therefore, it must represent a source of law of a normative character upon which the Parties and the Tribunal can rely'.[1096] Such a source of law of 'normative character' could be 'any legal reasoning, juridical principle, or precedent that would ascribe a normative component'.[1097] Based on this reasoning, the interpretation of the fair and equitable treatment standard would have a normative character when based on precedent.

The reasoning of the *Urbaser* Tribunal is quite clear in demonstrating how the two elements of customary international law – general practice and *opinio juris* – can be found in the practice of arbitral tribunals. As such, the Tribunal connects the

1092. Kingsbury and Schill, 'Investor-State Arbitration as Governance' (n 148) 5.
1093. *Urbaser S.A. and Consorcio de Aguas Bilbao Bizkaia, Bilbao Biskaia Ur Partzuergoa v. The Argentine Republic*, ICSID Case No. ARB/07/26, Award (8 Dec. 2016) para. 610 (The Tribunal added that 'any standard is a "minimum" compared to any other "broader standard"'.)
1094. *Urbaser*, Award (n 249) para. 610.
1095. *Ibid.* paras 611, 612, 616.
1096. *Ibid.* paras 613–633. The elements of the standard that the Tribunal makes reference to are the following: (a) The standard is not tied to one set of expectations since in a given situation, more than one solution can meet the threshold of being fair and equitable; (b)The standard encompasses the entire legal, social and economic framework of the investment; (c) The rights and expectations of the investor must have been affected in essential parts; (d) An unfair or inequitable treatment of such importance must affect the investor's expectations in actual terms; The threshold for a treatment not being fair and equal also results from its intensity or gravity, both factors being subject to variations in relation to the duration of their impact in the particular case.
1097. *Urbaser S.A. and Consorcio de Aguas Bilbao Bizkaia, Bilbao Biskaia Ur Partzuergoa v. The Argentine Republic*, ICSID Case No. ARB/07/26, Decision on Jurisdiction (19 Dec. 2012) para. 146.

interpretation of the fair and equitable minimum standard of treatment with two elements: its general nature that will lead to its application in investment cases in general; and its 'normative character' upon which tribunals and parties can rely on. This generality of application and the normative character of the CIL standard as interpreted in the investment-arbitration case seem to relate to the two elements of customary international law, general practice and *opinio juris*.

From a perspective of arbitral practice, when customary international law is applied in an arbitration dispute, it is interpreted by investment-arbitration tribunals. Although an answer to the question whether arbitral tribunals can create custom or they merely identify it, is not an easy one, what can be concluded is that customary international law should not be viewed as a pre-existing and pre-defined source of legal rights and obligations. On the contrary, it should be treated as a body of law developing through time. In this sense, when the tribunals proceed to an evolutionary interpretation of customary international law in the context of an investment dispute, they further contribute to the development of its general content. The reasoning of investment-arbitration tribunals may influence the general practice of other courts and tribunals, further leading to the development of customary international law through case law.

§6.05 POLICY ARGUMENTS

The Policy-based arguments bring arbitral decision-making in contact with its reality. Theorising over interpretation without contemplating the policies (itself a concept with many meanings) shaping its reality cannot reveal the full picture of legal decision-making. The policy element in legal decision-making may be refined or pushed back but a point always remains at which a choice has to be made, and the necessity arises to determine which factors influenced such a choice.[1098]

The focus on this type of interpretive arguments reveals how policies are used as the foundation of a specific interpretation. The decision-maker interpreting a legal concept exercises certain discretion that is legitimate since 'no system of interpretation can resolve every case presented to the interpreter'.[1099] Within this 'legitimate discretion' arbitrators also employ policy-based arguments. As will be demonstrated in the present section, the well-known and primary case-specific mandate of arbitrators may involve consideration of the policies of the investment-arbitration framework.[1100]

Policy in investment arbitration is a term with no defined content. This book recognises the multifaceted nature of policy and attempts to present and analyse these facets. Policy arguments in legal decision-making stem from the policies of the

1098. Wolfgang Friedmann, 'Legal Philosophy and Judicial Lawmaking' (1961) 61(5) ColumLRev 821, 826.
1099. Barak, *Purposive Interpretation in Law* (n 159) 219.
1100. For the purposes of this section, arbitrators are not viewed as policy-makers but as considering policies in their decision-making process. For an analysis of whether tribunals have policy-making powers, *see* Clasmeier, *Arbitral Awards as Investments* (n 91) 160 et seq.

investment-arbitration framework that are either directly expressed through the investment treaties, or indirectly expressed through the practice of arbitral tribunals. They may comprise policies connected to the behaviour of the State (e.g., transparent, unambiguous and non-contradictory governmental conduct) or policies connected to the investment-arbitration framework (e.g., stability and predictability for the investments).

Treaty policies can be divided into two broad categories: economic policy concerns and political policy concerns. This book proposes two more types of policies which are the legal policy concerns of the investment-arbitration framework and the emerging social policy concerns. In this sense, the arbitrator interprets legal concepts while in constant dialogue with the policies of the investment treaties and the arbitration framework as a whole.

[A] Policies Expressed in Investment Treaties

Investment law such as international law and generally every law is 'rarely neutral' encapsulating 'competing values and policy judgments'.[1101] The application of the rule is examined, not only based on the text of a provision but also through the prism of its social and economic consequences.[1102] On the one hand, such policy concerns may comprise the aims and values of a certain community, in our case of the investment-arbitration framework, the measures to address these concerns, and the actual implementation of the arrangements.[1103] On the other hand, the policies directly expressed in the investment treaties are mainly political and economic.

[1] Political Policies

The need for international cooperation in the investment law scene is linked to the policy of avoiding the solution of diplomatic protection. Dealing with an investor's claim in an international forum is a way to depoliticise the dispute and bring it within the realm of law rather than that of diplomacy and politics.[1104] The resolution of investment disputes in the particular forum avoids the confrontation of the home State

1101. Michael Waibel, 'Demystifying the Art of Interpretation' (2011) 22(2) EJIL 571, 573. Arbitrator G states that: '[...] legal prescriptions are efforts to achieve certain policy consequences and I think that the art of the arbitrator or any decision-maker is to identify the relevant policy consequences that have been sought and fashion a decision consistent with them, with the law which contributes to the realisation of those policies.' *See* Annex 'Interview Questions'.
1102. Reisman, *The Quest for World Order and Human Dignity in the Twenty-First Century* (n 142) 172; For the issue of discretion in arbitral decision-making *see* §1.02[D][3] 'Legal Interpretation and Arbitral Discretion'.
1103. Reisman, *The Quest for World Order and Human Dignity in the Twenty-First Century* (n 142) 171.
1104. Gabrielle Kaufmann-Kohler, 'Non-disputing State Submissions in Investment Arbitration: Resurgence of Diplomatic Protection' in Laurence Boisson de Chazournes, Marcelo G Kohen, and Jorge E Viñuales (eds) *Diplomatic and Judicial Means of Dispute Settlement* (Nijhoff 2012) 305.

with the host State.[1105] Diplomatic protection is not a tempting way of resolving the arising dispute as it requires the exhaustion of all local remedies and it depends on the will of the State to pursue the claim.[1106] Investment arbitration regulates the judicial settlement of disputes that were previously resolved in the political arena through diplomatic protection. However, as investor-state disputes involve a State, they are strictly connected with State policy and regulation maintaining their political aspect.[1107] The recourse to investment treaties is viewed as an act of international cooperation in an 'anarchic word of independent sovereign states'.[1108] Through such a political cooperation act individual interests of States, such as the facilitation of the flow of capital and economic development, can be advanced.[1109]

The reasoning of the *Banro* tribunal well illustrates such a political-oriented policy when noting that one of the main objectives of the Washington Convention is to deal with the international tension and crisis that even resulted in the use of force, caused by the diplomatic protection accorded to an investor by its home State.[1110] A secondary political objective of investment treaties is the creation and strengthening of the relationship between two countries. A developing country signing a BIT with a developed capital-exporting country may not only wish for investment flows but also for increased trade, foreign aid or security assistance.[1111] Against this background, political policies may vary depending on the perspective of a developed or developing State. For developed States, apart from the de-politicisation of investment disputes, a factor for entering into investment agreements may have also been the interests of multinational firms which influence policy outcomes on an international level.[1112]

Another political aspect connected to investment treaties is the creation of an international, extra jurisdictional substitute for domestic institutional quality.[1113] The quality of national judicial institutions varies – issues of judicial independence and in some case even corruption may arise – turning the route of international arbitration into a quality substitute for coping with the challenges of a foreign international investment dispute. The recourse to local courts is not the best solution for the investor

1105. Rudolf Dolzer and Christoph Schreuer, *Principles of International Investment Law* (n 338) 53.
1106. Schreuer and others, *The ICSID Convention: A Commentary* (n 269) 6.
1107. Sureda, *Investment Treaty Arbitration Judging Under Uncertainty* (n 162) 2.
1108. Robert O Keohane, *International Institutions and State Power: Essays in International Relations Theory* (Routledge 1989) 132; Salacuse, 'The Emerging Global Regime for Investments' (n 578) 427, 435.
1109. Salacuse, 'The Emerging Global Regime for Investments' (n 578) 427, 435.
1110. *Banro American Resources, Inc. and Société Aurifère du Kivu et du Maniema S.A.R.L. v. Democratic Republic of the Congo*, ICSID Case No. ARB/98/7, Award (1 Sep. 2000) para. 15.
1111. Salacuse, *The Law of Investment Treaties* (n 69) 113.
1112. Mark Manger, *Investing in Protection: The Politics of Preferential Trade Agreements Between North and South* (CUP 2009) discussing how foreign direct investment and services are a driving force behind preferential trading agreements; *See also* Bonnitcha and others, *The Political Economy of the Investment Treaty Regime* (n 938) 181 (examining whether the establishment of the institutional frameworks for the resolution of investment disputes was influenced by private commercial interests advanced by corporate lobby groups).
1113. Tom Ginsburg, 'International Substitutes for Domestic Institutions: Bilateral Investment Treaties and Governance' (n 11).

either, who would have to deal with a foreign legal and judicial system and the fear of prejudice or even government intervention in the judicial procedure.[1114]

Both States and investors view the investment treaties as a mechanism to control the risk a foreign investment entails. The rights and obligations contained into the BITs are linked to political interests such as the risk management of the domestic law modifications and governmental acts, and 'taming' the dangers of expropriation. A political risk entails the danger that political developments in the host State might damage the economic basis of the investment through nationalisation, forced renegotiation and obstacles to repatriation of capital and profits in foreign exchange.[1115] In this context, investment treaties can be seen as a risk management tool for States in order to attract investments. The development of international investment treaties came as an answer to the investor's concerns for a safe, secure and stable legal framework appropriate to facilitate, promote and protect their investments.

They are also a risk management tool for investors. Investors can choose from various risk management tools in order to protect their interests. These may vary from spreading the risk through the formation of joint venture for projects that entail high risks to insuring the risk in order to cover a change of the fiscal regime and guarantee fiscal exchange.[1116] Investment treaties constitute a tool for reassuring the stabilisation of the contractual framework negotiated with the State offering protection against legislative and administrative interference.[1117] The investor profits from the 'irrevocable offer' from the State to submit the dispute to an arbitral dispute resolution body independent from the control of the host State.[1118] Within the control of this political risk lies the discouragement of the host State in abusing its sovereign regulatory and administrative powers since a prospect of a negative arbitral award would wound the State's reputation.[1119]

[2] Economic Policies

An examination of investment treaties and conventions reveals the economic and political aims that the States targeted when concluding these international law instruments.[1120] The ICSID framework[1121] offers the most popular regulatory and institutional framework for the resolution of investment disputes between States and

1114. Salacuse, *The Law of Investment Treaties* (n 69) 109.
1115. Wälde, 'Investment Arbitration under the Energy Charter Treaty – From Dispute Settlement to Treaty Implementation' (n 350) 431.
1116. Thomas Wälde, 'Stabilizing International Investment Commitments: International Law versus Contract Interpretation' (1996) 31 Tex. Intl. LJ 215, 233–234.
1117. Wälde, 'Investment Arbitration under the Energy Charter Treaty – From Dispute Settlement to Treaty Implementation' (n 350) 432.
1118. Antonio Parra, 'Principles Governing Foreign Investment as Reflected in National Investment Codes' (1992) 7(2) ICSID Rev 428, 446.
1119. Wälde, 'Arbitration under the Energy Charter Treaty – From Dispute Settlement to Treaty Implementation' (n 350) 432.
1120. For a detailed theoretical discussion on the economic efficiency of investment treaties connected to the net economic benefit or cost associated with a policy or a decision of States and investors, *see* Bonnitcha and others, *The Political Economy of the Investment Treaty Regime* (n 938) 127 at seq.

investors. The Preamble of the ICSID Convention reveals the primary aim of the creation of the ICSID dispute resolution regime which is the 'international cooperation for economic development, and the role of private international investment therein'.[1122] The desire to strengthen the partnership between countries in the cause of economic development and the promotion of an atmosphere of mutual confidence, and thus the stimulation of a larger flow of private international capital, are emphatically mentioned in the Report of the Executive Directors.[1123]

An additional economic element attached to the policies of the ICSID dispute resolution framework is the founding role of the World Bank, which is an international agency for development as well as for the promotion of foreign direct investment.[1124] The preamble of the ICSID Convention in paragraph 5 states that the facilities for conciliation or arbitration are established 'under the auspices of the International Bank for Reconstruction and Development'.[1125] However, the decisions on the disputes are made by independent arbitrators and not by the World Bank itself. Rooting ICSID within the World Bank places the dispute resolution framework within the context of framing capital flows, emphasising at the same time on the benefits of investment in-flows for the development of the recipient States.[1126]

An area where the economic policies make their way into the legal decision-making process of ICSID tribunals is the definition of investment. It could be argued that the divergence in the case law as to the need for a requirement of development of the host State, within the meaning of 'investment' is in fact an economic policy choice to afford protection to certain interests or to exclude others. The Report of the Executive Directors on the Convention mentions that no attempt was made in order to define the term.[1127]

In the *Ceskoslovenska Obchodni Banka (CSOB)* case, the Tribunal addressed the issue of whether the legal dispute arose directly out of an investment. In the absence of the definition of an investment, the tribunal proceeded to a broad definition of the term supporting its reasoning by reference to the preamble of the ICSID Convention. It

1121. The term 'regime' is used as a synonym for the term 'framework' and does not imply the application of the regimes theory. For the use of regime theory to examine the investment treaties *see* Salacuse, *The Law of Investment Treaties* (n 69) 5. Following a 'consensus definition' from the scene of international relations the author describes an international regime as 'principles, norms rules and decision-making procedures around which actors' expectations converge in a given area of international relations'.
1122. ICSID, Preamble.
1123. Schreuer and others, *The ICSID Convention: A Commentary* (n 269) 4 citing 1 ICSID Reports 25.
1124. *Ibid.* 8.
1125. ICSID, Preamble, para. 5.
1126. Omar García-Bolívar, 'Economic Development at the Core of the International Investment Regime' in Chester Brown and Miles Kate (eds) *Evolution in Investment Treaty Law and Arbitration* (CUP 2011) 591.
1127. 'Report of the Executive Directors on the Convention' 1 ICSID Rep. 28 (1993) Article 25(4) stating: No attempt was made to define the term 'investment' given the essential requirements of consent by the parties, and the mechanisms through which Contracting States can make known in advance, if they so desire, the classes of disputes which they would or would not consider submitting to the Centre.

specifically noted that the need for 'international cooperation for economic development and the role of private international investment therein' opened the way to the conclusion that an international transaction which contributes to such a type of cooperation, could be characterised an investment for the purposes of the ICSID Convention.[1128]

Similarly, the *Salini* Tribunal, when identifying the criteria for defining an 'investment', coupled the doctrine with the Preamble of the Convention and the economic development of the State:

> The doctrine generally considers that investment infers: contributions, a certain duration of performance of the contract and a participation in the risks of the transaction [...]. In reading the Convention's preamble, one may add the contribution to the economic development of the host State of the investment as an additional condition.[1129]

Going a step further, the Tribunal connected the investment's contribution to the economic development of the host State with serving the public interest and contributing know-how in relation with the work to be undertaken.[1130]

The criterion to contribute to the development of the host State has been described by the *Alpha v. Ukraine* tribunal as requiring a 'post-hoc examination of the economic, financial and/or policy assessment that prompted the Claimants' activities.[1131] Some tribunals have followed a more restrictive interpretation of the term 'economic development',[1132] while others followed the Salini test, albeit with certain

1128. *Ceskoslovenska Obchodni Banka, AS v. The Slovak Republic,* ICSID Case No. ARB/97/4, Decision on Jurisdiction (24 May 1999) para. 64.
1129. *Salini Costruttori SpA and Italstrade SpA v. Morocco,* ICSID Case No. ARB/00/4, Decision on Jurisdiction (23 Jul. 2001) para. 51; *See also* Christoph Schreuer and others, *The ICSID Convention: A Commentary* (n 269), Article 25, paras 153–174.
1130. *Salini Costruttori SpA and Italstrade SpA v. Morocco,* ICSID Case No. ARB/00/4, Decision on Jurisdiction (23 Jul. 2001) para. 57.
1131. *Alpha Projektholding GmbH v. Ukraine,* ICSID Case No. ARB/07/16 (8 Nov. 2010) para. 312; Peng Wang, 'When Investor-State Arbitration Tribunal Becomes Policy Maker: Reflection on Jurisdiction Decision of Philip Morris v. Uruguay' (2013) <SSRN: https://ssrn.com/abstract=2296490 or http://dx.doi.org/10.2139/ssrn.2296490> (accessed 10 Jul. 2018) (commenting on the decision: *Philip Morris Brands Sàrl, Philip Morris Products S.A And Abal Hermanos S.A. V Oriental Republic of Uruguay,* ICSID Case No. ARB/10/07, Decision on Jurisdiction, (2 Jul. 2013).
1132. *See,* for example, the Pantechniki Tribunal which does not accept the definition given in Salini since: '[...] broadly acceptable descriptions cannot be elevated to jurisdictional requirements unless that is their explicit function. They may introduce elements of subjective judgment on the part of arbitral tribunals (such as "sufficient" duration or magnitude or contribution to economic development) which (a) transform arbitrators into policy-makers and above all (b) increase unpredictability about the availability of ICSID to settle given disputes'. *Pantechniki S.A. Contractors & Engineers (Greece) v. The Republic of Albania,* ICSID Case No. ARB/07/21, Award (30 Jul. 2009) para. 43; *See also Mr. Patrick Mitchell v. Democratic Republic of the Congo,* ICSID Case No. ARB/99/7, Decision on Annulment (1 Nov. 2006) para. 33 (The Tribunal stated that the economic development of the host State is essential but not an 'unquestionable criterion of the investment'. The Tribunal added that ICSID tribunals do not have to evaluate the real contribution but it suffices if there is a contribution 'one way or another' to the economic development of the host State).

variations, such as in the *Helnan International Hotels* case.[1133] The Tribunal based its reasoning on ICSID precedent adding the requirement for 'significant' contribution to the development of the State.[1134] It stated that a project is an investment when showing 'a certain duration, a regularity of profit and return, an element of risk, a substantial commitment and a significant contribution to the host State's development'. However, the tribunal did not specify the meaning of the phrase 'significant contribution'.

One year later, in the *Malaysian Historical Salvors Sdn Bhd v. Malaysia* case, Tribunal made reference to the condition of 'significant contribution'. The Tribunal stated that 'economic development' has the meaning of a contract making a significant contribution to the host State through enhancing the Gross Domestic Product of its economy.[1135]

In the bilateral treaty scene, the driving force for the expansion of BITs was the need to cope with the uncertainty created by the lack of consensus regarding customary international law applicable to foreign investments, by providing specific rules and effective enforcement mechanisms.[1136] The rights and obligations contained into the BITs are linked to economic interests such as the promotion of foreign direct investment and 'taming' the dangers of expropriation.[1137]

The *Maffezini* tribunal delimited the policies of the treaty defining what does not fall under the BIT's purposes. In particular, the tribunal emphasised that 'Bilateral Investment Treaties are not insurance policies against bad business judgments [...] and they cannot be deemed to relieve investors of the business risks inherent in any investment.'[1138] Similarly, the *CMS v. Argentina* tribunal referred to the object and purpose of the treaty in order to assess whether the BIT is applied or not in the case of necessity. The tribunal held that '[t]he Treaty in this case is clearly designed to protect

1133. *Helnan International Hotels A/S v. Arab Republic of Egypt*, ICSID Case No. ARB/05/19, Decision on Jurisdiction (17 Oct. 2006) para. 77.
1134. The Tribunal based its reasoning on the case law cited by the Respondent namely the *Salini v. Kingdom of Morocco* case and on the Commentary by Prof. Ch. Schreuer (Schreuer, *The ICSID Convention: A Commentary* (n 269) 140), and *Helnan International Hotels A/S v. Arab Republic of Egypt* para. 77.
1135. *Malaysian Historical Salvors, SDN, BHD v. The Government of Malaysia*, ICSID Case No. ARB/05/10, Decision on Jurisdiction (17 May 2007) para. 73. The decision was subsequently annulled but there was a dissenting opinion by Judge Mohamed Shahabuddeen. *See* the discussion by Omar García-Bolívar, 'Economic Development at the Core of the International Investment Regime' in Chester Brown and Miles Kate (eds) *Evolution in Investment Treaty Law and Arbitration* (n 1126) 597.
1136. Salacuse and Sullivan, 'Do BITS Really Work?' (n 341) 76.
1137. For example, Canada 2004 Model BIT, Preamble; *See* Bonnitcha and others, *The Political Economy of the Investment Treaty Regime* (n 938) 46 et seq (analysing the economic impact of foreign direct investment on host States which can vary across sectors and industries); Beata Javorcik, 'Does Foreign Direct Investment Increase the Productivity of Domestic Firms? In search of spillovers through backward linkages' (2004) AmEconRev 94, 605–27 (discussing the spillover effects such as the diffusion of technology and know-how); Emma Aisbett, 'Bilateral Investment Treaties and Foreign Direct Investment: Correlation versus Causation' in Karl Sauvant and Lisa Sachs (eds), *The Effect of Treaties on Foreign Direct Investment: Bilateral Investment Treaties, Double Taxation Treaties and Investment Flows* (OUP 2009) (assessing the benefits of investment liberalisation policies and questioning the strong correlation between BITs and investment flows).
1138. *Emilio Agustín Maffezini v. The Kingdom of Spain*, ICSID Case No. ARB/97/7, Award (13 Nov. 2000) para. 64.

investments at a time of economic difficulties or other circumstances leading to the adoption of adverse measures by the Government'.[1139] Based on this reasoning the tribunal concluded that 'the Argentine crisis was severe but did not result in total economic and social collapse' and, therefore, the purpose of the treaty will prevail over any plea of necessity.[1140]

The Energy Charter Treaty also strives for the promotion of economic development and international cooperation with emphasis, however, on the energy sector.[1141] The *Plama* Tribunal clearly stated that the ECT should be interpreted 'in a manner consistent with the aim of encouraging respect for the rule of law' and, as such, 'the substantive protections of the ECT cannot apply to investments that are made contrary to law'.[1142]

The economic aspect of these policy goals is connected to the promotion of economic development, the facilitation of private international investment through the creation of an investor-friendly climate, and the liberalisation of the developing country's economy via the entry of foreign investments.[1143] Apart from the protection of the investors, investment treaties aim further to increase the flow of capital and technology in a State in order to promote its economic development, business activity and increasing prosperity.[1144] These economic policies tend to differ based on the individual interests of capital-exporting and capital-importing States. As an example, capital-exporting countries use investment treaties as a tool for mitigating foreign State interference in the companies of their nationals, while capital-importing countries enter into investment agreements in order to reduce the investment risks and thus reduce the investment costs.[1145]

Going a step further, certain treaties such as the NAFTA seek to facilitate the entry and operation of investments through the abolition of national regulatory impediments and the creation of a single market for the free movement of capital.[1146] The *ADF* award is a fine illustration of how the Tribunal assessed the use of the NAFTA treaty policies in its decision-making process. Under the title of 'preliminary interpretive considerations', the tribunal commented on the interpreting task of NAFTA provisions the following:

> NAFTA's objectives, together with the statements set out in the Preamble of NAFTA, are necessarily cast in terms of a high level of generality and abstraction.

1139. *CMS Gas Transmission Company v. The Republic of Argentina,* ICSID Case No. ARB/01/8, Award (12 May 2005) para. 353.
1140. *Ibid.* paras 354–355.
1141. Energy Charter Treaty, 13–14.
1142. *Plama Consortium Limited v. Republic of Bulgaria,* ICSID Case No. ARB/03/24, Award (27 Aug. 2008) para. 139.
1143. Schreuer, *The ICSID Convention: A Commentary* (n 269) 4.
1144. Jeswald Salacuse (2015) 'The Emerging Global Regime for Investments' (n 578) 427, 434.
1145. Jeswald Salacuse (2015) 'The Emerging Global Regime for Investments' (n 578) 427, 430; Bonnitcha and others, *The Political Economy of the Investment Treaty Regime* (n 938) 192; Andrew T Guzman, 'Why LDCs Sign Treaties That Hurt Them: Explaining the Popularity of Bilateral Investment Treaties' (1998) 38 VaJIntlL 639, 687 (arguing that 'BITs, therefore, do not reflect a sense of legal obligation but are rather the result of countries using the international tools at their disposal to pursue their economic interests').
1146. NAFTA Agreement (Article 102 (1)(a)(b)).

> In contrast, interpretive issues commonly arise in respect of detailed provisions embedded in the extraordinarily complex architecture of the treaty. [...] We do not suggest that the general objectives of NAFTA are not useful or relevant. Far from it. Those general objectives may be conceived of as partaking of the nature of *lex generalis* while a particular detailed provision set in a particular context in the rest of a Chapter or Part of NAFTA functions as *lex specialis*. The former may frequently cast light on a specific interpretive issue; but it is not to be regarded as overriding and superseding the latter.[1147]

Based on these considerations, arbitral tribunals do take into account political and economic considerations in the context of deciding a dispute. The arbitrator's task of interpreting the treaties may very often include taking into account these considerations as expressed into the treaty text and its preambles. In practice, however, inserting policies in the decision-making task of the arbitrator and, even more, interpreting these policies, is not a straightforward process. Such a level of interpretational discretion brings to the surface two issues: The first one is on what basis do arbitrators take into account policy concerns when interpreting the law? Is it only on the basis of Article 31(1) VCLT which talks about the object and purpose of a treaty? The second one relates to the need to address the issue of conflicting policies that may arise in the interpretational task. Should an arbitrator and – if yes – how would an arbitrator evaluate conflicting policies? The next section deals with these questions picturing on what basis policy concerns are inserted in the decision-making process of arbitral tribunals.

[3] Evaluating the Effectiveness of Treaty Policies

Even though treaty preambles do not reflect binding obligations, they constitute one of the sources for identifying a treaty's objectives.[1148] Nonetheless, caution is necessary since preambles are not always drafted clearly and they may also need to be interpreted.[1149] Another source for identifying the treaty policies is the treaty text taken as a whole.[1150]

Article 31(1) VCLT makes reference to the interpretation of treaties based on their object and purpose. In the context of this teleological interpretation it has been expressed by commentators and arbitral case law that recourse to the object and purpose of a treaty cannot override the wording of the treaty text, and that it is used not as a means to determine the interpretation but rather as a means of confirming a specific interpretation.[1151]

1147. *ADF*, Award (n 1063) para. 147; *See also Metalclad Corporation v. The United Mexican States*, ICSID Case No. ARB(AF)/97/1, Award (30 Aug. 2000) para. 75. The tribunal held that 'an underlying objective of NAFTA is to promote and increase cross-border investment opportunities and ensure the successful implementation of investment initiatives (NAFTA Article 102(1))'.
1148. Dolzer and Stevens, *Bilateral Investment Treaties* (n 338) 20.
1149. Richard Gardiner, *Treaty Interpretation* (2nd ed., OUP 2015) 217.
1150. *Ibid.* 213.
1151. Romesh Weeramantry, *Treaty Interpretation in Investment Arbitration* (n 144) 68; *See Marvin Roy Feldman Karpa v. United Mexican States*, ICSID Case No. ARB(AF)/99/1, Decision on

However, arbitral tribunals do not always follow the VCLT but rely on non-conventional interpretation methods such as 'common sense', 'justice', 'fairness', 'policy implications', 'practical consequences', 'efficiency', or 'reasonableness'.[1152] In this context, practice reveals that when tribunals refer to policies in their reasoning, they do not always mention the VCLT interpretation rule and they do not necessarily make reference to the preamble of the treaty.[1153] In an empirical analysis of arbitral decisions, Fauchald found that of ninety-eight decisions, forty-eight referred to the 'object and purpose' interpretive argument while within these forty-eight decisions only thirteen referred to the preamble of the treaty as a source of identifying the purpose of a treaty.[1154] This lack of reference to the sources may be explained by the fact that the policies of the treaty were evident or that the tribunals put forward their own view on which were the treaty policies.[1155]

Additionally, the need may arise to refer to economic policies that are not connected with the treaties but with the national legal framework within which the investment takes place. As an example, the *Enron* Tribunal used policy-based arguments to address the foreseeability of the events underlying the issue of who bears the devaluation risk and the risk concerning the freeze of tariffs.[1156] In addressing the respondent's view that 'a risk is not the same as foreseeing that the events in question will necessarily take place' the tribunal used economic policy arguments.[1157] Referring to the economic policies behind the privatisation regulatory regime, which were to 'tak[e] cover against all kind of risks inspired by the economic history of the country and the instability of the 1980s, including country risk and devaluation', the tribunal concluded that this 'is in itself indicating that the parties were quite aware of the dangers ahead'.[1158]

Furthermore, resort to the VCLT 'object and purpose' is not always helpful when it comes to the need to evaluate policies and give answers to debates such as whether investment treaties primarily aim at protecting investors and investments or constitute an equally important means of promoting foreign investment and public interest.[1159] Emphasising on the first point may suggest that policies protecting the investor should prevail while the second way of thinking may require that the protection of the investor

jurisdiction (6 Dec. 2000) para. 35; Cf. The *Siemens* Tribunal used the object and purpose of the treaty which prevailed over the text of the treaty. *Siemens A.G. v. The Argentine Republic,* ICSID Case No. ARB/02/8, Decision on Jurisdiction (3 Aug. 2004) para. 92.

1152. *See* for example *Siemens*, Jurisdiction, para. 92. The Tribunal referred to 'common sense': 'The subjective element is just a matter of plain common sense, e.g., in clauses dealing with the transfer of payments, dispute settlement, and activities in relation to investments: these actions need to be taken by a person, physical or legal. The Tribunal finds that, for purposes of applying the MFN clause, there is no special significance to the differential use of the terms investor or investments in the Treaty.'; Weeramantry states that one-third (87 out of 258) of the arbitral awards do not refer directly or indirectly to the VCLT. Weeramantry, *Treaty Interpretation in Investment Arbitration* (n 144) 157–164; *See* §6.01 'Convention Arguments'.
1153. For example, *Urbaser,* Award (n 249) paras 145, 146.
1154. Fauchald, 'The Legal Reasoning of ICSID Tribunals – An Empirical Analysis' (n 401) 322.
1155. *Ibid.*
1156. *Enron,* Award (n 581) para. 216.
1157. *Ibid.* para. 216.
1158. *Ibid.*
1159. Roberts, 'Clash of Paradigms' (n 76) 9.

should be balanced with other policy goals.[1160] This situation is enhanced by the fact that investment treaties have complex goals which may appear to conflict.[1161] In this context, the 'object and purpose' of an investment treaty is a concept borrowed from the language if the VCLT. However, in the arbitration context, policy appears to have a broader meaning that not only encompasses the treaty objectives expressed in the preamble but also the process of weighing and according the suitable considerations to each policy.

The *Saluka* tribunal well depicts such a picture. While it first refers to the title and preamble of the treaty in order to identify its 'object and purpose', it states that such a reference 'is a more subtle and balanced statement of the Treaty's aims than is sometimes appreciated'.[1162] Based on this approach it identifies further treaty aims that need to be balanced:

> The protection of foreign investments is not the sole aim of the Treaty, but rather a necessary element alongside the overall aim of encouraging foreign investment and extending and intensifying the parties' economic relations. That in turn calls for a balanced approach to the interpretation of the Treaty's substantive provisions for the protection of investments, since an interpretation which exaggerates the protection to be accorded to foreign investments may serve to dissuade host States from admitting foreign investments and so undermine the overall aim of extending and intensifying the parties' mutual economic relations.[1163]

After proceeding to such a balance of policies, the tribunal concluded that the FET standard should be understood as a treatment which 'if not proactively stimulating the inflow of foreign investment capital, does at least not deter foreign capital by providing disincentives to foreign investors'.[1164]

Balancing such economic and political policies through the legal decision-making process is neither an intellectually nor a practically simple procedure. Predicting how the interpretation of a specific treaty issue would contribute to the realisation of a specific policy goal requires 'competence in highly sophisticated social and economic forecasting', a trait that arbitrators are not expected to own.[1165] But even if they possessed such a quality, such an exercise may be criticised as touching upon a legislative function.

As a solution to this situation, Wälde interestingly remarks that even though the tribunals cannot predict how a specific interpretation will fulfil the object of a treaty, what they can do is speculate about such a probability by identifying and bearing in mind both the main objective of a treaty and the specific purposes of a treaty

1160. *Ibid.* 9.
1161. Wälde characteristically mentions that the ECT has '50 or so items which would be relevant for the definition of the "object and purpose" under Article 31(1) VCLT [including] 14 objectives mentioned in the preamble; the preamble of the 1991 European Energy Charter (which the ECT refers to, accepts, and intends to implement) itself has another 21 [...] objectives in addition to approximately a further 20 objectives in its title I.' Wälde, 'Interpreting Investment Treaties' (n 673) 759.
1162. *Saluka*, Partial Award (n 377) paras 299, 300.
1163. *Ibid.* para. 300.
1164. *Ibid.* para. 301.
1165. Wälde, 'Interpreting Investment Treaties' (n 673) 761.

concept.[1166] Investment treaties, let alone multilateral ones, are comprised of various 'individual mechanisms, concepts and terms' which need to work altogether in order to construct a 'reasonably sensible and logical whole'.[1167] In this context, a functional interpretation which can be expressed through the principle of effectiveness is able to help these components work effectively together.

Certain tribunals have responded to such a need by inserting in their interpretation process the principle of effectiveness.[1168] A fine illustration is the *SGS v. Philippines* tribunal which proceeds to the effective interpretation of the object and purpose of the treaty in order to give priority to the protection of the investments. It particularly stated the following:

> The object and purpose of the BIT supports an effective interpretation of Article X(2). The BIT is a treaty for the promotion and reciprocal protection of investments. According to the preamble it is intended 'to create and maintain favourable conditions for investments by investors of one Contracting Party in the territory of the other'. It is legitimate to resolve uncertainties in its interpretation so as to favour the protection of covered investments.[1169]

Similarly, the *Noble v. Romania* tribunal employed the principle of effectiveness in order to support an interpretation of the umbrella clause exclusively in favour of the investor:

> The object and purpose rule also supports such an interpretation. While it is not *permissible, as is* too often done regarding BITs, to interpret clauses exclusively in favour of investors, here such an interpretation is justified. Considering, as pointed out above, that any other interpretation would deprive Art. II (2)(c) of practical content, reference has necessarily to be made to the principle of effectiveness, also applied by other Tribunals in interpreting BIT provisions (see *SGS v. Philippines*, para. 116 and *Salini v. Jordan*, para. 95). An interpretation to the contrary would deprive the investor of any internationally secured legal remedy in respect of investment contracts that it has entered into with the host State. While it is not the purpose of investment treaties per se to remedy such problems, a clause that is readily capable of being interpreted in this way and which would otherwise be deprived of practical applicability is naturally to be understood as protecting investors also with regard to contracts with the host State generally in so far as the contract was entered into with regard to an investment.[1170]

Arbitral tribunals have acknowledged that the principle of effectiveness 'is a cardinal rule of the interpretation of treaties that each and every operative clause of a treaty is to be interpreted as meaningful rather than meaningless'.[1171] Effectiveness as

1166. *Ibid.* 764.
1167. *Ibid.*
1168. James Crawford, 22nd Freshfields Lecture on International Arbitration, London, 29 Nov. 2007.
1169. *SGS*, Jurisdiction (n 351) para. 116.
1170. *Noble Ventures, Inc. v. Romania*, ICSID Case No. ARB/01/11, Award (12 Oct. 2005) para. 52; *See also Feldman* Award (n 935) para. 183; *Mondev*, Award (n 239) para. 91.
1171. *Granti Koza v. Turkmentisan*, ICSID Case No. ARB/11/20 (3 Jul. 2013) Laurence Boisson de Chazournes dissenting opinion para. 27; *Eureko BV v. Republic of Poland*, Partial Award (by Majority) of 19 Aug. 2005, para. 248; *See also, Pan American Energy LLC and BP Argentina*

a principle of interpretation is strongly connected to the teleological approach to interpretation and has a double meaning which is not always easily distinguished: its broader version aims at the interpretation that will effectively fulfil the goals of a treaty while its narrower version prescribes that the treaty provisions should be interpreted in a way that does not render the rest of the provisions superfluous or without a meaning (*effet utile*).[1172]

Effectiveness also appears as a treaty goal in certain BITs and multilateral treaties such as Article II (7) US–Ecuador BIT and Article 10(12) ECT requiring 'effective means of asserting claims and enforcing rights with respect to investment, investment agreements, and investment authorizations'. Tribunals have interpreted 'effectiveness' within this context as a 'systemic obligation' requiring from States 'to provide an effective framework or system for the enforcement of rights, but does not offer guarantees in individual cases'.[1173] Other tribunals interpreted similar provisions as requiring the effective enforcement of rights in every individual case as well as the availability of remedies in domestic courts for foreign investors.[1174]

The effectiveness of the protection accorded to foreign investors is not an absolute concept. It is confronted with the tension between the public-private interests involved in an investor-state arbitration dispute and the policies formed around these interests. The policies underlying the effective protection of the investment accorded by investment treaties does not *in abstracto* prevail the interests of the State and the law of State immunity. In the confines of a specific dispute, the process of balancing the policies around public and private interests will *in concreto* define which one of the two policies – investor-driven or State-driven – will have precedence over the other.

Based on these considerations, the importance of the policy-based arguments should not be obscured by the application of the VCLT 'object and purpose' rule. Securing the effectiveness of the general treaty objectives seems to fulfil a larger aspiration than an interpretation based on the object and purpose of the treaty.[1175] In

Exploration Company v. Argentine Republic, ICSID Case No. ARB/03/13, Decision on Preliminary Objections (27 Jul. 2006) para. 132; *Salini Costruttori S.p.A. and Italstrade S.p.A. v. Hashemite Kingdom of Jordan*, ICSID Case No. ARB/02/13, Decision on Jurisdiction (29 Nov. 2004) para. 95.

1172. Fauchald, 'The Legal Reasoning of ICSID Tribunals – An Empirical Analysis' (n 401) 317; Cf *Banro*, Award (n 1110) para. 6 which delimits the principle of effectiveness noting that such an interpretation should not go against the clear and explicit terms of the treaty.

1173. Schill, 'Cross-Regime Harmonization through Proportionality Analysis' (n 879) 105; *Limited Liability Company Amto v. Ukraine*, SCC Case No. 080/2005, ECT, Final Award (26 Mar. 2008) para. 88.

1174. *Duke Energy*, Award (n 960) paras 390–403; *Noble Ventures, Inc. v. Romania*, ICSID Case No. ARB/01/11, Award (12 Oct. 2005) para. 52 (invoking the principle in determining that 'any other interpretation [of the BIT article under dispute] would deprive [that article] of practical content'); *Kaiser Bauxite Company v. Government of Jamaica*, ICSID Case No. ARB/74/3, Decision on Jurisdiction and Competence (6 Jul. 1975) reported at 114 ILR 142 (1999), para. 24 (interpreting the ICSID Convention to find that Jamaica had consented since 'any other interpretation would very largely, if not wholly, deprive the Convention of any practical value'); Expert Opinion of Professor Steven R Ratner in case *Murphy Exploration and Production Company International, Claimant v. The Republic of Ecuador*, ICSID Case No. ARB/08/4 (15 Mar. 2013) para. 11.

1175. Gardiner, *Treaty Interpretation* (n 1149) 221.

this sense, advancing the aims of a treaty through a specific interpretation is dependent on but not identical to the mere identification of the treaty's objectives.[1176] The importance of properly appreciating the functions of the effectiveness principle, by both practice and doctrine, lies in its ability to put emphasis on the particular treaty policies that should be emphasised in the context of the specific dispute being at the same time aware of the treaty's broader context.

The next question that arises here is whether political motivations and economic objectives are the only policy consideration that may arise in the decision-making process. As will be demonstrated in the next sections, interpretive arguments may also be derived from legal and social policy considerations that *inter alia* promote the rule of law.

[B] Policies Revealed by Tribunals in Practice

Political and economic policies, as described above, constitute the basis for the creation and negotiation of dispute resolution outside the realm of diplomatic protection. They are entrenched in the drafting history and texts of the investment treaties. This section identifies policies that are not always directly referred to in the treaties but are expressed through the voice of arbitral tribunals. With the development of investment-arbitration case law and practice come to the surface concerns that are connected to the functioning of the dispute resolution framework and the way arbitrators interpret and apply the law. These concerns, even though not constituting a source of thorough contemplation and analysis in most of the investment treaties, made their gradual and strong appearance in the decisions of arbitral tribunals.

Such policies are characterised as 'legal policies' since they appear in the legal decision-making process of arbitrators and are connected to the interpretation of the law process. Arbitrators base a specific interpretation choice on legal policies such as consistency, predictability and stability. Since these policies are rarely codified into the treaties, they emanate from how arbitrators conceive the arbitration framework within which they are called upon to function. What is important, as a first step, is to reveal the existence of such legal policies and their role, and as a second step to justify their existence in the so-called case specific mandate of the arbitrator.

[1] Legal Policy Concerns

The emergence of legal policy concerns is strongly connected to the legal nature of the dispute and the legal decision-making process. Investor-state disputes are above all legal disputes. Article 25 (1) of ICSID refers to the existence of a 'legal dispute' making the legal nature of the conflict between the parties an indispensable element of investment arbitration. The Executive Directors clarified in their report that '[t]he

1176. *Ibid.* 211.

dispute must concern the existence or scope of a legal right or obligation, or the nature or extent of the reparation to be made for breach of a legal obligation'.[1177]

The ICSID Convention emphasises the legal characteristics of the dispute resolution framework that contrasts with the purely contractual focus of commercial arbitration. The 'legal dispute' requirement is pictured by investment tribunals as concerning 'legal rights or obligations or the consequences of their breach', as 'legal rights stemming from contracts, legislation and the BIT' or as a 'disagreement about legal rights or obligations'.[1178]

As a consequence, the legal aspect of the dispute is important for the private judging mechanism and should be treated with due consideration. It goes without saying that facts play a major role from which emanates the existence of the dispute to be resolved through arbitration. It is also common in practice that the legal nature of disputes may be described through the use of facts and their consequences.[1179] However, what determines the legal nature of the dispute are not the fact patterns alone but the type of claim and the remedy that is invoked.[1180]

Based on the above considerations, even though parties are the main actors in an arbitration, one must not disregard the importance of the legal framework governing inevitably the dispute resolution process. Arbitral tribunals operate in and are constrained by a legal framework consisting of international treaties, general principles of law, customary international law, national laws and contracts.[1181] The case law of the investment tribunals, through which the aims and policies of this legal framework are illustrated from a practical perspective, recognises not only the political and economic policy issues but also the legal ones. Legal policy considerations are used as interpretive arguments in the legal decision-making process. Considerations regarding the way the interpretation of the law fosters consistency, certainty and predictability of the dispute resolution system find their foundation in the importance of the legal nature of the disputes and the mandate of the arbitrators to interpret and eventually apply the law.

[a] Consistency, Predictability, Legal Stability

The public scrutiny of the published awards has led to the questioning of the predictability of investment law especially in those cases where arbitrators render contradictory awards. The heterogeneity of the substantive law applied in each dispute, the different factual scenarios as well as the ad hoc nature of the arbitral

1177. Schreuer, *The ICSID Convention: A Commentary* (n 269) 98 citing 1 ICSID Reports 8.
1178. *See* respectively *CSOB v. Slovakia*, ICSID Case No. ARB /97/4, Decision on Jurisdiction (24 May 1999) paras 60, 61; *Continental Casualty v. Argentina*, ICSID Case No. ARB /03/9, Decision on Jurisdiction (22 Feb. 2006) para. 37; Christoph Schreuer, 'What Is a Legal Dispute?' in Isabelle Buffard and others (eds), *International Law Between Universalism and Fragmentation: Festschrift In Honour Of Gerhard Hafner* (Nijhoff 2009) 970.
1179. Schreuer, 'What Is a Legal Dispute?' (n 1178) 966.
1180. *Ibid.*
1181. Kingsbury and Schill, 'Investor-State Arbitration as Governance' (n 148) 50.

tribunals constitute the main reasons for a divergent investment-arbitration case law and contradictory legal outcomes.[1182]

Consistency, conceived as 'a logical coherence among arbitral decisions' has also been an issue of heated debate in investment-treaty arbitration.[1183] Certain commentators argue that the current dispute resolution framework is not totally inconsistent but it is not as coherent as it could be.[1184] Investment arbitration is still in its early stages of development giving a convincing justification of why a degree of incoherency exists in this rather new body of law and jurisprudence. Even though they are not generally established as a policy goal of investment treaties, the need to pursue consistency and predictability is acknowledged both in theory as well as in practice by arbitral tribunals. Consistency in the application of the law fosters predictability enabling the members of the legal community to plan their actions, relying on the pronouncements about the law that appear in published opinions.[1185] These judicial policies, foster confidence in the dispute resolution framework and boost its legitimacy and justice perception.[1186] The decision-making process of arbitrators is, in this context, linked to concerns regarding the stability of the investment-arbitration legal framework which in its turn enhances the effectiveness of economic and political policy goals pursued in the investment treaties.

Based on the above considerations, arbitral tribunals have connected the interpretation of the investor protection standards with the concepts of 'consistency', 'stability', 'certainty' and 'predictability'. Each of these concepts expresses policies associated with the legal framework governing investment arbitration and is revealed through the legal decision-making function of arbitrators. They have also been described as 'statements about the adjudicatory policy' followed by the tribunals.[1187]

As analysed above, arbitral tribunals find guidance for the interpretation of vague treaty concepts in the investment-arbitration case law.[1188] Legal certainty, consistency, predictability and the rule of law constitute the policy rationales in favour of following

1182. *See* for example the conflicting awards that were issued in the context of the Argentine economic crisis in 2001 on whether Argentina could invoke the defense of necessity: *CMS*, Award (n 1139); LG&E Energy, *Decision on Liability* (n 374); *Enron*, Award (n 581).
1183. Gabrielle Kaufmann-Kohler, 'Is Consistency a Myth?' in Emmanuel Gaillard and Yas Banifatemi (eds) *Precedent in International Arbitration* (Juris 2008) 137, 138; *See generally* Amalia Amaya, *The Tapestry of Reason* (Hart 2015) (discussing coherence approaches to both normative and factual reasoning in law).
1184. Caron, 'Investor State Arbitration: Strategic and Tactical Perspectives on Legitimacy' (n 459) 516.
1185. Ten Cate, 'The Costs of Consistency' (n 804) 456 et seq.
1186. August Reinisch, 'The Role of Precedent in ICSID Arbitration' (2008) 1 <http://investmentarbitration.univie.ac.at/fileadmin/user_upload/int_beziehungen/Personal/Publikationen_Reinisch/role_precedents_icsid_arbitrationaayb_2008.pdf> (accessed 8 Mar. 2018).
1187. Sureda, *Investment Treaty Arbitration Judging under Uncertainty* (n 162) 11.
1188. *See* §6.03 'Precedent Arguments'; *See*, for example, *Burlington v. Ecuador* where the tribunal commented on the relevance of previous ICSID decisions and awards: 'At the same time, it is of the opinion that it must pay due consideration to earlier decisions of international tribunals. The majority believes that, subject to compelling contrary grounds, it has a duty to adopt solutions established in a series of consistent cases' *Burlington Resources Inc. v. Ecuador*, ICSID Case No. ARB/08/5, Decision on Jurisdiction (2 Jun. 2010) para. 100.

previous awards.[1189] Amongst the various reasons underlying a State's investment obligations is the maintenance of a transparent and predictable legal framework for the investment.[1190]

Kaufman-Kohler also remarks that 'arbitral precedent is a necessity for certain types of disputes, if not only for the sake of rule of law'.[1191] Striving for predictability and consistency though does not constitute a way to impose the same solution to similar disputes. In contrast, it is more fruitful to view these aspirations as a means to prove whether a line of cases decided in the same way is convincing based on the strength of the awards' reasoning and not as a duty to follow prior awards only for the sake of promoting consistency.[1192] In this context, the *ADC* tribunal stated that the cautious reliance on principles developed through the international case law on the issue of expropriation constitute persuasive authority and may advance the body of law and serve predictability in the interests of both States and investors.[1193]

Similarly, the tribunal in the *Suez* case stated that the establishment of a 'predictable, stable legal framework' for investments is a 'recognized goal of international investment law' and a 'factor that justifies tribunals in giving due regard to previous decisions on similar issues'.[1194] The policy of establishing a predictable legal framework along with considerations of justice were emphasised in the context of making use of case law in arbitral decisions. The tribunal specifically stated that:

> [...] considerations of basic justice would lead tribunals to be guided by the basic judicial principle that 'like cases should be decided alike,' unless a strong reason exists to distinguish the current case from previous ones. In addition, a recognized goal of international investment law is to establish a predictable, stable legal framework for investments, a factor that justifies tribunals in giving due regard to previous decisions on similar issues. Thus, absent compelling reasons to the contrary, a tribunal should always consider heavily solutions established in a series of consistent cases.[1195]

The *CMS* tribunal connected the standards of investment protection accorded by the investment treaties with the use of the interpretive arguments of stability and predictability of the 'investment environment' notably the State's legal framework.[1196] Stability and predictability however, also embrace legal policies connected not only to

1189. *See generally* Kaufmann-Kohler, *Arbitral Precedent: Dream, Necessity or Excuse?* (n 812).
1190. Ortino, 'Refining the Content and Role of Investment "Rules" and "Standards": A New Approach to International Investment Treaty-Making' (n 224) 6.
1191. Kaufmann-Kohler, *Arbitral Precedent: Dream, Necessity or Excuse?* (n 812) 378.
1192. Ten Cate, 'The Costs of Consistency' (804) 473; Arbitrator J confirms this by stating: 'I don't follow the school of consistency for consistency's sake. I think the first task of a tribunal is to decide the case before it. Ideally the interpretation of treaties will be consistent with that of other tribunals' whose work I respect because it is well reasoned and I agree with the outcome. If it is the right consistency, it will lead to more predictability for parties'.
1193. *ADC Affiliate Limited and ADC & ADMC Management Limited v. Republic of Hungary*, ICSID Case No. ARB/03/16, Award (2 Oct. 2006) para. 293.
1194. *Suez, Decision on Liability* (n 959) para. 189; Michael Reisman, '"Case Specific Mandates" Versus "Systemic Implications": How Should Investment Tribunals Decide? – The Freshfields Arbitration Lecture' (2013) 29(2) ArbIntl 131, 141.
1195. *Suez, Decision on Liability* (n 959) para. 189.
1196. *CMS*, Award (n 1139) paras 267, 276, 284.

State conduct but also to the investment-arbitration legal framework in particular. In this sense, when the tribunal referred to the restrictive application of the state of necessity it considered the 'stability and predictability of the law' emphasising on the State's international obligations under the investment treaties.[1197]

Equally, in determining the meaning of the 'full protection and security' guarantee, the *Siemens* tribunal interpreted the term security as referring to 'legal security'. The policy behind legal security is a qualitative legal system implying certainty in its norms and, consequently, predictability in their application.[1198] Similarly, the *M.C.I Power* annulment committee made reference to the past decisions of ad hoc committees cited by the parties. It stated that it would take them into consideration since arbitral case law promotes consistency and legal certainty as a means of ensuring trust in the dispute settlement system and predictability for both States and investors.[1199] Going a step further, the *Urbaser* Tribunal made a strong connection between the FET protection guarantee and consistency as an inherent objective of FET:

> The meaning of the requirement of fair and equitable treatment cannot be left for the exclusive discretion of the arbitral tribunal seized with a particular case. Such an approach would lead to arbitrary divergence between investor tribunals, which, while not avoidable in all cases, cannot be considered as an inherent objective of a fair and equitable treatment clause. It would also be in a striking contrast to the objective of creating a secure environment for investment protection.[1200]

Based on the above, consistent adjudication constrains arbitrary decision-making fostering predictability, enhancing the perception of legitimacy of dispute resolution, and develops the content of substantive law. Legal interpretation and precedent have a double legal policy mission which is the need to maintain the stability of the legal system and at the same time being armed with the competence to evolve alongside with the environment within which it operates. As a result, there is a paradox of legal rules being at the same time stable and changeable.[1201]

Legal rules gain stability through the interconnection of the substance given to them through the process of their interpretation. This substance may vary according to the facts of the legal dispute. However, the interconnection between the different interpretations demonstrates that there is a core that remains stable fostering the internal consistency of the legal norm. This need for internal legal consistency should

1197. *CMS*, Award (n 981) para. 317; The *Enron* Tribunal also referred to the principle of stability when characterising the Argentinian legal system: 'Stability of rights and contracts is thus a central feature of the applicable domestic law'. The tribunal clarified, however, that this stability did not signify that contractual obligations are forever unchanged irrespective of the circumstances. *Enron*, Award (n 581) paras 213, 214.
1198. *Siemens*, Award (n 1063) para. 303 (citations omitted).
1199. *M.C.I. Power Group L.C. and New Turbine Inc. v. Republic of Ecuador*, ICSID Case No. ARB/03/6, Decision on Annulment (19 Oct. 2009) para. 25.
1200. *Urbaser* Award (n 249) para. 621.
1201. Simon Deakin, 'Legal Evolution: Integrating Economic and Systemic Approaches' (2011) Faculty of Law and Centre for Business Research, University of Cambridge Comparative Law and Economics Forum, 13.

characterise the workings of a legal system in order to enhance its efficiency.[1202] Arbitrator I clearly illustrates the relevance of consistency when stating that:

> It is useful for everyone, those who are considering claims, those who are defending claims and those who are deciding claims, to identify a direction of the law which can be followed. Consistency and enforceability of outcome is an important feature of the rule of law and I don't think that that is inconsistent with recognising that every dispute deserves its own resolution. Every dispute deserves its own resolution but when you are applying the same principles, then consistency is important.[1203]

Based on these considerations, the use as interpretive arguments of the legal policies found in decisions made by investment tribunals such as consistency, predictability and stability enhance the internal cohesiveness of the investment-arbitration framework while promoting at the same time its legitimacy, and thus external effectiveness.

[b] Legal Policies and the Rule of Law

The exploration of the rule of law commonly relates either to the qualification of a system of governance as a legal system or to the investigation of the rule of law as a moral ideal.[1204] Focusing on the first aspect of the rule of law, the concept of 'formal legality' plays a central role. Under this concept, rules, which are the distinctive form of the law, have certain characteristics that enable them to function as general guides of behaviour.[1205] These characteristics are: (1) generality of the rules, (2) promulgation of the rules to the people whose conduct will be assessed through them, (3) authoritative formulation and clarity of the language of the rules, (4) logical consistency of one norm with another, (5) the requirements of the norms are not beyond the capabilities of those subject to them, (6) prospectivity which is the non-retroactivity of the rules, (7) steadiness of the content of the norms, (8) consistent formulation and application of the laws in practice meaning an impartial application of the rules.[1206]

This last characteristic of 'consistency' fostering the rule of law can well be associated with the dispute resolution function in general and that of arbitral tribunals in particular. In this context, the promotion of the rule of law is examined through the lens of the arbitral decision-making process and the way the arbitrator interprets the

1202. *See* Deakin mentioning that 'it is, moreover, the need for consistency in its internal operations, and not its alignment with the economy or the political system, that above all drives the workings of the legal system and defines its "efficiency". It follows that some degree of misalignment of systems is unavoidable'. *Ibid.* 13.
1203. *See* Annex 'Interview Questions'.
1204. Matthiew Kramer, *Objectivity and the Rule of Law* (CUP 2007) 105.
1205. Brian Tamanaha, *On the Rule of Law: History, Politics, Theory* (CUP 2004) 97.
1206. Kramer, *Objectivity and the Rule of Law* (n 1204) 104.

applicable legal concepts. The emphasis here is placed on the promotion of the rule of law in its systemic 'formal legality' form.[1207]

According to Fuller, there is a certain threshold of conformity to the above-mentioned elements which underlie the existence of a legal system. Each of these characteristics cannot be perfectly fulfilled. The threshold is not possible to be defined in a precise way, as it is different for each legal regime.[1208] From a commercial arbitration perspective, the focus is put on the private nature of the arbitration. The rule of law is translated as 'faithfulness to party consent, party autonomy, and sanctity of contracts'.[1209] A precise rule of law design with its length and width measured accurately would be an unruly horse in the field of investment arbitration where flexibility, arbitral discretion and ad hoc decision-making constitute the triptych of arbitration's attractiveness. However, although not clearly defined by treaties, rule of law thresholds are sketched through the practice of arbitral tribunals when expressing legal policy concerns.

The effects of the tribunals' dispute resolution functions have been described as sustaining or enhancing the predictability of the investment framework 'by providing a forum where the rules are applied in a cognitively reliable way through competent and impartial adjudication'.[1210] When it comes to the dispute resolution function, the rule of law is commonly examined from a procedural prism, mainly the principle of due process and the impartiality of the judicial authority when deciding on a case.[1211]

However, apart from procedural safeguards, there is also a rule of law aspect connected to substantive issues and the way investment protection standards are interpreted and applied.[1212] Legal policies such as consistency, stability and predictability of a legal framework have been described as 'normative principles' which constitute an expression of the rule of law in various legal systems.[1213] The exigencies for consistency and predictability do not seem at first sight to be directly fulfilled by an

1207. Thomas Schultz, 'Against Consistency in Investment Arbitration', King's College London Law School Research Paper No. 2013-3, 7 <http://ssrn.com/abstract=2318358> (accessed 02 Apr. 2018).
1208. Kramer, *Objectivity and the Rule of Law* (n 1204) 105.
1209. Schill, 'The Sixth Path: Reforming Investment Law from Within' (n 628) 12; *See also* Andrea Menaker, *International Arbitration and the Rule of Law: Contribution and Conformity* (Kluwer Law International 2017).
1210. The authors refer to this function as a hypothesis of their research, concluding to the confirmation of such a hypothesis with the caveat that tribunals may seem to be harder on poorer countries than on richer countries. Thomas Schultz and Cédric Dupont, 'Investment Arbitration: Promoting the Rule of Law or Over-empowering Investors? A Quantitative Empirical Study' (2014) King's College London Dickson Poon School of Law Legal Studies Research Paper Series, Paper No. 2014-16 23, 28.
1211. *See* generally Lord Tom Bingham, *The Rule of Law* (Penguin 2011) 137 et seq.
1212. Arbitrator B confirms the fact that 'the interpretation process is part of the rule of law'. *See* Annex 'Interview Questions'; *See also* Susan D Franck, Anne van Aaken, James Freda, Chris Guthrie, and Jeffrey J Rachlinski, 'Inside the Arbitrator's Mind' (2017) 66 *Emory Law Journal* 1115 (discussing how normative debates on global dispute resolution should focus 'not on decisionmaker identity or title but rather on structural safeguards and legal protections to enhance quality rule of law based decisionmaking').
1213. Kingsbury and Schill, 'Investor-State Arbitration as Governance' (n 148) 10; Arbitrator D argues that 'the rule of law should operate to give effect to the legitimate expectations of the parties and there is probably nothing more important than that because seeing that your

ad hoc dispute resolution mechanism. However, in practice, investment tribunals have made multiple references to the way these policies contribute to the certainty of the rule of law in the context of interpreting a legal concept. The policy syllogism of the *Duke Energy* case reveals how the duty of the tribunal is linked to rule of law concerns marking that a tribunal:

> [...] has a duty to consider the solutions consistently established in prior similar cases. Subject to the specifics of a given treaty and of the circumstances of the case it has a duty to seek to contribute to the harmonious development of investment law, and thereby to meet the legitimate expectations of the community of States and investors towards establishing certainty in the rule of law.[1214]

In a similar context, the *Saipem* tribunal connects the relevance of previous awards to issues of consistency, harmonious development of investment law and the rule of law. Specifically, it is mentioned that the arbitrator has the duty to duty pay due consideration to consistent cases and 'seek to contribute to the harmonious development of investment law and thereby to meet the legitimate expectations of the community of States and investors towards certainty of the rule of law'.[1215]

In a similar wording, the *Noble Energy* tribunal marks that:

> [...] subject to a specific provision of a given treaty, to the circumstances of the actual case and the evidence tendered, it should seek to foster the harmonious development of investment law and thereby to meet the legitimate expectations of the community of States and investors towards certainty of the rule of law.[1216]

The tribunal in the *Burlington Resources* case also speaks about the arbitrator's duty to 'seek to contribute to the harmonious development of investment law, and thereby to meet the legitimate expectations of the community of States and investors towards the certainty of the rule of law'.[1217]

Such arbitral case law, created principally on an ad hoc and individualist basis, harbours within it systemic integrity perspectives striving for acknowledgement.[1218] Consistency and predictability reveal the need for legal stability and development through the application and interpretation of the law. A process of interpretation that focuses on effectiveness, consistency, and evolution of terms through the 'more

legitimate expectations are respected is a test of stable institutions that hold our societies together – otherwise we would have chaos'. *See* Annex 'Interview Questions'.

1214. *Duke Energy,* Award (n 960) para. 117; Arbitrator I interestingly marks: 'I don't think investment arbitration should be considered in any way outside of the manifestation of the rule of law. It is an expression of the international rule of law and so I would see it as contributing to the international rule of law rather as something separate from the international rule of law. The question is how does investment treaty jurisprudence contribute to the rule of law.' *See* Annex 'Interview Questions'.
1215. *Saipem S.p.A. v. The People's Republic of Bangladesh,* ICSID Case No. ARB/05/07, Decision on jurisdiction and Recommendation of Provisional Measures (21 Mar. 2007) para. 67.
1216. *Noble Energy, Inc. and Machalapower Cia. Ltda. v. The Republic of Ecuador and Consejo Nacional de Electricidad,* ICSID Case No ARB/05/12, Decision on Jurisdiction (5 Mar. 2008) para. 50.
1217. *Burlington Resources Inc. v. Ecuador,* ICSID Case No ARB/08/5, Decision on Jurisdiction (2 Jun. 2010) para. 100.
1218. For the systemic integrity concept *see* below §6.01[B][1][c] 'Systemic Integrity'.

low-key polishing of the treaty's textual machinery, elimination of inconsistencies, clarification of the operation of treaty mechanisms, and developing a subtly modernized meaning to incrementally evolving concepts' constitutes an 'interpretative updating [which] takes place – and needs to take place – all the time'.[1219]

[c] Systemic Integrity

Legal policy concerns require that the arbitrators are aware not only of their mandate but also of the framework within which they are called to operate. In this context however, the dispute-oriented mandate of the arbitrator may seem to conflict with any legal policy considerations of the investment-arbitration framework. At first sight, any consideration of legal policies in the decision-making of arbitrators may seem an anathema to the principle of party autonomy and to the effectiveness of the dispute resolution mechanism. However, the role legal policy plays in the field of investment arbitration depends on the meaning given to the term and the specific role it plays in the decision-making process.

In the field of investment arbitration, the parties – within the concept of party autonomy – confine the arbitrator to a specific mandate to resolve a particular dispute. The dispute-oriented mandate of the arbitrator requires the decision-maker to decide a case solely based on the particular facts of the case and applicable law. Within this background, the idea that prevails is that investor-state arbitration constitutes a 'party-owned process'.[1220] However, with the possibility to submit *amicus curiae* briefs as well as the possibility of third-party intervention, the word 'owner' of the investment dispute seems to acquire a relative meaning.[1221]

The *Glamis* tribunal describes its mandate under Chapter 11 of the NAFTA with reference to the case-specific mandate normally found in international commercial arbitration. The tribunal specifically states that '[i]n the normal contractual setting, a tribunal is a creature of contract, tasked with resolving a particular dispute arising under a particular contract'.[1222]

However, the undertaking of a case-specific arbitration constitutes only one side of the *Glamis* tribunal's task. The resolution of a specific dispute is effectuated with simultaneous awareness of the 'larger context in which [the tribunal] operates'.[1223] The *Glamis* tribunal indicates the importance of each tribunal rendering 'its case-specific decision with sensitivity to the position of future tribunals and an awareness of other systemic implications'.[1224] The tribunal continues clarifying that the awareness of the 'NAFTA Chapter 11 System' does not signify a departure from a case-specific mandate but rather it constitutes 'a discipline upon its reasoning that does not alter the

1219. Wälde, 'Interpreting Investment Treaties' (n 673) 759.
1220. Schill, 'The Sixth Path: Reforming Investment Law from Within' (n 628) 3.
1221. *See* §6.01[D] 'Expanding the Dialogue Through Third Parties'.
1222. *Glamis Gold, Award* (n 407) para. 3.
1223. *Ibid.* para. 4.
1224. *Ibid.* para. 6.

Tribunal's decision, but rather guides and aids the Tribunal in simultaneously supporting the system of which it is only a temporary part'.[1225]

The specific 'context' in which NAFTA tribunals operate is described by the *Glamis* tribunal as follows:

> Tribunals are not only aware of the objectives and experience of the NAFTA; they are aware that the NAFTA State Parties: decided to allow the two non-disputing States in any particular arbitration to submit observations, established procedures for the possible consolidation of arbitrations involving the same questions of fact or law, more recently decided to make the record and awards of all arbitrations publicly available, and – in response to the requests of interested parts of civil society – made possible limited submissions by such non-parties.[1226]

The 'awareness of the context' is further analysed as 'aiding' the case-specific mandate of the tribunal in terms of five principles.[1227] The first principle requires that the tribunal 'confine[s] its decision to the issues presented by the dispute before it' instead of making statements that are not required by the issues presented. According to the second principle, the tribunal should explicitly address the *amicus curiae* submissions in the award only to the extent that they are related to the decisions that the tribunal should take. Third, the NAFTA tribunals are called to provide 'detailed' and 'persuasive' reasons for the awards rendered. The fourth principle requires that the award not only includes detailed reasoning but also 'succinctly' communicates its conclusions. Within the context of this last principle, even though there is no formal doctrine of precedent in the field of investment arbitration, the NAFTA tribunals should specifically state the reasons for departing from 'major trends' in previous decisions.

The 'systemic implications' approach followed by the Glamis tribunal has been criticised for turning arbitrators into 'lawmakers' rather than only being 'law-appliers' as authorised.[1228] Such an approach is connected to lawmaking functions requiring 'taking account of the systemic implications of alternative possible legal arrangements'.[1229] Under these circumstances, it has been argued that investment arbitrators should not mix their 'case-specific mandate' with a 'system's implication' approach except when three 'narrow exceptions' arise:

> (i) thoughtful consideration of previous awards that are on-point; (ii) consideration of the objects and purposes of the BIT or investment chapter in question, but only within the scope prescribed by the canon of treaty interpretation; and (iii) disciplined supplementative interpretation but only when confronted by a lacuna

1225. *Ibid.* para. 7.
1226. *Ibid.* para. 4 (citations omitted).
1227. *Ibid.* para. 8.
1228. Reisman, '"Case Specific Mandates" Versus "Systemic Implications"' (n 1194) 131. Cf Kahn, arguing: 'Glamis is the gold standard for investor-state arbitration. Future proceedings should model themselves after its commendably transparent process. [...] Glamis's analyses, while subject to future refinement, are golden contributions to international law.' Jordan Kahn, 'Striking NAFTA Gold: Glamis Advances Investor-State Arbitration' (2009) 33(1) FordhamIntlLJ 101, 155.
1229. Reisman, '"Case Specific Mandates" Versus "Systemic Implications"' (n 1194) 132.

in the applicable law. Subject to these narrow exceptions, international investment tribunals should confine themselves to a case-specific methodology.[1230]

The question that may arise here is whether these three circumstances are issues that typically and repeatedly appear in an investment-arbitration case, turning the exception into the general rule. Political and economic policy concerns arise through the object and purpose of the treaty that is omnipresent in the interpretation of open-ended treaty standards. Going a step further, the rule of law exigencies from a dispute resolution framework treating public law issues brings to the surface concerns about the predictability and stability of the legal framework within which tribunals operate. As a consequence, since policy considerations do exist and make their way in the decision-making process, what is necessary is the conscious treatment of these policies by the tribunals.

Instead of connecting the 'systemic implication' approach to lawmaking functions, it would be useful to approach the legal policy issues as 'systemic integrity' concerns connected to the process of law-interpretation. A lawmaking function entails considerations connected to policies and the future implication of any choice for the relevant system as a whole. On the contrary, in the law-interpretation function, considerations regarding the framework within which each arbitrator is called to render a specific decision acquires a different meaning expressed through the methodology arbitrators use in order to interpret the vague treaty standards. Replacing the phrase 'systemic implication' and its lawmaking connotations with that of 'systemic integrity' reflects a more accurate representation of the role of legal policies in arbitral decision-making. 'Systemic integrity' in this context expresses concerns of an investment-arbitration framework which is unified and coherent through common values whether legal, political, economic or social. In such a case, taking into consideration internal systemic integrity will foster external legitimacy and effectiveness of the arbitration framework. Going a step further, if investment arbitration will at some point be described as a proper system of law, embracing core systemic values is an important element of any legal system.

Based on these considerations, policy concerns do not necessarily lead to directly making law in the field of investment arbitration but to considering the policies of the investment framework in the decision-making process in order to respect not only the object and purpose of a treaty but also of the rule of law. The interest of investor-state arbitrators in being part of a (perceived) 'functional' dispute resolution system has been described as a professional interest that 'may lead an arbitrator not only to seek to make "balanced" (or "rebalanced") decisions in individual cases, but to strive for coherence and consistency across different investment disputes'.[1231] In this context, the main focus of investment arbitration is the resolution of the specific dispute but

1230. *Ibid.*
1231. Alex Mills, 'The Balancing (and Unbalancing?) of Interests in International Investment Law and Arbitration' in Zachary Douglas, Joost Pauwelyn, and Jorge E Viñuales (eds), *The Foundations of International Investment Law: Bringing Theory into Practice* (OUP 2014) 437, 454; Michael Waibel, 'Interpretive Communities in International Law' in Andrea Bianchi, Daniel Peat, and Matthew Windsor (eds) *Interpretation in International Law* (n 59) 160.

subsequent functions arise which are connected to the characteristics and specificities of investment arbitration such as the need for consistency, predictability and stability.[1232]

Interpretation is not a neutral exercise but depends upon 'the social and interpretive context – the background against which the members of an institution or adjudicative body decide'.[1233] As such, not only political and legal policies affect the interpretation process but also social policies that may provide a background for interpretation.[1234]

[2] Emerging Social Policy Concerns

As mentioned above, despite the fact that an investment-arbitration procedure begins to operate from the aim to resolve a specific dispute, subsequent functions may arise in practice that are expressed through the interpretive arguments used by tribunals.[1235] These subsequent functions refer to the role the adjudicatory body plays in society and in particular the broader societal consequences the resolution of disputes has.

In this context, when the decision-makers decide, for instance, a contract dispute, they promote at the same time economic relations through the enforcement of the contract.[1236] The promotion of substantive values of the society aims in bringing reality closer to the ideals the society has collectively chosen to embody into authoritative legal texts.[1237] The aims of a legal system pursued through a specific form of justice colours the interpretation of specific rules in individual cases.[1238] In the field of investment arbitration certain subsequent functions – either seen in a descriptive form of what the dispute resolution mechanism does or in a normative form of what it should do – are the promotion of sustainable development in a transparent, predictable and legitimate manner.

The previous sections revealed the need to make a distinction between the political and economic policies that motivated the creation of a treaty and the function served by the operation of the tribunal[1239] that gave rise to legal policy concerns.

1232. Arbitrator H particularly mentioned that 'my concern is that my result is fair, that the party understands why I have decided, how I have decided; that to me is all, that's my job; if that means that I am upholding the rule of law, then great; so it's consequence for me'; *See* Annex Interview Questions; Caron also speaks about the immediate 'direct' function of deciding a case and the 'consequential function' for society of the court doing so. Caron, 'International Courts and Tribunals' (n 72) 4.
1233. Michael Waibel, 'Interpretive Communities in International Law' in Andrea Bianchi, Daniel Peat, and Matthew Windsor (eds) *Interpretation in International Law* (n 59) 149.
1234. *ibid*; *See also* Gregory Shaffer and Joel Trachtman, 'Interpretation and Institutional Choice at the WTO' (2011) 52 VaJIntlL 103, 131.
1235. *See* §6.01[B][1][c] 'Systemic Integrity'.
1236. Caron, 'International Courts and Tribunals' (n 72) 4.
1237. Schultz, 'The Three Pursuits of Dispute Settlement' (n 74) 228.
1238. H L A Hart, 'Positivism and the Separation of Law and Morals' (1958) 71 HarvLRev 593, 622.
1239. Caron, 'International Courts and Tribunals' (n 72) 9.

However, the policies pursued might change and evolve, calling for the reassessment of the tribunal's role when resolving a dispute.[1240] As such, the policy concept is equipped with a temporal perspective. Given the fact that the law – or better the perception somebody has about the law – is not stable but changes depending on the values and needs of the society, the process of applying and interpreting the law is also called to adjust to such a change. The so-called currency of the underlying normative framework 'may change over time, growing or shrinking depending on actors' evaluations of the normative regime's evolution as compared to their interests and values'.[1241]

When a dispute resolution framework has been described as a secret organisation having unknown members[1242] its social perspective is more than evident. The social criticism of arbitration has become more ardent when characterised as a 'multimillion-dollar, self-serving industry' created by Western governments.[1243]

Civil society, through think tanks, lobby groups and NGOs, plays an important role in the emergence of social concerns while organising political pressure through the media and participating on consultative bodies.[1244] Their strong interest and involvement in arbitration reveals a non-statist transnational element in investment arbitration since the State is not the main and only actor in the field.[1245] The importance in

1240. *See also* the UNCTAD Report referring to the principle of dynamic policy-making which 'recognizes that national and international investment policies need flexibility to adapt to changing circumstances, while recognizing that a favourable investment climate requires stability and predictability' UNCTAD Report 'World Investment Report: Towards a New Generation of Investment Policies' (United Nations 2012) 108.

1241. Grossman, 'Legitimacy and International Adjudicative Bodies' (n 463) 143.

1242. Quote From New York Times, 'NAFTA's Powerful Little Secret; Obscure Tribunals Settle Disputes, But Go Too Far, Critics Say' (11 Mar. 2001) <http://www.nytimes.com/2001/03/11/business/nafta-s-powerful-little-secret-obscure-tribunals-settle-disputes-but-go-too-far.html?_r=0> (accessed 14 Oct. 2018).

1243. Eberhardt and Olivet, *Profiting from Injustice* (n 13) 7.

1244. Wälde, 'The Specific Nature of Investment Arbitration' (n 873) 92; The UNCTAD World Investment Report 2018 analyses the interaction between new industrial policies and investment policies. It particularly states that: 'The investment policy regime does not exist in a vacuum; it interacts with other areas of economic law and policy (e.g., competition, finance, intellectual property, development, taxation and trade), as well as with areas of law and policy that are typically considered "non-economic" (e.g., culture, environment, health, labour, social or gender-related issues; land rights; national security issues).' UNCTAD 'World Investment Report 2018: Investment and New Industrial Policies' 106, <http://unctad.org/en/PublicationsLibrary/wir2018 _en.pdf> (accessed 30 Jun. 2018).

1245. This is also evident with the *amicus curiae* submissions. *See* §6.01[D] 'Expanding the Dialogue Through Third Parties'; *See also* David Neuberger, "Judgment and Judgments – The Art of Forming and Writing Judicial Decisions" Denning Society Lecture 2017 <https://www.lincolnsinn.org.uk/images/pdf/denning/denningsocietylecture2017.pdf> (accessed 1 Sep. 2018) (The author focuses on judicial decisions. He maintains that a trial judge has not merely to decide the point of law and facts, but to give reasons, and to do so in public. Accordingly, any judgment is open to media criticism, to appeal to superior court, and to academic scorn. And reasons can be problematic).

identifying their existence lays in fact that these social actors may directly or indirectly influence the interpretation process.[1246]

A stark illustration is the process of negotiation of the trade agreement between the US and EU, the Transatlantic Trade and Investment Partnership (TTIP) that has given impetus to a broad array of comments questioning not only its legitimacy but also the promotion and protection of social welfare including human rights. The EU recognised the social implications of such a treaty launching a public consultation on investment protection and ISDS in the TTIP. The consultation mobilised EU civil society to extraordinary levels of public involvement receiving a total of nearly 150,000 responses.[1247] NGOs consider that arbitrators should also have experience in the social or environmental fields since there are calls for stronger investor obligations regarding human rights, job creation, sustainable development and corporate social responsibility.[1248]

In the US arena, the Subcommittee of Advisory Committee on International Economic Policy was established in 2009 to review the US Model BIT. The participation of a group of representatives from the academia, business and labour area as well as environmental NGOs ensured that the content of the US investment rules were suitably adapted to 'changing societal preferences'.[1249]

In this context, the recognition of the role of State actors in the investment-arbitration scene verifies the emergence of a transnational legal decision-making process where not only public but also private actors, NGOs and individuals interact.[1250]

1246. The concept of 'interpretive communities' represents exactly the way social groups 'whose shared comprehension of a context makes possible the common interpretation of socially relevant texts'. The interpretive communities are considered to 'discipline and channel interpretation', Eben Moglen and Richard Pierce, 'Sunstein's New Canons: Choosing the Fictions of Statutory Interpretation' (1990) 57 U Chi L Rev 1203, 1207; Michael Waibel, 'Interpretive Communities in International Law' in Andrea Bianchi, Daniel Peat, and Matthew Windsor (eds) *Interpretation in International Law* (n 59) 151.

1247. 'Online Public Consultation on Investment Protection and Investor-to-state Dispute Settlement (ISDS) in the Transatlantic Trade and Investment Partnership Agreement (TTIP)' European Commission Report (13 Jan. 2015) 9; *See also* Mary Mitsi and others, 'A Response to the Criticism Against ISDS by EFILA'(2016) 33(1) JIntlArb.

1248. *Online Public Consultation on Investment Protection and Investor-to-state Dispute Settlement (ISDS) in the Transatlantic Trade and Investment Partnership Agreement (TTIP)* (n 1247) 20, 137.

1249. Jürgen Kurtz, 'Building Legitimacy Through Interpretation in Investor-State Arbitration: On Consistency, Coherence, and the Identification of Applicable Law' in Zachary Douglas, Joost Pauwelyn, and Jorge Viñuales (eds) *The Foundations of International Investment Law: Bringing Theory into Practice* (OUP 2014) 259.

1250. Koh, 'Jefferson Memorial Lecture – Transnational Legal Process after September 11th' (n 93) 339.

[a] Sustainable Development-Environmental Rights

The protection of human rights and especially the protection of the environment in the framework of investment treaties constitute a primary social concern.[1251] There are strong calls for broader investor obligations regarding social and environmental regulation and human rights. The strong emphasis on both social and environmental policies is in line with the concept of 'sustainable development' evolving in the neo-liberal economic arena.[1252] Economic policies constitute a means of achieving sustainable development. However, the focus on these should be tempered in order to avoid the detriment of equally significant social and environmental policies.[1253] The idea is that sustainable development focuses on the integration of all economic, social and environmental policies into governmental, administrative and judicial decision-making processes.[1254] The International Institute on Sustainable Development (IISD) also published a Model International Agreement aiming to promote global sustainable development through investments, essential for the further development of national and global economies.[1255]

In this context, in certain investment treaties, social and environmental policies appear in the preamble as having the same importance with investment policy objectives.[1256] The preamble of the 2004 US Model BIT stresses that the objective of the parties is to protect the foreign investor 'in a manner consistent with the protection of health, safety, and the environment, and the promotion of internationally recognized labour rights'.[1257] Similarly, the preamble of the NAFTA requires that State parties

1251. *See generally:* Bruno Simma, 'Foreign Investment Arbitration: A Place for Human Rights?' (2011) 60(3) ICLQ 573; Pierre-Marie Dupuy, Ernst-Ulrich Petersmann, and Francesco Francioni, *Human Rights in International Investment Law and Arbitration* (OUP 2009); Patrick Dumberry and Gabrielle Dumas-Aubin, 'When and How Allegations of Human Rights Violations can be Raised in Investor-State Arbitration' (2012) 13(3) The Journal of World Investment & Trade 349; James Harrison, 'Environmental Counterclaims in Investor-State Arbitration: *Perenco Ecuador Ltd v. Republic of Ecuador*, ICSID Case No. ARB/08/6, Interim Decision on the Environmental Counterclaim, 11 Aug. 2015 (Peter Tomka, Neil Kaplan, J Christopher Thomas)' (2016) 17(3) The Journal of World Investment & Trade 479; *Azurix Corp. v. The Argentine Republic*, ICSID Case No. ARB/01/12, Award (14 Jul. 2006) paras 254, 311, 442.
1252. *See* generally Marie-Claire Cordonier Segger, Markus Gehring, and Andrew Newcombe (eds), *Sustainable Development in World Investment Law* (Kluwer Law International 2011).
1253. Suzanne Spears, 'The Quest for Policy Space in a New Generation of International Investment Agreements' (2010) 13(3) JIEL 1037, 1067.
1254. *Ibid*; Muthucumaraswamy Sornarajah, *The International Law on Foreign Investment* (3rd ed., CUP 2010) 224.
1255. Sustainable development is understood as being 'a development that meets the needs of the present without compromising the ability of future generations to meet their own needs; Until the adoption of rules of arbitration consistent with the IISD Agreement, the ICSID rules will govern the arbitration irrespective of whether the host and home States are parties to the ICSID Convention' (Article 3 IIDS Agreement) IISD Model International Agreement on Investment for Sustainable Development, Preamble <http://www.italaw.com/sites/default/files/archive/ita1027.pdf> (accessed 30 Sep. 2018).
1256. The 2018 'UNCTAD IIA Issues Note' revealed that since 2012, over 150 States have taken steps to formulate a new generation of sustainable development oriented IIAs, <http://unctad.org/en/PublicationsLibrary/diaepcbinf2018d1_en.pdf> (accessed 1 Jun. 2018).
1257. US Model BIT (2004) Preamble.

'promote sustainable development' and 'strengthen the development and enforcement of environmental laws and regulations'. Based, *inter alia*, on this last policy, the tribunal in the *SD Myers case* stated that NAFTA's investment regulations should be interpreted in the light of certain general principles such as the right of the parties to create a level of high environmental protection, the avoidance of distorting trade and the mutually supportive relationship between economic development and environmental protection.[1258]

In its reasoning, the *Urbaser* Tribunal eloquently connected the claimant's legitimate expectations with social interest and, in particular, human rights obligations.[1259] Since the case addressed a dispute arising from a water supply concession contract, the right to water was described by the Tribunal as a 'universal basic human right'.[1260] The Tribunal concluded that the FET standard does not only focus on legal expectations but also includes 'the actual social and economic environment of the host State, which is also part of the expectations the investor has to acknowledge when making its business decision'.[1261] As such, the protection of the right to water supply constitutes part of the framework within which the Claimant should frame its expectations.[1262]

Social policies such as the protection of the environment and sustainable development become part of the broader investment policy not only through the Preambles of the investment treaties but also through methods of treaty interpretation.[1263] Article 31(3)(c) VCLT requires the interpretation of a treaty in accordance with international law. Although 'sustainable development' has not yet been fully recognised as customary international law, principles such as the principle of integration, which closely relate to it, may be blending into binding rules of international law.[1264]

As the dilemma between accepting a social intervention and transforming the arbitral proceeding into a 'court of public opinion',[1265] leading potentially to the re-politicisation of disputes, continues to be an issue of strong academic debate, 'pubic legitimacy [features as a] double edged sword'.[1266] What remains necessary is to

---

1258. *SD Myers Inc. v. Government of Canada*, Merits (13 Nov. 2000) 8 ICSID Report 4, para. 221; Spears, *The Quest for Policy Space in a New Generation of International Investment Agreements* (n 1253) 1068.
1259. *Urbaser* Award (n 249) para. 624.
1260. For an analysis of the case *see* §6.04[C] 'Reciprocal Communication'.
1261. *Urbaser* Award (n 249) para. 623.
1262. *Ibid.* para. 624; *See also SAUR International SA v. Republic of Argentina*, ICSID Case No. ARB/04/4, Decision on Jurisdiction and Liability (6 Jun. 2012) para. 328 (the Tribunal recognised the human rights and in particular the right to clean water, as part of the general principles of law that should be respected by the State).
1263. Marie-Claire Cordonier Segger, 'Integrating Social and Economic Development and Environmental Protection in World Trade Law', in Segger, Gehring and Newcombe (eds) *Sustainable Development* (n 1252) 134.
1264. *Ibid.* 133, 466–467.
1265. Kyla Tienhaara, 'Third Party Participation in Investment-Environment Disputes: Recent Developments' (2007) 16 RECIEL 230, 230.
1266. Jorge Vifluales, 'Amicus Intervention in Investor-State Arbitration' (2007) 61 DispResolJ 72, 75.

cautiously find the most effective way of considering social policies in the decision-making of arbitral tribunals.[1267]

In this context, it becomes useful to approach investment protection guarantees such as FET from a holistic perspective encompassing both economic and non-economic considerations.[1268] Such a perspective will not transform investment treaties into pure social and environmental regulation instruments but will bring investment protection in connection with emerging social and environmental concerns.

1267. Vadi argues that the judicial dialogue among international tribunals may promote the consideration of non-economic values in investment-treaty arbitration such as human rights. Vadi, *Analogies in Investment Treaty Law and Arbitration* (n 277) 74.

1268. Ortino, 'Refining the Content and Role of Investment "Rules" and "Standards": A New Approach to International Investment Treaty-Making' (n 224) 15.

Conclusion to Part IV

This part analysed the legal decision-making process of investment-arbitration tribunals through the perspective of 'Dialogue'. Arbitrators have the complicated task of considering the involvement of various national and international legal orders. In combination with the specialised dispute resolution procedure and the interaction between public and private interests, they face different challenges than those appearing in other dispute resolution scenes. This transnational legal architecture of the investment-arbitration framework has shaped the legal decision-making process accordingly in order to accommodate the specific features of investment arbitration.

From a theoretical perspective, Chapter 5 presented the novel dialogical network approach describing its purpose and function for the analysis of legal decision-making. This approach identified five interpretive arguments which arbitrators use when interpreting and eventually applying the law: narrative, convention, precedent, customary law and policy.

Bringing theory into the practice of arbitral decision-making, Chapter 6 described the dialogues formed within the use of each of these interpretive arguments through the analysis of arbitral case law. First, the Narrative arguments described the types of communication between the arbitrators and the parties of a dispute. The stories presented by the parties through their submissions constitute the basis of the legal decision-making process and keep the interpretation process connected to the specific dispute.

On a second note, the Convention arguments revealed an awareness of the international treaty system within which an investment dispute arises and is connected to the need to interpret investment treaties using the VCLT. However, the traditional rules of the VCLT do not give answers regarding further interpretational issues that may arise such as the interpretation of precedents and customary international law or the role of policy in decision-making.

This gap brought the analysis to the Precedent-based arguments which reflected the importance of arbitral case law and the interactions with national and international legal orders. Such interactions are not realised in vacuum but they are further adapted to the specific interpretation needs that may arise in the context of the dispute and to the idiosyncratic characteristics of investment arbitration. As an example, when confronting the need to balance private and public interests in the course of interpretation, arbitral tribunals resort to the ECtHR case law for information on the content of the 'proportionality' concept. However, tribunals further enhance the proportionality methodology with concepts such as 'reasonableness' and 'legitimacy' adapting this concept to the needs of investment arbitration. This cross-fertilisation between arbitrators and, national and international legal orders goes both ways since the latter also profit from such an interaction. Investment tribunals are considered to influence the approaches to State behaviour followed by specialised regimes such as human rights and trade law in the context of balancing public and private interests as well as influencing the development of customary international law. Arbitral case law also helps domestic courts better understand the functioning of the investment-arbitration framework resulting in a more conscious balancing of domestic and investment protection interests when this need arises in national jurisdictions. Dialogue in this context, expresses a dynamic transnational decision-making process which forms links between arbitration and other legal orders but at the same time preserves the specificities of the investment-arbitration framework.

Arbitral tribunals also recognise the need to resort to Customary International Law for the interpretation of treaty protection guarantees and to fill in the gaps of the treaties. Case law reveals that tribunals approach Customary International Law through an evolutionary perspective. The consideration of the evolutive elements characterising the content of investment protection guarantees such as FET demonstrates that their meaning is not stable in time but acquires a dynamic interpretation which is linked to the way they evolve over time. Such a perspective has led to the steady emergence of 'customary international investment law' thus attributing to arbitral decision-making its transnational, specifically normative, character.

Last but not least, the use of policy-based arguments demonstrates the role of policy in legal interpretation. This includes not only political and economic treaty goals but also legal and social policies. Considerations such as consistency, predictability, the rule of law, human rights and sustainable development have made their gradual appearance in the arbitral decision-making process. In addition, civil society, through think tanks, lobby groups and NGOs plays an important role in the emergence of social concerns. Their strong interest and involvement in arbitration reveals a non-statist element since the State is not the main and only actor in the field. In this context, dispute resolution may be the main function of arbitral tribunals but subsequent functions may arise connected to legal and social policy concerns.

Based on the above findings, the analysis of arbitral decision-making through the 'dialogical network' approach has revealed on the one hand the use of arbitral interpretation approaches adapted to the specificities of the investment-arbitration framework, and on the other hand the relations that can be formed amongst various legal and judicial orders. In this context, it demonstrates that investment arbitration is a developing dispute resolution framework presenting the need to interact with domestic and international legal orders in order to obtain guidance and exchange legal ideas, opinions and doctrines. This interaction is pictured through the use of interpretive arguments functioning in a dialogical network. However, the investment-arbitration framework has its own physiognomies, policies and functions that motivate the arbitrators to adapt exogenous influences to the needs and characteristics of investment arbitration. This adaptation process, clearly pictured in the decision-making of arbitral tribunals, constitutes a filter that permits a transnational dialogue on the one hand and preserves the idiosyncratic characteristics of the investment-arbitration framework on the other. Investment tribunals demonstrate a need to acknowledge what is already out there and at the same time canvass the intellectually defensible esoteric characteristics of the investment-arbitration framework.

Going a step further, the dialogical network methodology can be used as a theoretical framework for studying legal decision-making of other international courts and tribunals. It offers a working method for exploring how judicial bodies interpret treaties, national laws, policies, precedents and customs in the context of a specific dispute and how these interpretation issues further interact between them in order to reach to a specific decision. It also helps understanding how specialised dispute resolution bodies interact with their broader international environment but at the same time preserve their particularities.

Conclusions

Arbitral decision-making is an important and topical issue as various economic, political and legal interests depend on the arbitral award. Investor-state arbitration is requested to give answers to complex issues connected to the public interest of a State and its economic progress. The outcome of an arbitral award may also affect the public works and the everyday life of the State's citizens as well as the investment strategies of private investors.

While the popularity of investment arbitration as a means to resolve investor-state disputes is growing, important criticisms have been raised not only by the legal community but also by the civil and political circles. Such criticisms include the questioning of the legitimacy of the investment-arbitration framework in general and of the decision-making process in particular. The broader issues that underpin such criticisms are the wide discretion arbitrators have when deciding on a specific dispute and as a corollary the existence of checks and balances when such dispute resolution functions are performed.

Due to the decentralised form of investor-state arbitration and the absence of a standing judicial body, arbitral tribunals have the mandate to resolve each dispute on an ad hoc basis. In addition, despite the fact that the terms used in the investment treaties are characterised by a certain degree of vagueness and generality, there are no specific guidelines on how arbitrators interpret and apply the law in the investment-arbitration context. This wide discretion of arbitral tribunals when interpreting the law is enhanced by the absence of a doctrine of binding precedent that could guide the legal decision-making process. Going a step further, the lack of an appeals mechanism entrusted with the correction of errors of law may question the importance of a correct legal interpretation in the course of rendering an arbitral award.

Based on these considerations, the process arbitrators follow to render an award raises important questions regarding how arbitrators interpret and eventually apply the law, the adequate reasoning of the awards, the consistent interpretation of investment guarantees and the persuasive authority of arbitral case law. Addressing these issues is important not only for the sake of legal analysis but even more so for the long-term well-being of the whole dispute resolution process. An effective dispute resolution process requires a transparent and reliable decision-making process that will solidify investment arbitration as an alternative to court proceedings.

This book purported to shed light and critically analyse these issues connected to the legal decision-making process of arbitrators. Its aim was to present how investment-arbitration tribunals interpret the law. On this basis, the book revealed that arbitrators have developed a specialised way of legal decision-making which is adapted to the specific needs and transnational characteristics of investment arbitration.

As a first step for such an analysis, Part I of the book acknowledged and described the particularities of the investment-arbitration framework within which arbitral decision-making takes place. Investment arbitration encompasses both private and public interests and lies at the intersection of the national and international legal cosmos. It is comprised of public and private actors coming from various legal and political systems and of different sets of laws including public international law, administrative decisions and host State regulations. From a functional perspective, investment arbitration is considered to have developed into a dynamic dispute resolution process with unique sets of procedures that largely operate independently from national and international law. Structurally it is not entirely positioned either in the sphere of national, international or in the field of private or public law.

As such, the assessment of the dispute resolution function of arbitral tribunals within the international and domestic arena becomes more complicated. With this background in mind, picturing investment arbitration as solely a microcosm of party-centred dispute resolution appears to be at odds with reality. The ad hoc and case-specific dispute resolution process may be the obvious target of decision-making but a comprehensive analysis of the legal decision-making process cannot ignore the gap between the obvious target and what exists in symbiosis with it. As an example, symbiotic issues that may arise are the way national and international legal orders interact in the context of interpretation or the role of policy and third-parties therein. For this reason, and in an attempt to offer proper insight into how decision-making in investment arbitration takes place, this book approached the legal decision-making process of arbitral tribunals through the wider perspective of transnational dispute resolution. This approach placed arbitral decision-making at the crossroad of international and national legal orders and the intersection of private and public interests.

A transnational dispute resolution process can find its theoretical basis in what Koh describes as a 'transnational legal process':

> a process whereby public and private actors, including nation States, corporations, international organizations, non-governmental organizations, and individuals, interact in a variety of fora to interpret, enforce, and ultimately internalize, rules of international law.[1269]

1269. Koh, 'Jefferson Memorial Lecture – Transnational Legal Process after September 11th' (n 93) 339; *See* §1.01 'Dispute Resolution Function: A Transnational Perspective'.

Going a step further, a transnational legal process has four main characteristics being: non-traditional, non-statist, dynamic, and normative.[1270] These four elements can also be traced in the legal decision-making of investment-arbitration tribunals.

Within this transnational context, the book explored the legal decision-making process analysing the legal arguments arbitral tribunals used in their awards in order to interpret the law. Legal argumentation theories and specifically the triptych of language–rhetoric–dialogue constituted the theoretical framework for such an analysis. Each one of these aspects analysed the decision-making process from a different angle. The language aspect focused on the language arbitrators use when interpreting the law while the rhetoric aspect of legal argumentation revealed the way arbitrators externalise the decision-making process through the reasoning of arbitral awards. Last but not least, the dialogue aspect demonstrated the interactions of laws, judges and arbitrators in legal decision-making.

Starting from the perspective of 'Language', Part II analysed the legal language arbitrators use in the interpretation process. In particular, it examined the meaning they give to legal concepts such as 'rights', 'principles' and 'standards'. The overall objective was to reveal the legal decision-making process of arbitrators analysing the legal terminology they use and whether such terminology contributed in developing a specialised legal decision-making process.

In investment arbitration the main models of normative arrangements contained in set rules or customary international law are primarily externalised as 'principles', 'standards' and 'rights'. The study of investment-arbitration cases revealed that arbitrators treat these concepts in an idiosyncratic way. As an example, the decision-makers may characterise FET interchangeably as a 'standard', 'right' or 'principle'. Especially in the situations where investment treaties and arbitration rules avoid such legal characterisations, the arbitrators' discretion on how to address the normative arrangements in the decision-making process becomes even wider. This interchangeability demonstrates a non-consistent legal characterisation of the investment protection guarantees.

However, despite such inconsistency, there is an underlying pattern of how they are interpreted by investment tribunals. The analysis showed that arbitrators make purposive use of language connecting the investment protection guarantees with the interpretive technique used. The term 'standard' is used when the tribunal proceeds to the assessment of whether a specific level of protection has been attained while the term 'right' signifies the need to balance between the investor's and State's rights. Similarly, the use of the term 'principle', in particular 'general principle of law', is connected on the one hand, to the transnational comparative methodology of identifying general principles through various legal systems and on the other hand, to the interpretation of these principles as specialised principles of investment arbitration.

The diversification of the use of these terms further demonstrates the cyclical and dynamic nature of the interpretation language. An arbitral tribunal resolving a particular dispute will turn for guidance to case law in order to identify the purpose of using

1270. Harold Koh, 'Transnational Legal Process' (1996) 75 NebLRev 181, 183.

a specific legal terminology. The purposive use is further enhanced by the parties' submissions. When a party will refer to FET as a 'standard' and to the degree of protection to be accorded, the tribunal will use the same characterisation in order to make the specific assessment. As a consequence, the meaning of a specific term is formed both with a look at the legal precedents as well as in the context of the present dispute.

The study of juridical language can reveal not only the way a juridical field operates but also an autonomy of thought. According to the above findings, the analysis of legal decision-making from a language perspective demonstrates that arbitrators have developed a common use of language which is formed based on the interpretational needs that arise in the context of the specific dispute and the experience provided from case law. Such a language is both non-traditional and dynamic. Non-traditional as it is adapted to the specificities and needs of investment arbitration, the latter not entirely fitting in the private or public international law sphere; and dynamic as it is formed and transformed through the practice of arbitral tribunals.

Nevertheless, while the analysis of language as sketched in Part II becomes more of an esoteric issue of legal decision-making, the analysis of 'Rhetoric' as effectuated in Part III introduced an exoteric view of the legal decision-making process revealing how arbitral tribunals externalise their legal decision-making process through the awards' reasoning.

In particular, 'Rhetoric' is strongly connected to an audience-oriented legal argumentation scheme. Drawing on this approach the legal decision-making process was examined based on the functions of the reasoning process for specific audiences and for the investment-arbitration framework in general. Consistent with the findings in the 'Language' Part, this part revealed that arbitral tribunals approach the issue of reasoning in a specialised way, based on the characteristics and needs of investment arbitration. These needs stem from the transnational elements of investment arbitration, the arising demands for external and internal legitimacy and the existence of an annulment – rather than appeal – mechanism.

The transnational characteristics of the dispute resolution framework have largely influenced the connection of reasoning with concerns such as acceptability and legitimacy. The interaction of States, private investors, international institutions, domestic courts and international tribunals, national and international laws, and public and private interests creates the image of a decentralised and non-hierarchical dispute resolution framework. In this setting, reasoning plays a significant role since it is connected to the acceptability of the award not only by the internal audience – the parties of the dispute which are offered an explanation of why the won of lost – but also by the external audience – third parties such as States, international institutions or NGOs.

Going a step further, the acceptability of the award fosters in its turn legitimacy. Reasoning is capable of expressing the validity and legitimacy of the award's arguments and outcome. As such, it plays the important role of expressing the legitimacy of the decision-making process. Legitimacy in this context, encompasses the way investment arbitration appears not only to the inside players but also to the outside viewers of the field.

This way, reasoning brings to the surface the non-statist element of decision-making in investment arbitration since not only States but also private parties, international institutions and organisations take interest in the reasoning of arbitral awards influencing the legitimacy perceptions of the dispute resolution process.

Within this background, the analysis of arbitral case law revealed two functions of reasoning. The first function is the persuasion-oriented function. The debate over a high or low reasoning standard for annulment in case law illustrates the different approaches of arbitral tribunals and annulment committees regarding the tribunal's discretion to express its reasoning in certain ways. Arbitral practice reveals that the reasoning of arbitral awards primarily aims at persuading the parties, the ad hoc committees and the reader in general that they understand what they read. In this context, the understanding of a tribunal's reasoning is based on persuasion rather than direct communication with the reader; persuasion that the tribunal followed a specific logical process in order to move from a set of arguments to a certain final decision, irrespective of the correctness of such arguments.

However, what is also revealed is that the function of reasoning is not limited to how well parties understand the awards when reading them but it is also important for expressing how arbitrators interpreted and eventually applied the law. The development function of reasoning pictures clearly this concern. Apart from persuasion, reasoning has the important function of developing the content of investment protection guarantees and, even more, their consistent development through the de facto use of precedent by future tribunals. The interpretation of abstract legal norms requires thorough legal argumentation expressed in the reasoning of the award. This is further confirmed by the case law and interview data both stressing out the importance of picturing the interpretation process in the award's reasoning despite the absence of an appeals mechanism. As a consequence, this function reveals the normative character of decision-making since apart from persuasion, reasoning has the role of developing the content of vague norms and guiding future tribunals in their interpretations.

Both the analysis of decision-making through the 'Language' and 'Rhetoric' lens revealed that legal interpretation is a process strongly linked to the characteristics of investment arbitration. Specificities such as legitimacy concerns, arbitral discretion in interpretation, balancing public and private interests, and the importance of correct legal interpretation despite the lack of an appeals facility have all led to the gradual development of a dynamic, non-statist and normative dispute resolution process. However, an additional element that requires attention when analysing the legal decision-making is the fact that arbitrators have the complicated task of considering the involvement of various national and international legal orders.

The existence of disputes requiring the consideration of different national and international legal frameworks coupled with the spread of international courts and tribunals has led to the development of judicial practices that are not expressly referred to in national and international laws.[1271] Such practices may include the dialogue between courts for solving transnational cases and the cross-citation between courts

1271. *See* §5.03 'From Legal Transplants to Legal Dialogues'.

belonging to different judicial systems. In line with these developments, Part IV of the book analysed arbitral decision-making through the third lens, that of 'Dialogue'. It has particularly proposed a novel 'dialogical network' approach, identifying five argument types which arbitrators use in their decision-making process and picturing the dialogues formed therein. The interpretation process was viewed as one combined operation where each argument may contribute to the overall interpretation process.[1272] Each legal argument focuses respectively on five elements: narrative techniques, the VCLT, precedent, customary international law and policy:

- The *Narrative arguments* portrayed the dialogues formed between the parties, the members of the tribunal, and the arbitrators with the parties. The narratives presented by the parties through their submissions constitute the basis of the legal decision-making process and provide the reassurance that the interpretation process will stay connected to the specific dispute. Additionally, the gradual appearance of third parties submitting *amicus curiae* briefs has expanded the dialogue interlocutors. The *amici* may inform the decision-maker of the different legal frameworks that may be associated with the specific dispute introducing a dynamic and non-statist transnational decision-making aspect.
- The analysis of the *Convention-based arguments* revealed that arbitral decision-making remains connected with its traditional international law background through reference to the VCLT. However, investment arbitration presents challenges stemming from its specialised nature such as the need to find a balance between public and private interests. In addition, the VCLT does not give answers regarding further interpretational issues that may arise in practice such as the interpretation of precedents and customary international law or the role of policy in decision-making. Based on these considerations arbitrators employ further interpretation arguments in order to deal with the additional interpretational needs that arise in the context of a specific dispute.
- As such, the analysis of the *Precedent arguments* revealed the important role of case law as a method of interpretation. It specifically demonstrated the dialogue with international and national legal orders and the insertion of traditional international and domestic law concepts such as 'proportionality' and 'legitimate expectations' in the investment-arbitration context. This cross-fertilisation goes both ways since international and national legal orders also profit from such an interaction. Arbitral case law helps international and domestic courts better understand the functioning of the investment-arbitration framework resulting in a more conscious balancing of investment protection and other interests when this need arises in various jurisdictions. 'Dialogue' in this context, expresses a dynamic transnational decision-making process which on the one hand preserves the specificities of the investment-arbitration framework and on the other hand carves the way for mutual recognition amongst arbitration and other legal orders.

1272. *See* §1.02[D][2] 'The Science and Art of Legal Interpretation'.

- Arbitral tribunals also resort to customary international law in the course of legal interpretation. The use of *customary law arguments* revealed that in the process of clarifying the content of the treaty terms, reference to general international law, specifically to customary international law, becomes necessary. The dialogue unveils that arbitrators use customary international law as an interpretive tool for treaty provisions, as auxiliary to other legal concepts, as filling gaps in investment treaties, or as delimiting the content of vague treaty standards. However, its flexibility and adaptability has led arbitrators to approach customary international law through an evolutionary perspective adapted to the needs of investment arbitration. As an example while FET has its origin in customary international law, arbitral tribunals proceed to an evolutionary interpretation of customary international law in the context of investment-treaty arbitration. This evolutionary perspective has set the basis for the gradual emergence of a customary international investment law attributing to arbitral decision-making its normative character. The use of these arguments also demonstrates a non-traditional decision-making process which preserves its connections with international legal orders but also takes a different specialised approach when needed.
- Finally, the analysis of how *Policy-based arguments* are used revealed the role of policy in the legal decision-making process of arbitral tribunals. As demonstrated in this section, the policies of the investment-arbitration framework were primarily established as political and economic goals. With the spread of investment arbitration as a means for resolving investment disputes, legal and social policies arose urging the need to be addressed. Legal considerations such as consistency, predictability and the rule of law stem from the public law nature of the interests involved and the function of the investment-arbitration dispute resolution procedure as a private, however, justice mechanism. On the other hand, civil society, through think tanks, lobby groups and NGOs plays an important role in the emergence of social concerns while organising political pressure through the media and participating in consultative bodies. Their strong interest and involvement in arbitration reveals a non-statist element since the state is not the main and only actor in the field. The policy-based arguments depict exactly this evolution of policies of the investment-arbitration framework and as a corollary of the functions of the dispute resolution bodies. The dispute resolution function may be the main function of the decision-making process but one cannot ignore the subsequent functions that may arise due to emerging legal and social policy concerns. An example of such subsequent functions may be the need to address the legitimacy concerns by producing awards of a high reasoning standard that clearly depict the decision-making process followed.

The analysis of arbitral decision-making through the dialogical network approach has revealed on the one hand, the use of arbitral interpretation approaches adapted to the specificities of the investment-arbitration framework and on the other hand, the various interactions formed in the decision-making process. The dialogical networks formed and the adaptation process of the products of the dialogue, demonstrate the development of a transnational method of decision-making.

Investor-state tribunals have developed a specialised legal decision-making process adjusted to the transnational characteristics of the investment-arbitration framework and the interpretational needs that arise in the context of the specific dispute. These characteristics and needs can be summarised as including the interaction of private and public actors, domestic and international laws,[1273] the vague content of investment protection guarantees of investment treaties,[1274] the wide discretion of arbitrators when interpreting the law,[1275] the need to balance private and public interests,[1276] and last but not least the need to respond to political, economic, legal and social concerns.[1277]

Against this background, investor-state tribunals interpret the law in a way that shows the gradual development of a transnational decision-making process which is non-traditional, non-statist, dynamic and normative:

It is *non-traditional* because decision-making is adapted to the specificities of investment arbitration. Arbitral tribunals have created an idiosyncratic interpretation language which is strongly connected to the way they interpret standards, principles and rights.[1278] Furthermore, despite the use of the traditional interpretation rules of the VCLT, tribunals have also introduced interpretation methods that fill in conventional gaps such as the need to interpret precedents and customary international law, and take into account policies.[1279] Last but not least, investment tribunals recognise the need to communicate with national and international legal orders through case law but they further adapt such an interaction to the specificities of the investment-arbitration context.[1280]

Additionally, the decision-making process is effectuated in a *non-statist* environment since the State is not the only actor with an important role in the process. Private parties, international institutions and organisations show a strong interest in the reasoning of arbitral awards thus shaping the legitimacy perceptions of the decision-making process. This in its turn may influence the way arbitral awards are reasoned.[1281] In addition, civil society, through think tanks, lobby groups and NGOs plays an important role in the emergence of social and even legal policy concerns which can be traced in the legal decision-making process.[1282]

The analysis of arbitral case law demonstrated that it is also a *normative* decision-making process in the sense that arbitral tribunals develop the context of vague protection guarantees through legal interpretation. This is confirmed both by the importance of a correct interpretation despite the lack of an appeals mechanism and by

1273. Part I: 'Arbitral Decision-Making' and Part IV: 'Dialogue'.
1274. Part I: 'Arbitral Decision-Making' and Part II: 'Language'.
1275. *Ibid.*
1276. Part II: 'Language' and Part IV: 'Dialogue'.
1277. Part III: 'Rhetoric' and Part IV: 'Dialogue'.
1278. Part II: 'Language'.
1279. Part IV: 'Dialogue'.
1280. Part IV: 'Dialogue'.
1281. Part III: 'Rhetoric'.
1282. Part IV: 'Dialogue'.

the emergence of a *de facto* doctrine of precedent connected to the extensive citation practices of arbitral tribunals when interpreting the law.[1283] Additionally, the evolutionary interpretation of customary international law standards by arbitral tribunals, reveals the steady development of specialised customary law applied to investment arbitration disputes.[1284]

Finally, it is a *dynamic* decision-making process that is formed and transformed through the practice of arbitral tribunals. The language arbitrators use and the purpose of using specific legal terms are mainly identified through previous case law. In this context, any new elements in such language will again appear in legal precedents.[1285] Moreover, the dialogue between investment arbitration and national and international legal orders is reciprocal.[1286] Such interactions picture the broader dynamic process of a 'give-take-adapt' relationship amongst decision-makers in the dispute resolution scene.

This gradual development of a transnational decision-making process creates the broader picture of a dispute resolution process that is progressively acquiring its own special place in the legal and judicial firmament. On the one hand, it is developing based on its specificities while on the other hand, it is creating communication channels with international and national legal orders. Decision-making in investment arbitration opts neither for isolation nor for complete homogenisation.

Finally, this book should be viewed as an integral part of the wider debate and research developed regarding the way arbitral tribunals reach their decisions. Nevertheless, for the first time, this book supplements the existing scholarship on legal arbitral decision-making focusing on the specificities of investment arbitration and drawing on legal argumentation theories. The analysis developed can further constitute the theoretical framework for studying the legal decision-making of other international courts and tribunals. It is helpful for identifying the emergence of specific judicial practices such as the use of a specialised language when interpreting the law or the use of reasoning as a means to persuade an audience. It is also suitable for exploring how judicial bodies interpret treaties, national laws, policies, precedents and customs in the context of a specific dispute. Going a step further, such an analysis could be useful for studying how domestic courts deal with international and cross-border matters. After all, knowledge of the interpretation practices constitutes knowledge of how a dispute resolution body operates and, even more, knowledge of how the legal framework it forms part of gradually matures.

1283. Part III: 'Rhetoric' and Part IV: 'Dialogue'.
1284. Part IV: 'Dialogue'.
1285. Part II: 'Language'.
1286. Part IV: 'Dialogue'.

Annex Interview Questions

The interview questions follow an open-ended, semi-structured method. Below are presented the main interview questions put to all interviewees. Any deviation or further elaboration, is not included here.

1) What tools do you use to interpret the law in investor-state disputes?
2) Do you think that the reasoning of the awards depicts the whole interpretation and application process arbitrators follow?
3) Do you think that errors of law are common? What criteria do arbitrators use when they conclude that there is an erroneous interpretation or misapplication of the law?
4) Do the submissions of the parties affect the way the arbitrators interpret and apply the law? If yes, in what way?
5) What risks do you see in tribunals' striving for consistency through interpretation? Would it take the arbitrators away from their case-specific mandate?
6) Do you think that decoding the methodology of interpretation arbitrators use is important for the investment-arbitration framework?
7) How would you describe the decision-making process of arbitral tribunals with one phrase?

Bibliography

Books

Aguilar-Alvarez G and Reisman M, The Reason's Requirement in International Investment Arbitration (Nijhoff 2008)

Alvarez J, The Public International Law Regime Governing International Investment (Brill/Nijhoff 2011)

Alexy R, A Theory of Legal Argumentation. The Theory of Rational Discourse as Theory of Legal Justification (Clarendon 1989)

Alexy R, A Theory of Legal Argumentation. The Theory of Rational Discourse as Theory of Legal Justification (Ruth Adler and Neil MacCormick tr, Clarendon 2009)

Amaya A, The Tapestry of Reason (Hart 2015)

Amsterdam A and Bruner J, Minding the Law (HUP 2002)

Aristotle, Eudemian Ethics

Aristotle, On Rhetoric: A Theory of Civic Discourse (George Kennedy tr, OUP 2007)

Barak A, Purposive Interpretation in Law (Sari Bashi tr, PUP 2005)

Beaulac S, The Power of Language in the Making of International Law (Nijhoff 2004)

Berg B, Qualitative Research Methods for the Social Sciences (Pearson 2007)

Berger B and Schneider M, Inside the Black Box: How Arbitral Tribunals Operate and Reach Their Decisions (Juris 2013)

Bhatia V, Candlin C and Engberg J, Legal Discourse Across Cultures and Systems (HKUP 2008)

Bianchi A, Peat D, and Windsor M (eds) Interpretation in International Law (OUP 2015)

Bonnitcha J, Skovgaard Poulsen LN, and Waibel M, The Political Economy of the Investment Treaty Regime (OUP 2017)

Bingham T Lord, The Rule of Law (Penguin 2011)

Bishop D and Kehoe E G (eds) The Art of Advocacy in International Arbitration (2nd ed., Juris 2010)

Brown C, A Common Law of International Adjudication (CUP 2007)

Brownlie I, Principles of Public International Law (6th ed., OUP 2003)

Bücheler G, Proportionality in Investor-State Arbitration (OUP 2015)

Burton S, An Introduction to Law and Legal Reasoning (Little, Brown & Co 1985)

Burton S, Judging in Good Faith (CUP 1994)
Calliess G-P and Zumbansen P, Rough Consensus and Running Code: A Theory of Transnational Private Law (Hart 2010)
Candlin C and Gotti M, Discourse and Practice in International Commercial Arbitration (Ashgate 2012)
Carlson L, Dialogue Games: An Approach to Discourse Analysis (Reidel Publishing Company 1983)
Caron D, Schill S, Smutny A and Triantafilou E (eds), Practising Virtue: Inside International Arbitration (OUP 2015)
Carton J, The Culture of International Arbitration (OUP 2013)
Cassese A, Self-Determination of Peoples: A Legal Reappraisal (CUP 1995)
Channell J, Vague Language (OUP 1994)
Cheng B, General Principles of Law as Applied by International Courts and Tribunals (CUP 1953)
Clasmeier J, Arbitral Awards as Investments: Treaty Interpretation and the Dynamics of International Investment Law (Kluwer 2016)
Cohen L, Manion L and Morrison K, Research Methods in Education (6th ed., Routledge 2007)
Cope E and Sandys J, Aristotle: Rhetoric, vol 1 (CUP 2009)
Crawford J, The Creation of States in International Law (Clarendon 1979)
Dahlman C and Feteris E (eds), Legal Argumentation Theory: Cross-Disciplinary Perspectives (Springer 2013)
Damme I van, Treaty Interpretation by the WTO Appellate Body (OUP 2009)
Delmas-Marty M, Ordering Pluralism (Hart 2009)
Dezalay Y and Garth B, Dealing in Virtue: International Commercial Arbitration and the Construction of a Transnational Legal Order (UCP 1996)
Dolzer R and Stevens M, Bilateral Investment Treaties (Nijhoff 1995)
Dolzer R, Stevens M and Schreuer C, Principles of International Investment Law (2nd ed., OUP 2012)
Dugan C, Wallace D Jr, Rubins N and Sabahi B, Investor-State Arbitration (OUP 2012)
Dworkin R, Taking Rights Seriously (HUP 1978)
Dworkin R, Law's Empire (HUP 1986)
Eemeren F van (ed.), Crucial Concepts in argumentation theory (AUP 2001) Eemeren F van (ed.) and Grootendorst R, A Systematic Theory of Argumentation: The pragma-dialectical approach (CUP 2004)
Eemeren F van (ed.), Grootendorst R, Henkemans F, Blair J, Johnson R, Krabbe E, Plantin C, Walton D, Willard C, Woods J, Zarefsky D, Fundamentals of Argumentation Theory: A Hand-book of Historical Backgrounds and Contemporary Developments (LEA 1996)
Elkouri F and Elkouri E, How Arbitration Works (4th ed., BNA 1985)
Emiliou N, The Principle of Proportionality in European Law: A Comparative Study (KLI 1996)
Feteris E, Fundamentals of Legal Argumentation: A Survey on Theories of the Justification of Judicial Decisions (Springer 1999)
Fuller L, Anatomy of the Law (Penguin 1971)

Gaillard E, Legal Theory of International Arbitration (Nijhoff 2010)
Gaillard E, Aspects Philosophiques du Droit de l'Arbitrage International (Nijhoff 2008)
Gardiner R, Treaty Interpretation (2nd ed., OUP 2015)
Garzone G and Degano C, Arbitration Awards: Generic Features and Textual Realisations (Cambridge Scholars Publishing 2012)
Gazzini T, Interpretation of International Investment Treaties (Bloomsbury 2016)
Goode R, Kronke H, Mckendrick E (eds), Transnational Commercial Law: Texts, Cases and Materials (2nd ed., OUP 2015)
Gerbay R, The Functions of Arbitral Institutions (Kluwer 2016)
Gubrium J and Holstein J (eds), Handbook of Interview Research (Sage 2002)
Halliday M, McIntosh A and Strevens P, The Linguistic Sciences and Language Teaching (Longmans 1964)
Harari O, Knowledge and Demonstration: Aristotle's Posterior Analytics (Springer 2004)
Hart H, The Concept of Law (OUP 1961)
Hartwieg O, Tatsachen und Normarbeit im Rechtsvergleich (Mohr Siebeck 2003)
Hintikka J, Analysis of Aristotle (KLI 2004)
Jessup P, Transnational Law (YUP 1956)
Kalinowski G, La Logique des norms (PUF 1972)
Kennedy D, A Critique of Adjudication (HUP 1997)
Keohane R., International Institutions and State Power: Essays in International Relations Theory (Routledge 1989)
Kidane W L, The Culture of International Arbitration (OUP 2017)
Klabbers J, Treaty Conflict and the European Union (CUP 2009)
Knop K, Diversity and Self-Determination in International Law (CUP 2002)
Koskenniemi M, Sources of International Law (Ashgate 2000)
Koskenniemi M, From Apology to Utopia. The Structure of International Legal Argument (Reissue with a new Epilogue, CUP 2006)
Kramer M, Objectivity and the Rule of Law (CUP 2007)
Kulick A, Global Public Interest in International Investment Law (CUP 2012)
Lauterpacht H Sir, The Function of Law in the International Community (Clarendon 1933)
Lauterpacht H Sir, The Development of International law by the permanent court of international justice (Longmans 1934)
Le Quinio A, Recherche sur la circulation des solutions juridiques: le recours au droit comparé par les juridictions constitutionnelles (Fondation Varenne 2011)
MacCormick N, Legal Reasoning and Legal Theory (OUP 1978)
MacCormick N, Rhetoric and the Rule of Law: A Theory of Legal Reasoning (OUP 2005)
MacCormick N, The Rule of Law and the Arguable Character of Law (OUP 2005) MacCormick N, and Summers R (eds), Interpreting Statutes: A Comparative Study (Dartmouth 1991)
MacCormick N, and Summers R (eds), Interpreting Precedent: A Comparative Study (Ashgate: Dartmouth, 1997);
McConville M, and Chui W (ed.), Research Methods for Law (EUP 2007)

McLachlan C, Shore L and Weiniger M, International Investment Arbitration: Substantive Principles (OUP 2008)
Morth U, Soft Law in Governance and Regulation: An interdisciplinary Analysis (Edward Elgar Publishing 2004)
Nobles R and Schiff D, Observing Law Through Systems Theory (Hart 2012)
Orakhelashvili A, The interpretation of Acts and Rules in Public International Law (OUP 2008)
Orrego Vicuña F, International Dispute Settlement in an Evolving Global Society (CUP 2004)
Perelman C, Justice, Law and Argument (Reidel 1980)
Perelman C, Droit, Morale et Philosophie (2nd edn, LGDJ/Pichon et Durand-Auzias 1976)
Perelman C, The New Rhetoric and the Humanities: Essays on Rhetoric and its Applications (Reidel 1979)
Perelman C, Le Champ de l' Argumentation (Presses Universitaires de Bruxelles 1970)
Posner R, How Judges Think (HUP 2008)
Prakken H, Logical Tools for Modelling Legal Argument (Springer 1997)
Reinisch A (ed.), Standards of Investment Protection (OUP 2008)
Reisman M, The Quest for World Order and Human Dignity in the Twenty-first Century: Constitutive Process and Individual Commitment (Brill 2012)
Richards I. A., The Philosophy of Rhetoric (OUP 1936)
Rieke R, Sillars M and Peterson T, Argumentation and Critical Decision Making, (6th ed., Peachpit 2013)
Rorty R, The Linguistic Turn: Essays in Philosophical Method (UCP 1992) 409
Salacuse J, The Law of Investment Treaties (OUP 2010)
Salacuse J, The Three Laws of International Investment, National, Contractual, and International Frameworks for Foreign Capital (OUP 2013)
Sasson M, Substantive Law in Investment Treaty Arbitration. The Unsettled Relationship Between International Law And Municipal Law (KLI 2010)
Schachter O, International Law in Theory and Practice (Nijhoff 1991)
Schill S, International Investment Law and Comparative Public Law (OUP 2010)
Schlesinger R, The Common Core of Legal Systems, an Emerging Subject of Comparative Study (A.W. Sijthoff 1961)
Schreuer C, The ICSID Convention A Commentary (2nd ed., CUP 2009)
Schubert G, The Judicial Mind: The Attitudes and Ideologies of Supreme Court Justices 1946–1963 (NUP 1965)
Schultz T, Transnational Legality: Stateless Law and International Arbitration (OUP 2014)
Segal J and Spaeth H (eds), The Supreme Court and the Attitudinal Model Revisited (CUP 2002)
Segger M, Gehring M and Newcombe A, Sustainable Development in World Investment Law (KLI 2011)
Shany Y, The Competing Jurisdictions of International Courts and Tribunals (OUP 2003)
Sornarajah M, The International Law on Foreign Investment (2nd ed., CUP, 2004)

Sornarajah M, The International Law on Foreign Investment (3rd ed., CUP 2010)
Sourgens F, A Nascent Common Law: The Process of Decisionmaking in International Legal Disputes Between States and Foreign Investors (Brill/ Nijhoff 2015)
Spranzi M, The Art of Dialectic Between Dialogue and Rhetoric, The Aristotelian Tradition (John Benjamins 2011)
Stelmach J and Brozek B, Methods of Legal Reasoning (Springer 2006)
Stiglitz J, Globalization and Its Discontents (WWNorton 2002)
Sunstein C, Legal Reasoning and Political Conflict (OUP 1998)
Sureda A, Treaty Arbitration Judging under Uncertainty (CUP 2012)
Tamanaha B, On the Rule of Law: History, Politics, Theory (CUP 2004)
Toulmin S, The Uses of Argument (CUP 1958)
Vadi V, Analogies in International Investment Law and Arbitration (CUP 2015)
Venzke I, How Interpretation Makes International Law: On Semantic Change and Normative Twists (CUP 2012)
Venzke I, Makes International Law: On Semantic Change and Normative Twists (OUP 2012)
Ward J, Aristotle on Homonymy: Dialectic and Science (CUP 2008)
Watkins D and Burton M, Research Methods in Law (Routledge 2013)
Watson A, Legal Transplants: An Approach to Comparative Law (2nd ed., UGA 1993)
Webb P, International Judicial Integration and Fragmentation (OUP 2013)
Weeramantry R, Treaty Interpretation in Investment Arbitration (OUP 2012)
Weiler T, The Interpretation of International Investment Law Equality, Discrimination and Minimum Standards of Treatment in Historical Context (Brill 2013)
Zappen J, The Rebirth of Dialogue: Bakhtin, Socrates, and the Rhetorical Tradition (SUNYP 2004)
Zeiler G, Jurisdiction, Competence and Admissibility in International Investment Law for the 21st Century, Essays in Honour of Christoph Schreuer (OUP 2009)

Chapters in Edited Books

Abi-Saab G, 'The Appellate Body and Treaty Interpretation' in Giorgio Sacerdoti, Alan Yanovich, and Jan Bohanes (eds), The WTO at Ten – The Contribution of the Dispute Settlement System (CUP 2006)
Aguilar-Alvarez G, 'Written Advocacy' in Albert Jan Van den Berg (ed.), Arbitration Advocacy in Changing Times (KLI 2011)
Avila G, 'ICSID annulment procedure: A balancing exercise between correctness and finality' in Albert Jan van den Berg (ed.), Arbitration Advocacy in Changing Times, ICCA Congress Series, 2010 Rio Volume 15 (KLI 2011)
Bermann G, 'Writing the Award-An Arbitrator's Perspective' in Grant Hanessian and Lawrence Newman (eds), International Arbitration Checklists (2nd ed., Juris 2009)
Bernhardt R, 'Interpretation in international law' in Rudolf Bernhardt (ed.), Encyclopedia of Public International Law vol. 2 (North–Holland 1994)

Bhatia V, Candlin C, and Engberg J, 'Concepts, Contexts and Procedures in Arbitration Discourse' in Vijay Bhatia, Christopher Candlin and Jan Engberg (eds), Legal Discourse Across Cultures and Systems (HKUP 2008)

Bradney A, 'The Place of Empirical Research in the Law School Curriculum' in Peter Crane and Herbert Kritzer (eds), The Oxford Handbook of Empirical Legal Research (OUP 2010)

Braun T, 'Part V Chapter 21: Globalization: The Driving Force in International Investment Law' in Michael Waibel, Asha Kaushal, Kyo-Hwa Liz Chung and Claire Balchin (eds), The Backlash Against Investment Arbitration (KLI 2010)

Büthe T and Milner H, 'Bilateral Investment Treaties and Foreign Direct Investment: A Political Analysis.' in Karl Sauvant and Lisa Sachs (eds), The Effect of Treaties on Foreign Direct Investment Bilateral Investment Treaties, Double Taxation Treaties, and Investment Flows (OUP 2009)

Cantegriel J, 'The Final Award in *Mondev International v. United States of America*', in Guillermo Aguilar-Alvarez and Michael Reisman (eds), The Reason's Requirement in International Investment Arbitration (Nijhoff 2008)

Carton J, 'International Arbitration Culture and Global Governance' in Walter Mattli and Thomas Dietz (eds), International Arbitration and Global Governance: Contending Theories and Evidence (OUP 2014)

Casanovas P, 'Legal Electronic Institutions and ONTOMEDIA: Dialogue, Inventio, and Relational Justice Scenarios' in Pompeu Casanovas, Ugo Pagallo, Giovanni Sartor and Gianmaria Ajani (eds), AI Approaches to the Complexity of Legal Systems Comp lex Systems, the Semantic Web, Ontologies, Argumentation and Dialogue (Springer 2010)

Chang-fa Lo 'Difference and Relations Between Interpretation and Application of Treaties and the Possible Codification' in Chang-fa Lo (ed.), Treaty Interpretation Under the Vienna Convention on the Law of Treaties A New Round of Codification' (Springer 2017)

Clodfelter M, 'Written Proceedings in International Investment Arbitration' in Chiara Giorgetti (ed.), Litigating International Investment Disputes: A Practitioner's Guide (Brill/Nijhoff 2014)

Damme I van, 'Jurisdiction, Applicable Law, and Interpretation' in Daniel Bethlehem, Donald McRae Rodney Neufeld and Isabelle Van Damme (eds), The Oxford Handbook of International Trade Law (OUP 2009)

D'Aspremont J, 'The Multidimensional Process of Interpretation' in Andrea Bianchi, Daniel Peat, and Matthew Windsor (eds) Interpretation in International Law (OUP 2015)

Degano C, 'Indicators of Argumentation in Arbitration Awards: A Diachronic Perspective' in Vijay Kumar Bhatia, Christopher Candlin and Maurizio Gotti (eds), The Discourses of Dispute Resolution (Peter Lang 2010)

Digon R, '*The Decision on Liability in LG&E v. Argentina*' in Guillermo Aguilar-Alvarez and Michael Reisman (eds), The Reason's Requirement in International Investment Arbitration (Nijhoff 2008)

Donovan D, 'The Transnational Advocate' in Albert Jan van den Berg (ed.), Arbitration Advocacy in Changing Times, ICCA Congress Series, vol 15 (KLI 2011)

Dyzenhaus D and Taggart M, 'Reasoned Decisions and Legal Theory' in Douglas Edlin (ed.), Common Law Theory (CUP 2007)

Engberg J and Heller D, 'Vagueness and Indeterminacy in Law' in Vijay Bhatia, Christopher Candlin and Jan Engberg (eds), Legal Discourse Across Cultures and Systems (HKUP 2008)

Engel H, 'The Transatlantic Business Dialogue: The Perspective of the European Chemical Industry' in George Bermann, Matthias Herdegen and Peter Lindseth (eds), Transatlantic Regulatory Cooperation: Legal Problems and Political Prospects (OUP 2000)

García-Bolívar O, 'Economic Development at the Core of the International Investment Regime' in Chester Brown, Miles Kate (eds) Evolution in Investment Treaty Law and Arbitration (CUP 2011)

Georgiev G, 'The Award in *Saluka Investments v. Czech Republic*' in Guillermo Aguilar-Alvarez and Michael Reisman (eds), The Reason's Requirement in International Investment Arbitration (Nijhoff 2008)

Gill J, 'The Development of Legal Argument in Arbitration' in David Caron, Stephan Schill, Abby Smutny and Epaminontas Triantafilou (eds), Practising Virtue: Inside International Arbitration (OUP 2015)

Hérnandez G, 'Interpretative Authority and International Judiciary' in Andrea Bianchi, Daniel Peat, and Matthew Windsor (eds) Interpretation in International Law (OUP 2015)

Jennings R, 'The Differences Between Conducting a Case in the ICJ and in Ad Hoc Arbitration Tribunal – An Inside View' in Liber Amicorum Judge Shigeru Oda (Brill 2002)

Kaufmann-Kohler G, 'Interpretive Powers of the Free Trade Commission and the Rule of Law' in Emmanuel Gaillard and Frédéric Bachand (eds), Fifteen Years of NAFTA Chapter 11 Arbitration (Juris 2001)

Kaufmann-Kohler G, 'Is Consistency a Myth?' in Emmanuel Gaillard and Yas Banifatemi (eds), Precedent in International Arbitration 137 (Juris 2008)

Kaufmann-Kohler G, 'Non-Disputing State Submissions in Investment Arbitration: Resurgence of Diplomatic Protection' in Laurence Chazournes, Marcelo Kohen and Jorge Viñuales (eds), Diplomatic and Judicial Means of Dispute Settlement (Nijhoff 2012)

Kennedy D, 'The Rule of Law, Political Choices, and Development Common-Sense', in David Trubek and Alvaro Santos (eds), The New Law and Economic Development (CUP 2006)

Kingsbury B and Schill S, 'Public Law Concepts to Balance Investors' Rights with State Regulatory Actions in the Public Interest – The Concept of Proportionality' in Stephan Schill (ed.), International Investment Law and Comparative Public Law (OUP 2010)

Koniaris M, Anagnostopoulos I and Vassiliou Y, 'Network Analysis in the Legal Domain: A complex model for European Union legal sources' in Rinke Hoekstra (ed.), Legal Knowledge and Information Systems (IOSPBV 2014) 143

Koskenniemi M, 'General Principles: Reflections on Constructivist Thinking in International Law', in Martti Koskenniemi (eds), Sources of International Law (Ashgate 2000)

Krishan D, 'Thinking About BITs and BIT Arbitration: The Legitimacy Crisis that Never Was' in Todd Weiler and Freya Baetens (eds), New Directions in International Economic Law (Brill 2011)

Kurtz J, 'Building Legitimacy Through Interpretation in Investor-State Arbitration: On Consistency, Coherence, and the Identification of Applicable Law' in Zachary Douglas, Joost Pauwelyn and Jorge Viñuales (eds), The Foundations of International Investment Law: Bringing Theory into Practice (OUP 2014)

Landau T, 'Reasons for Reasons: The Tribunal's Duty in Investor-State Arbitration' in Albert Jan van den Berg (ed.), 50 Years of the New York Convention: ICCA International Arbitration Conference (KLI 2009)

Laurent Lévy, 'The Chairman's Role in the Arbitral Tribunal's Dynamics' in Bernard Hanotiau and Alexis Mourre (eds), Dossier IX: Players' Interaction in International Arbitration (Dossiers of the ICC Institute of World Business Law 2012) 67-85

Mairal H, 'Legitimate Expectations and Informal Administrative Representations' in Stephan Schill (ed.), International Investment Law and Comparative Public Law (OUP 2010)

Maupin J, '*The Awards in Wena Hotels Limited v. Arab Republic of Egypt*' in G Aguilar-Alvarez and Michael Reisman (eds), The Reason's Requirement in International Investment Arbitration (Nijhoff 2008)

Merkouris P, 'Interpretation is a Science, is an Art, is a Science', in Malgosia Fitzmaurice, Olufemi Elias and Panos Merkouris (eds), Treaty Interpretation and the Vienna Convention on the Law of Treaties: 30 Years on (Brill/Nijhoff 2010)

Mosk R, 'Deliberations of Arbitrators' in David Caron, Stephan Schill, Abby Smutny and Epaminontas Triantafilou (eds), Practising Virtue: Inside International Arbitration (OUP 2015)

Mosler H, 'General Principles of Law' in Rudolf Bernhardt (ed.), Encyclopedia of Public International Law, Vol. II (E-I) (North-Holland-1995)

Nelken D, 'Towards a Sociology of Legal Adaptation' (2001) in David Nelken and Johannes Feest (eds), Adapting Legal Cultures (Hart 2001)

Paulsson J, 'Awards – and Awards' in Andrea Bjorklund, Ian Laird and Sergey Ripinsky (eds), Investment Treaty Law Current Issues III (BIICL 2009)

Peters P, 'The Arbitrator and the Arbitration Procedure – Presiding Arbitrator, Deciding Arbitrator: Decision-Making in Arbitral Tribunals' in Christian Klausegger, Peter Klein, Florian Kremslehner, Alexandre Petsche and Nikolaus Pitkowitz (eds), Austrian Yearbook on International Arbitration 2011 (Manz'sche Verlags-Universitätsbuchhandlung 2011)

Rieke R, 'Argumentation in the Legal Process' in Robert Cox and Charles Arthur Willard (eds), Advances in Argumentation Theory and Research (SIUP 1982)

Schill S, 'Fair and Equitable Treatment, the Rule of Law, and Comparative Public Law', in Stephan Schill (ed.), International Investment Law and Comparative Public Law (OUP 2010)

Schill S, 'Conceptions of Legitimacy of International Arbitration' in David Caron, Stephan Schill, Abby Smutny and Epaminontas Triantafilou (eds), Practising Virtue: Inside International Arbitration (OUP 2015)

Schreuer C, 'Preliminary Rulings in Investment Arbitration', in Karl Sauvant (ed.), Appeals Mechanism in International Investment Disputes (OUP 2008)

Schreuer C, 'What Is a Legal Dispute?' in Isabelle Buffard, James Crawford, Alain Pellet and Stephan Wittich (eds), International Law Between Universalism and Fragmentation: Festschrift In Honour Of Gerhard Hafner (Nijhoff 2008)

Schreuer C, 'Interaction of International Tribunals and Domestic Courts in Investment Law' in Arthur Rovine (ed.), Contemporary Issues in International Arbitration and Mediation: The Fordham Papers, vol 4 (Brill/Nijhoff 2010)

Schreuer C, 'The Future of Investment Arbitration' in Mahnoush Arsanjani, Jacob Katz Cogan, Robert Sloane and Siegfried Wiessner (eds), Looking to the Future: Essays on International Law in Honor of W Michael Reisman (Brill/Nijhoff 2011)

Schreuer C, and Weiniger M, 'A Doctrine of Precedent', in Peter Muchlinski, Federico Ortino and Christoph Schreuer (eds), The Oxford Handbook of International Investment Law (OUP 2008)

Schultz T, 'Against Consistency in Investment Arbitration' in Zachary Douglas, Joost Pauwelyn and Jorge Viñuales (eds) KCL Law School Research Paper No 2013-3

Scobbie I, 'Rhetoric, Persuasion, and Interpretation in International Law' in Andrea Bianchi, Daniel Peat, and Matthew Windsor (eds) Interpretation in International Law (OUP 2015)

Segger M, 'Integrating Social and Economic Development and Environmental Protection in World Trade Law', in Markus Gehring and Marie-Claire Segger (eds), Sustainable Development in World Trade Law (KLI 2005)

Simmons B and Martin L, 'International Organizations and Institutions', in Handbook of International Relations (WalterCarlsnaesetal 2002)

Sipiorski E, 'Evidence and the Principle of Good Faith in Investment Arbitration: Finding Meaning in Public International Law' in Dário Vicente (ed.), Towards a Universal Justice? Putting International Courts and Jurisdictions into Perspective (Brill / Nijhoff 2016)

Slaughter A, 'Government Networks: The Heart of the Liberal Democratic Order' in Gregory Fox and Brad Roth (eds), Democratic Governance and International Law (CUP 2000)

Spaeth H, 'The Attitudinal Model' in Lee Epstein (ed.), Contemplating Courts (CQP 1995)

Sureda A, 'Precedent in Investment Treaty Arbitration' in Christina Binder, Ursula Kriebaum, August Reinisch and Stephan Wittich (eds), International Investment Law for the 21st Century: Essays in Honor of Christoph Schreuer (OUP 2009)

Teubner G, 'Global Bukowina': Legal Pluralism in the World Society, in Gunther Teubner (ed.), Global Law Without a State (Dartmouth Publishing 1997)

Trosborg A, 'Rhetorical Strategies in Arbitration Law', in Vijay Bhatia, Christopher Candlin, and Jan Engberg (eds), Legal Discourse Across Cultures and Systems (HKUP 2010)

Waibel M, 'Interpretive Communities in International Law' in Andrea Bianchi, Daniel Peat, and Matthew Windsor (eds) Interpretation in International Law (OUP 2015)

Waibel M, 'Empirical Research on International Arbitrators: Benefits and Challenges' in Stavros Brekoulakis, Julian Lew and Loukas Mistelis (eds), The Evolution of International Arbitration (Kluwer 2016)

Wälde T, 'The Specific Nature of Investment Arbitration', in Philippe Kahn and Thomas Wälde (eds), New Aspects of International Investment Law (Brill 2007)

Wälde T, 'Interpreting Investment Treaties: Experiences and Examples' in Christina Binder, Ursula Kriebaum, August Reinisch and Stephan Wittich (eds), International Investment Law for the 21st Century: Essays in Honour of Christoph Schreuer (OUP 2009)

Wälde T, 'Equality of Arms' in Investment Arbitration: Procedural Challenges' in Katia Yanacca Small (ed.), Arbitration under International Investment Agreements – A Guide to the Key Issues (OUP 2012)

Wongkaew T, 'The Transplantation of Legitimate Expectations in Investment Treaty Arbitration' in Shaheeza Lalani and Rodrigo Lazo (eds), The Role of the State in Investor-State Arbitration (Brill/Nijhoff 2014)

Zumbansen P, 'Transnational Comparisons: Theory and Practice of Comparative Law as a Critique of Global Governance', in Maurice Adams and Jacco Bomhoff (eds), Practice and Theory in Comparative Law (CUP 2012)

Journal Articles

Aaken A van, 'Fragmentation of International Law: The Case of International Investment Protection' (2008) USGL&Econ Working Paper No 2008-01, vol XVII 91.

Aguilar-Alvarez G and Park W, 'The New Face of Investment Arbitration: NAFTA Chapter 11' (2003) 28 YaleJIntlL 365

Ahdieh R, 'Between Dialogue and Decree: International Review of National Courts' (2004) 79 NYULRev 2019

Alpa G, 'General Principles of Law' (1994) 1(1) Annual Survey of International & Comparative Law

Alvarez J, 'A BIT on Custom' (2009) 42 New York University Journal of International Law and Policy 17

Anderson B, 'Current Views on Legal Reasoning: The Problem of Communication' (1997 15(2) Method: Journal of Lonergan Studies

Arsanjani M and Reisman M, 'Interpreting Treaties for the Benefit of Third Parties: The "Salvors Doctrine" and the Use of Legislative History in Investment Treaties' (2010) 104 AJIL 597

Arsanjani M and Reisman M, 'The United Nations and International Law Making' (2012) 362 RecdesCours 9

Ashenfelter O and Bloom D, 'Models of Arbitrator Behavior: Theory and Evidence' (1984) 74 AmEconRev 111

Azubuike EC, 'The Place of Treaties in International Investment' (2013) 19(1) Annual Survey of International & Comparative Law 155

Baird D and Weisberg R, 'Rules, Standards, and the Battle of the Forms: A Reassessment of § 2-207' (1982) 68 VaLRev 1217
Bartholomeusz L, 'The Amicus Curiae Before International Courts and Tribunals' (2005) 5 NSAIL 209
Bekker P, 'Recalibrating the Investment Treaty Arbitration System Through Non-Compartmentalized Legal Thinking' (2013) 55 HarvIntlLJ Online 1, 12
Benvenisti E, 'Reclaiming Democracy: The Strategic Uses of Foreign and International Law by National Courts' (2008) 102 AJIL 241
Berkowitz D, Pistor K and Richard J-F, 'Economic Development, Legality, and the Transplant Effect' (2003) 47 EurEconRev 165
Berman F Sir, 'International Treaties and British Statutes' (2005) 26 StatuteLRev 1
Berman P, 'Global Legal Pluralism' (2007) 80 SCalLRev 1155
Bernardini P, 'UNIDROIT Principles and International Investment Arbitration' (2014) 19(4) Uniform Law Review 561
Bingham T Lord, 'Reasons and Reasons for Reasons: Differences Between a Court Judgment and an Arbitral Award' (1988) 4 ArbIntl 141
Blackstone W T, 'Criteria of Adequacy for Judicial Reasoning' (1971) (53) Logique Et Analyse 14
Blankenburg E, 'Patterns of Legal Culture: The Netherlands Compared to Neighboring Germany' (1998) 46 AmJCompL 1
Bloom D, 'Empirical Models of Arbitrator Behaviour under Conventional Arbitration' (1986) 68 RevEcon&Stat 578
Bogdandy A von and Venzke I, 'Beyond Dispute: International Judicial Institutions as Lawmakers' (2012) 12 GLJ 979
Bogdandy A von and Venzke I, 'On the Functions of International Courts: An Appraisal in Light of the Burgeoning Public Authority' (2012) Amsterdam Law School Legal Studies Research Paper No 2012-69, 1
Bohoslavsky J and Justo J, 'The Conventionality Control of Investment Arbitrations: Enhancing Coherence Through Dialogue' (2013) 10 TDM 1
Bourdieu P, 'The Force of Law: Toward a Sociology of the Juridical Field' (1987) 38 HLJ 814
Brekoulakis S, 'Systemic Bias and the Institution of International arbitration: A New Approach to Arbitral Decision-Making' (2013) JIDS 553
Brekoulakis S, 'Collective Biases and International Arbitral Tribunals' (2013) QMUL School of Law Legal Studies Research Paper No. 131/2013
Brekoulakis S, 'International Arbitration Scholarship and the Concept of Arbitration Law' (2013) 36(4) FordhamIntlLJ
Brower C, 'Structure, Legitimacy and NAFTA's Investment Chapter' (2003) 36 VandJTransnatL 37
Burdeau G, 'Nouvelles perspectives pour l'arbitrage le contentieux economique interessant l'Etat' (1995) 1 RevArb 3
Burke-White W, 'International Legal Pluralism' (2003) 25 MichJIntlL 963
Cameron C and Lewis K, 'Rational Choice Attitudinalism? A Review of Epstein, Landes and Posner's The Behavior of Federal Judges: A Theoretical and Empirical Study of Rational Choice' (2015) NYUL&Econ Research Paper No. 15-15

Carbonneau T, 'Rendering Arbitral Awards with Reasons: The Elaboration of a Common Law of International Transactions' (1984) 23 ColumJTransnatlL 579

Caron D, 'Investor State Arbitration: Strategic and Tactical Perspectives on Legitimacy' (2008) 32 SuffolkTransnatlLJ 513

Caron D, 'International Courts and Tribunals: Their Roles Amidst a World of Courts' (2011) 26(1) ICSID Rev 3

Cass R, 'Judging: Norms and Incentives of Retrospective Decision-Making' (1995) 75 BULRev 941

Cassese S, 'Beyond Legal Comparison' (2012) AnnuarioDirComp 387

Catá Backer L, 'The Emerging Normative Structures of Transnational Law: Non-State Enterprises in Polycentric Asymmetric Global Orders' (2016) 31 BYU Journal Public International Law 1

Cate I, 'The Costs of Consistency: Precedent in Investment Treaty Arbitration' (2013) 51 ColumJTransnatlL 418

Claes M and Visser M De, 'Are You Networked Yet? On Dialogues in European Judicial Networks' (2012) 8 Utrecht LR 100

Cotterrell R, 'What Is Transnational Law?' (2012) 37(2) Journal of the American Bar Foundation Issue 500

Charney J, 'Is International Law Threatened by Multiple International Tribunals?' (1998) 271 RecdesCours 101

Charney J, 'Sources of International Law' (1998) 271 Recueil Des Cours 189

Cheng T, 'Precedent and Control in Investment Treaty Arbitration' (2006) 30 FordhamIntlLJ 1014

Choudhury B, 'Recapturing Public Power: Is Investment Arbitration's Engagement of the Public Interest Contributing to the Democratic Deficit?' (2008) 41 VandJTransnatL 775Cheng T and Trisotto R, 'Reasons and Reasoning in Investment Treaty Arbitration' (2008–2009) 32(2) SuffolkTransnatlLRev 409

Choudhury B, 'Recapturing Public Power: Is Investment Arbitration's Engagement of the Public Interest Contributing to the Democratic Deficit?' (2008) 41 VandJTransnatL 775

Clements C, 'Perception and Persuasion in Legal Argumentation: Using Informal Fallacies and Cognitive Biases to Win the War of Words' (2013) BYULRev 319

Coe J, 'Fair and Equitable Treatment in the NAFTA's Investment Chapter' (2002) 96 ASILPROC 17

Coe J, 'The State of Investor-State Arbitration-Some Reflections on Prof. Brower's Plea for Sensible Principles' (2005) 20(5) AmUIntlLRev 929

Coe J, 'Taking Stock of NAFTA Chapter 11 in Its Tenth Year: An Interim Sketch of Selected Themes, Issues, and Methods' (2003) 36 VandJTransnatL 1381

Commission J, 'Precedent in Investment Treaty Arbitration – A Citation Analysis of a Developing Jurisprudence' (2007) 24(2) JIntlArb 129

Commission J, 'Precedent in Investment Treaty Arbitration: The Empirical Backing' (2007) 4(5) TDM 1

Cooter R, 'The Objectives of Private and Public Judges' (1983) 41 Public Choice 107

Coulson R, 'The Decision-Making Process in Arbitration' (1990) 45(3) ArbJ 37

Cover R, 'Foreword: Nomos and Narrative' (1983) 97(1) HarvLRev 4

Crawford J, 'The ILC's Articles on Responsibility of States for Internationally Wrongful Acts: A Retrospect' (2002) 96 (4) AJIL 874

Cremades B, 'Good Faith in International Arbitration' (2012) 27(4) Am.U. L. Rev.

Crow S and Logan J, 'Arbitrators' Characteristics and Decision-Making Records, Gender of Arbitrators and Grievants, and the Presence of Legal Counsel as Predictors of Arbitral Outcomes (1994) 7 ERRJ 169

Dahlquist J, 'Beside the Point. On Obiter Dicta in Investment Treaty Arbitration' (2016) 1 ArbIntl 1.

D'Alterio E, 'From Judicial Comity to Legal Comity: A Judicial Solution to Global Disorder?' (2011) 9 IntlJConstL 394

Đajic´ S, 'Mapping the Good Faith Principle in International Investment Arbitration: Assessment of its Substantive and Procedural Value' (2012) 46 Zbornik Radova 207

Deakin S, 'Legal Evolution: Integrating Economic and Systemic Approaches' (2011) University of Cambridge Faculty of Law Research Paper No. 41/2011

Del Mar M, 'The Role and Value of Coherence in Theories of Legal Reasoning' (2017) 30(4) Ratio Juris

Dilts D and Elsea S, 'What Do Arbitrators Do: Empirical Results and Ethical Considerations in Interest Arbitration' (1992) 27(3) Indian Journal of Industrial Relations 279

Douglas Z, 'The Hybrid Foundations of Investment Treaty Arbitration' (2003) 74 BYIL 151

Douglas Z, 'Can a Doctrine of Precedent Be Justified in Investment Treaty Arbitration?' (2010) 25(1) ICSID Rev 104

Douglas Z, 'The Plea of Illegality in Investment Arbitration' (2014) 29(1) ICSID Rev 1

Drobak J and North D, 'Understanding Judicial Decision-Making: The Importance of Constraints on Non-Rational Deliberations' (2008) 26 WashUJL&P 131

Dryzek J, 'Rhetoric in Democracy: A Systemic Appreciation' (2010) 38(3) Political Theory 319

Dumberry P, 'The Role and Relevance of Awards in the Formation, Identification and Evolution of Customary Rules in International Investment Law' (2016) 33(3) JIntlArb 269

Dworkin R, 'Hard Cases' (1976) 88 HarvLRev 1057

Edwards L, 'The Convergence of Analogical and Dialectic Imaginations in Legal Discourse' (1996) 20 LegalStudF 7

Edwards H T, 'Public Misperceptions Concerning the 'Politics' of Judging: Dispelling Some Myths About the D.C. Circuit' (1985) 56 University of Colorado Law Review 619

Farber H and Bazerman M, 'The General Basis of Arbitrator Behavior: An Empirical Analysis of Conventional and Final-Offer Arbitration' (1986) 54 Econometrica 819

Fauchald O, 'The Legal Reasoning of ICSID Tribunals – An Empirical Analysis' (2008) 19 EJIL 301

Feteris E, 'A Survey of 25 Years of Research on Legal Argumentation' (1997) 11 Argumentation 355

Fischer-Lescano A and Teubner G, 'Regime-Collisions: The Vain Search for Legal Unity in the Fragmentation of Global Law' (2004) 25 MichJIntlL 999

Fitzmaurice G, 'The General Principles of International Law Considered from the Standpoint of the Rule of Law' (1957) 92(II) RecdesCours 5

Flader D, 'Aspects of Legal Argumentation' (2007) 4(1) TDM 1.

Fowler J, Johnson T, Spriggs J, Jeon S and Wahlbeck P, 'Network Analysis and the Law: Measuring the Legal Importance of Supreme Court Precedents' (2007) 15(3) Political Analysis 324

Franck S, 'Book Review: The Public International Law Regime Governing International Investment, by Jose E. Alvarez, The Hague: Hague Academy of International Law, 2011, pp. 502 (October 4, 2012)' (2012) Wash&LeeLRev Paper No 2012-34

Franck S, 'Development and Outcomes of Investment Treaty Arbitration' (2009) 50 HarvIntlLJ 435

Franck S, 'The Legitimacy Crisis in Investment Arbitration: Privatizing Public International Law Through Inconsistent Decisions' (2005) 73 FordhamLRev 1521

Franck S, 'The Nature and Enforcement of Investor Rights under Investment Treaties: Do Investment Treaties have a Bright Future?' (2005) 12 UCDJIntlL&Poly 47

Franck S, 'Empirically Evaluating Claims About Investment Treaty Arbitration' (2007) 86 NCLRev 1

Franck S D, van Aaken A, Freda J, Guthrie C and Rachlinski J, 'Inside the Arbitrator's Mind' (2017) 66 Emory Law Journal 1115

Friedmann W, 'The Uses of "General Principles" in the Development of International Law' (1963) 57 AJIL 279

Freund O, 'On Uses and Misuses of Comparative Law' (1974) 37 ModLRev 1

Friedmann W, 'Legal Philosophy and Judicial Lawmaking' (1961) 61(5) ColumLRev 821

Gaffney J, 'Going to Pieces Without Falling Apart: Wälde's Defence "Specialisation" in the Interpretation of Investment Treaties' (2012) 9 TDM 55

Gaillard E, 'Transnational Law: A Legal System or a Method of Decision-Making?' (2000) 17(1) ArbIntl 59

Gaillard E, 'The Sociology of International Arbitration' (2015) 31(1) ArbIntl 3 et seq.

Gaillard E and Yas Banifatemi, 'The Meaning of 'and' in Article 42(1), Second Sentence, of the Washington Convention: The Role of International Law in the ICSID Choice of Law Process' (2003) 18 ICSID Rev 375

Gantz D, 'The Evolution of FTA Investment Provisions: From NAFTA to the United States – Chile Free Trade Agreement' (2003) 19(4) AmUIntlLRev 679

Gerarld F, 'The General Principles of International Law Considered from the Standpoint of the Rule of Law' (1957) 92(II) RecdesCours 5

Gill J, 'Is There a Special Role for Precedent in Investment Arbitration?' (2010) 25(1) ICSID Rev 87

Gillies P and Selvadurai N, 'Reasoned Awards: How Extensive Must the Reasoning Be?' (2008) 74 Arbitration 125

Gilles C, 'Enhancing Judicial Reputation Through Legal Transplants – Estoppel Travels to France' (2012) 60(2) AmJCompL 383

Gilmore G, 'Security Law, Formalism and Article 9' (1968) 47 NebLRev 659

Ginsburg T, 'International Substitutes for Domestic Institutions: Bilateral Investment Treaties and Governance' (2006) University Illinois Law & Economics Research Paper No LE06-027, 28

Giorgetti C, 'Who Decides Who Decides in International Investment Arbitration?' (2013) 35 UPaJIntlL 431

Giraldo-Carrillo N, 'The "Repeat Arbitrators" Issue: A Subjective Concept' (2011) 19 Revista Colombiana de Derecho Internacional 75

Glass A, 'Interpretation/Application/Decision-Making' (2005) 25 AJLP 97

Goldman S, 'Voting Behavior on the United States Courts of Appeals, 1961–1964' (1966) 60 AmPolSciRev 374–383

Gourgourinis A, 'The Distinction Between Interpretation and Application of Norms in International Adjudication' (2011) 2(1) JIDS 31

Greenwood L and Baker M, 'Getting a Better Balance on International Arbitration Tribunals' (2012) 28(4) ArbIntl 653

Grossman N, 'Legitimacy and International Adjudicative Bodies' (2009–2010) 41 GeoWashIntlLRev 107

Guillaume G, 'The Use of Precedent by International Judges and Arbitrators' (2011) 2(1) JIDS 5

Guthrieetal C, 'Inside the Judicial Mind' (2001) 86 CornellLRev 777

Gutteridge H C, 'Comparative Law and the Law of Nations' (1944) 21(1) BYCL 5

Guzman A, 'Why LDCs Sign Treaties That Hurt Them: Explaining the Popularity of Bilateral Investment Treaties' (1998) 38 VaJIntlL 639

Haddad M, 'Adequacy of Reasons in Arbitral Awards' (2008) 5 Macquarie J. Bus. L. 353

Hanessian G, 'General Principles of Law in the Iran-U.S. Claims Tribunal' (1989) 27 ColumJTransnatlL 309

Hart H, 'Positivism and the Separation of Law and Morals' (1958) 71 HarvLRev 593

Helfer L and Slaughter A, 'Toward a Theory of Effective Supranational Adjudication' (1997) 107 YaleLJ 273

Henckels C, 'Indirect Expropriation and the Right to Regulate: Revisiting Proportionality Analysis and the Standard of Review in Investor-State Arbitration' (2012) 15 JIntlEconL 223

Hogg P and Bushell A, 'Charter Dialogue between Courts and Legislatures, (Or Perhaps the Charter of Rights Isn't Such a Bad Thing after All)' (1997) 35(1) Osgoode-HallLJ 75

Horn P, 'A Matter of Appearances: Arbitrator Independence and Impartiality in ICSID Arbitration' (2014) 11 (2) JLB 249

Huhn W, 'The Use and Limits of Syllogistic Reasoning in Briefing Cases' (2001) 42(3) SantaClaraLRev 813

Infantino M, 'International Arbitral Awards' Reasons: Surveying the State-of-the-Art in Commercial and Investment International Dispute Settlements' (2014) 5 JIDS 175

Jalet F F, 'The Quest for the General Principles of Law Recognised by Civilised Nations' (1963) 10 UCLA 1041

Jans J, ''Proportionality Revisited' (2000) 27 LIEI 239

Jenks W, 'The Conflict of Law-Making Treaties' (1953) 30 BYIL 401

Kahn J, 'Striking NAFTA Gold: Glamis Advances Investor-State Arbitration' (2009) 33(1) FordhamIntlLJ 101
Kahn-Freund O, 'On Uses and Misuses of Comparative Law' (1974) 37 ModLRev 1
Kapeliuk D, 'Repeat Appointment Factor: Exploring Decision Patterns of Elite Investment Arbitrators' (2010–2011) 96 CornellLRev 47
Kapeliuk D, 'Collegial Games: Analyzing the Effect of Panel Composition on Outcome in Investment Arbitration' (2012) 31 Rev Litig 267
Kaplow L, 'Rules Versus Standards: An Economic Analysis' (1992) 42 DukeLJ 557
Kaufmann-Kohler G, 'Arbitral Precedent: Dream, Necessity or Excuse? – The 2006 Freshfields Lecture' (2007) 23(3) ArbIntl 357
Keer S and Naimark R, 'Arbitrators Do Not "Split the Baby": Empirical Evidence from International Business Arbitrations' (2001) 18 J. Int'l Arb. 573
Kennedy D, 'Form and Substance in Private Law Adjudication' (1976) 89 HarvLRev 1685
Khalil M, 'Treatment of Foreign Investment in Bilateral Investment Treaties' (1992) 7 ICSID Rev 339
Klabbers J, 'Re-inventing the Law of Treaties: The Contribution of the EC Courts' (1999) 30 NYIL 45
Kishoiyian B, 'The Utility of Bilateral Investment Treaties in the Formulation of Customary International Law' (1994) 14 NJILB 327
Klein-Bronfman M, 'Fair and Equitable Treatment an Evolving Standard' (2006) 10 MaxPlankUNYB 609
Kleinberg J, 'Authoritative Sources in a Hyperlinked Environment' (1999) 46(5) JACM 604
Kock C, Defining Rhetorical argumentation' (2013) 46(4) Ph&Rh 437
Koh H, 'Transnational Legal Process' (1996) 75 NebLRev181
Koh H, 'Jefferson Memorial Lecture – Transnational Legal Process after September 11th' (2004) 22(3) BerkeleyJIntlL 337
Koszowski M, 'The Scope of Application of Analogical Reasoning in Precedential Law' (2016) 37 Liverpool Law Rev 19
Krisch N and Kingsbury B, 'Introduction, Global Governance and Global Administrative Law in the International Legal Order' (2006) 17 EJIL 1
Lalive P, 'On the Reasoning of International Arbitral Awards' (2010) 1 JIDS 55
Lalive P, 'Threats to International Investment Arbitration' (1986) 1(1) ICSID Rev 26
Landau T, 'Luncheon Address: Advocacy in International Arbitration' (2011) 5 WAMR 351
Langer M, 'From Legal Transplants to Legal Translations: The Globalization of Plea Bargaining and the Americanization Thesis in Criminal Procedure' (2004) 45 HarvIntlLJ 1
Leonhardsen E, 'Looking for Legitimacy: Exploring Proportionality Analysis in Investment Treaty Arbitration' (2011) 3(1) JIDS 95
Levine E, 'Amicus Curiae in International Investment Arbitration: The Implications of an Increase in Third-Party Participation' (2011) 29 BerkeleyJIntlL 200
Lévy L, 'L'interprétation arbitrale' (2013) Revue de l'arbitrage, 861-952

Linderfalk U, 'Is the Hierarchical Structure of Arts 31 and 32 of the Vienna Convention Real or Not? Interpreting the Rules of Interpretation' (2007) 54 NILR 133

Linderfalk U, 'Is Treaty Interpretation an Art or a Science? International Law and Rational Decision Making' (2015) 26 EJIL 169

Lowenfeld A, 'Investment Agreements and International Law' (2003) 42 ColumJTransnatlL 123

Lupu Y and Voeten E, 'Precedent in International Courts: A Network Analysis of Case Citations by the European Court of Human Rights' (2012) 42 BrJPoliticalSci 413

Lyke S, 'Brown Abroad: An Empirical Analysis of Foreign Judicial Citation and the Metaphor of Cosmopolitan Conversation' (2012) 45 VandJTransnatL 83

Maniruzzaman M, 'The Concept of Good Faith in International Investment Disputes – The Arbitrator's Dilemma' (2012) 89 Amicus Curiae 16

Markesinis B, 'Judicial Style and Judicial Reasoning in England and Germany' (2000) 59(2) The Cambridge Law Journal 294

Maupin J, 'Public and Private in International Investment Law: An integrated Systems Approach' 54(2) Virginia Journal of International Law 367

Mbengue M, 'Rules of Interpretation (Article 32 of the Vienna Convention on the Law of Treaties)' (2016) 31(2) ICSID Rev

McLachlan C, 'The Principle of Systemic Integration and Article 31(3)(c) of the Vienna Convention' (2005) 54 ICLQ 279

McLachlan C, 'Investment Treaties and General International Law' (2008) 57 ICLQ 361

Mitsi M, Spiteri-Gonzi E, Wiliński P, Alvarez G, van Hoolwerff T, Koutouzi K, Lavranos N, Mena Verdegay A, Błasikiewicz B, 'A Response to the Criticism against ISDS by EFILA' (2016) 33(1) JIntlArb

Nelson N and Kim S M, 'A Model of Arbitral Decision Making: Facts, Weights, and Decision Elements' (2008) 47(2) Industrial Relations: A Journal of Economy and Society 266

Nelson N and Earl M, Curry, J, 'Arbitrator Characteristics and Arbitral Decisions' (1981) 20 Industrial Relations: A Journal of Economy and Society 3

Newman L and Zaslowsky D, 'The Party-Appointed Arbitrator Dialectic' (2009) 242(20) International Litigation 2

Oellers-Frahm K, 'Multiplication of International Courts and Tribunals and Conflicting Jurisdictions – Problems and Possible Solutions' (2001) 5 MaxPlanckUNYB 67

Ogus A, 'The Economic Basis of Legal Culture: Networks and Monopolization' (2002) 22(3) OJLS 419

Ortino F, 'Legal Reasoning of International Investment Tribunals: A Typology of Egregious Failures' (2012) 3 (1) JIDS 31

Örücü E, 'Law as Transposition' (2002) 51(2) ICLQ 205

Palmer V V, 'From Lerotholi to Lando: Some Examples of Comparative Law Methodology' (2004) 4(2) Global Jurist Frontiers 16

Paparinskis M, 'Investment Treaty Arbitration and the (New) Law of State Responsibility' (2013) 24(2) EJIL 617

Parra A, 'Principles Governing Foreign Investment as Reflected in National Investment Codes' (1992) 7(2) ICSID Rev 428

Paulsson J, 'Metaphors Maxims, and Other Mischief the Freshfields Arbitration Lecture' (2014) 30(4) ArbIntl 615

Paulsson J, 'Arbitration in Three Dimensions' (2011) 60(2) ICLQ 291

Paulsson J, 'International Arbitration and the Generation of Legal Norms: Treaty Arbitration and International Law' (2006) 3(5) TDM 11

Pellet A, 'The Case Law of the ICJ in Investment Arbitration' (2013) 28(2) ICSID Rev

Peter H and Alison B 'Charter Dialogue Between Courts and Legislatures, (Or Perhaps the Charter of Rights Isn't Such a Bad Thing after All' (1997) 35 OsgoodeHallLJ 75

Ponce J and Cevallos R, 'Good Faith in Investment Arbitration' (2016) 5 TDM

Ponzetto G and Fernandez P, 'Case Law Versus Statute Law: An Evolutionary Comparison' (2008) 37 JLS 379

Posner E, 'Standards, Rules, and Social Norms' (1997-1998) 21 HarvJL&PubPol'y 101

Posner R, 'Judicial Behavior and Performance an Economic Approach' (2005) 32 FlaStULRev 1259

Prakken H, 'A Formal Model of Adjudication Dialogues.' (2008) 16(3) AI&L 305

Pritchett C H, 'Divisions of Opinion among Justices of the U.S. Supreme Court 1939–1941' (1941) 35 AmPolSciRev 890

Radin M, 'Reconsidering the Rule of Law' (1989) 69 BULRev 781

Rau A, 'Integrity in Private Judging' (1997) 38 TLR 485

Ranjan P, 'Using the Public Law Concept of Proportionality to Balance Investment Protection and Regulation in International Investment Law: A Critical Appraisal' (2014) 3(3) CJICL 853

Reed L, 'The 2013 Hong Kong International Arbitration Centre Kaplan Lecture – Arbitral Decision-Making: Art, Science or Sport?' (2013) 30(2) JIntlArb 85

Reisman M, 'Canute Confronts the Tide: States versus Tribunals and the Evolution of the Minimum Standard in Customary International Law' (2015) 30(3) ICSID Rev 616

Reisman M, '"Case Specific Mandates" Versus "Systemic Implications": How Should Investment Tribunals Decide? – The Freshfields Arbitration Lecture' (2013) 29(2) ArbIntl 131

Risse T, 'Let's Argue! Communicative Action in World Politics' (2000) 54 IO 1

Roberts A, 'Clash of Paradigms: Actors and Analogies Shaping the Investment Treaty System' (2013) 107 AJIL 45

Roberts A, 'Triangular Treaties: The Nature and Limits of Investment Treaty Rights' (2015) 56 (2) HarvIntlLJ 353

Rodgers M, 'Bilateral Investment Treaties and Arbitration: An Argument and a Proposal for the ICSID's Implementation of a System of Binding Precedent' (2008) 5(3) TDM 24

Rogers C A, 'The Politics of International Investment Arbitrators' (2013) 12 SantaClaraIntlLRev, Penn State Law Research Paper No. 52-2013

Rogers C, 'The Vocation of the International Arbitrator' (2005) 20(5) AmUIntlLRev 957

Rosenfeld F, 'The Trend from Standards to Rules in International Investment Law and Its Impact upon the Interpretive Power of Arbitral Tribunals' (2014) 108 The Effectiveness of International Law 191

Sacerdoti G, 'Bilateral Investment Treaties and Multilateral Instruments on Investment Protection' (1997) 269 RecdesCours 251
Sacerdoti G, 'Precedent in the Settlement of International Economic Disputes: The WTO and Investment Arbitration Models', Bocconi Legal Studies Research Paper No. 1931560 1
Salacuse J, 'The Treatification of International Investment Law' (2007) 13 Law & Bus. REV. AM. 155
Salacuse J, 'The Emerging Global Regime for Investments' (2015) 51(2) HarvIntlLJ 427
Salacuse J and Sullivan N, 'Do BITS Really Work?: An Evaluation of Bilateral Investment Treaties and Their Grand Bargain' (2005) 46 HarvIntlLJ 67
Saldarriaga A, 'Investment Awards and the Rules of Interpretation of the Vienna Convention: Making Room for Improvement' (2013) 28(1) ICSID Rev 97
Sanders A, 'Of All Things Made in America Why Are We Exporting the Penn Central Test?', (2010) NJILB 30
Schachter O, 'The Relation of Law, Politics and Action in the United Nations' (1963) 109 HagueRec 169
Schatz S, 'The Effect of the Annulment Decisions In *Amco v. Indonesia* and *Klöckner v. Cameroon* on the Future of the International Centre for the Settlement of Investment Disputes' (1988) 3(2) AmUIntlLRev 481
Schill S, 'Revisiting a Landmark': Indirect Expropriation and Fair and Equitable Treatment in the ICSID Case Tecmed' (2006) 3 TDM 10
Schill S, 'Cross-Regime Harmonization through Proportionality Analysis: The Case of International Investment Law, the Law of State Immunity and Human Rights' (2012) 27(1) ICSID Rev 87
Schill S, 'Deference in Investment Treaty Arbitration: Reconceptualising the Standard of Review' (2012) 3(3) JIDS
Schlag P, 'Rules and Standards' (1985) 33 UCLA L Rev 379.
Schneiderman D, 'Judicial Politics and International Investment Arbitration: Seeking an Explanation for Conflicting Outcomes.' (2010) 30 NJILB 383.
Schreuer C, 'What Is a Legal Dispute?' (2009) 6 TDM 1.
Schreuer C, 'Interaction of International Tribunals and Domestic Courts in Investment Law' (2010) 4 Contemporary Issues in International Arbitration and Mediation: The Fordham Papers 71–94
Schultz T, 'The Three Pursuits of Dispute Settlement' (2010) 1 CYArb 227
Schultz T, 'The Concept of Law in Transnational Arbitral Legal Orders and some of its Consequences', 2(1) JIDS (2011) 59
Schultz T, 'Arbitral Decision-Making: Legal Realism and Law & Economics' (2015) King's College London Dickson Poon School of Law Legal Studies Research Paper Series: Paper No. 2015-28
Schultz T, and Dupont C, 'Investment Arbitration: Promoting the Rule of Law or Over – Empowering Investors? A Quantitative Empirical Study' (2014) King's College London Dickson Poon School of Law Legal Studies Research Paper Series, paper no. 2014-16-23.
Schultz T, and Kovacs R, 'The Law Is What the Arbitrator Had for Breakfast: How Income, Reputation, Justice, and Reprimand Act as Determinants of Arbitrator

Behaviour' (2014) King's College London Dickson Poon School of Law Legal Studies Research Paper Series: Paper No. 2014-36.
Schultz T, 'Arbitral Decision-Making: Legal Realism and Law & economics' (2015) King's College London Dickson Poon School of Law Legal Studies Research Paper Series: Paper No. 2015-28.
Schwebel M, 'The Influence of Bilateral Investment Treaties on Customary International Law' (2004) 98 ASIL PROC 27
Sclesinger R, 'Research on General Principles of Law Recognised by Civilised Nations' (1957) 51(4) The AJIL 734
Shaffer G and Trachtman J, 'Interpretation and Institutional Choice at the WTO' (2011) 52 VaJIntlL 103
Silveira L, 'Discovery and Justification of Judicial Decisions: Towards More Precise Distinctions in Legal Decision-Making' (2014) Law and Method
Simma B, 'Universality of International Law from the Perspective of a Practitioner' (2009) 20(2) EJIL 265
Slaughter A, 'The Real New World Order' (1997) 76 Foreign Affairs 183
Slaughter A, 'A Global Community of Courts' (2003) 44 HarvIntlLJ 191
Spears S, 'The Quest for Policy Space in a New Generation of International Investment Agreements' (2010) 13(3) JIEL 1037
Stein T, 'Jurisprudence and Jurists' Prudence: The Iranian-Forum Clause Decisions of the Iran-U.S. Claims Tribunal' (1984) 78(1) AJIL 32
Sullivan K, 'Foreword: The Justices of Rules and Standards' (1992–1993) 106 HarvLRev 22
Tai-Heng C, 'Precedent and Control in Investment Treaty Arbitration' (2006) 30 FordhamIntlLJ 1014
Tai-Heng Cheng and Robert Trisotto, 'Reasons and Reasoning in Investment Treaty Arbitration' (2008–2009) 32(2) Suffolk Transnational Law Review 409, 414
Tienhaara K, 'Third Party Participation in Investment-Environment Disputes: Recent Developments' (2007) 16 RECIEL 230
Timmermans C, 'The European Union's Judicial System' (2004) 41(2) CMLRev 393
Tordesillas A, 'Justice, Argumentation and Ancient Rhetoric' (1990) 4(1) Argumentation 109
Trachtman J, 'The Domain of WTO Dispute Resolution' (1999) 40 HarvIntlLJ 333
Twining W, 'Social Science and Diffusion of Law' (2005) 32 JL&Soc'y 203
Vadi V, 'Towards Arbitral Path Coherence & Judicial Borrowing: Persuasive Precedent in Investment Arbitration' (2008) 5(3) TDM 14
Vadi V, 'Critical Comparisons: The Role of Comparative Law in Investment Treaty Arbitration' (2010) 39 DJILP 89
Vadi V, 'The Migration of Constitutional Ideas to Regional and International Economic Law: The Case of Proportionality' (2015) 35(3) NJILB 557
Van Harten G, 'Five Justifications for Investment Treaties: A Critical Discussion' (2010) 2 Trade L and Development 19
Vázquez-Orta I, 'Authoritative Intervention in Legal Discourse: A Genre-Based Study of Judgements and Arbitration Awards' (2013) RESLA 9hv1
Vifluales J, 'Amicus Intervention in Investor-State Arbitration' (2007) 61 DispResolJ 72

Voigt C, 'The Role of General Principles in International Law and Their Relationship to Treaty Law' (2008) 121 NR Retfærd Årgang

Waibel M, 'Demystifying the Art of Interpretation' (2011) 22(2) EJIL 571

Wälde T, 'Investment Arbitration under the Energy Charter Treaty – From Dispute Settlement to Treaty Implementation' (1996) 12 (6) ArbIntl 429

Wälde T, 'Stabilizing international investment Commitments: International Law Versus Contract Interpretation' (1996) 31 TexIntlLJ 215

Walker G, and Daniels S, 'Argument and Alternative Dispute Resolution Systems' (1995) 9 Argumentation 693

Walker H, 'Modern Treaties of Friendship, Commerce and Navigation' (1957–1958) 42 Minn LR 805 307

Weidemaier M, 'Toward a Theory of Precedent in Arbitration' (2010) 51 Wm&MaryLRev 1895

Wiener J, 'Something borrowed for something blue: Legal transplants and the evolution of global environmental law' (2001) 27 EcologyLQ 1295

Wilson H, 'The Use and Limits of Syllogistic Reasoning in Briefing Cases' (2001) 42(3) SantaClaraLRev 813

Wróblewski J, 'Legal Decision and Its Justification' (1971) 14(53) *Logique et Analyse* 409

Yuan J, Yao L, Hao Z and Wang Y, 'Multi-party Dialogue Games for Dialectical Argumentation' (2012) 7(10) JC 25

Zhengruia H and Xiaoyu lI, 'Discourse of International Commercial Arbitration: The Case of Mainland China' (2011) 43 JPragmat 1380

Zumbansen P, 'Defining the Space of Transnational Law: Legal Theory, Global Governance & Legal Pluralism' (2011) Osgoode CLPE Research Paper No. 21/2011 1.

Online Resources

Aristophanes, 'The Clouds' <http://classics.mit.edu/Aristophanes/clouds.html> (accessed 3 October 2018)

Aristotle, Rhetoric (W. Rhys Roberts Tr) <http://rhetoric.eserver.org /aristotle/rhet1 -1.html #1354a> (accessed 5 December 2018)

Aristotle, 'Posterior Analytics' <http://classics.mit.edu/Aristotle/posterior.html> (accessed 4 January 2018)

Aristotle, 'Prior Analytics' <http://classics.mit.edu/Aristotle/prior.1.i.html> (accessed 3 January 2018)

Bassiouni M C, 'A Functional Approach to General Principles of International Law' (1990) 11 MichJIntlL 768 <http://repository.law.umich.edu/mjil /vol11/iss 3/3> (accessed 10 June 2018)

Cameron C M and Kornhauser L A, 'Rational Choice Attitudinalism? A Review of Epstein, Landes and Posner's The Behavior of Federal Judges: A Theoretical and Empirical Study of Rational Choice' (2015). NYU Law and Economics Research

Paper No. 15-15 <http://ssrn.com/abstract = 2640600> (accessed 10 June 2018)

Cosbey A, 'Investment and Sustainable Development: A Guide to the Use and Potential of International Investment Agreements' (2004) International Institute for Sustainable Development, 38 <https://www.iisd.org/pdf/2004/investment_invest_and_sd.pdf> (accessed 15 March 2018)

Dalhuisen J, 'Legal Reasoning and Powers of International Arbitrators' (2015) <SSRN: https://ssrn.com/abstract = 2393705> (accessed 10 September 2018)

Drahozal C, 'A Behavioral Analysis of Private Judging' (Paper prepared for a symposium on 'The Coming Crisis in Mandatory Arbitration: New Perspectives and Possibilities' Duke University School of Law (2002) <http://papers.ssrn.com/sol3/ papers.cfm? abstract_id= 380021> (accessed on 11 May 2018)

Eberhardt P and Olivet C, 'Profiting from Injustice: How Law Firms, Arbitrators and Financiers are Fuelling an Investment Arbitration Boom' (2012) Brussels/Amsterdam: Corporate Europe Observatory and the Transnational Institute <https://www.tni.org/files/download/ profitingfrominjustice.pdf> (accessed 10 June 2018)

FTC, 'Statement of the Free Trade Commission on non-disputing party participation' <http://www.state.gov/documents/organization/38791.pdf> (accessed 8 November 2018)

Gourgourinis A, 'The Nature of Investor's Rights under Investment Treaties: A Rejoinder to Martins Paparinskis' (EJIL 2013) <http://www.ejiltalk.org/the-nature-of-investors-rights-under-investment-treaties-a-rejoinder-tomartins-paparinskis/> (accessed 4 Mar. 2018)

Gupta R and Limond K, 'Who is the Most Influential Arbitrator in the World?' (GAR, 2016) <http://globalarbitrationreview.com/journal/article/34478/who-influential- arbitrator-world> (accessed 20 May 2018)

Hafner-Burton E, Steinert-Threlkeld Z, and Victor D, 'Transparency of Investor-State-Arbitration' (2013) <http://irworkshop.sites.yale.edu/sites/default/ files/HafnerBurton_YaleIR_9.25.pdf> (accessed 11 May 2018)

ICSID statistics <http://documents.worldbank.org/curated/en/2013/01/1880 1881/icsid-caseload-statistics> (accessed 4 April 2018)

John McArthur, 'Growing Pains: Building Arbitration's Legitimacy Through Everyday Arbitral Decisionmaking' (2010) Lenox Institute of Water Technology 43–44. <http://works.bepress.com/john_mcarthur/3/> (accessed 3 June 2018)

Kingsbury B and Schill S, 'Investor-State Arbitration as Governance: Fair and Equitable Treatment, Proportionality and the Emerging Global Administrative Law' (2009) Public Law & Legal Theory Research Paper Series Working Paper <No. 09-46, 21 http://ssrn.com/abstract = 1466980> (accessed 4 July 2018)

Mann H, 'International Institute for Sustainable Development and World Wildlife Fund, 'Private Rights, Public Problems: A Guide to NAFTA's Controversial Chapter on Investor Rights' (2001) 46 <http://www.iisd.org/pdf/trade_citizensguide.pdf> (accessed 2 September 2018)

Neuberger D, 'Judgment and Judgments – The Art of Forming and Writing Judicial Decisions' Denning Society Lecture 2017 <https://www.lincolnsinn.org.uk/images/pdf/denning/denningsocietylecture2017.pdf> (accessed 1 Sep. 2018)

OECD, 'Improving the System of Investor-State Dispute Settlement: An Overview' (12 December 2005) <https://www.oecd.org/investment/internatio nalinvestment agreements/35808448.pdf> (accessed 28 May 2018)

Orsinger R, 'The Role of Reasoning and Persuasion in Legal Argumentation' (2013) <http://www.orsinger.com/PDFFiles/constructing-a-persuasive-argument-version-three.pdf> (accessed 2 October 2018)

Oxford dictionaries <www.oxforddictionnaries.com> (accessed 10 May 2018)

Reinisch A, 'The Role of Precedent in ICSID Arbitration' (2008) 1 <http://investm entarbitration.univie.ac.at/fileadmin/user_upload/int_beziehungen/Personal/Publikationen_Reinisch/role_precedents_icsid_arbitrationaayb_2008.pdf> (accessed 8 March 2018)

Rogers C, 'The Ethics of International Arbitrators' Bocconi Legal Studies Research Paper No. 08/01 <http://ssrn.com/abstract=10O81436> (accessed 20 June 2018)

Schill S, 'From Sources to Discourse: Investment Treaty Jurisprudence as the New Custom?' <http://www.biicl.org/files/5630_ stephan_schill.pdf> (accessed 22 July 2018)

Schreuer C, 'The Relevance of Public International Law in International Commercial Arbitration: Investment Dispute' <http://www.univie.ac.at/intlaw/wordpress/pdf/81_csunpublpaper_1.pdf> (accessed 24 February 2018)

Schultz T, 'Against Consistency in Investment Arbitration' King's College London Law School Research Paper No 2013-3, 7 <http://ssrn.com/abstract=2318358> (accessed 2 April 2018)

Spiller P and Gely R, 'Strategic Judicial Decision Making' (2007) NBER Working Paper No. 13321 <http://www.nber.org/papers/w13321> (accessed 2 October 2018)

Van Harten G, 'The (Lack of) Women Arbitrators in Investment Treaty Arbitration' (2012) Columbia FDI Perspectives No 59 <https://academiccommons.colum bia.edu/doi/10.7916/D8HT2XHM> (accessed 6 February 2018)

Van Harten G, 'Fairness and Independence in Investment Arbitration: A Critique of Susan Franck's "Development and Outcomes of Investment Treaty Arbitration"' (2011) <http://ssrn.com/abstract=1740031> (accessed 10 June 2018)

Van Harten G, 'The Public-Private Distinction in the International Arbitration of Individual Claims Against the State' (2009) 29 <http://ssrn.com/abstract=146 1125> (accessed 9 January 2018)

Veznke I, 'The Role of International Courts as Interpreters and Developers of the Law Working Out the Jurisgenerative Practice of Interpretation' (2011) Loyola of Los Angeles International and Comparative Law Review, Forthcoming, 7 <http://ssrn.com/abstract= 1868423> (accessed 3 November 2018)

Yaraslau K, 'Counterclaims in Investor-State Arbitration' (2011) LSE Law, Society and Economy Working Papers 8/2011 London School of Economics and Political Science Law Department 24 <http://ssrn.com /abstract=1891935> (accessed 28 February 2018)

Zumbansen P, 'Defining the Space of Transnational Law: Legal Theory, Global Governance & Legal Pluralism; (2011) Osgoode CLPE Research Paper No. 21/2011 <http://ssrn.com/abstract=1934044> (accessed 6 August 2018)

Conference Papers

Drahozal C, 'A Behavioral Analysis of Private Judging' (Paper prepared for a symposium on 'The Coming Crisis in Mandatory Arbitration: New Perspectives and Possibilities' Duke University School of Law, 2002) <http://papers.ssrn.com/sol3/papers.cfm?abstract_id= 380021> (accessed 11 May 2018)

Escobar A, The *Use of ICSID Precedents by ICSID and ICSID Tribunals*, at The British Institute of International and Comparative Law (BIICL) Annual Meeting panel, 'Used and Abused: The Role of Precedent in Investment Protection Arbitration' (19 June 2005)

Gaillard E, 'Annulment of ICSID Awards' (a Joint IAI-ASIL Conference Bern, 2004) <http://archive-ouverte.unige.ch/unige:14377> (accessed 15 August 2018)

Kraus M, 'Arguing or reasoning? Argumentation in rhetorical OSSA Conference Archive Paper 97 <http://scholar.uwindsor.ca/cgi/viewcontent. cgi?article= 2067& context=ossaarc hive> (accessed 17 January 2018)

Mclachlan C, 'Fragmentation and Custom in Investment Treaty Law' (2007) BIICL Investment Treaty Forum

Ortino F, 'Refining the Content and Role of Investment 'Rules' and 'Standards': A New Approach to International Investment Treaty-Making' (2012) Society of International Economic Law (SIEL), 3rd Biennial Global Conference 3 <http://ssrn.com/abstract= 2181426> (accessed 21 March 2018).

Schill S, 'The Sixth Path: Reforming Investment Law from Within' (2014) Fourth Biennial Global Conference of the Society of International Economic Law (SIEL) Working Paper. No 2014/02

Lloyd, 'Globalization and Harmonization of the Basic Notions in International Arbitration' (1997) 13 Int'lConstrLRev. 144

Reports

Draft Articles on the Law of Treaties with commentaries 1966, ILC Yb. 1966, II, 177 as part of Report of the International Law Commission on the work of its eighteenth session (4 May–19 July 1966) (ILC Draft Articles (1966)), Doc A/6309/Rev.1 (1966) ILC Yb. II, 218

European Commission, 'Online public consultation on investment protection and investor-to-state dispute settlement (ISDS) in the Transatlantic Trade and Investment Partnership Agreement (TTIP)' Report (13 January 2015)

European Commission Press Release, 'Investment Court System for TTIP and other EU trade and investment negotiations' (16 September 2015) <http://europa.eu/rapid/press-release_IP-15-5651_ en.htm> (accessed 21 April 2018)

'Fragmentation of International Law: Difficulties Arising from Diversification and Expansion of International Law' Report of the Study Group of the International Law Commission finalised by Martti Koskenniemi, United Nations (2006) UN Doc. A/CN/4/L.68

Higgins R, 'Speech on the Occasion of the Opening of the Judicial Year' European Court of Human Rights Annual Report 2009 Rosalyn Higgins, 'Speech on the Occasion of the Opening of the Judicial Year' (2009) <http://www.echr.coe.int/ Documents/ Annual_report_ 2009_ENG.pdf> (accessed 6 December 2018)

ICSID, Documents Concerning the Origin and Formulation of the Convention (1970) (History vol II)

IISD Model International Agreement on Investment for Sustainable Development (2005) <http://www.italaw.com/sites/default/files/archive/ita 1027.pdf> (accessed 30 September 2018)

North American Free Trade Agreement 'Notes of Interpretation of Certain Chapter 11 Provisions' (31 July 2001) <http://www.sice.oas.org/tpd/nafta /Commission/ CH11understand ing_e.asp accessed> (5 September 2018)

Report of the Executive Directors on the Convention on the Settlement of Investment Disputes between States and Nationals of Other States <https://icsid.world bank.org/ICSID/StaticFiles/basicdoc/partB.htm> (accessed 16 March 2018)

'Report of the International Law Commission covering the work of Its Twelfth Session' (1960) 2 Yearbook of the International Law Commission 145, UN Doc. A/4425

The IBA Guidelines on Conflict of Interest in International Arbitration (2014) <http:/ /www.ibanet.org/Publications/publications_IBA_guides_and_free_materials. aspx> (accessed 19 June 2018)

The Commission's proposal on a new Investment Court System for TTIP and other EU trade and investment negotiations (16 September 2015) <http://europa.eu/ rapid/press-release_IP-15-5651_en.htm> (accessed 21 April 2018)

The International Law Commission Second report on Identification of Customary International Law, by Michael Wood (A/CN.4/672, 2014)

The EU Commission's press release: 'CETA: EU and Canada agree on new approach on investment in trade agreement' (29 February 2016) <http://europa.eu/rapid/ press-release_IP-16-399_en.htm> (accessed 21 April 2018)

UNCTAD Report, 'Interpretation of IIAs: What States Can Do', IIA Issues Note No. 3 (2011) <http://unctad.org/en/docs/webdiaeia2011d10_en.pdf> (accessed 2 October 2018)

UNCTAD Report 'Most-Favoured Nation Treatment (United Nations 2010) <http:// unctad.org/en/ docs/diaeia20101_en.pdf> (accessed 15 October 2018)

UNCTAD, IAA Issues Note No 1, 'Recent Trends in IIAs and ISDS' (February 2015) <http://unctad.org/en/PublicationsLibrary/ webdiae pcb2015d1_en.pdf> (accessed 30 September 2018)

UNCTAD, 'Reform of Investor State Dispute Settlement: In search of a roadmap, IIA Issues Note No 2 (June 2013) <http://unctad.org/en/ PublicationsLibrary /webdiaepcb2013d4_ en.pdf> (accessed 30 September 2018)

UNCTAD, World Investment Report, 'Non-equity modes of international production and development' (2011) < https://unctad.org/en/PublicationsLibrary/wir2011overview_en.pdf> (accessed 4 May 2018)

UNCTAD, World Investment Report, 'Towards a New Generation of Investment Policies' (2012) < https://unctad.org/en/PublicationsLibrary/wir2012_embargoed _en.pdf > (accessed 3 May 2018)

Wälde T, 'International Investment Law: An overview of Key Concepts and Methodology' (Report of the 2004 Research Seminar on International Investment Law, Hague Academy of International Law, October 2005)

Wood Michael 'The International Law Commission Second report on Identification of Customary International Law' (2014) A/CN.4/672

WTO Appellate Body Report, 'International Trade Law – Role of Dispute Settlement Decisions in WTO Law – WTO Appellate Body Reaffirms WTO-Inconsistency of 'Zeroing.' – Appellate Body Report, 'United States – Final Anti-Dumping Measures on Stainless Steel from Mexico', WT/DS344/AB/R (Apr. 30, 2008).' (2009) 122(7) HarvLRev 1993

Table of Cases

Caribbean Court of Justice

The British Caribbean Bank Limited v. The Attorney General, CCJ 4, Appeal (25 June 2013), 195

Court of Justice of the European Union

Slovakia Republic v. Achmea B.V. Case C-284/16 (6 March 2018), 3

European Court of Human Rights

Banković v. Belgium, ECtHR, Decision as to the admissibility of Application no. 52207/99 (12 December 2001), 173

James and Others v. The United Kingdom, ECtHR, Judgment (21 February 1986), 180

Matos e Silva, *Lda., and Others v. Portugal*, ECtHR, Judgment (16 September 1996), 180

Mellacher and Others v. Austria, ECtHR, Judgment (19 December 1989), 180

Pressos Compañía Naviera and Others v. Belgium, ECtHR, Judgment (20 November 1995), 180

ICSID Decisions

Abaclat and others (Case formerly known as Giovanna a Beccara and others) v. The Argentine Republic, ICSID Case No. ARB/07/5, Decision on Jurisdiction and Admissibility (4 August 2011) (Albert Jan van den Berg, Georges Abi-Saab, Pierre Tercier, President), 56

ADC Affiliate Limited and ADC & ADMC Management Limited v. Republic of Hungary, ICSID Case No. ARB/03/16, Award (2 October 2006) (Charles Brower, Albert Jan van den Berg, Neil Kaplan, President), 230

ADF Group Inc. v. United States of America, ICSID Case No. ARB (AF)/00/1, Award (9 January 2003) (Armand de Mestral, Carolyn Lamm, Florentino Feliciano, President), 208

AES Corp v. The Argentine Republic, ICSID Case No. ARB/02/17, Decision on Jurisdiction (26 April 2005) (Karl-Heinz Böckstiegel, Domingo Bello Janeiro, Pierre-Marie Dupuy, President), 78

Alapli Elektrik B.V. v. Republic of Turkey, ICSID Case No. ARB/08/13, Decision on Annulment (10 July 2014) (Karl-Heinz Böckstiegel, Makhdoom Ali Khan, Bernard Hanotiau, President), 91

Alex Genin, Eastern Credit Limited, Inc. And A.S. Baltoil v. The Republic Of Estonia, ICSID Case No. ARB/99/2 Award (25 June 2001) (Meir Heth, Albert Jan van den Berg, L. Yves Fortier, President), 58

Amco Asia Corporation and others v. Republic of Indonesia, ICSID Case No. ARB/81/1, Resubmitted Case: Award (5 June 1990) (Edward W. Rubin, Isi Foighel, Berthold Goldman, President), 69

Amco Asia Corporation and others v. Republic of Indonesia, ICSID Case No. ARB/81/1, Resubmitted Case: Decision on Jurisdiction (10 May 1988) (Edward W. Rubin, Isi Foighel, Berthold Goldman, President), 69, 70

Amco Asia Crop. v. the Republic of Indonesia, ICSID Case No.ARB/81/1, Decision on Annulment, (16 May 1986) (Florentino Feliciano, Andrea Giardina, Ignaz Seidl-Hohenveldern, President), 114

American Manufacturing and Trading, Inc. v. Republic of Zaire, ICSID Case No. ARB/93/1, Award (21 February 1997) (Heribert Golsong, Kéba Mbuye, Sompong Sucharitkul, President), 76

Archer Daniels Midland Company and Tate & Lyle Ingredients Americas, Inc. v. The United Mexican States, ICSID Case No. ARB(AF)/04/05, Award (21 November 2007) (Arthur Rovine, Eduardo Siqueiros, Bernardo Cremades, President), 76, 212

Asian Agricultural Products Ltd. v. Sri Lanka, ICSID Case ARB/87/3, Award (27 June 1990) (Berthold Goldman, Samuel Asante, Ahmed El-Kosheri, President), 64, 158

Azurix Corporation v. The Argentine Republic (Azurix v. Argentina), ICSID Case No. ARB/01/12, Award (14 July 2006) (Marc Lalonde, Daniel Martins, Andrés Rigo Sureda, President), 241

Banro American Resources, Inc. and Société Aurifère du Kivu et du Maniema S.A.R.L.v. Democratic Republic of the Congo, ICSID Case No. ARB/98/7, Award (1 September 2000) (Carveth Harcourt Geach, Alioune Diagne, Prosper Weil, President), 216

Bayindir Insaat Turizm Ticaret Ve Sanayi A.S. v. Islamic Republic of Pakistan, ICSID Case No. ARB/03/29, Award (27 August 2009) (Karl-Heinz Böckstiegel, Franklin Berman, Gabrielle Kaufmann-Kohler, President), 169, 191

Bosh International, Inc and B&P Ltd Foreign Investments Enterprise v. Ukraine, ICSID Case No ARB/08/11, Award (25 October 2012) (Philippe Sands, Donald McRae, Gavan Griffith QC, President), 152

Burlington Resources Inc. v. Ecuador, ICSID Case No. ARB/08/5, Decision on Jurisdiction (2 June 2010) (Francisco Orrego Vicuña, Brigitte Stern, Gabrielle Kaufmann-Kohler, President), 229, 234

Camuzzi International S.A. v. The Argentine Republic, ICSID Case No. ARB/03/2, Decision on objection to jurisdiction (11 May 2005) (Marc Lalonde, Sandra Morelli Rico, Francisco Orrego Vicuña, President), 155, 212

Caratube International Oil Company LLP v. The Republic of Kazakhstan, ICSID Case No. ARB/08/12, Decision on Annulment (21 February 2014) (Tan Sri Dato Cecil W.M. Abraham, Hans Danelius, Juan Fernández-Armesto, President), 91

CDC Group plc v. Republic of Seychelles, ICSID Case No. ARB/02/14, Decision on Annulment (29 June 2005) (Michael Hwang, David Williams QC, Judge Charles Brower, President), 109

Ceskoslovenska Obchodni Banka, AS v. The Slovak Republic, ICSID Case No ARB/97/4, Jurisdiction (24 May 1999) (Andreas Bucher, Piero Bernardini, Thomas Buergenthal, President), 219

CMS Gas Transmission Co. v. Argentine Republic, ICSID Case No. ARB/01/8, Decision on Annulment (25 September 2007) (James Crawford, Nabil Elaraby, Gilbert Guillaume, President), 113

CMS Gas Transmission Company v. The Republic of Argentina [2003], ICSID Case No. ARB/01/8, Decision on Jurisdiction (17 July 2003) (The Honorable Marc Lalonde, H.E. Judge Francisco Rezek, Professor Francisco Orrego Vicuña, President), 78

CMS Gas Transmission Company v. The Republic of Argentina, ICSID Case No. ARB/01/8, Award (12 May 2005) (The Honorable Marc Lalonde, H.E. Judge Francisco Rezek, Professor Francisco Orrego Vicuña, President), 221

Compania de Aguas del Aconquija SA and Vivendi Universal (formerly Compagnie General des Eaux) v. Argentine Republic, ICSID Case No. ARB/97/3, Decision on Annulment (3 July 2002) (James Crawford, José Carlos Fernández Rozas, L. Yves Fortier, President), 195

Continental Casualty v. Argentina, ICSID Case No. ARB/03/9, Decision on Jurisdiction (22 February 2006) (V.V. Veeder, Michell Nader, Giorgio Sacerdoti, President), 228

Desert Line Projects LLP v. Yemen, ICSID Case No. ARB/05/17, Award (6 February 2008) (Jan Paulsson, Ahmed S. El-Kosheri, Pierre Tercier, President), 178

Duke Energy Electroquil Partners & Electroquil S.A. v. Republic of Ecuador, ICSID Case No. ARB/04/19, Award (18 August 2008) (Enrique Gómez-Pinzón, Albert Jan van den Berg, Gabrielle Kaufmann-Kohler, President), 191

EDF International S.A., SAUR International S.A. and León Participaciones Argentinas S.A. v. Argentine Republic, ICSID Case No. ARB/03/23, Decision on Annulment (5 February 2016) (Teresa Cheng, Yasuhei Taniguchi, Christopher Greenwood, President), 91

El Paso Energy International Company v. The Argentine Republic, ICSID Case No ARB/03/15, Award (31 October 2011) (Prof. Piero Bernardini, Prof. Brigitte Stern, Prof. Lucius Caflisch, President) 62, 66, 181, 198

Emilio Agustín Maffezini v. The Kingdom of Spain, ICSID Case No. ARB/97/7 Decision on Jurisdiction (25 January 2000) (Professor Francisco Orrego Vicuña, Judge Thomas Buergenthal, Mr Maurice Wolf), 188

Emilio Agustín Maffezini v. The Kingdom of Spain, ICSID Case No. ARB/97/7, Award (13 November 2000) (Thomas Buergenthal, Maurice Wolf, Francisco Orrego Vicuña, President), 159, 188, 220

Empresas Lucchetti, S.A. and Lucchetti Peru, S.A. v. The Republic of Peru, ICSID Case No. ARB/03/4, Decision on Annulment, Dissenting opinion Sir Franklin Berman (5 September 2007) (also known as: Industria Nacional de Alimentos, *A.S. and Indalsa Perú S.A. v. The Republic of Peru*), 112

Empresas Lucchetti, S.A. and Lucchetti Peru, S.A. v. The Republic of Peru, ICSID Case No. ARB/03/4 (also known as: Industria Nacional de Alimentos, *A.S. and Indalsa Perú S.A. v. The Republic of Peru*) Decision on Annulment (5 September 2007) (Sir Franklin Berman, Prof. Andrea Giardina, Justice Hans Danelius), 35

Enron Corporation and Ponderosa Assets, L.P. v. The Argentine Republic, ICSID Case No. ARB/01/3, Decision on Jurisdiction (14 January 2004) (Pierre-Yves Tschanz, Héctor Gros Espiell, Francisco Orrego Vicuña, President), 160

Enron Corporation and Ponderosa Assets, L.P. v. Argentine Republic, ICSID Case No ARB/01/3, Award (22 May 2007) (Albert Jan van den Berg, Pierre-Yves Tschanz, Francisco Orrego Vicuña, President), 129

Enron Creditors Recovery Corp. Ponderosa Assets, L.P. v. The Argentine Republic, ICSID Case No. ARB/01/3, Decision on Annulment (30 July 2010) (Judge Patrick L. Robinson Judge Per Tresselt, Gavan Griffith QC, President), 90

Europe Cement Investment & Trade S.A. v. Republic of Turkey, ICSID Case No. ARB(AF)/07/2, Award (13 August 2009) (Julian Lew QC, Laurent Lévy, Donald McRae, President), 65

Fireman's Fund v. Mexico, ICSID Case No. ARB(AF)/02/1, Award (17 Jul. 2006) (Andreas Lowenfeld, Alberto Guillermo Saavedra Olavarrieta, Albert Jan van den Berg, President), 158

Generation Ukraine, Inc. v. Ukraine, ICSID Case No. ARB/00/9, Award (16 September 2003) (Dr Eugen Salpius, Dr Jürgen Voss, Jan Paulsson, President), 152, 197

Granti Koza v Turkmentisan, ICSID Case No. ARB/11/20 (3 July 2013) Laurence Boisson de Chazournes, Dissenting Opinion, 225

Hochtief AG v Argentina, ICSID Case No. ARB/07/31, Decision on Jurisdiction (24 October 2011) (Charles Brower, J. Christopher Thomas, Vaughan Lowe, President), 74

Hochtief AG v Argentina, ICSID Case No. ARB/07/31, Award (19 December 2016) (Charles Brower, J. Christopher Thomas, Vaughan Lowe, President), 56

Hussein Nuaman Soufraki v. United Arab Emirates, ICSID Case No ARB/02/7, Decision on Annulment (5 June 2007) (Omar Nabulsi, Brigitte Stern, Florentino Feliciano, President), 106

Inceysa Vallisoletana, S.L. v. Republic of El Salvador, ICSID Case No. ARB/03126, Award (2 August 2006) (Burton Landy, Claus von Wobeser, Rodrigo Oreamuno Blanco, President), 63

Ioannis Kardassopoulos v. The Republic of Georgia, ICSID Case No. ARB/05/18 Decision on Jurisdiction (6 July 2007) (Professor Francisco Orrego Vicuña, Sir Arthur Watts, K.C.M.G., QC, L. Yves Fortier QC President), 176

Jan de Nul NV and Dredging International NV v. Arab Republic of Egypt, ICSID Case No. ARB/04/13, Award (6 November 2008) (Pierre Mayer, Brigitte Stern, Gabrielle Kaufmann-Kohler, President), 158

Joan Micula and others v Romania, ICSID Case No. ARB/05/20, Award (11 December 2013) (Stanimir Alexandrov, Georges Abi-Saab, Laurent Lévy, President), 65, 68

Klöckner Industrie-Anlagen GmbH and others v. United Republic of Cameroon and Société Camerounaise des Engrais, ICSID Case No. ARB/81/2, Award (21 October 1983) (Dominique Schmidt, William D. Rogers, Eduardo Jiminez de Arechaga, President), 69

Klöckner v. Industrie-Anlagen GmbH and others v. Republic of Cameroon, ICSID Case No. ARB/81/2, Decision on Annulment (3 May 1985) (Dominique Schmidt, William D. Rogers, Eduardo Jiminez de Arechaga, President), 62

LG&E Energy Corp., LG&E Capital Corp., and LG&E International, Inc. v. Argentine Republic, ICSID Case No. ARB/02/1, Decision on Liability (3 October 2006) (Albert Jan van den Berg, Francisco Rezek, Tatiana de Maekelt, President), 78

Loewen Group, Inc. and Raymond L. Loewen v. United States of America, ICSID Case No. ARB(AF)/98/3, NAFTA, Award (26 June 2003) (Lord Mustill, Abner Mikva, Anthony Mason, President), 76

Malicorp Limited v. The Arab Republic of Egypt, ICSID Case No. ARB/08/18, Award (7 February 2011) Luiz Olavo Baptista, Pierre-Yves Tschanz, Pierre Tercier, President), 70, 72

Maritime International Nominees Establishment v. Republic of Guinea, ICSID Case No. ARB/84/4 Decision on Annulment (22 December 1989) (Aron Broches, Kéba Mbaye, Sompong Sucharitkul, President), 106

Marvin Roy Feldman Karpa v. United Mexican States, ICSID Case No. ARB(AF)/99/1 (also known as Marvin Feldman v. Mexico) Award (16 December 2002) (Prof. Konstantinos D. Kerameus, Jorge Covarrubias Bravo, Prof. David A. Gantz), 188

Marving Roy Feldman Karpa v. United Mexican States, ICSID Case No. ARB(AF)/99/1. NAFTA, Decision on jurisdiction (6 December 2000) (David Gantz, Jorge Covarrubias Bravo, Konstantinos Kerameus, President), 222–223

Metaclad Corporation v. The United Mexican States [2000] ICSID Case No. ARB(AF)/97/1, NAFTA-ICSID Additional Facility, Award (30 August 2000) (Benjamin R. Civiletti, José Luis Siqueiros, Professor Sir Elihu Lauterpacht, President), 190, 222

Mihaly International Corporation v. Democratic Socialist Republic of Sri Lanka, ICSID Case No. ARB/00/2, Award (15 March 2002) (David Suratgar, Andrew Rogers, Sompong Sucharitkul, President), 202

Mondev International Ltd. v. United States of America, ICSID Case No. ARB(AF)/99/2 Award (11 October 2002) (Professor James Crawford, Judge Stephen Schwebel, Sir Ninian Stephen, President), 56, 136, 202

Mr Patrick Mitchell v. the Democratic Republic of Congo, ICSID Case No. ARB/99/7, Decision on Annulment (1 November 2006) (Robert Dossou, Andrea Giardina, Antonias Dimolitsa, President), 107

Noble Energy, Inc. and Machalapower Cia. Ltda. v. The Republic of Ecuador and Consejo Nacional de Electricidad, ICSID Case No. ARB/05/12, Decision on Jurisdiction (5

March 2008) (Henri Alvarez, Bernardo Cremades, Gabrielle Kaufmann-Kohler, President), 234

Noble Ventures, Inc. v. Romania, ICSID Case No. ARB/01/11, Award (12 October 2005) (Jeremy Lever, Vincenzo Porcasi, Karl-Heinz Böckstiegel, President), 225, 226

Occidental Petroleum Corporation and Occidental Exploration and Production Company v. The Republic of Ecuador, ICSID Case No. ARB/06/11, Award (5 October 2012) (David Williams, Brigitte Stern, L. Yves Fortier, President), 180

Pan American Energy LLC and BP Argentina Exploration Company v. Argentine Republic, ICSID Case No. ARB/03/13, Decision on Preliminary Objections (27 July 2006) (Albert Jan van den Berg, Brigitte Stern, Lucius Caflisch, President), 225–226

Phoenix Action Ltd v. Czech Republic, ICSID Case No. ARB/06/5, Award (15 April 2009) (Juan Fernández-Armesto, Andreas Bucher, Brigitte Stern, President), 65

Plama Consortium Limited v. Republic of Bulgaria, ICSID Case No. ARB/03/24, Award (27 August 2008) (Albert Jan van den Berg, V.V. Veeder, Carl Salans, President), 221

Philippe Gruslin v. Malaysia, ICSID Case No. ARB/99/3, Award (27 November 2000) (Gavan Griffith QC, Sole Arbitrator), 159

Rumeli Telekom A.S. and Telsim Mobil Telekomunikasyon Hizmetleri A.S. v. Republic of Kazakhstan, ICSID Case No. ARB/05/16, Decision on Annulment (25 March 2010) (Campbell McLachlan, Eduardo Silva Romero, Stephen Schwebel, President), 109

Saipem S.p.A. v. The People's Republic of Bangladesh, ICSID Case No. ARB/05/07, Decision on jurisdiction and Recommendation of Provisional measures (21 March 2007) (Christoph Schreuer, Philip Otton, Gabrielle Kaufmann-Kohler, President), 234

Saipem S.p.A. v. The People's Republic of Bangladesh, ICSID Case No. ARB/05/7, Award (30 June 2009) (Prof. Christoph H. Schreuer, Sir Philip Otton, Gabrielle Kaufmann-Kohler, President), 136

SGS Société Générale de Surveillance SA v. Philippines, ICSID Case No. ARB/02/6, Decision on Jurisdiction (29 January 2004) (Antonio Crivellaro, James Crawford, Ahmed El-Kosheri, President), 75

Siemens A.G. v. The Argentine Republic, ICSID Case No. ARB/02/8, Decision on Jurisdiction (3 August 2004) (Charles Brower, Domingo Bello Janeiro, Andrés Rigo Sureda, President), 223

Siemens AG v. Argentina, ICSID Case No. ARB/02/8, Award (17 January 2007) (Judge Charles N. Brower, Professor Domingo Bello Janeiro, Dr Andrés Rigo Sureda, President), 208

Southern Pacific Properties (Middle East) Ltd. v. Arab Republic of Egypt, ICSID Case No. ARB/98/4, Award (20 May 1992) (Robert F. Pietrowski, Mohamed Amin Elabassy El Mahdi, Eduardo Jimenez De Arechaga, President), 172

Suez, Sociedad General de Aguas de Barcelona S.A., and InterAguas Servicios Integrales del Agua S.A. v. The Argentine Republic, ICSID Case No. ARB/03/17, Decision on liability (30 July 2010) (Gabrielle Kaufmann-Kohler, Pedro Nikken, Jeswald Salacuse, President), 191

Suez, Sociedad General de Aguas de Barcelona, S.A .and Vivendi Universal, S.A. v. Argentine Republic, (formerly Aguas Argentinas, *S.A., Suez, Sociedad General de Aguas de Barcelona, S.A.and Vivendi Universal, S.A. v. Argentine Republic,* ICSID, Case No. ARB/03/19, Order in Response to Transparency and Amicus Curiae Petition (19 May 2005) (Gabrielle Kaufmann-Kohler, Pedro Nikken, Jeswald Salacuse, President), 153

Técnicas Medioambientales Tecmed, S.A. v. The United Mexican States, ICSID Case No. ARB(AF)/00/2, Award (29 May 2003) (Prof. José Carlos Fernandez Rozas Mr Carlos Bernal Verea, Dr Horacio A. Grigera Naon, President), 36, 136

TECO Guatemala Holdings LLC v. Republic of Guatemala, ICSID Case No. ARB/10/23, CAFTA-DR, Decision on Annulment (5 April 2016) (Ms. Tinuade Oyekunle Professor Klaus Sachs, Professor Bernard Hanotiau, President), 107

Tokios Tokelés v. Ukraine, ICSID Case No. ARB/02/18, Jurisdiction (29 April 2004) (Piero Bernardini, Daniel M. Price, Prosper Weil, President), 198

Total SA v. The Argentine Republic, ICSID Case No ARB/04/1, Decision on Liability (27 December 2010) (Professor Giorgio Sacerdoti, President, Mr Henri C. Alvarez, Dr Luis Herrera Marcano), 181

Toto Costruzioni Generali S.p.A. v. The Republic of Lebanon, ICSID Case No. ARB/07/12, Award (7 June 2012) (Fadi Moghaizel, Stephen Schwebel, Hans van Houtte, President), 191

Urbaser S.A. and Consorcio de Aguas Bilbao Bizkaia, Bilbao Biskaia Ur Partzuergoa v. The Argentine Republic, ICSID Case No. ARB/07/26, Award (8 December 2016) (Pedro Martinez-Fraga, Campbell McLachlan, Andreas Bucher, President), 58, 213

Waste Management, Inc. v. United Mexican States ('Number 2'), ICSID Case No. ARB(AF)/00/3, Jurisdiction (26 June 2002) (Benjamin Civiletti, Guillermo Aguilar-Alvarez, James Crawford, President), 62, 67, 68

Wena Hotels Ltd v. Arab Republic of Egypt, ICISD Case No ARB/98/4, Proceeding on the Merits (8 December 2000) (Ibrahim Fadlallah, Hamzeh Ahmad Haddad, Monroe Leigh, President), 96

Wena Hotels Ltd v. Arab Republic of Egypt, ICSID Case No. ARB/98/4, Proceeding on Jurisdiction (25 May 1999) (Ibrahim Fadlallah, Hamzeh Ahmad Haddad, Monroe Leigh, President), 96

Wena Hotels Ltd v. Arab Republic of Egypt, ICSID Case No. ARB/98/4, Annulment Proceeding (28 January 2002) (Andreas Bücher, Francisco Orrego Vicuña, Konstantinos Kerameus, President), 96

Wintershall AG v. Argentina, ICSID Case No. ARB/04/14, Award (8 December 2008) (Piero Bernardini, Santiago Torres Bernárdez, Fali Nariman, President), 76

World Duty Free Company Limited v. the Republic of Kenya, ICSID Case No. Arb/00/7, Award (4 October 2006) (V.V. Veeder, Andrew Rogers, Gilbert Guillaume, President), 67

International Court of Justice Decisions

Ahmadou Sadio Diallo (Republic of Guinea v. Democratic Republic of the Congo), Joint dissenting opinion of Judges Al-Khasawneh and Yusuf (30 November 2010), 80
LaGrand Case (*Ger. v. U.S.*) ICJ, Merits (27 June 2001), 74
Polish Postal Service in Danzig PCIJ, Ser. B, No. 11 (1925), 68
Portugal v. India, Case concerning the Right of Passage over Indian Territory, ICJ, Preliminary Objections (26 November 1957), 175

Ontario Court of Appeal

Canada (AG) v. Ontario (AG), 326, Appeal (Labour Conventions) (1937), 194
The Council of Canadians et als v. Attorney General of Canada, Supreme Court of Canada, C43995, Appeal (30 November 2006), 194

Royal High Court of Justice

Republic of Ecuador v. Occidental Exploration and Production Co, Case No: 04/656 QB (Queen's Bench, Commercial court) (2 March 2006), 195

Stockholm Chamber of Commerce

Limited Liability Company Amto v. Ukraine, SCC Case No. 080/2005, Final Award, (26 March 2008), 226

UNCITRAL Decisions

CME Czech Republic B.V. v. Czech Republic, UNCITRAL, Partial Award (13 Sep. 2001) (Judge Stephen M. Schwebel, Jaroslav Hándl, Dr. Wolfgang Kühn, President), 5
Chemtura Corporation v. Canada, UNCITRAL, Award (2 August 2010) (Charles Brower, James Crawford, Gabrielle Kaufmann-Kohler, President), 55
Chevron Corporation and Texaco Petroleum Company v Ecuador, UNCITRAL PCA Case No 2009-23, Partial Award (30 March 2010) (Dr Horacio A. Grigera Naón, Professor Vaughan Lowe QC, V.V. Veeder, President), 66
Eureko B.V. v. Republic of Poland, UNCITRAL, Partial award (19 August 2005) (Stephen Schwebel, Jerzy Rajski, L. Yves Fortier, President), 74
Glamis Gold, Ltd. v. The United States of America, UNCITRAL, Award (8 June 2009) (Professor David D. Caron, Kenneth D. Hubbard, Michael K. Young, President), 91
International Thunderbird Gaming Corporation v. The United Mexican States, UNCITRAL, Award (26 January 2006) (Professor Dr Albert Jan van den Berg (President), Lic. Agustín Portal Ariosa, Professor Thomas W. Wälde), 71

International Thunderbird Gaming Corporation v. The United Mexican States, UNCITRAL, Separate Opinion of Thomas Wälde (1 December 2005), 137
Lauder v. Czech Republic, UNCITRAL, Final Award (3 September 2002) (Lloyd Cutler, Bohuslav Klein, Robert Briner, President), 5
Merrill & Ring Forestry L.P. v. The Government of Canada, UNCITRAL, ICSID Administered Case, Award (31 March 2010) (Professor Kenneth W. Dam, J. William Rowley QC, Professor Francisco Orrego Vicuña, President), 203
Occidental Exploration and Production Co v. Republic of Ecuador, UNCITRAL, LCIA Administered Case No UN3467, Award (1 July 2004) (The Honorable Charles N. Brower, Dr Patrick Barrera Sweeney, Professor Francisco Orrego Vicuna, President), 188
Pope & Talbot Inc. v. The Government of Canada, UNCITRAL, Award in Respect of Damages (31 May 2002) (Benjamin Greenberg, Murray Belman, Lord Dervaird, President), 206
Pope & Talbot, Inc. v. The Government of Canada, UNCITRAL, Award on the Merits of Phase 2 (10 April 2001) (Benjamin Greenberg, Murray Belman, Lord Dervaird, President), 206
Saluka Investments BV (The Netherlands) v. Czech Republic, UNCITRAL, Partial Award (17 March 2006) (L. Yves Fortier, Peter Behrens, Arthur Watts, President), 79

United States Supreme Court

Magno Santovincenzo v. James F. Egan, United States Supreme Court, Decision (23 November 1931), 188
Penn Central Transportation Co. v. New York City' United States Supreme Court, Decision (26 June 1978), 188

United States Court of Appeals

John Koufakis v. Carvel, 425 F 2d 892, US Court of Appeals for the Second Circuit (24 April 1970), 189
Kevin Pappas v. Middle Earth Condominium Association, 963 F 2d 534, US Court of Appeals for the Second Circuit (8 May 1992), 189
Spanish Supreme Court
Estudio v. Puma Judgment of the Spanish Supreme Court, No. 102/2017 (15 February 2017), 141

Swedish Court of Appeal

Czech Republic v. CME Czech Republic, B.V. Case No. T 8735-01, Svea Court of Appeal Judgment, Challenge of arbitral award, (15 May 2003), 151

Table of Legislation

BIT Fra La Repubblica Italiana E La Repubblica Argentina Sulla Promozione E Protezione Degli Investimenti (1990), 56
Canada Model BIT (2004), 220
Energy Charter Treaty (1994), 75, 217, 221
ICSID Convention (1966) (2006), 4, 39, 61–65, 75, 89, 112, 153, 161, 162, 168, 185, 202, 216, 218–221, 226, 228, 241
ICSID Rules of Procedure for Arbitration Proceedings (Arbitration Rules) (1968) (2006), 89, 142, 143, 147, 153
Italy-Russia BIT (1996), 74
Kazakhstan-Turkey BIT (1992), 57
NAFTA Agreement (1993), 39, 221
The Dominican Republic – Central America – United States Free Trade Agreement (DR-CAFTA) (2004), 115
UNCITRAL Arbitration Rules (2010), 112, 143
US – Australia Free Trade Agreement (2004), 205
US – ESTONIA BIT (1994), 58
US – Rwanda BIT (2008), 198
US Model BIT (2004), 188, 205, 241
Vienna Convention on the Law of Treaties (1968-1969), 1, 2, 5, 17, 37, 41, 76, 121, 123, 127, 128, 138, 155–164, 175–178, 222–224, 226, 242, 245, 254, 256

Index

A

Actors, 2–4, 6, 24–27, 32, 43, 72, 124, 134, 137, 153, 162, 187, 196, 200, 201, 203, 212, 228, 239, 240, 246, 250, 255, 256
Adaptation, 12, 64, 66, 98, 132, 134–140, 181, 189, 190, 210, 247, 256
Administrative law, 146, 184, 192, 212
Advocacy, 146, 189
Agreement, 39, 63, 65, 74, 75, 77, 139, 160, 186, 195, 201, 202, 205, 206, 216, 221, 226, 240, 241
Amicus curiae, 43, 97, 152–154, 235, 236, 254
Analogical reasoning, 134, 171
Analogy, 11, 13, 76, 87, 178
Annulment, 35, 62, 89, 90, 92, 104–106, 108–110, 112–115, 118, 185, 231, 252, 253
Antithesis, 128, 144
Appeal, 5, 94, 105, 106, 110–116, 118, 123, 151, 166, 193, 194, 249, 252, 253, 256
Arbitral awards/arbitration awards, 1, 3, 4, 13, 16, 67, 84, 89–92, 95, 97, 98, 103, 106, 110, 116, 118, 145, 147, 157, 158, 167–169, 183, 201, 203, 204, 217, 251, 253, 256
Arbitral tribunals/Arbitration tribunals, 1–2, 5, 12, 14–16, 21, 23, 24, 36–41, 43, 52–54, 57–59, 61, 62, 67–69, 72, 74, 75, 78, 83, 84, 87, 88, 92, 97, 101, 104–106, 110–112, 114, 116–118, 121, 122, 123, 125, 132, 135, 138, 141, 143, 148, 152, 156–161, 164–166, 168, 174, 176, 180, 181, 183–186, 191, 193–195, 197, 198, 201, 203–206, 210–215, 222, 223, 225, 227–229, 231–233, 243, 245- 247, 249–257
Arbitrators, 149–152
Argumentation, 6–16, 23–41
Arguments
  convention, 121, 127, 131, 155–164, 245
  customary law, 128, 129, 196–214, 255
  narrative, 17, 121, 127, 129, 139, 141–154, 245, 254
  policy, 17, 121, 127–129, 131, 139, 214–243, 246, 255
  precedent, 17, 127–129, 131, 132, 164–196, 254
Aristotle, 7–11, 103
Audience, 3, 6, 8, 9, 11, 13, 16, 17, 88, 93–99, 103, 110, 114, 115, 117, 163, 252, 257
Authority, 21, 28, 38, 61, 67, 91, 93, 99, 105, 111, 116, 166, 167, 171, 183, 184, 193, 201, 230, 233, 249
Autonomy, 84, 194, 233, 235, 252

B

Background, 2, 14, 27, 29, 30, 43, 51, 55, 123, 131, 134, 137, 147, 170–172, 175, 180, 186, 187, 192, 196, 197, 200, 202, 216, 235, 238, 250, 253, 254, 256
Balance of rights, 64, 77–79, 83, 190, 251

C

Certainty, 36, 50, 90, 157, 228, 229, 231, 234
Commercial arbitration, 13, 98, 158, 167, 194, 228, 233, 235
Commission, 39, 139, 153, 157, 162, 201, 205, 207, 209
Communication, 3, 9, 11, 26, 36, 107, 124, 125, 134–137, 143, 147, 151, 153, 165, 172, 174, 177, 183–184, 186, 190, 193–196, 211–214, 245, 253, 257
Conflict, 7, 11, 31, 36, 39, 61, 132, 133, 154, 163, 172, 174, 182, 222, 224, 227, 235
Consistency, 228–232
Constitutional law, 34, 138, 174, 193
Court of Appeal, 112, 151, 193
Courts/domestic courts/international courts, 4, 6, 10, 15, 17, 23, 62, 66–68, 74, 90–92, 96, 99, 110, 112, 115, 116, 124, 130, 133, 135, 136, 137, 146, 151, 153, 160, 161, 165, 166, 172–175, 180, 182–189, 193–196, 201, 214, 216, 226, 242, 246, 247, 250, 252–254, 257
Cultural, 4, 181, 192
Culture, 8, 32, 134, 135
Customary law, 17, 121, 127–131, 139, 144, 175, 190, 196–214, 255, 257

D

Decision-maker, 17, 28, 29, 31, 33, 37, 40, 41, 47, 50–55, 57, 61, 65, 68, 69, 78, 83, 94, 95, 97, 98, 116, 124, 129, 134–136, 139, 141, 142, 144–157, 161, 164, 168, 169, 171, 172, 174, 177, 179, 182, 185, 196, 198, 199, 214, 235, 238, 257
Decision making, 1–17, 21, 23–44, 47, 50–53, 59, 61, 68, 70, 72, 83, 84, 87, 88, 91–94, 96, 99–101, 109, 111, 114, 115, 117, 118, 121, 122, 124–126, 128, 135, 136, 138–140, 142, 148, 149, 154, 156, 158, 161, 165–169, 172, 175, 178, 179, 186, 187, 190, 193, 198, 200, 201, 203, 204, 212, 214, 221, 222, 224, 227–237, 240, 243, 245–247, 249–257
Decision making genres, 16, 28–41
Development, 110–116, 241–243
Dialectic, 7–13, 124, 145, 174, 183, 184, 187
Dialogical, 11, 13, 16, 17, 121–243, 245–247, 254, 255
Dialogue, 12–16, 124–125, 133–135, 141–243
Dialogue des juges, 124
Discourse, 6, 8, 25, 144, 165, 204
Discretion, 1, 10, 34, 37–41, 44, 50, 52, 53, 59, 83, 96, 111, 118, 133, 153, 157, 164, 205, 213, 214, 222, 231, 233, 249, 251, 253, 256
Domestic decisions, 193
Domestic legal system, 61, 191, 193
Due process, 57, 58, 64, 183, 187–190, 209, 233
Dynamic, 17, 24, 27, 30, 37, 83, 84, 87–101, 117, 118, 154, 200, 208, 209, 246, 250–254, 256, 257

E

Errors of law, 110, 112–116, 249
European Court of Human Rights (ECtHR), 36, 136, 165, 174, 178, 180, 182, 190, 246
European Court of Justice (ECJ), 137, 174, 178, 180
Evolutionary interpretation, 204–210
Expropriation, 54–56, 58, 73, 78, 79, 97, 132, 144, 145, 148, 170, 179–181, 190, 198, 202, 217, 220, 230

F

Fair and Equitable treatment (FET), 53, 55–58, 73, 77, 131, 132, 179, 184, 189, 190, 192, 198, 202, 206–210, 213, 231
Fragmentation, 35, 166, 174, 175, 184
Functions, 23–27, 49–52, 103–116

G

General practice, 162, 196, 201, 203, 212–214
General principles of law, 62–63, 65–68
Globalisation, 196
Good faith, 11, 57, 64, 67, 68, 70–72, 75, 95, 129, 131, 145, 155, 190

H

Hermeneutics, 37, 181
Human rights, 74, 136, 154, 173, 178, 182, 184, 190, 210, 213, 240–242, 246

I

ICSID Convention, 39, 62–64, 75, 89, 112, 168, 185, 202, 218, 219, 228
Idiosyncratic characteristics, 2, 3, 209, 245, 247
Indeterminacy, 38
International courts, 17, 23, 66, 68, 74, 110, 133, 135, 136, 160, 161, 165, 166, 173, 175, 183, 201, 247, 253, 257
International judges, 125, 135, 136, 177–183, 193
International legal system, 24, 125, 134, 145, 184, 191
Interpretation, 34–41, 204–210
Interpretive arguments, 61, 63–65, 127–129, 132, 135, 138, 161, 164, 165, 177, 178, 187, 200, 211, 214, 223, 227, 228, 230, 232, 238, 245, 246
Interpretive communities, 26, 237, 238, 240
Investment arbitration framework, 2–5, 13, 16, 17, 24, 60, 68, 69, 92–101, 117, 121, 123, 124, 127–129, 135, 136, 138, 140, 145, 159, 161, 164, 177, 181–184, 190, 193, 195, 199, 200, 201, 204, 207, 210, 214, 215, 232, 235, 237, 245–247, 249, 250, 252, 255, 256
Investment treaties, 215–227
Investors, 3, 4, 24, 53, 55–57, 72–75, 77, 78, 80, 99, 129, 130, 138, 139, 161–164, 173, 178, 179, 183, 185, 187, 188, 94, 197, 201, 203, 206, 210, 213, 217, 218, 220, 221, 223–226, 230, 231, 234, 239, 249, 252

J

Judges, 4, 5, 9–11, 28–32, 36, 47, 96, 115, 125, 133, 135, 136, 151, 160, 164, 165, 173, 174, 177–184, 186–193, 200, 251
Judgment, 9, 14, 15, 35, 37, 41, 55, 59, 68, 93, 106, 136, 151, 165, 167, 174, 195, 215, 220
Judicial borrowing, 134, 165

Jurisdiction, 25, 34, 35, 55, 78, 113, 133, 137, 152, 157, 166, 168, 170, 176, 182, 185, 186, 189, 196, 198, 216, 246, 254
Jurisprudence, 36, 66, 68, 90, 111, 135, 138, 145, 168, 169, 170, 172, 177, 178, 180, 183, 184, 190–193, 195, 196, 203, 229
Jurisprudence constante, 166, 167, 203
Justice, 2, 49, 62, 65, 74, 96, 107, 116, 137, 167, 180, 190, 191, 193, 194, 209, 223, 229, 230, 238, 239, 255

L

Language, 10, 12–16, 40, 41, 47, 49–81, 83, 84, 87, 93, 109, 111, 114, 124, 147, 166, 171, 177, 206, 211, 212, 224, 232, 251–253, 256, 257
Legal argumentation theories, 6, 9–14, 16, 251, 257
Legal arguments, 6, 9, 11–13, 16, 17, 40, 41, 87, 93, 121, 127–132, 142–144, 251
Legal reasoning, 9, 10, 13, 79, 91–93, 103, 105, 112, 115, 134, 168, 175, 193, 213
Legal transplants, 133–135
Legitimacy, 99–101
Legitimate expectations, 57, 71, 180, 181, 190–193, 234, 242, 254
Lex specialis, 60, 139, 157, 173, 198, 199, 210, 212, 222
Logic, 10–12

M

Measures, 33, 53, 55–57, 73, 76, 78, 99, 126, 129, 179, 180, 189, 197, 206, 213, 215, 221
Methodology, 1, 2, 5–8, 10, 12, 13, 17, 26, 34, 40, 56, 65, 66, 68, 72, 83, 121, 129, 136, 138, 156, 159, 164, 180, 181, 187, 237, 246, 247, 251
Most Favoured Nation Clause (MFN), 52, 53, 56, 73, 188, 194, 197, 199

N

Narrative, 13, 17, 103, 121, 123, 127–129, 139, 141–154, 245, 254
National courts, 112, 116, 151, 189, 201
National judges, 186–193
National law, 185–186
Network, 123–243
Non-statist, 27, 154, 203, 239, 246, 251, 253–256
Non-traditional, 27, 84, 251, 252, 255, 256
Normative, 49–52, 110–116
  decision-making, 118, 256

O

Object and purpose, 137, 155, 159, 160, 176, 208, 220, 222–226, 237
Opinio juris, 200–204, 212–214

P

Parties, 2, 4, 5, 8, 17, 21, 23, 30–34, 38, 39, 43, 57–59, 63, 70, 77, 79, 80, 83, 89–90, 93, 95–100, 103, 108, 112, 116–118, 121, 124, 125, 127, 129, 132, 135, 138, 139, 141–150, 152–155, 160–163, 167–170, 172, 175, 178, 182, 186, 201, 203, 206, 207, 211, 213, 214, 223, 224, 227, 228, 230, 235, 236, 241, 242, 245, 250, 252, 253, 254, 256
Party submissions, 5, 59, 83, 121, 127, 132, 139, 142, 143, 145, 146, 148, 152–154, 178, 245, 252, 254

Persuasion, 103–110
Pluralism, 135–140, 165
Policies, 214–243
Power of arbitrators, 96
Powers, 6–8, 11, 26, 31, 33, 38, 39, 53, 64, 69, 76, 79, 93, 96, 99, 101, 105, 107, 110, 111, 131, 137, 138, 152, 157, 166, 178, 179, 194, 201, 202, 206, 213, 217, 231
Practice/arbitral practice, 1–3, 17, 70, 169, 141–243, 253
Precedent arguments, 164–196
Precedent, 1, 2, 5, 17, 34, 38, 66, 84, 97, 118, 121, 123, 127–132, 135, 138, 151, 160, 161, 164–196, 201, 204, 209, 213, 220, 230, 231, 236, 245, 247, 249, 252–254, 256, 257
Predictability, 2, 5, 6, 43, 90, 98, 115, 128, 167, 190, 215, 227–234, 237–239, 246, 255
Principles, 2, 8, 11, 13, 16, 34, 36, 37, 41, 47–72, 77, 78, 83, 130, 136, 138, 139, 143, 144, 155–157, 160–165, 172, 175–177, 183–185, 190, 192, 194, 202, 206, 208, 211, 228, 230, 232, 233, 236, 242, 251, 256
Private interest, 75, 78, 79, 96, 99, 132, 161, 181, 182, 184, 212, 226, 245, 246, 252–254
Procedural law, 69
Procedural rights, 64, 73, 75
Proportionality, 36, 78, 79, 132, 178–182, 190, 246, 254
Public interest, 3, 4, 78–80, 81, 97–99, 124, 134, 179, 180, 182, 190, 213, 219, 223, 246, 249, 250, 256
Public policy, 3, 67, 78, 90, 92, 190, 192, 203, 213
Purposive use, 59, 77, 83, 251, 252

R

Rationality, 10, 11, 95, 100
Reasoning standards, 92, 104–109, 112, 114, 115, 117, 118, 253, 255
Reciprocity, 211
Res judicata, 62, 67, 69
Rhetoric, 10–16, 103–110
Rights, 72–81, 241–243
Rule of law, 232–235

S

Socrates, 7
Soft law, 25, 136
Sources, 8, 25, 28, 33, 34, 61–65, 80, 138, 161, 162, 164, 175, 176, 202, 209, 222
Stability, 3, 131, 190, 192, 227–234, 237, 238
Standards, 53–59, 77–79, 104–110
Stare decisis, 111, 165, 167
State practice, 200–204
Substantive law, 80–81, 151, 172, 228, 231
Substantive rights, 70, 72, 77–81, 182
Sustainable development, 43, 238, 240–243, 246
Syllogism, 8, 9, 17, 129, 138, 145, 180, 188, 189, 208, 234
Synthesis, 121, 123, 128, 139, 148
Systemic integration, 175–176
Systemic integrity, 234–238

T

Teleological interpretation, 108, 222
Theory, 1–3, 6–10, 12–14, 16, 33, 71, 75, 99, 122–140, 142, 164, 166, 229, 245, 251, 257
Thesis, 1, 128, 129, 144
Third parties, 2, 23, 97, 117, 127, 152–154, 250, 252, 254

Transnational characteristics, 2, 3, 14, 16, 21, 99, 135, 146, 250, 252, 256
Transnational decision-making, 26, 154, 154, 156, 157
Transnational law, 25, 65–68, 72, 111, 201
Transparency, 3, 39, 43, 57, 98, 99, 114, 128, 139, 143, 187, 188, 190, 192

V

Vagueness, 38, 40, 53, 65, 198, 249
Value, 23, 30, 32, 33, 50–52, 66, 67, 101, 107, 137, 149, 159, 160, 164, 167–169, 181, 190, 192, 215, 237, 238, 239
Vienna Convention on the Law of Treaties (VCLT), 1, 2, 5, 17, 37, 41, 76, 121, 123, 127, 128, 138, 155–164, 175–178, 222–224, 226, 242, 245, 254, 256

W

WTO Appellate body, 174

INTERNATIONAL ARBITRATION LAW LIBRARY

1. Moshe Hirsch, *The Arbitration Mechanism of the International Center for the Settlement of Investment Disputes,* 1993 (ISBN 07-923-1993-1).
2. Aida B. Avanessian, *Iran-United States Claims Tribunal in Action,* 1993 (ISBN 18-533-3902-4).
3. Isaak I. Dore, *The UNCITRAL Framework for Arbitration in Contemporary Perspective,* 1993 (ISBN 18-533-3573-8).
4. Vesna Lazić, *Insolvency Proceedings and Commercial Arbitration,* 1998 (ISBN 90-411-1115-8).
5. Joachim Frick, *Arbitration in Complex International Contracts,* 2001 (ISBN 90-411-1662-1).
6. Katherine Lynch, *The Forces of Economic Globalization: Challenges to the Regime of International Commercial Arbitration,* 2003 (ISBN 90-411-1994-9).
7. Christoph Liebscher, *The Healthy Award: Challenge in International Commercial Arbitration,* 2003 (ISBN 90-411-2011-4).
8. Hamid G. Gharavi, *The International Effectiveness of the Annulment of an Arbitral Award,* 2003 (ISBN 90-411-1717-2).
9. Abdulhay Sayed, *Corruption in International Trade and Commercial Arbitration,* 2004 (ISBN 90-411-2236-2).
10. Gabrielle Kaufmann-Kohler & Thomas Schultz, *Online Dispute Resolution: Challenges for Contemporary Justice,* 2004 (ISBN 90-411-2318-0).
11. Christopher R. Drahozal & Richard W. Naimark (eds), *Towards a Science of International Arbitration: Collected Empirical Research,* 2005 (ISBN 90-411-2322-9).
12. Ali Yeşilirmak, *Provisional Measures in International Commercial Arbitration,* 2005 (ISBN 90-411-2353-9).
13. Christian Bühring-Uhle, *Arbitration and Mediation in International Business,* second revised edition, 2006 (ISBN 978-9-041-12256-8).
14. Bernard Hanotiau, *Complex Arbitrations: Multiparty, Multicontract, Multiissue and Class Actions,* 2006 (ISBN 978-9-041-12442-5).
15. Loukas A. Mistelis & Julian D.M. Lew (eds), *Pervasive Problems in International Arbitration,* 2006 (ISBN 978-9-041-12450-0).
16. Julian D.M. Lew & Loukas A. Mistelis (eds), *Arbitration Insights – Twenty Years of the Annual Lecture of the School of International Arbitration, Sponsored by Freshfields Bruckhaus Deringer,* 2006 (ISBN 978-9-041-12606-1).
17. Mark Kantor, *Valuation for Arbitration: Compensation Standards, Valuation Methods and Expert Evidence,* 2008 (ISBN 978-9-041-12735-8).
18. Christoph Brunner, *Force Majeure and Hardship under General Contract Principles: Exemption for Non-Performance in International Arbitration,* 2009 (ISBN 978-90-411-2792-1).

19. Loukas A. Mistelis & Stavros L. Brekoulakis (eds), *Arbitrability: International & Comparative Perspectives*, 2009 (ISBN 978-90-411-2730-3).
20. Sam Luttrell, *Bias Challenges in International Commercial Arbitration: The Need for a 'Real Danger' Test*, 2009 (ISBN 978-90-411-3191-1).
21. Monique Sasson, *Substantive Law in Investment Treaty Arbitration: The Unsettled Relationship Between International Law and Municipal Law*, Second Edition, 2017 (ISBN 978-90-411-6103-1).
22. Ileana M. Smeureanu, *Confidentiality in International Commercial Arbitration*, 2011 (ISBN 978-90-411-3226-0).
23. Won Kidane, *China-Africa Dispute Settlement: The Law, Economics and Culture of Arbitration*, 2011 (ISBN 978-90-411-3674-9).
24. Karel Daele, *Challenge and Disqualification of Arbitrators in International Arbitration*, 2012 (ISBN 978-90-411-3799-9).
25. Crina Baltag, *The Energy Charter Treaty: The Notion of Investor*, 2012 (ISBN 978-90-411-3428-8).
26. Alexandra Diehl, *The Core Standard of International Investment Protection: Fair and Equitable Treatment*, 2012 (ISBN 978-90-411-3869-9).
27. Manuel Indlekofer, *International Arbitration and the Permanent Court of Arbitration*, 2013 (ISBN 978-90-411-4766-0).
28. Günther J. Horvath & Stephan Wilske (eds), *Guerrilla Tactics in International Arbitration*, 2013 (ISBN 978-90-411-4002-9).
29. Albert Badia, *Piercing the Veil of State Enterprises in International Arbitration*, 2014 (ISBN 978-90-411-5162-9).
30. Nadja Erk, *Parallel Proceedings in International Arbitration: A Comparative European Perspective*, 2014 (ISBN 978-90-411-5264-0).
31. Simon Vorburger, *International Arbitration and Cross-Border Insolvency: Comparative Perspectives*, 2014 (ISBN 978-90-411-5419-4).
32. Ahmad Ali Ghouri, *Interaction and Conflict of Treaties in Investment Arbitration*, 2015 (ISBN 978-90-411-5417-0).
33. Reto Marghitola, *Document Production in International Arbitration*, 2015 (ISBN 978-90-411-5159-9).
34. Alfonso Gómez-Acebo, *Party-Appointed Arbitrators in International Commercial Arbitration*, 2016 (ISBN 978-90-411-6671-5).
35. Jonas von Goeler, *Third-Party Funding in International Arbitration and Its Impact on Procedure*, 2016 (ISBN 978-90-411-5015-8).
36. Dean Lewis, *The Interpretation and Uniformity of the UNCITRAL Model Law on International Commercial Arbitration: Focusing on Australia, Hong Kong and Singapore*, 2016 (ISBN 978-90-411-6700-2).
37. Stavros Brekoulakis, Julian D.M. Lew & Loukas Mistelis (eds), *The Evolution and Future of International Arbitration*, 2016 (ISBN 978-90-411-7004-0).
38. Rémy Gerbay, *The Functions of Arbitral Institutions*, 2016 (ISBN 978-90-411-6217-5).

39. Maximilian Clasmeier, *Arbitral Awards as Investments: Treaty Interpretation and the Dynamics of International Investment Law*, 2017 (ISBN 978-90-411-8357-6).
40. Tony Cole (ed.), *The Roles of Psychology in International Arbitration*, 2017 (ISBN 978-90-411-5921-2).
41. Pietro Ferrario, *The Adaptation of Long-Term Gas Sale Agreements by Arbitrators*, 2017 (ISBN 978-90-411-8232-6).
42. Jacob B. van de Velden, *Finality in Litigation: The Law and Practice of Preclusion – Res Judicata (Merger and Estoppel), Abuse of Process and Recognition of Foreign Judgments*, 2017 (ISBN 978-90-411-8342-2).
43. Dolores Bentolila, *Arbitrators as Lawmakers*, 2017 (ISBN 978-90-411-8354-5).
44. Giacomo Marchisio, *The Notion of Award in International Commercial Arbitration: A Comparative Analysis of French Law, English Law, and the UNCITRAL Model Law*, 2017 (ISBN 978-90-411-8391-0).
45. Csaba Kovács, *Attribution in International Investment Law*, 2018 (ISBN 978-90-411-9675-0).
46. Mary Mitsi, *The Decision-Making Process of Investor-State Arbitration Tribunals*, 2019 (ISBN 978-90-411-9600-2).